MW00625130

TRIBAL

T

TRIBAL

HOW THE CULTURAL INSTINCTS THAT DIVIDE US CAN HELP BRING US TOGETHER

MICHAEL MORRIS

THESIS

Thesis / Penguin
An imprint of Penguin Random House LLC
penguinrandomhouse.com

Copyright © 2024 by Michael Morris
Penguin Random House values and supports copyright. Copyright fuels creativity, encourages diverse voices, promotes free speech, and creates a vibrant culture. Thank you for buying an authorized edition of this book and for complying with copyright laws by not reproducing, scanning, or distributing any part of it in any form without permission. You are supporting writers and allowing Penguin Random House to continue to publish books for every reader. Please note that no part of this book may be used or reproduced in any manner for the purpose of training artificial intelligence technologies or systems.

Thesis with colophon is a trademark of Penguin Random House LLC.

Most Thesis books are available at a discount when purchased in quantity for sales promotions or corporate use. Special editions, which include personalized covers, excerpts, and corporate imprints, can be created when purchased in large quantities. For more information, please call (212) 572-2232 or email specialmarkets@penguinrandomhouse.com. Your local bookstore can also assist with discounted bulk purchases using the Penguin Random House corporate Business-to-Business program. For assistance in locating a participating retailer, email B2B@penguinrandomhouse.com.

Image credits: page xxi, *The Asahi Shimbun* / Getty Images; page 4, Professor Matthew Bennett / Bournemouth University; page 21, courtesy of Professor Ying-yi Hong; page 34, iStock; page 57, photo by Professor Jean Clottes / Chauvet Cave Scientific Team; page 89, courtesy of Shiry Ginosar; page 111, Bettmann / Getty Images; page 144, Wikimedia Commons via CC BY-SA 3.0; page 165, by Jan Collsiöö via Wikimedia Commons; page 209, Str Old / Reuters Pictures.

LIBRARY OF CONGRESS CATALOGING-IN-PUBLICATION DATA
Names: Morris, Michael W., author.
Title: Tribal : how the cultural instincts that divide
us can help bring us together / Michael Morris.
Description: New York : Portfolio/Penguin, [2025] |
Includes bibliographical references and index.
Identifiers: LCCN 2024007382 (print) | LCCN 2024007383 (ebook) |
ISBN 9780735218093 (hardcover) | ISBN 9780735218116 (ebook)
Subjects: LCSH: Tribes—Social aspects. | Tribes—Psychological aspects. |
Culture—Psychological aspects. | Loyalty—Psychological aspects.
Classification: LCC GN490 .M67 2025 (print) |
LCC GN490 (ebook) | DDC 305.01/9—dc23/eng/20240610
LC record available at https://lccn.loc.gov/2024007382
LC ebook record available at https://lccn.loc.gov/2024007383

Printed in the United States of America
1st Printing

BOOK DESIGN BY CHRIS WELCH

To Tatjana

CONTENTS

Introduction: The Riddle of Hiddink   ix

PART I
TRIBAL TRIGGERS

1   Syncing Up   3

2   Slaying Giants   33

3   Visiting the Temple   56

PART II
TRIBAL SIGNALS

4   The Rise and Fall of Prohibition   83

5   Soap Operas and Social Change   103

6   Inside the History Factory   126

PART III

TRIBAL RIPPLES

7   When Change Spreads, and When It
Fizzles Out   151

8   Toxic Tribalism and Its Antidotes   178

Acknowledgments   217

Notes   221

Index   291

THE RIDDLE OF HIDDINK

A year and a half before South Korea would host the 2002 World Cup, the Land of the Morning Calm was anything but. Its national soccer team, usually a regional power, had faltered in the 2000 Asian Cup, failing to beat lightweights like Kuwait. Meanwhile, its archrival and cohost, Japan, had gone undefeated to claim the trophy.

More than sports was at stake. After a difficult century of colonization, war, and political unrest, South Korea had ascended to the elite tier of economies. Its ethos of success through striving and sacrifice helped it land the Cup. Then the 1997 financial crisis crushed its economy, exposed corruption, and brought a humiliating bailout from abroad. In the wake of this, leaders held out hope that an impressive showing could restore the country's reputation for competence. But now the world's oddsmakers were betting that it would be the first-ever host nation to fail to advance beyond group play to the tournament rounds. Yet another humiliation loomed.

The worried chief of the Korean Football Association (KFA), Chung Mong-joon, placed a long-distance call to the Netherlands. On the other end of the line was Guus Hiddink, a graying Dutch coach with a dog-eared passport, a rumpled tracksuit, and a track record for bringing out the talent in teams. In the 1998 World Cup, he led a formerly divided Dutch squad to the semifinals. Along the way, they thrashed South Korea's Reds 5–0, which both depressed and impressed its soccer overlords. Now, those overlords were asking him to come coach their stumbling team at its moment of truth. From game tapes, Hiddink saw that the team's style of play remained slow and outdated. He had heard that the KFA meddled in roster decisions, sometimes inserting players based on their social backgrounds rather than just their talents. He called Chung back, apologizing for his Dutch bluntness, and made some unprecedented provisos: absolute roster control, extra-long training camps, and a budget to invite the world's best for exhibition games.

A month later, the ruddy-faced Hiddink landed in Seoul for his unveiling to the sports press. "I don't know much about Korea," he began. This was not false modesty, they later realized, when he didn't recognize some names of prominent players. However, that lack of recognition might as well have been intentional. Hiddink's first official act was to announce "open tryouts," welcoming not only the country's A-listers but also unknowns just out of high school. All had to prove themselves in demanding drills—and some famous names didn't make the cut. This riled players and rankled fans in a society with a deep respect for age and experience.

Hiddink taught a tactical system called *totaalvoetbal* ("total football"), a fast, pressing style in which players move fluidly around the field to create unexpected plays. Perfected by the Dutch, it was increasingly adopted by elite clubs in other countries. From the scrimmages at the first training camp, however, Hiddink could see that this freewheeling style wouldn't come easily. His players moved the ball in more regimented ways, often predictably passing to more senior teammates. Worse yet, the youngsters he had selected for their speed would balk in front of the net when they had clear shots. Then they'd apologize to the veterans for their mistakes, sometimes reprising this self-criticism in press interviews afterward.

The squad was playing poorly, but Hiddink didn't cut the underperformers or chide them from the sidelines. Instead, he called a formal meeting. His Korean translator winced when relaying the coach's gloomy assessment that their current form would result in an early exit from the tournament. To underscore this threat, he reminded them that the Reds had never won a game in five previous World Cup appearances. But if they would commit to a grueling regimen of advanced fitness workouts throughout their long training camp, there was hope. They might gain a stamina advantage like the one that had carried the miracle North Korean team into the 1966 tournament. The men in red met eyes for a moment and answered: "*Ye!*" They would do whatever it takes.

The coach then stunned the team with a new set of ground rules. The next round of training would be held halfway across the world—at an international soccer facility in the United Arab Emirates—where cutting-edge kinesiologists would lead them through next-level workouts. The Korean press would be ceremoniously *un*invited. The changes extended even to matters of grammar: the Korean language's honorific formulations (which he had learned rookies were using to address their veteran teammates, even in fast-moving situations on the field) were henceforth banned. Hiddink rationalized all these policies in terms of efficiency, but they also transformed the cultural cues surrounding players. Onlookers started to question the coach's sanity—or at least his sensitivity. Was he "ignoring the cultural differences and asking Koreans to work, play and train like

Europeans overnight," as a *New York Times* reporter questioned? "Maybe you are right," Hiddink replied, "or maybe these players can adapt quicker than you think."

Soon, Hiddink's bet seemed to be paying off. The changed setting brought out different sides of his players' identities and fostered their learning. Players carried themselves like the other international pros who were training there. The Korean social habits that had been slowing their play—deference and self-criticism—surfaced less frequently on the field. Veterans became less attached to regimented set pieces. Rookies felt freer to react spontaneously and take scoring opportunities.

Still, as the Reds started their summer 2001 schedule against the world's best teams, their *totaalvoetbal* often lapsed into total chaos. A central tactic is swapping positions with a teammate to throw off defenders. But the Reds didn't have enough experience playing this way to read each other's minds and mesh with their moves. In May, they fell to France 5–0. After another 5–0 loss in August to the Czech Republic, the Korean press branded Hiddink "Oh Dae Young" (Mr. 5–0). The Reds were losing worse than ever. A retired Reds manager blamed it on the "ignorant" foreigner. The team's major sponsor, Samsung, canned a pricey TV commercial it had shot featuring the beleaguered coach.

During the extended camp that followed, Reds players continued to hone their skills and build their stamina. However, daily social interactions began to settle into old grooves of the team's traditions. Veterans like Hong Myung-bo (who had played in three previous Cups) guided the rest through the old-fashioned warm-ups the Reds had always done. Longtime staffers regaled players with tales of heroes from past squads. Rituals of camp life reconfigured themselves, such as rookies waiting at meals for veterans to first take a table. Some days they even polished the veterans' shoes. All of this hit home for Hiddink one day when a rookie confided that it felt somehow wrong—against the Reds' way—to swap places with a veteran famous for playing his position.

Traditions are invaluable for unifying a team, but these rituals were teaching the wrong lessons. Deference to seniority (whether from Korean habits or now from Reds traditions) impeded *totaalvoetbal* fluidity. But Hiddink kept faith in adaptation. If these Reds traditions had coalesced in the hothouse environment of training camp, then surely new traditions could be forged the same way. Once again, Hiddink imposed strange policies, this time transforming their daily social interactions. He nixed the veteran-led warm-up routines as too "robotic." He appointed younger players to captain-like roles. He assigned seats for all meals, interweaving rookies and veterans. He sat them together on flights and roomed them together at hotels. He started calling fouls on innocent players repeatedly until they finally protested, then he lauded them for standing up to authority. For players from a culture where even meeting the eyes of an elder can come across as insolent, these were unfamiliar and uncomfortable experiences. But after months of this every day, interacting as equals became the new normal: the new Reds tradition.

As their culture evolved—and their fitness training reached completion—the Reds' game finally began to gel. In an exhibition game, they crushed Scotland 4–1. In the friendly matches leading up to the Cup, they fought England to an impressive draw. Then the Reds stayed within a goal of reigning champ France. In the sportsbooks, they were still 150-to-1 no-hopers, but the players began to believe.

In the initial group play, their first draw was a towering Polish squad, which to the soccer savants in the broadcast booth portended doom. However, the Reds' explosive attacks kept the Poles on defense. Thirty-three-year-old Hwang Sun-hong struck first to establish a precarious lead, then after halftime thirty-year-old Yoo Sang-chul added a swerving shot into the net. The home crowd of fifty thousand fans, including President Kim Dae-jung, rose to their feet for the rest of the game, clapping steadily to rally their team on to a historic victory. Next, the Reds faced a tough American squad and fell behind, placing tournament hopes in jeopardy. Yet their fan club, the Red Devils, carried on with its rhythmic chant—"*Dae-Han-Min-Guk*" (Republic of Korea), *clap-clap clap-clap clap*—drowning out any sound of "U-S-A!" The Reds kept pressing in aggressive runs. Finally, in the closing minutes, a graceful header by twenty-six-year-old Ahn Jung-hwan (more famed for his movie-star looks than late-game heroics) sealed a draw. Screens all across Korea replayed the glorious goal, and popular excitement mounted for the final group match against powerhouse Portugal. From the very start, the stadium shook with the beat of *buk* drums from the Devils section. The veteran sweeper Hong lofted elegant passes to tee up headers that kept falling *just* wide of the net, keeping fans on the edge of their seats. Then in the seventieth minute, the tireless twenty-one-year old Park Ji-sung took a cross in midair, deflected it off a defender, and then drilled a winner through the keeper's legs. The crowd's applause rose to a frenzied roar. The team fed off this energy to attack again and again, while the exhausted Portuguese struggled to keep pace.

The Reds won the game and, thereby, won their group. The team had shown steely resolve under pressure. What's more, it had sparkled with style, dazzling fans with artful passes and acrobatic goals. The host nation that had braced itself for disgrace instead felt exultation.

▼

Every World Cup, the soccer sages of the media soliloquize about a clash of cultures on the field: German industriousness versus Brazilian samba, Italian artistry versus British pragmatism. To Hiddink, these "national character" stereotypes never quite rang true.

Hiddink believed that cultural backgrounds and identities influence players, but not so rigidly that they are limited to one style. He had faith, born of his own experience playing in different countries, that the role of culture is variable, not constant. When he first coached in the Dutch league, he tried importing a star from abroad. Grizzled coaches scoffed that it would never work, a Brazilian would never fit *totaalvoetbal*. But after experimenting with many minor adjustments in practice, the synergy finally clicked, and the club went on to championships. Then he and others tried bringing the "Dutch style" to Spanish teams supposedly unsuited to it, forging new variants of the style in the process.

Most coaches of the time regarded cultures as something too sacrosanct to touch. Hiddink, in his down-to-earth way, saw them as *manageable* and even *malleable*. While many coaches believed that national culture was an influence on playing style, few intuited that they could switch on or switch off cultural forces through architecting the cues that surrounded players. While many coaches had sought to harness their team's organizational culture, few dared to think that they could reprogram this culture through choreographing the players' social interactions.

After his 2002 run in South Korea, Hiddink repeated the trick, coaching Australia's Socceroos to its first-time tournament rounds in the 2006 World Cup and then leading underdog Russia to the semifinals of the 2008 Euro Cup. Each time, he managed and molded cultures through cryptic policies and crafty messages. The Socceroos brimmed with athleticism but lacked tactical coordination. Hiddink quashed their boisterous cheering from the bench (which was hampering communication on the field) and imposed strict zones for defenders (so they stopped running all over the field). He reined in selfish stars by invoking the Aussie taboo against "tall poppies." The Russian squad had a somewhat opposite syndrome of rigid risk aversion, so Hiddink introduced playful routines at practices to loosen them up. He sold them on the *totaalvoetbal* system by showing them tapes of its earliest incarnation: the pressing defense of a 1960s Moscow coach. Their Russian pride became a force for learning rather than an obstacle to it. Later, Hiddink took over a squabbling squad of international stars at Chelsea, remolded the team culture, and compiled the best coaching record in the English Premier League.

Consistent success—all around the world, at different levels—can't be just luck. There must be a method to Hiddink's madness, a means of unlocking talent through selectively evoking and adjusting cultural patterns. Like a horse whisperer, he found ways to summon traits that helped performance and to subdue traits that hindered it. He found ways to gradually reshape each team's image of itself. And this cultural alchemy—the secrets to the riddle of Hiddink—could make a difference far beyond the soccer pitch.

Around the same time that Hiddink was developing his heretical views about culture on the soccer field, the scientists who study culture were shifting their paradigms in somewhat parallel ways. Not unlike the "old guard" soccer coaches, the older generation of scholars presumed that cultural landscapes were permanent fixtures. Anthropology portrayed Indigenous societies in terms of timeless institutions (e.g., the Haida people hold *potlatch* feasts before putting up totem poles). Psychology compared individual traits (e.g., achievement-oriented personalities were rife in the US and rare in India). These approaches reduced cultures to stable patterns—age-old institutions or fixed character traits.

However, by the late twentieth century, it became hard to miss that cultural patterns—of societies and of individuals—were in flux. Across the world, societies were evolving as globalized generations developed new lifestyles through selective retention of their parents' ways and heightened borrowing from other traditions. Individuals were migrating more than ever but not always assimilating—instead, maintaining multiple cultural worldviews that they switched between situationally. Scholars began to appreciate that it was not simply collective institutions or individual psychologies that determined culture, but the interplay between them. Cultural institutions shape the individual's mind, and the individual's mind shapes cultural institutions. Culture and psyche are inexorably intertwined.

Over the past two decades, this fusion of anthropology and psychology has produced a new science called "cultural psychology." Its scholars study many different kinds of cultural groups—from hunter-gatherer clans to corporations to nations—investigating cognitive structures, social structures, biases, and behaviors. It is an interdisciplinary crossroads where scholars from different scientific and cultural backgrounds collaborate. I've been fortunate to play a part in the exciting growth of this field. Through the luck of good timing, I've conducted some of the pathbreaking studies that shaped the field's trajectory. A major lesson from the hundreds of studies that I have conducted is that cultural patterns are mutable and malleable, and that with the right tools, we—like Hiddink—can harness them.

Though science is increasingly adopting this dynamic paradigm, the practical world still tends to construe cultural patterns as unchanging (and unchangeable). Politicians reference Appalachia's "culture of poverty" to imply that economic aid won't help. Journalists warn of "rape culture on campus," "gun culture in Texas," or "drug culture in Hollywood." Leaders trace their group's success to its cultural essence: art "runs in the blood" of the Italian people; loyalty is "bred into the bone" by the Marine Corps; innovation is in IBM's "cultural DNA." These familiar phrases posit an underlying essence inside members of a tribe that makes them who they are and enables their distinctive talents.

But essentialism gets cultures wrong—sometimes *tragically* wrong. When a nation, corporation, or team chalks up its success to an immutable essence, it's a recipe for complacency. The scrap heap of history is full of invincible empires, corporations "built to last," and perennial champs. Conversely, when we trace an adversary's sins to immutable imprinting, we become prone to heavy-handed and unhelpful reprisals. After 9/11, US hawks targeted madrassas (Islamic schools that cater to the poor) as "breeding grounds for terrorists," assuming that jihadi ideals must be inculcated at a mullah's knee. But radicalism is more a product of resentment than religiosity. *None* of the attackers attended a madrassa; they studied technical subjects at Western universities (Mohammed Atta studied urban restoration, of all things) and were radicalized then. Likewise, ISIS recruitment came largely from the disenfranchised, not the devout. Its breeding grounds were not madrassas but military prisons and marginalized neighborhoods (revealed by a purchase left behind in a recruit's London flat: *Islam for Dummies*). Counterterrorism measures that target whole religions and their basic institutions miss the real sources of radicalization. Worse yet, they play into the hands of extremists by alienating moderates.

Contrary to essentialist views of cultural character as set in stone, people's cultural conditioning and convictions change over time. We internalize new cultural identities and codes with every new community we join. You may have noticed this in a college freshman who returned home for Thanksgiving with a new persona—listening to new music, spouting new expressions, dressing in a different style, perhaps attesting to different politics. Or you may know someone who joined the army—or joined an ashram—and similarly acquired a fresh identity and outlook. The human brain is wired to automatically encode the ways of the communities that nurture us. We pick up cultural patterns unconsciously, without even trying to. These automatic learning processes play this same role when a group's changed experiences precipitate new patterns of collective behavior. When Hiddink roomed Reds rookies with veterans, banned Socceroo shouting, and revealed *totaalvoetbal*'s Russian roots, he was cultivating transformed team cultures.

In addition to learning new cultures, people switch between their multiple cultural mindsets situationally. Walt Whitman said it best: "I am large, I contain multitudes." A person's many cultural selves can't all rule at once; they have to take turns. When our freshman friend returns home, her newfound campus persona isn't on display every day. It surfaces when her college roommate visits, but not when she hangs out with her childhood friends. Cultural codes spring to the fore of our minds when they are triggered by the situation. This is another key to the riddle of Hiddink. When he transported the Reds to an international training facility abroad, he was placing them in a setting that would call forth their occupational norms as soccer pros and give a rest to their national habits as Koreans. At that stage, the team needed a mindset conducive to learning the unfamiliar tactics required for world-class play.

Tribal will elucidate the hidden dynamics of cultural codes that are drawn upon by Hiddink and other changemakers. I've developed frameworks for understanding and managing these dynamics over many years of teaching about related topics at top business schools (a decade at Stanford's Graduate School of Business in Silicon Valley, another at Columbia Business School in New York City, and shorter stretches at leading institutions in London, Paris, Barcelona, Hong Kong, Singapore, and elsewhere). I've worked on the side as a consultant to tech firms, global banks, media conglomerates, and other companies, helping to change organizational cultures, foster diversity, and develop cross-cultural skills. Likewise, I've worked with military leaders to develop better models of cultural challenges among allies and adversaries, with the State Department and foreign ministries to understand diversity dynamics, and with the Intelligence Community to trigger the cultural biases of hackers. I've worked with public health experts and NGOs seeking to change cultural norms related to health and gender in the developing world. I've advised political campaigns about culture-relevant policies and messaging, including the presidential campaigns of Barack Obama, Hillary Clinton, and Joe Biden. I can't claim to have worked Hiddink-level miracles in these roles, but I do have a wide range of experience putting these ideas into practice.

Despite this work to share insights with practitioners, cultural dynamics are still not very widely understood. While elite corporations are catching on, the tools are just as useful for schools, restaurants, design studios, and many other workplaces where cultural capital matters. Almost everywhere these days, cultural differences can divide, or they can be leveraged for performance and innovation. Many of the relevant research findings about this exist only in technical journals where few can access them. That's the reason for this book. I've tried to leave the jargon behind and convey the practical insights through stories about culture shifters and shapers like Coach Hiddink.

▼

As the tournament rounds began in the 2002 World Cup, South Korea drew top-ranked Italy. The Italians scored early to take the lead and their famed defenders stopped repeated Korean efforts to answer. Yet the ever-swelling section of Red Devils, now wearing face paint and waving flags, rallied their team with propulsive cheering and drumming: *"Dae-Han-Min-Guk," boom-boom boom-boom boom!* As the game wore on in the summer humidity, the Reds' fitness edge began to show, and in the closing minutes the quick reflexes of twenty-three-year-old forward Seol Ki-hyeon found the net to send the match into extra time. Hiddink kept calling out "Sudden death!" to summon vigilant defense and killer instinct. Meanwhile, the Italians began to fatigue and commit fouls. Finally, in the 117th minute, the striker Ahn found a burst of energy to somehow out-jump defender Paolo Maldini and spin a header past the helpless keeper.

The stadium exploded into rapture. Fans of all ages shook outstretched

fists, Hiddink's signature goal celebration. The victory set off shock waves across the country, literally: "When Ahn scored the golden goal, I could feel the apartment building vibrate from the cheering," a Seoul retiree told reporters. An estimated four million revelers in team regalia filled the streets, soused on *soju*, chanting *"Dae-Han-Min-Guk"* as gridlocked cabbies tooted along with their horns (*Beep-beep beep-beep beep!*). Fans hung signs from their balconies that read "Hiddink for President." Posters and figurines of the once-reviled foreign coach flew out of the shops. The formerly canceled Samsung ad began airing every hour.

The quarterfinal against undefeated Spain was another taut affair. Gwangju Stadium was a sea of red. Korean fans clapped but also wrung their hands as Spain found the net twice, but the goals were disallowed by referees. The game remained scoreless through ninety minutes and then extra time. Finally, in the penalty shoot-out, Korea's composure prevailed once again. After the veteran Hong converted the winning kick, he looked up to see forty thousand fans on their feet applauding manically. Unsure of what to do, the team bowed like actors at a curtain call, to one side of the stadium, then the other, to one goal, then the other. The crowd's roar resolved itself into two syllables—*Hee-dink, Hee-dink, Hee-dink!*—and the coach finally trotted out to center field. His players lifted him and tossed him high into the air. Thousands of flashbulbs froze the moment. The image fronted every newspaper the next morning. With transformed tactics and traditions, they became the first Asian team to reach the semis!

This wasn't just a feel-good story for football fans; it became a signal moment for the nation. Spontaneous celebrations broke out in every city and village, a final liberation from the lingering malaise of the economic crisis. Journalists described the team's triumph as "the greatest moment since the end of Japanese colonial rule." President Kim went further, calling it "the greatest day since Dangun" (the legendary king who founded Korea four thousand years ago).

The Reds' run eventually ended in a semifinal loss to Germany, but the chain reaction had gone critical and there was no stopping it. This transformed team was trumpeted in the press as a model for schools, companies, and agencies. The wavy-haired star Ahn, who married Miss Korea, became a celebrity, while Coach Hiddink became something more than that. His statue was erected in parks, and Gwangju Stadium became renamed "Guus Hiddink Stadium." Journalists compared him to Hendrick Hamel, the seventeenth-century Dutch sailor who introduced Korea to the West. The government emblazoned his visage on a Korean postage stamp, then (in order to make him an honorary citizen) they changed the country's age-old ethnic restriction: "the conquest of blood-lineage nationalism." Symbolically and literally, South Korea opened itself up to the outside world. It was a critical step toward the confident, cosmopolitan South Korea that we know today—a cultural exporter whose soap operas delight the Middle East, whose K-pop bands top the charts, and whose films win Oscars for Best Picture.

Hiddink's coaching policies, intended to sharpen a single team for one tournament, had much broader ripple effects. New social patterns spread from the soccer pitch to the stands, then the streets, and then the institutions of education, business, and government.

This speaks to the power—and also the danger—of cultural change. Culture is not just malleable; it can be labile and sometimes downright volatile. Hiddink never imagined he'd become an icon of Korean cosmopolitanism, but that happened within months of the Cup. Because of the way cultural patterns are cued and encoded, they sometimes spread through domino effects. Hence, changemakers need to understand not just how to initiate changes, but also how changes can take on a life of their own—for better or for worse. To harness these mysterious ripple effects, we need to consider more deeply what culture is and how it affects us. How did humans evolve to connect this way in the first place?

▼

Aristotle called our species "the social animal." But we are not the *only* social animal. Wolves run in packs. Penguins huddle together for warmth. Elephants call out to each other when lost.

Humans are not even the *most* social animal. Ants, bees, and termites put humanity to shame on many metrics of sociality. Myriad relatives live together with seamlessly meshing behavior and collectively care for their young. But while insect colonies are impressively social places, it's not *our* kind of social life. Bees always build hexagonal hives, ants march in lines, and termites swarm in zigzag strides. These patterns recur predictably because they are tightly programmed genetically and propelled pheromonally. We humans are more free, less tightly programmed genetically, so our social patterns can be more diverse and dynamic. Every group dances a slightly different dance, and these choreographies change across generations. We still think and act in ways that mesh with others around us, but it is through patterns that are more shaped by nurture, not just nature.

Our closest evolutionary relatives, chimpanzees, have some of this same behavioral freedom. Chimps can choose whether to cooperate or compete with a neighbor. To lock in cooperation, a chimp needs to bond with each chimp in the group through mutual grooming, a time-consuming process. This need for direct friendship limits how large the circle of cooperation can grow. When a chimpanzee troop expands beyond fifty members, cooperation breaks down into clashing factions. Put a hundred unrelated chimpanzees on an island, and the result would be a bloodbath. A chimpanzee Manhattan, with millions of strangers rubbing shoulders, is inconceivable.

Humans, too, cooperate based on kinship and friendship, but we also have more powerful forms of social glue that other species lack. From the early Stone Age, we started evolving specialized brain systems that facilitated sharing knowledge in groups. If someone in your foraging band figured out how to dislodge coconuts from a tree, you would learn by watching, and soon the whole group would share the skill. Then you could work in closer coordination with each other by following this shared script. In this way, groups living in different ecologies developed different pools of common knowledge: different cultures. Members of each group gained increased mutual understanding; even if the topic wasn't coconuts, the common ground of shared coconut expertise could help in learning other survival-relevant skills. Group membership became increasingly manifest in behavior, making peers more similar, predictable, and sympathetic. Our forebears began to experience the elevating sense of "Us," an expansion of identity beyond close kinship and direct friendship to a broader group. In these larger clans, they began to highlight their membership through distinctive styles of dress and self-adornment. At the same time, human brains kept evolving to share new kinds of knowledge, such as reputation in these broader groups, all of which further boosted our fitness as social animals. In time, interactions using new forms of knowledge, such as ritual, coalesced across clans to forge broad networks of sharing in mates, resources, and knowledge. Humans began feeling solidarity with these large communities (thousands of other people living in small groups nested within larger groups) held together by the glue of common cultural knowledge. This form of social organization is not a hive or a troop but a *tribe*.

Surviving through sharing knowledge in these solidaristic, nested groups is tribal living. With apologies to Aristotle, it's misleading to call humans "the social animal." We are more accurately "the tribal animal."

The word "tribe," however, has taken on considerable baggage. It originated in the Latin term *tribus*, for the cultural and regional groups that made up ancient Rome. It came into English (and other languages) with biblical translations for the twelve tribes of Israel. By Shakespeare's time, it referred to the Jewish people, to Germanic clans, and to New World societies. Only during the era of colonialist expansion did "tribe" take on pejorative connotations of primitivism. European explorers had a vested interest in categorizing the Indigenous peoples they met as at different stages of societal development—"savage" or "barbaric" tribes rather than civilized societies. Left behind by the march of history, they needed the civilizing influence of European armies, missionaries, and schools. These categories were politics, not science.

As anthropology developed as a field, it dropped the evolutionary stage frameworks, and the tribe concept came to be used very broadly. Successive efforts were made to clarify the concept structurally in terms of kinship, authority, or continuity—but without definitive progress. As more and more Indigenous peoples were studied, exceptions rose against every structural criterion: tribes without a chief, tribes with members mostly adopted from other groups, tribes that changed their language, religion, or origin story. The evidence from careful ethnographies diverged so sharply from the classical image of tribes with standard structures of leadership, kinship, and tradition that many anthropologists abandoned the tribe concept, surmising that the notion was just a colonialist mirage. Some even abandoned the theory of culture as a driver of behavior, explaining India's "sacred cows" in terms of soil conditions rather than Hindu myths.

By the late twentieth century, the pervasive wave of cultural change spelled the end for theories of tribes as rigid structures, but it awakened renewed curiosity about cultural evolution. An exciting new strain of theory and research emerged, providing novel explanations of how tribal living originated in our Stone Age forebears and developed across the ages. Human cultural evolution and genetic evolution have been intimately intertwined from the start of our species, and they continue to affect each other. As early humans learned more and more adaptive lessons from experience (*eat red berries, not green berries*), mutations conferring brain systems for social learning and imitation became adaptive. As a result of these new psychological adaptations, the pools of shared knowledge in human communities became richer, and this cultural evolution then created new selection pressures for further genetic adaptations. And so on and so on. This cycle of enriched cultures and enhanced brains spawned new human species throughout the Stone Age—each one brainier, more cultural, and more cooperative than the previous. This upward spiral of co-evolution is nothing less than a new origin story for our kind, one that places tribes and tribal psychology at the center of the plot.

The new science of cultural evolution also sheds light on the complex ways that tribes change across generations. While theories about these processes of cultural evolution are expressed in complex mathematical models, one of the central insights is that cultural transmission hinges on learning processes. A culture evolves as some elements are learned and others are overlooked as the rising generation re-creates the society. Close studies implicate particular biases in social learning. Conformity bias means that widespread customs are more likely to be learned than rare customs. Prestige bias means that those associated with success and status are more likely to be learned and passed on. Anthropologist Lawrence Rosen suggested that the ways tribes evolve may be what best distinguishes them—tribes are best defined not "in their structural manifestations but in the capabilities that allow them to adapt."

Other quirks of social learning, such as a bias toward continuity with deep tradition, might seem to inhibit cultural change. Yet when hijacked by political movements that mythologize halcyon eras, the drive for continuity can turn into an engine for reactionary change. Some scholars prefer media theorist Marshall McLuhan's term of "re-tribalization." To understand the many twists and turns of cultural change, we can look to the biases of learning within our tribal psychology.

In this book, I peel the onion of our special human talent for sharing with groups to distinguish three layers of "tribal instincts." They originated in the Stone Age, but we can still recognize these evolved systems in our minds and hearts today. Our sideways glances at classmates, coworkers, and neighbors are part of the *peer instinct*, as is our impulse to mesh with their patterns in our everyday inferences and actions. Our upward-directed fascination with celebrities, CEOs, MVPs, and other elites comes from the *hero instinct*, as do our aspirations for glory and our drive to contribute. Our backward-gazing nostalgia is part of the *ancestor instinct*, as is the comfort we find in traditions and the duty we feel to maintain them. These instincts are like three characters inside every person: the conformist who seeks belonging and understanding, the contributor who dreams of esteem and tribute, and the traditionalist who cherishes continuity. Each of these systems has its fallibilities, but—as we'll see—each generally guides people in adaptive directions.

The real wonder, though, is what the three systems create in combination. Once all three tribal instincts were in place, in the last hundred thousand years, our forebears began to thrive and to live in recognizably human ways. Within an evolutionary eyeblink, they suddenly had much more sophisticated tools, weapons, arts, and rituals. After millions of years of achingly slow change, cultural complexity began to expand exponentially. The pools of shared knowledge in human communities began to accumulate across generations and adapt to local ecologies. This tribe-level learning (not heightened individual brainpower) is the secret to how our kind adapted to widely differing different climates and terrains. Humans became the earth's dominant species, threatened only by our own success.

In *Tribal*, I hope to reclaim the original meaning of the word as community enabled by shared culture. This is how humankind first transcended the narrow bonds of kith and kin to accomplish bigger things in clans. And it's how we later ventured into exchange and collaboration with strangers in the broader networks called "tribes." In these nested groups, our forebears first felt the empowering experience of access to myriad individuals and ideas, the ongoing experiment that we call society. It was an engine for group change and differentiation. By showing that tribal living is the source of cultural change and progress, I hope to put to rest any lingering association of tribes with stasis and primitivism. Tribal living is what made us truly human.

Just as the word "tribe" largely vanished from anthropology, it began to proliferate in popular parlance. The term and its cognates are used by creedal communities (the Jewish tribe, Amish tribes) and Indigenous nations (the Navajo tribe, the Zulu tribe). Companies chose the term to honor their "power users" (the Mac tribe) and devoted employees (the Zappos tribe). Political analysts applied it to partisan factions. Marketers saw neo-tribes in consumer networks (gamers, environmentalists, extreme sports enthusiasts). Professions, occupations, and vocations found the term felicitous, as did communities formed around shared tastes—Deadheads, surfers, swingers, cyclists, and the like. Likewise for alumni groups, fan clubs, Mardi Gras bands, and Burning Man camps. More than any other English noun, "tribe" captures the sense of meaning and motivation that people find in communities united by shared ideologies, expertise, or aesthetics. I use this concept in search of general principles governing all of these communities—from cave-painting clans to the book clubs, tech firms, and nation-states of today.

Especially in a time of powerful and shifting politics, we shouldn't ignore our quintessential human capacities to bond with our communities. Nor should we delude ourselves that the thin gruel of rationality and universalism will mobilize people to accomplish desired goals. Guus Hiddink didn't lead his teams to success through appealing to rational self-interest. He led by harnessing tribal motivations—the pull to mesh with peers, the drive to be a hero, and the ache to maintain traditions. Focusing his players temporarily on their team identity or their occupational identity didn't eliminate their ethnic and national identities; it ultimately reinforced them. Leaders who can harness tribal impulses can lift a team to greatness and, under the right conditions, this can reverberate in ways that heal a nation. In other words, we shouldn't fight tribalism—we should channel it.

I write as a convert to the advocacy of tribalism. I used to consider group-related instincts as a detrimental force in human affairs. I was raised (as you may have been too) to see rationality, creativity, and morality as the hallmarks of humanity, and I viewed conformity, status-seeking, and traditionalism as fallibilities. But based on what I've learned from decades as a behavioral scientist, I've come to see my former humanities worldview as naive, or at least incomplete. Our tribal instincts are not *bugs* in the system that hinder an otherwise intelligent species. They are the distinguishing *features* of our kind that enabled its evolutionary ascent— and still drive many of its greatest achievements today. They are not human foibles that hold us back; they are human superpowers that create our distinctive cultures.

In this book, we'll get to know the three basic tribal instincts one at a time, opening their hoods to see the underlying mechanisms that make them run. That humans are inclined to imitate peers, emulate heroes, and perpetuate traditions is not exactly news. But what will surprise you is just how powerful and pervasive these familiar instincts are. They sustain cultures of very different kinds—religious, regional, occupational, and more. These instincts reveal hidden levers for aligning, inspiring, and emboldening people. And we'll demystify the paradoxes of change, seeing why many ambitious change initiatives stall out while other movements take off and spread beyond their founders' wildest dreams.

This book unfolds in several sections. In part I, "Tribal Triggers," we'll look back at how our forebears evolved each instinct and gained new social breakthroughs as a result. Because cultural codes can't all operate at once, they are activated by triggers. Peer, hero, and ancestor codes are triggered by both situational cues and our inner needs. These are the keys that Hiddink turned in his varied training camps to activate or deactivate cultural codes. We'll see how figures as diverse as Joan of Arc, Martin Luther King Jr., and Singapore's Lee Kuan Yew used cues to lift groups to face epic challenges. Sometimes triggers arise organically to unlock the cultural strengths needed for a challenge, as when a team of senior-citizen engineers, the Fukushima 50, rallied around the samurai code to save a nuclear plant teetering on the brink of catastrophe.

In part II, "Tribal Signals," the three layers of culture—peer, hero, and ancestor codes—reveal themselves as not just manageable but also malleable. Hiddink reshaped the Reds' team norms through changed routines and reshaped the Russians' sense of tradition by informing them about a Moscow team from generations past. These are examples of how cultural codes get shaped—or reshaped—by informational signals. The unconscious effects of tribal signals elucidate many dramatic and mysterious changes, such as how Brazil defused its population bomb without a family planning policy, how soft-spoken Satya Nadella restored Microsoft to the top of the tech industry, and how Nelson Mandela led the rainbow nation through its collective trauma and into a democratic future.

Part III, "Tribal Ripples," builds on these previous sections to explore how cultural change spreads more broadly. The opening chapter considers how chain reactions work in models for managing change. A "grassroots movement" is a bottom-up sequence of changes, from ordinary people's habits to collective ideals to public institutions. "Shock therapy" prescribes an opposite, top-down progression. Tribal psychology shows us how each sequence creates ripple effects of change and the conditions to which each strategy is best suited. We'll see why the grassroots strategy worked for same-sex marriage but not for the Occupy movement. We'll see why a shock-wave strategy helped Mary Barra jumpstart change at GM but back-fired for Ellen Pao at Reddit.

The closing chapter considers unwanted chain reactions in the escalating group conflicts of our day—political, racial, and sectarian. In the past few years, political pundits increasingly blame these pressing problems on toxic tribalism, implying that a primal hate for out-groups has somehow resurfaced to tear our world apart. While it's an engaging theme that the "Us" instincts inevitably create hostility toward "Them," it doesn't square with evolutionary or psychological evidence. A better way to understand escalating conflicts, and the role of evolved psychology therein, is to look for the signature processes of the three familiar tribal instincts, each of which can cycle out of control under certain conditions in dysfunctional ways. Fortunately, our understanding of triggers and signals suggests interventions to break the cycles. To be sure, tribal psychology is part of the problem in many of today's conflicts—but it can also be part of the solution. We'll see how some citizen groups are bridging the divide between peers of red and blue persuasions, how heroes like maestro Gustavo Dudamel have catalyzed ethnic inclusion in workplaces, and how interventions that remind Christians and Muslims about themes of tolerance in their scriptures can reverse their defensive responses to threats, allaying the escalation of sectarian violence.

At a time of ethnic strife, pandemics, and climate crisis, our human capacity to act collectively is more important than ever. We must transcend the Manichean paranoia that our greatest evolutionary blessing carries with it an ineluctable curse. Our tribal instincts are our greatest tool for group cooperation—we should not fear them but learn to harness them. They offer some hope to save us from ourselves. Ultimately, this is a book about how we change—together.

PART I

TRIBAL
TRIGGERS

1

Syncing Up

Alone we can do so little; together we can do so much.

—HELEN KELLER

When mud is just the right consistency, it can stop time in its tracks. In 2007, near Kenya's Lake Turkana, archaeologist Jack Harris, who had worked for decades at the site, brushed away layers of sand to uncover traces of long-ago life. Indentations in the mud had hardened into stone. Among many tracks of birds and antelopes were some familiar oblong prints: ninety-seven impressions of human feet so well preserved that all the toes were visible. Carbon dating revealed, astonishingly, that these prints had been frozen in time for 1.5 million years. They were the oldest human footprints ever discovered.

These fossilized prints offered a tantalizing glimpse into the life of *Homo erectus*, who roamed the earth throughout the early Stone Age. While tried-and-true archaeological techniques could identify the species involved, they couldn't discern what activity the tracks reflected. They

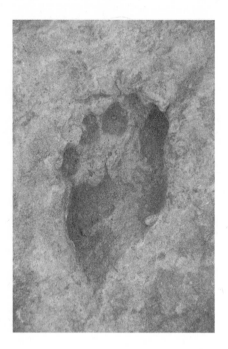

could have been left by a band of passing nomads, by one thirsty individual's repeated water runs, or by any number of other lakeside scenarios.

To plumb this mystery, young scientists flocked to the Turkana site to try
new techniques that had been revitalizing the study of human origins. To
experts on human anatomy and locomotion, minute structural details of
the well-preserved prints spoke volumes. Neil Roach and Kevin Hatala
used precise digital measuring tools and 3D modeling software to match
prints from the same individuals and simulate the strides connecting
them. In a behavioral science approach, they recruited volunteers of different ages and genders from the nearby Daasanach people to walk and
run on some lakeside mud. From these reference points, they could

identify the sex, age, and height of the paleo pedestrians, as well as their timing and pace. The tracks were created by a group of young men trekking quickly together—the earliest evidence of a human sex-segregated group activity. Tellingly, the group traversed the shore like hunters in pursuit of prey, rather than converging on it like seekers of water. The totality of the Turkana evidence points to an intriguing explanation—a hunting party stalking antelope.

Archaeologists had long noticed antelope bones in *erectus* living sites, but had no clue *how* our forebears came by this bounty. Antelopes startle at the slightest sound and sprint away at sixty miles per hour. Not even Usain Bolt could catch one! This early species lacked any weapons that could close the distance. They invented only one tool in their million years on the planet: a handheld chunk of flint used for chopping, pounding, and smashing. This staggering technological stasis gave archaeologists the impression of *erectus* as little beyond apes in intelligence. Some surmised that they came by their occasional venison as scavengers (by scrounging carrion from the savanna after the big cats had had their fill).

But the Turkana tracks raised a more exalted possibility. The San people of the Kalahari Desert (the world's oldest tribe) can stalk antelopes through a technique called "persistence hunting." Several hunters work to separate an animal from its herd and then chase it, track it, and chase it again—repeatedly, until it overheats and collapses (evolution built antelopes to be sprinters, not marathoners). The key to this hunting method is *coordinating* on the same target; it does no good to chase different antelopes around all afternoon. The hunters must form a shared plan. Biologist and professional tracker Louis Liebenberg proposed that early humans like *erectus* could have collaborated this way to hunt antelopes. Roach and Hatala's findings provide supporting archaeological evidence.

The hunting explanation implies that *erectus* enjoyed a larger leap in brain evolution than previously assumed. Our closest ape relatives, chimpanzees, are impressively inventive but not collaborative. A chimp may figure out how to move logs to feast on the termites underneath, but never do two chimps work together to move a log that is too heavy for one of them. Nor do they ever point to inform a peer about something. This is one reason why they can't coordinate to hunt antelopes—they can't point out the intended target. We can't be sure exactly what the young male humans were doing that day long ago near Lake Turkana, but their tracks tell of a level of teamwork beyond what prior primates could muster.

At later sites, archaeologists found hints of coordinated activity in gathering as well as hunting. In Israel's Hula Valley, Naama Goren-Inbar excavated a lakeside site where a soil layer from eight hundred thousand years ago that shows extensive evidence of human inhabitation. Her team uses laboratory techniques to analyze microscopic bits of plants, bones, and stones. From the elevated presence of botanical fragments in these soil layers (relative to earlier and later layers), they infer the foraging of fifty-five different plant species. This harvest was not just low-hanging fruit, mind you, but also included nuts from tall trees, tubers from deep underground, and even water lilies that blossom far from shore. The sheer range and challenge of their foraging bespeaks coordinated work. The haul even included plants that are inedible unless cooked, suggesting that these *erectus* women may have also gathered fire—the glowing embers after a lightning strike that could be used to start cooking fires. In 2004 Goren-Inbar's microscope first discovered bits of charred wood and bone in soil samples, but her team couldn't be sure they weren't from natural fires. Three years later, they discovered "phantom hearths," rings of stone fragments scarred from repeated exposure to fire. A decade earlier, biological anthropologist Richard Wrangham had pondered the evolutionary paradox that *erectus* brains expanded while their jaws and guts shrank (i.e., an increased demand for calories, yet reduced capacity to supply them) and posited that the advent of cooking could be the explanation. Archaeologists at the time scoffed because no hearths could be seen at *erectus* sites, but Goren-Inbar's microscope revealed the smoking gun. We can't reconstruct these primeval barbecues in full detail, but we can bet that roasting an antelope was not a one-caveman (or cavewoman) job. Not even survivalists like Bear Grylls would try that. For the butchery, fire-building, and browning, you'd want a cooking crew working in close coordination.

A final surprise about *erectus* involves language. Chimps use gestural signals to communicate fixed messages but lack grammar for combining these into sentences that express novel ideas (likewise, sign-language training experiments succeed in teaching them many words but not in teaching grammar). This shortcoming is understandable because chimps lack the specialized brain structures that we humans use for syntactic processing. This left-hemisphere circuitry is, neuroscientists believe, the reason that 90 percent of humans are right-handed. Interestingly, studies of *erectus* skeletal asymmetries reveal that they, too, were predominantly right-handed. Paleodental analyses of tooth wear concur: 90 percent stuffed their faces from the right side. This "righty" predominance is not present in chimps or in the australopiths of three million years ago (which immediately preceded the first humans). Its presence in *erectus* suggests the emergence of syntactic circuitry and capacity, likely a gestural language that built on preexisting signals. Contrary to linguist Noam Chomsky's long-dominant theory that language evolved recently and discontinuously in a massive mutation, these findings about handedness (among other discoveries) now place it far deeper in the human cultural past.

Footprints, water lilies, fire scars, tooth wear. Separately, such clues are open to various interpretations. But together, they provide converging evidence that our primordial human predecessor has been grossly underestimated. *Erectus* was not the single-tool simpleton that archaeologists have long portrayed. It was the first hominin to operate in coordinated groups, a critical step toward tribal living. By coordinating—melding minds and meshing actions—*erectus* groups foraged more efficiently, fed themselves, and forged the solidarity that comes from working in concert. Its evolutionary breakthrough was not walking upright (as its name forever implies) but working as a team. Its great innovation was not the hand axe (which all the textbooks trumpet) but the hunting party, the gathering squad, the cooking crew—and the linguistic communication that made them all possible.

These revelations of *erectus* teamwork are part of a dawning scientific awareness that humans' social smarts (and social lives) are more central to our ascent—from prehistory to the present—than previously understood.

Classically, the science of human origins was all about how the *body* evolved. A famed illustration, entitled *The March of Progress*, portrays it as a succession of silhouettes: *Australopithecus* on all fours, then knuckle-dragging *Homo habilis*, *Homo erectus* standing more straight, *Homo heidelbergensis* carrying a crude spear, *Homo neanderthalensis* with a more fine-tooled club, and then finally the upstanding profile of our own kind, *Homo sapiens*. It was progress in terms of posture, at least!

Yet even this triumphalist diagram can't hide that there were trade-offs involved. Across millions of years, our forebears gradually lost apes' thick fur, sharp fangs, crushing grip, and four-legged speed. This was a lot to lose, survival-wise. Big cats could catch them in one pounce. Cave bears could tear them to shreds. But while they lost their physical defenses, they gained brain size. Apes were already brainiacs compared to other mammals, but humans evolved brains three times larger. These freakishly large thinking organs are "gas guzzlers": 2 percent of our body weight that consumes 20 percent of our calories. Anything so resource-consuming must have been very helpful—somehow—to survival.

Thoughts don't leave fossils, so archaeologists didn't have evidence about *how* bigger brains helped. Most presumed that hominid brains ballooned to provide greater mastery over the physical environment. That is, chimps evolved big brains so they could navigate large terrains, devise ways of cracking nuts, and find trees with ripe fruit. Early humans developed even bigger brains to avoid quicksand, craft spears, and build shelters. This explanation seemed so self-evident that it remained untested through most of the twentieth century.

It took a scientist versed in both physiology and primatology to test it. For every primate species, from tiny spider monkeys to hulking mountain gorillas, Robin Dunbar calculated an "encephalization index"—brain size as a proportion of body size. Then he analyzed whether braininess is related to how these primate species live and survive—their range, diet, group size, mating habits, and so forth. The correlations revealed, surprisingly, that brainier species *don't* cover more territory, crack more nuts, or eat more fruit. But they *do* mate more judiciously, maintain longer "pair bonds," and cooperate in larger groups. Brainier primates have more complex social lives. Dunbar proposed a new theory: big brains evolved for mastery of the *social environment*, not mastery of the physical environment.

This "social brain hypothesis" gained further traction as behavioral scientists adopted neuroscience tools for imaging brain activity. A wave of revolutionary studies hooked people up to fMRI machines while they engaged in different kinds of thinking tasks. They found that social judgments (e.g., reading a person's intentions, or anticipating their feelings) are handled by different parts of the brain than judgments about the physical world. The forebrain regions that handle social thinking (e.g., the prefrontal cortex) are the ones that expanded most dramatically in the evolution from apes to us.

Then, in the mid-aughts, another offbeat study sealed the case for social aptitudes as our species' signature strength. An expert on both child cognition and primate cognition, Michael Tomasello decided to conduct the ultimate standardized test. His lab administered a broad battery of aptitude tests to three groups of test-takers: humans, chimps, and orangutans. The humans were preschoolers, so education wouldn't give them an edge. The tests were administered as puzzles with food treats as rewards. Perhaps this seems a foolish study—surely humans (with much bigger brains) were much smarter across the board? Surprisingly not. On standard tests of cognitive capacities relevant to physical things (e.g., object permanence, shape rotation), chimps didn't differ from humans, and orangutans were not far behind. But on tests of social cognitive capacities (e.g., inferring intention from an action, learning a skill from a demonstration), humans performed almost perfectly, whereas the chimps and orangutans floundered. For instance, after watching someone pop open the end of a plastic tube to access the treat inside, all of the human toddlers reproduced this method to solve the puzzle. Chimps and orangutans watched the same demonstration but somehow missed the lesson. When given their turn, they tried to break the tube or bite it open, grimacing with frustration at their inability to get the treat.

It's easy to take social inferences for granted because they come so naturally to us. We can read intentions and reproduce demonstrated actions effortlessly. But they are computationally complex problems for which our brains just happen to have dedicated chips. Our innate wiring for social cognition largely consists of several *tribal instincts*: the human-specific adaptations that evolved to enable our distinctive form of social living. As we'll see, three major tribal instincts evolved at different stages of the Stone Age. They helped our forebears learn the ways of their group and act upon them. In more academic terms, they *encode* group patterns and then *enact* these patterns. You can think of these systems as both a radar that continually scans the social environment and an autopilot that helps you steer safely through it.

Tribal instincts changed the human experience of group living in several ways. First, they accelerated the acquisition of learned skills. With tribal instincts, I don't have to rely on effortful trial-and-error experience, as I can pick up many skills through observation. If I see a peer knocking fruit from a high branch with a stick, my brain encodes this action so that when I am next in the situation I feel impelled to try it. If other group members witness me, *they* can pick up the skill in the same way, and so on and so on, until everyone in the group knows it. As a practice becomes common to a group this way, it takes on meanings and functions beyond its original instrumental value. It's what "we" do. It contributes to similarity within the in-group and distinctiveness from out-groups, heightening feelings of connection and loyalty. It also powerfully enables collaboration. When I learn a skill through observing groupmates, the code is tagged in my head as *shared* by the group. Because *I know* that *they know* it, I can anticipate their moves, understand their intentions, and make complementary contributions. The power of such *known knowns* has been discovered independently in many different fields—linguists call it "common ground," game theorists call it "common knowledge," cognitive scientists term it "second-order knowledge," and psychologists prefer "metacognition."

This transformative tribal wiring—honed by a million years of evolution—put our Stone Age forebears on the path to living in highly cultural and highly collaborative groups. You may have heard the well-worn twentieth-century notion that our forebears knew only small bands of close relatives who lived and foraged together (like a chimpanzee troop) until the "agricultural revolution" of about ten thousand years ago enabled permanent settlements, surplus production, and the time for impractical symbolic activities (such as building the Stonehenge temples). The new

science of the past decade has upended this theory of social development—
not just its chronology but even its phylogeny. Archaeologists have uncovered "princely burials" and temple-building that occurred tens of thousands
of years before any agriculture. Temples paved the way for farms and settlements, not the other way around. Discoveries of large-scale hunts from
hundreds of thousands of years ago show the start of clan-level cooperation.
And fully a million years ago, our forebears already foraged in communicating teams, with coordination far beyond that of other primates. These
discoveries cast the human journey in a new and ennobling light. From
almost the very start of humanity, we have lived as tribal animals.

The breakthroughs of *Homo erectus*, specifically, owe to the first of
these psychological systems, the *peer instinct*. This is an adaptation for
copying learned responses of others, particularly habits shared by multiple
others. Once this brain system was in place, early humans began encoding
how the others in their band hunt game, gather plants, evade predators,
seek mates, and so forth. They also felt impelled to follow these codes,
particularly when in the presence of peers who could coordinate in these
activities. In survival-relevant tasks like foraging and self-defense, working collectively boosts returns and reduces risks. The peer instinct helped
early humans reap the rewards of coordinated effort.

This development of peer codes also made human experience funda-
mentally more social. We are less alone than other primates because we
carry around our peers in our heads. We are continually reminded by our
peer codes of what others in our group tend to do or think. We are kept
company—and sometimes feel suffocated—by the steady stream of suggestions from our unconscious about what's normal to think, normal to
do, or normal to say in a situation. Other primates can collaborate in the
minimal sense of foraging side by side, sometimes mutually benefiting
each other, such as by spooking prey. But it's only as social as the parallel

play of young toddlers. They are not cognitively intertwined and working together from a common plan.

Peer codes pop up automatically in relevant situations, thanks to the brain's associational engine. We don't always follow them, but we feel more motivated to do so when our peers are present. If you grew up in the US, you've probably encoded the response of smiling for a camera. If so, you don't have to *try* to smile; it happens on autopilot, especially if it's a group photo. Conforming to the cultural code helps you mesh with others, and you will be acceptable and understandable to them. In Russia, there is a different cultural code: it's normal to wear a serious expression for the camera (which is why Putin and his henchmen often appear so dour).

The peer instinct makes us far more sensitive to the others around than other primates are. When preschoolers who have learned to solve a puzzle one way see peers who solve it another way, they tend to switch to the method of their peers. Chimps and orangutans put through the same procedure *don't switch*; they stick to the method that has worked for them in the past. So much for "monkey see, monkey do." It's we humans who are the chief copycats and conformists.

We can imitate peers' actions adeptly, in part because we can read their minds. If we observe someone reaching toward a fruit-laden branch with a stick, we immediately "perceive" their intention (from where they are looking, we infer they are *trying* to knock loose some fruit). We then adopt this intention when reproducing the stick trick, and enact the movements needed to accomplish it. Evolutionists trace this capacity to the uniquely "readable" anatomy of our eyes. (They're the "windows to the soul," after all!) When a fellow human directs their gaze at something, their dark irises move against their white sclera. We reflexively track their gaze, which usually reveals its object and strongly hints at their intention. Other apes, such as chimps, have dark sclera (and hence less "readable" eyes).

Accordingly, they lack our gaze-tracking reflex. When a chimp sees some-one knock loose a banana with a stick, they encode the objects and move-ments involved but often miss the precise intention. When trying to reproduce the outcome, they will swing the stick but not follow the precise method. If a third chimp imitates this second chimp, the performance degrades further—it becomes a staticky game of telephone and the skill doesn't spread far. As a result, only very basic learned skills (e.g., using a rock to crack nuts) spread through chimpanzee troops. They can't develop more complex cultures because they lack our special human superpowers for encoding peers' actions and states of mind.

The psychological processes of the peer instinct—attention to peers, mind reading, learning from observation, conformist motivations—are the underappreciated foundation of human culture. We internalize a clus-ter of peer codes for each cultural community we belong to, and they spring up in situations to guide us toward socially safe actions. It's why your mannerisms at church are different than at the gym. It's why, without even realizing it, you greet people and talk differently at Coachella than at a corporate mixer. That said, it doesn't produce original or optimal choices. It explains my changing morning proclivity over the years for egg-white omelets, cold-pressed juices, and avocado toast—a mirror of my peers. It's why crypto investments go suddenly from boom to bust, and bank runs still spread like wildfire. We are not independent rational actors. We are tribal creatures wired to enact peer patterns.

Our peer code conformity helps organizations run, though not without some drawbacks. "Work from home" is ending because firms noticed that, while individual productivity increased, collective productivity declined. The office setting cues the organization's culture (particularly its peer codes) in ways needed for coordinated work. Yet firms still hold their brainstorming retreats "off-site" to cue different ways of thinking. Usually, peer codes and conformity are considered an obstacle to change, but they can be a changemaker's secret weapon when leveraged in the right way. As we'll see, triggering peer codes can spark change in teams, organizations, and even whole societies.

In 1965, Singapore, the newly independent city-state at the tip of the Malay Peninsula, faced a future filled with uncertainties. After escalating ethnic conflicts, it had been summarily expelled from the Federation of Malaysia, leaving it a small island with no hinterland. It had few natural resources— mostly consisting of malarial swamps, without even a source of fresh water. Its port was plagued with corruption. Unemployment was high, education levels were low, and the economy was moribund. International observers were skeptical of the territory's prospects for survival.

It had not always been this way. Singapore was founded in the early nineteenth century by Englishman Thomas Stamford Raffles as a free port. To outcompete Dutch colonies nearby, all ships were equally welcome— the island was free of tariffs and safeguarded by the British navy. The port flourished as a trading post until World War II, when it was occupied and shuttered by Japan, forcing locals into smuggling and operating black markets. After the war, a political movement grew against British rule and eventually threw off British dominion. Singapore then joined its regional neighbors in the Federation of Malaysia. Port operations drifted increasingly into partiality and graft. Merchants greased the palms of officials to expedite dock access and cargo loading, a regional custom known as *suap* or *kumshaw*; otherwise, they risked inventory losses and distorted invoices.

The prime minister charged with rescuing the struggling nation was Lee Kuan Yew. He had begun life in colonial times as Harry Lee, the scion of an Anglophile family. After studying law at Cambridge University, finishing first in his class, he worked as a London lawyer. Then he returned home to lead the anti-colonial movement and the ill-fated union with Malaysia. Now he needed to craft a strategy for the nascent nation.

His vision was not unlike that of Raffles. A "free port" attracts trade. If he could eradicate favoritism and graft from port operations, then trade would increasingly flow through Singapore rather than its regional rivals. It was a practical calculation: "We knew that if we were just like our neighbors, we would die." "I was trying to create," Lee said, looking back, "in a third-world situation, a first-world oasis."

Lee's anti-graft strategy included the usual legal measures, raised penalties against bribery. But anti-corruption laws would not suffice by themselves. In neighboring countries, the penalties on the books included large fines, life imprisonment, and even death. Nonetheless, graft was endemic. It's all too easy to slip a cash-stuffed envelope or a shiny Rolex under the table without getting caught. Lee understood that corruption is partly cultural. It's prone to developing in collectivistic cultures like those of Southeast Asia, as customs of gift-giving and relationship-based business easily slip over the line. The officials and merchants involved were not immoral people; they were following cultural customs of the region.

The cultural dimension was salient to Lee from his personal experience. After seeing Singapore's devolution into black markets and graft in his formative years, he left to study in England. He was impressed that British citizens abided the law because they believed that everyone else did too (the faith in "rule of law"). While Lee opposed British colonialism, he also internalized their cultural codes. One side of his cultural identity was Chinese and another side was English. British foreign secretary George Brown once famously called him "the best bloody Englishman east of Suez."

Lee believed that his fellow Singaporeans were bicultural too. They had become accustomed to the Southeast Asian relationship-based approach to business, but they also remembered the British rule-based approach. With the right cues, these memories could be reawakened. His political party donned white cotton uniforms, like the British navy, and this became the dress of all government officials. Lee also reinstated English as the language of government business. Port officials who had been conducting meetings in Malay wearing a flowing *baju kurong* now were speaking like the British and dressing like their midshipmen. (In case anyone missed these cues of language and attire, Lee also erected a twenty-foot statue of Raffles looming over the port.) The changed sights and sounds cued the free port norms of the antebellum era—not the customs of *kumshaw* or *suap*. Fewer officials hinted about favors and fewer merchants arrived with cash-stuffed envelopes. Backed by anti-corruption laws and role models of rectitude like Lee, these changed cultural cues evoked the codes of the "free port" era.

Over time the change became contagious. There was less reason for merchants to offer bribes when they saw that their peers were no longer doing it. And port officials became hesitant to ask for them. The port became busier and busier, which bolstered related industries. After "clean" norms consolidated in the port, they spread to other connected industries such as storage, trains, and trucking. Within a decade, Singapore had become the "cleanest" business environment in Asia, and soon Transparency International's index showed it as among the cleanest in the world. Foreign investment poured in, and by 1975 it had developed a skilled manufacturing and services industry. Its standard of living reached that of European countries (and has since risen beyond them). Lee's use of biculturalism and tribal triggers was a critical step in mobilizing the change.

Some politicians accept that corruption is largely cultural. Others hold out hope that a community's level of corruption can be changed. Lee Kuan

Yew was perhaps the only politician of his time who believed both of these things: that corruption is largely cultural *and* (in part for that reason) changeable.

Only recently has behavioral science caught up with his prescient approach. In 2006 a colleague of mine, economist Ray Fisman, found a clever way to investigate the cultural roots of corruption. Merging UN personnel records with NYPD parking ticket tallies, he found that UN diplomats hailing from countries with higher corruption rates were more prone to abusing their diplomatic immunity by running up unpaid parking tickets. You can take the diplomat out of the corrupt country, but you can't take the corruption out of the diplomat!

In a paper entitled "Who Doesn't?" psychologist Paul van Lange and his team argued that people's perceptions that "almost everybody does it" precipitate their own corrupt behaviors. The team measured these perceptions in some studies and experimentally manipulated them in another. Similar studies have varied what players in a game are told about the prevalence of bribery (almost nobody bribes or almost everybody bribes) and also varied information about the penalty if caught (very low or very high). The prevalence information, which informs peer codes, mattered more than the penalty information, which is relevant to rational cost-benefit calculations. This confirmed it: peer codes (not rational calculations) propel many acts of corruption.

Abigail Barr's lab at Oxford University in England recruited international students from countries around the world to play a corruption game. As with Fisman's diplomats, propensity to bribe correlated with having grown up in a society of high corruption. But Barr also found an exception to the rule: Students who'd spent years in the UK, as opposed to short-term visitors, made choices less reflective of their heritage-country norms. Perhaps these long-stayers had become bicultural and internalized local peer codes. Given the setting, their British peer codes would have been triggered and would have guided their decision in the game.

These examples help to flesh out the situational cues of peer codes. Because the peer instinct evolved for in-group coordination, one cue is the presence of tribemates, familiar compatriots, or those recognizable by telltale in-group attributes. But other triggers are ambient *signs* of the tribe. You can't walk across campus in Oxford without sensing signs of the British tribe (e.g., plummy accents, tweed jackets, dreaming spires). Minor details in a setting that are diagnostic of a culture can trigger us, but it's hard to recognize because it happens unconsciously. It took someone as self-observant as novelist Marcel Proust to describe the experience: In *Swann's Way*, an aging Parisian sophisticate scarcely thinks of the provincial town of his youth until one day he tastes a petite madeleine teacake dipped in tea and the town's milieu and mentality "sprang into being" in his mind. Chancing upon a culinary reminder of this provincial culture reawakened its social codes and preconceptions in his thinking.

Signs of a tribe are powerfully evocative, but only for insiders to the culture. Malaysia tried to spark a tech boom to rival the Singaporean miracle by spending billions on Cyberjaya, a tech corridor near two universities. A delegation had toured Silicon Valley and copied every detail—low-slung glass buildings on manicured lawns, open-plan offices, conference rooms in primary colors, whiteboards, and beanbag chairs. An incubator program called MaGIC (Malaysian Global Innovation and Creativity Centre) used all the standard jargon. Cyberjaya looked and sounded like a setting of the "tech" tribe. Despite all this, no tech boom was evoked. The sleek buildings became occupied by mundane call centers and sales offices—not the hoped-for high-tech startups.

They built it, but innovation didn't come. Why not? Let's imagine a Malaysian Mark Zuckerberg, an ambitious young coder. Would a tour of

Cyberjaya have prompted him to start Malaysbook? Not likely. Internet innovation wasn't "a thing" there; it wasn't in young people's minds as an option. The same government trying to summon innovation had been limiting internet freedoms for years. Malaysians hadn't internalized startup culture, so they weren't provoked by Cyberjaya's many cues. A cue can only trigger habits that are already latent inside people. It can't conjure up new behaviors—or new startups—out of thin air.

The question of how culture shapes thinking has intrigued me since my student days. I lived one summer with housemates freshly arrived from China. When we talked about politicians or gossiped about neighbors, our explanations for behavior often starkly diverged. I usually traced a person's success or failure to character traits and credited or blamed the person accordingly. My Chinese friends tended to refer to more contextual pressures on the actor—whether from family, friends, or coworkers—and shared credit or blame with these groups surrounding the central figure. At first I thought they were just being polite, but eventually I realized that they really saw the world that way.

Meanwhile in my psychology classes, I was learning about a cognitive bias called the "fundamental attribution error." Many studies had found that participants asked to explain someone else's behavior tended to focus on properties of the person, even if there were situational factors present sufficient to explain the outcome. When the new quarterback is sacked repeatedly, we judge "slow" even though some of the offensive linemen are out sick. When the history teacher rattles off the answers to every question on the quiz, we judge "brilliant" even though it's her quiz. Psychologists at the time believed this bias to be a biologically rooted, universal blind spot that gives rise to universal human misunderstandings and conflicts. But it sure seemed that my Chinese friends were less plagued by it. Could this "fundamental" human bias be largely just a by-product of Western culture?

At the time, in the early 1990s, psychology experiment evidence from outside of Western settings scarcely existed. Culture wasn't considered to be relevant to basic processes like cognitive biases. I set to work in collaboration with a visiting scholar from Beijing named Kaiping Peng who was equally fascinated by this question. We started by comparing news articles about the same crimes, finding more person-centered explanations in English-language papers and more group-centered explanations in Chinese-language papers. But to convince research psychologists, we needed to develop a laboratory test and one not so dependent on language. I used an animation program to compose cartoons of fish swimming in ambiguous social interactions. It was like a Rorschach test, but designed to assess this bias in causal understandings of others' behavior.

When asked what was going on in the video, American high school students tended to answer that the leftmost fish was leading the others or acting on its own initiative. Chinese students tended to answer that the group was chasing it or pressuring it somehow. They interpreted the same activity through different cultural lenses. They diverged in attributions of causality and the narratives that followed. These findings with the fish test made quite a splash. I continued to work on this topic for years with

collaborators around the world, and we discovered that this perception-warping power of cultures comes primarily from peer codes. When we measured many facets of cultural identities and codes, we found that the biggest difference between our American and Chinese participants was their perception of their peers' beliefs; and these differing views of peers, more than any differences in personal convictions, statistically accounted for their differing biases in explanations for behavior.

This cultural lens model of social judgment biases was fairly controversial at first. Bias researchers thought they were part of the natural sciences, the "hard" sciences, and didn't all take kindly to my conjecture that culture was a factor in their findings. Just as the sufficient results rolled in to support this model, however, my daily experience began to show me that it was pitifully incomplete; the force of culture was far more dynamic than a fixed divide between Western and Eastern worldviews or peer codes. I lived and worked that year in Hong Kong, where many residents (including my students) crossed the East/West cultural divide on a daily basis—living in traditionally Chinese families and neighborhoods but thriving all day at culturally Western companies or universities. Every morning, I'd see students heading in toward campus: walking in small groups, chatting softly in Cantonese, waving politely to friends, giving way to any passersby. Once inside the gates, they were speaking in English, laughing more loudly, spreading out on the sidewalk, and greeting friends with okay signs, thumbs-ups, and high-fives. They morphed from Chinese mode to Western mode without breaking stride. As an American struggling to comport myself in Chinese settings, I felt awed by their bicultural dexterity.

But when I asked how they managed this cultural crossing, they just shrugged and said it happens naturally. Looking for clues in social science research, I read about code-switching among bilinguals to gain insight about how it happens and how far it goes. Classic studies by Susan Ervin-

Tripp found that Japanese American "war brides" told slightly different narratives and answered questions differently when interviewed in English as opposed to when interviewed in Japanese. Similarly, an experiment with international students at a US campus varied whether pairs were assigned to hold a "get acquainted" chat in their native language or English. It found that Venezuelans sat more closely together when speaking in Spanish whereas Japanese sat farther apart when speaking in Japanese. This suggested that language cued the proxemic norms of these cultures. Most poignant were interviews with bicultural adolescents:

> At home with my parents and grandparents the only acceptable language was Spanish; actually that's all they really understood. Everything was really Mexican. . . . But at school, I felt really different because everyone was American, including me. Then I would go home in the afternoon and be Mexican again.

These findings hinted that bicultural individuals switch situationally in ways that go far beyond the language they speak. But the studies didn't test the most interesting part of what I had been seeing in Hong Kong—that the switching occurred automatically rather than deliberately. To investigate the fascinating cultural chameleons of Hong Kong, I teamed up with two of them, a brilliant pair of young psychologists, Ying-yi Hong and Chi-yue Chiu. We reasoned that switching starts as a deliberate decision but becomes automatized in response to cultural cues—what I now call "tribal triggers." To test this, we invited bicultural Hong Kongers into the psychology laboratory and put them through the fish test or other social judgment tasks. But beforehand, they were surreptitiously exposed to a cultural cue, such as English- versus Chinese-language instructions or incidental pictures of football players in their helmets versus kung-fu masters in their robes. We repeatedly found that the same perceivers—students with a bicultural background—would explain behavior in the Western way when that culture was cued and would explain behavior in the Eastern way when that culture was cued. They were adept at both logics of explaining behavior or casting a narrative. Even more remarkably, they were switching cultural frames reflexively without any awareness of the cues triggering them.

These studies shifted the paradigm of cultural psychology. While scholars had known about linguistic code-switching, this was switching in the basic biases of social sensemaking. Since then, hundreds of studies have replicated this effect with different judgment tasks and different bicultural populations, such as Mexican Americans, Greek immigrants in the Netherlands, and Aboriginal Australians. My lab has applied techniques to check that this cognitive switching occurs automatically and unconsciously. We tested that cues work by activating peer codes associated with different identities, not through altering peer codes. Before these studies, psychology tended to portray bicultural individuals as dwelling halfway between two cultures and often torn between them; since then, the field has appreciated that people can be fully at home in two or more cultures and relatively unburdened by the transitions. Further research has found that not all bicultural individuals are alike in this respect: those who feel their two identities to be compatible tend to mesh with the cues of a setting (like chameleons), whereas those who feel identity conflict tend to resist the peer cues (like contrarians). Each of these identity orientations has been found to be advantageous in different occupational roles.

As a presidential candidate, Barack Obama attracted notice for winning over white crowds in a Midwestern newscaster accent but moving Black audiences in African American Vernacular English. At first, critics accused him of putting on personas for political gain. Then videos emerged of him switching the same way in ordinary, unstaged interactions, showing that he shapeshifts spontaneously, not strategically. Obama chalked up his adaptability to being less self-conscious about racial/cultural identities than prior politicians. Perhaps through his writing about his identities, he had worked through conflicts to enable more ease in adaptation.

But anything that automatic can go haywire sometimes. A video of Obama in the locker room of the Olympic basketball team went viral for how differently he greeted a white assistant coach (a firm handshake) and player Kevin Durant (an embrace with a tap on the back). This inspired a *Key & Peele* sketch with Obama working his way down a receiving line, alternating starkly between "Nice to meet you, sir" handshakes with whites and "Bring it in, fam" daps with Blacks.

Automatic triggering can create awkwardness in some settings. A problem experienced by new immigrants in the US is difficulty speaking English fluently in interactions with Americans, particularly those of their own background, ironically. Research in my lab identified that it's a problem of spurious triggering: these ethnically familiar faces trigger the immigrant's heritage-culture codes, including linguistic structures, which then cognitively interfere with their second-language processing. You may not be a politician on the stump or an immigrant speaking a second language, but you've experienced some version of spurious triggering. If you've ever taken a quick call from your mother at work, you may have lapsed into a dialect of your youth ("I'm fixing to go" or "I gotta pahk my cah") that differs from the office voice that your coworkers know. You don't realize that you've code-switched until you look up and see them staring at you like you've just turned into a different person.

While the facial features of your audience can be a spurious trigger, physiognomy is not as strong a cue as language or attire, even though it might seem a deeper feature. In Western societies, racial characteristics align with major cultural fault lines, but this is not true in much of the world. Skin color and facial features don't reliably distinguish Russians from Ukrainians, Palestinians from Jews, or Hutus from Tutsis. Nor did facial features demark tribal boundaries for our Stone Age forebears. In experiments that pit them against each other, race is trumped by language (even accent) in determining who a preschooler prefers to befriend. Even preverbal infants are oblivious to race, but they prefer strangers who speak their mother's language (and accent). They notice what people eat and expect that people of the same tongue like the same foods. While a person's skin color affects many judgments by adult observers, their language and attire matter even more. More obviously, language and attire are the primary cues for tribes other than ethnic groups. For bankers, surfers, or hipsters, it's how a person talks and dresses that marks them as one of the tribe and triggers in-group codes when interacting with them.

The primacy of language as a cue helps us understand why language policies can change behavior. In 1965, Lee Kuan Yew declared English the language of government in Singapore. He felt a language of the ethnic groups—Chinese, Malay, and Indian—would lend itself to favoritism, so better to use an external lingua franca. He hoped English would evoke norms of the free-port era to make Singapore attractive to ships of all nations. Later, in the 1980s, Lee's "Speak Mandarin" policy sought to trigger Chinese identity and customs, which had become economically invaluable given the rise of Taiwan and China.

A corporate example of language policies is Korean Air. The company had a terrible safety record in the first decades of 747 jets (which require equal collaboration of copilots and pilot). After Boeing reported that safety problems were sharpest for hierarchical cultures, and cockpit-transcript analyses indicated problems of deferential communication by copilots, Korean Air changed its official language to English (which pilots already knew, as it's used in air traffic control). The airline hasn't crashed since. The same people communicate more equally when free from linguistic cues to hierarchical norms.

Other companies have adopted English-only policies even without their employees speaking it. In 2012, the CEO of Japanese e-tailer Rakuten gave a speech (in English) announcing an English-language policy to help his dream of rapid expansion to the West. It did help the firm's hiring abroad, but it created huge morale problems in Japan, rendering managers outsiders in their own country, and the Japanese market share declined. Laboring to conduct meetings in rudimentary English didn't magically give Japan-based executives any special insight into Western customs or markets. Many of the Western businesses it started have failed. As iconic companies of non-Anglophone nations like Nokia, Renault, and Volkswagen follow, one wonders whether the loss in heritage-culture cues is worth the gain in cues to Anglophone cultures.

Dress policies are another way to trigger peer codes, often those of an occupational or organizational culture. Nothing says "You're in the army now!" like pulling on green fatigues. The attire triggers military habits, like discipline and obedience. Hospital studies find that nurses who wear uniforms adhere to protocols more than non-uniformed nurses. Even premeds who put on a doctor's white coat start conducting themselves more like physicians, meticulously and self-assuredly. For soldiers, cops, or EMTs responding to a crisis, the uniforms of their professional peers cue shared frameworks and protocols that enable coordinated work. Undercover agents instead adopt the attire of the networks they infiltrate, often ones they can infiltrate because of their ethnic or religious background. Dressing the part is designed to affect the criminals but it can also affect the agent, as they sometimes start to identify with the criminals they have been sent to spy upon. Dressing like a mafioso or an Islamist doesn't just trigger related codes in the criminals they approach, but also sometimes in themselves.

You and I may not be polyglot pilots or undercover agents, but we all contain multitudes—every person has encoded multiple peer groups. These codes take turns guiding us, activating in situations that cue them. We think and talk one way when playing pool and another way at a church group meeting. As we traverse these differing cultural worlds, we respond to cues in people's faces but especially in their words, in what they wear, and in other signs of their tribes.

Imagine that you are driving to a countryside inn. Your car's navigation system suggests a path to your destination—a well-traveled route that most drivers take. When the disembodied voice says, "Turn right on Interstate Twelve in four hundred feet," you might just do that. But many times you might not. If you have time to kill, you would prefer the scenic back roads. Or if you feel adventurous, you might try a shortcut via a little-known bridge that's sometimes closed.

Now imagine the same decision with a different context. You're leading a convoy of wedding guests to the inn. Hence you prefer a route that is *certain* rather than iffy, and one clearly understandable, so no one gets lost. In this case, the normal route that the navigation system provides appeals more than the other options.

These cases differ in the inner needs that color your decision-making, your "epistemic motivations." In the second case, you crave certainty and clarity, which the navigation system's standard route offers. These needs related to understanding also affect how we navigate social situations. The peer instinct prompts you toward paths that are normal or typical for your group. When we want to be original, we ignore its advice. But when we crave certainty and understandability, we tend to follow the peer-code path.

Picture a busy restaurant kitchen, full of workers chopping, boiling, and searing ingredients. People yell out "chef" and "corner" as they bustle around the space, and they hand off plates to each other in practiced, stylized gestures. With knives and flames in close quarters, and time pressure, it's not the place for experimentation or idiosyncratic methods. Chefs need to handle tasks in ways that are certain to work and understandable to their coworkers—even to new hires whom they haven't worked with before. Fortunately, they are surrounded by signs of the chef tribe—its lingo ("eighty-six it," "heard"), uniforms (white toques, aprons, and sleeve tattoos), and artifacts (ovens, pans, and knives)—which prime the shared protocols of their profession. At home, they may not adhere to these habits, but in the busy restaurant kitchen they surely do.

Yearning for certainty attracts us to peer codes because we gain a feeling of certainty from consensus. Slogans like "50,000,000 Elvis fans can't be wrong" leverage this psychology—people feel "in the know" when they follow the crowd. Needs intensify from deprivation, and the need for certainty is no exception. After an agonizing spell of uncertainty, like an inclement day at the airport with several canceled flights, you may find yourself gravitating toward more conformist choices—ordering what most other customers order at the restaurant, streaming Hollywood hits instead of quirky indies. A related play in marketing is known as "FUD" (fear, uncertainty, and doubt). A pitch like "Nobody ever got fired for buying IBM" sounds innocuous on the surface, but the more menacing subtext is that people *do* get fired for choosing less-well-known brands. The slogan stoked uncertainty in purchasing managers to heighten their attraction to the safe conformist choice. Even temporary pressures that reduce the feeling of certainty—like deadlines or distractions—induce more culturally conformist information processing. When US students are put under time pressure, their attributions for behavior become more individualistic. When Chinese students are put under time pressure, their attributions for the same behaviors become more collectivistic. Pressure heightens conformity to the salient peer codes, whether it's Western or Eastern codes of inference or the chef profession's protocols of cooking.

Craving for certainty is also a matter of temperament. Psychologist

Arie Kruglanski and his team developed a personality scale that measures certainty-seeking (or "need for cognitive closure"). Among college students, accounting majors (who keep a sharp pencil) score higher than art majors (who paint with broad brushstrokes). Scores on this test predict cultural conformity—how much people gravitate toward peer codes as a guide to their behavior. A study of immigrants to Italy found that certainty-seekers were faster to conform to Italian customs, except if they settled in a group from their heritage country, in which certainty-seekers adhered more to the heritage-country customs and were *slower* to practice Italian customs. In further experiments with Hong Kong biculturals, my lab found that higher certainty-seekers conform more to Western or Eastern codes when exposed to corresponding cues. Likewise, studies of bicultural MBA students found that higher certainty-seekers conformed more to Chinese norms when allocating rewards in China and conformed more to American norms when allocating rewards in the US. Individuals who constantly crave certainty are particularly prone to seize upon the peer codes that are cued in a setting as a guide to their response.

Whether this conformity to peer codes is helpful depends on what job needs to be accomplished. In intelligence work, where zealous scrutiny of each new data point is imperative, a pull toward conformist conclusions can be disastrous. Kruglanski has studied the Israeli intelligence officers who missed clues of the 1973 Yom Kippur attack and the CIA analysts who dismissed warnings of the 9/11 attack. They were time-pressured decision-makers who jumped to the conformist judgment—"no attack coming"—instead of deliberating carefully on all the data coming in. How did Israel brush off signs of Hamas's preparation for its October 7, 2023, attack? The certainty-seeking culture of military forces may make it hard to judge unprecedented risks as real.

In many endeavors, however, it's less important to make the right choice than to make the choice right. Optimization is less important than implementation, including coordination. Pressure can help with this latter matter because conforming to cultural codes helps coordination. It's a familiar sight in sports that a team finally gels under clutch conditions. NFL fans may remember an epic comeback by the Vikings at the end of the 2022 season. They were highly favored over the Colts and played in front of a purple-clad home crowd, but they couldn't connect on the simplest plays. Star back Dalvin Cook outran his blockers and got clobbered, losing the ball. Quarterback Kirk Cousins kept trying to throw it deep, but his receivers would switch their routes one too many times. Punter Ryan Wright was blocked in his first attempt and next time bobbled the snap before trying to pass to an unaware teammate. The home team trailed 36–7 as the third quarter ended. With the playoffs on the line, the crowd began singing their anthem "Don't Stop Believin'," and in the last quarter the Vikings finally found their "purple power." Cousins began "throwing dimes," methodically hitting one receiver after another on the numbers for a series of touchdowns, most impressively Cook on a sixty-four-yard touchdown play. Cousins says the problem was overactive thinking; success comes when he "turns his brain off" and trusts the process. That didn't come until mounting pressure changed the needs weighing on players' minds and they started following peer codes instead of trying to be creative. They stuck to the plays that they knew best, and the teamwork snapped into place.

One can picture a similar scene, eons ago, on the shore of Lake Turkana. A herd of antelope gathers warily at the water's edge. Three *erectus* men appear from behind a ridge—one gestures toward the lake or points to a vulnerable-looking antelope. Or maybe they just meet eyes and read each other's minds. They've all done this before, and their peer codes are triggered by the sights and sounds of the setting: the shimmering turquoise lake, the snorts and grunts of the nearby herd, the eager expressions on the faces of their fellow hunters. The urgency of the moment—if they don't hunt, they'll starve—only intensifies their motivation to meld minds and mesh efforts toward success. They morph into a seamless unit; everyone understands, and everyone is understood. They leap into action and the game of repeated chase begins, working as a team that never tires. Hours later, the antelope collapses and is vanquished, their teamwork the decisive weapon. These hunters and the band of several families that they return to with their kill have scored another victory in the game of survival, delivered to them by the peer instinct—the first step in the million-year march toward tribal living.

2

Slaying Giants

Reputation, reputation, reputation!
O, I have lost my reputation!
I have lost the immortal part of myself,
and what remains is bestial.

—WILLIAM SHAKESPEARE, *Othello*

In 2012 an eleven-year-old boy in Siberia made a gruesome discovery while climbing an icy bluff overlooking the Arctic Ocean. A giant bone wrapped in bristly hair and sinew protruded from the retreating permafrost. It was the leg of a woolly mammoth that had been preserved by the tundra. After excavating the giant carcass, scientists ascertained that it had been slain by human hands. Its eye sockets, ribs, legs, and jaw had been battered by stones. Critically, its cheekbone, near the base of its trunk, had been punctured by a stone spearpoint, an assault that would have staggered the animal. Given its thick hide, the spear must have been razor-sharp, solidly made, and hurled from point-blank range.

These bones likely record an act of Stone Age valor. A spear-thrower got right in the face of a fourteen-foot-tall pachyderm to deliver a stunning blow. Mammoths didn't sprint away like antelopes when startled; they charged with crushing strength—so this lead hunter was risking life and limb. He wasn't doing "what most people do." Most people hang back at a safer distance, until the prey has been weakened. But if everyone tries to play it safe, the encounter won't be safe for anyone. The heroic action of the lead hunter points to something new in human psychology, beyond what previously enabled them to coordinate in the chase of antelopes. It wasn't just *working as a team*; someone *took one for the team*.

And where did the lethal weapon come from? It's a painstaking process to craft a spear that can fly straight, pierce a hide, and sink into the bone. You must chip flint into a point using a harder stone, straighten a tree branch into a shaft by stripping, carving, and sanding, and lash them together with twine or sinew. The stone-tip spears that appeared starting half a million years ago were not ubiquitous, like the hand axe. Some communities had this tool whereas others did not, and some that did no longer had it generations later. This cultural forgetting suggests that spear-making was a specialized craft, one not easily learned by just looking around at one's peers; it required extended attention to the master of the craft. If this failed to happen before the experts in a group died, the community could lose the expertise.

Traces of behaviors that involve individual sacrifices to help the group—valorous hunting, sedulous tool-making, shelter-building, care for the infirm—appear in the fossil record about half a million years ago. This was when a new species, *Homo heidelbergensis*, arrived on the scene. They were nearly as tall as we are today, had brains 90 percent as large, and ascended to the top of the food chain. In 1994, coal miners in Schöningen, Germany, discovered a cache of finely crafted throwing spears near a copious array of butchered bones from large game. Archaeologists took over and identified the quarry as wild horses, elephants, and bison from three hundred thousand years ago. They reconstructed that hunters hid in the reeds near a summer watering hole to ambush their prey, slaying game on a scale far beyond that to feed a single band. This points to the start of clan-level cooperation that brought together neighboring bands.

These social breakthroughs of *heidelbergensis* reflect a side of human psychology that I call the "hero instinct." While the peer instinct encodes what most people in the group do and prompts conformity, the hero instinct registers what the most respected people do and stirs aspirations to contribute similarly. These forebears became concerned not just with what's normal in their group but with what's normative. Contributing to a community requires noticing what behaviors its members approve and admire, and, conversely, what they reject and scorn. Behavioral scientists call these evaluative social rules "ideals," "mores," or "injunctive norms," but a simpler term is "hero codes." They are images of virtue that we encode from the example of esteemed members of our cultural community, and they frame our aspirations to gain similar esteem.

For evolutionary theory, altruism has long been an enigma. Natural selection favors survival of the *fittest*, not survival of the nicest, so how would generosity ever evolve? Charles Darwin himself struggled to understand how "noble savages" willing to die for their tribe would have passed on their prosocial traits. After Gregor Mendel discovered genes, fitness became understood in terms of gene propagation probabilities. Sacrifice for kin, which occurs in many species, pays off to the extent that your kin share your genes. Helping selected others that one has bonded with is also seen in a number of species; it pays off because these friends reciprocate in *your* hour of need, which increases your reproductive odds. But giving more broadly to the group (beyond kith and kin) doesn't "pay off" in this same way, so it remained a mystery how prosocial impulses evolved. Theorists eventually worked out the math to show that prosociality pays off in a reputation-minded species. If members of a community evaluate each other's behaviors, share these judgments with others, and treat people according to their reputations, then prosociality helps reproductive prospects and would be selected for. This theory explains why prosociality doesn't occur in other primate species—they lack some of the chops for sharing knowledge in their groups.

But can reputation-mindedness explain prosociality that started in the Stone Age? It's obvious that people *today* think about reputations. We volunteer for service positions in our community to gain approval and respect. We work hard to make a name for ourselves in our fields as it "opens doors" for us professionally. We engage with others or avoid them based on their reputations. This system of collective evaluation and reward is institutionalized in criminal records, credit scores, and app-specific reputation ratings. While we may worry that technology is taking the reputation game too far, research increasingly reveals that its elements have been part of human nature from the very start. Psychologist Jonathan Haidt discovered that people's moral evaluations do not derive from abstract reasoning (as past theorists of moral psychology had assumed) but from emotional responses. Seeing moral violations elicits the same feelings and facial expression as tasting something disgusting. It elicits the same inner neural activation too. Disgust originated as a primate reflex to toxic substances (the wrinkled nose, pursed lips, and spitting to expel the substance), but disgust became co-opted by evolution as a response to immoral behavior. Our positive evaluations arise also from adapted primal emotions. Psychologist Dacher Keltner finds that people feel awe in response to acts of great skill or virtue and then engage and explore, while in apes this feeling of reverie and interest is elicited by lush landscapes. Equally primal is our urge to share our positive and negative evaluations about others. Robin Dunbar posits that gossip emerged to replace mutual grooming as our forebears lost their fur. "Eavesdropping" studies consistently find that gossip (evaluative talk about others) accounts for 70 percent of all public conversation—regardless of whether the community studied is a Mayan Indigenous village, a Montana ranching town, or the Oxford University faculty. Because humans have been morally judgmental and gossipy from the start, it's plausible that Stone Age communities were reputation-minded.

We don't have *direct* evidence of how reputations affected our paleo predecessor's choices, but scholars of human origins also reference the indirect evidence of antiquity and anthropology. In the oldest narratives, reputation is dearly sought and dearly rewarded. In the *Mahābhārata*, Arjuna joined the battle, against his own kinsmen, to avoid losing reputation and respect. In the Bible, King Solomon's wisdom brought a tribute of seven hundred wives and five hundred tons of gold. In the *Iliad*, Achilles fought the Trojans to bring glory to his name. In Athens, the wealthy would fund needed public works (e.g., a new bridge or amphitheater) in order to earn hero status.

In the Indigenous societies of the Pacific Northwest, the path to prestige was hosting a generous potlatch feast. In Melanesia, sustained largesse earned the status of "Big Man" (or "Big Woman"), which came with political privilege. Many writers insist that hunter-gatherer societies are free of reputation and status concerns, but even cultures that are egalitarian on the surface have ways of rewarding high contributors. The Aché of Paraguay, for instance, don't publicly recognize status distinctions and allocate food purely according to need, but more productive foragers receive better medical care when injured or sick. The !Kung bushmen are famed for mocking successful hunters ("insulting the meat"), but long-term studies reveal that more productive hunters manage to have more offspring. Even when a culture engages in status-leveling on the surface, heroes get rewarded in the end. Reputational rewards serve the giver and the group.

Society's tribute to heroes—mates, meat, or money—enabled our prosocial instinct to evolve. But this doesn't mean that our subjective motivations to give focus solely on these extrinsic rewards. Our species also evolved appetites for intrinsic rewards such as esteem and pride. Purely transactional motives wouldn't spur as many prosocial acts or attract as many rewards. At most moments when a community needs a contribution, rewards are not certain or immediate. Also, communities respect a contribution more when it is done without anticipation of rewards—it's more heroic. Intrinsic motivations for prosocial giving may have evolved, ironically, because these "selfless acts" bring much richer streams of societal rewards.

In addition to processes that motivate acts of contribution, the hero instinct system also required learning heuristics to discern what the community admires and desires. It's hard to learn by observing or asking each person, especially as the size of communities expanded from bands of several dozen members to clans of several hundred. A handy shortcut is focusing on the behavior of those members with most status. Sometimes this is marked by titles or tokens of success; sometimes by informal prestige. Individuals with high status exemplify qualities that the community appreciates, so we can learn from their example. They are beacons that show us paths to public approval. This adaptation of attending to and emulating the heroes of our communities is why we get pulled in by clickbait about what CEOs eat for breakfast and by "human interest" articles about whether a politician wears boxers or briefs. We can't always pinpoint a hero's prowess, what brings them such renown, so our hero-learning process errs on the side of inclusion. We emulate all of their distinctive actions. Elizabeth Holmes was hardly the first young tech founder to don Steve Jobs's trademark black turtlenecks. This emulation of arbitrary quirks occurs even in professions that you might expect to be more self-aware; at conferences of psychoanalysts, it's striking how many wear beards just like Freud's.

The hero instinct, a suite of status-related motivations and learning heuristics, brought a new dimension to our forebears' tribal living. Instead of just social learning from peers, there was social learning from heroes (attention to and emulation of high-status members). Instead of just motivation to act normally, there was motivation to act normatively. Individuals looked for exemplary ways to contribute to the good of the group, even if personal sacrifice was required. This generated new tools, like stone-tip spears, and new practices, like large-game hunting and shelter-building. It enabled the expansion of cooperation to larger groups (by reducing the "free-rider problem" that hinders cooperation among purely self-interested agents). It lifted *heidelbergensis* to a lifestyle more social, sophisticated, and secure than prior humans had enjoyed. In the modern world, too, the hero instinct remains a powerful force for community, motivating our aspirations to gain skills, uphold ideals, and distinguish ourselves. We can't sacrifice our self-interests every day, but sometimes—"when the spirit moves us"—we step up and act as heroes. The challenge in harnessing this instinct lies in understanding the social contexts that shape and spark these aspirations in our minds. Whether people step up depends on the subtleties of how a situation *triggers* the relevant hero code.

Leading up to his most famous speech, Reverend Martin Luther King Jr. didn't plan on saying "I have a dream." He and his fellow organizers of the 1963 March on Washington had planned a dry lecture about the Civil Rights Movement from the Capitol steps (its working title: "Normalcy— Never Again"). But as August twenty-eighth approached, the plan began to shift. The Lincoln Memorial seemed a more fitting site, and Reverend King wanted to include content that would resonate with broader audiences rather than just fellow activists. The night before, King talked to many people about it and stayed up revising the draft until four a.m., crossing out phrases and adding new ones, over and over again.

Meanwhile, buses, trains, and planes converged in DC from all over the country, bringing in political, religious, and labor groups involved in the cause. As the day dawned with searing heat and pea-soup humidity, rumors spread of a disappointing turnout—only 25,000 people, not the hoped-for 100,000. It reached 87 degrees by noon. But groups kept arriving throughout the day. By late afternoon, a record crowd of 250,000 strong filled the National Mall to hear a series of musical performances and remarks.

King was the last speaker on the agenda. By the time he ascended the steps to take the podium, the crowd was wilting and many were packing up to leave. Flanked by the red, white, and blue of towering flags, the black-suited minister began by acknowledging the "symbolic shadow" of the great president who, a century before, signed the Emancipation Proclamation. Clenching the podium, King deemed this "a promissory note" to America's citizens of color—one that had yet gone unpaid. He called upon activists to press on in their demands for "the riches of freedom" while withstanding the temptation to hatred and violence. It was an apt analogy, but it didn't *move* people the way his sermons often did. Nearing the end of his draft, King paused before another cerebral reference, when Mahalia Jackson, a gospel singer who had performed earlier, called out: "Tell them about *the dream*, Martin!" This was a metaphor he sometimes used in sermons about the cause.

King put aside his notes and began to speak about his hope of a more equal future, "a dream deeply rooted in the American dream." The country would live up to its founding creed that "all men are created equal." With hope rising in his voice, he recited the lines of the country's first anthem about a "sweet land of liberty" and "let freedom ring." As affirmations rang out from the audience ("Tell it, Martin"), he layered on allusions to biblical psalms and parables about equality before the eyes of God. He rose into a reverie about the day when "*all* of God's children, black men and white men, Jews and Gentiles, Protestants and Catholics, will be able to join hands and sing in the words of the old Negro spiritual: Free at last. Free at last. Thank God almighty, we are free at last."

This peroration captivated and unified the crowd, infusing it with a sense of collective will. The speech also radiated through television wires across the country into Americans' living room televisions. President Kennedy watched in the White House (exclaiming, "He's damned good. Damned good.") and invited King and others over to meet. The clarion call moved many types of citizens—from college students to sanitation workers—to join the movement's marches, strikes, and voter drives. This groundswell of popular support emboldened Congress to pass the Civil Rights Act of 1964 and the Voting Rights Act of 1965. In recognition, King became the youngest recipient of the Nobel Peace Prize. In the years since, his refrain, "I have a dream," has rooted itself in the American vernacular, a catchphrase for aspirations to an ideal.

The original plan of a political speech from the Capitol steps would have accomplished none of this. It would have interested some of the audience, but it would not have inspired them. Instead of an abstract lecture, the crowd experienced an opera of visual and verbal symbols. The steps were flanked by the Stars and Stripes and backed by Lincoln staring down from his marble temple. They heard iconic phrases of the nation's founding fathers, familiar lyrics about a "sweet land of liberty," and echoes of age-old Bible verses. King surrounded his audience with cherished symbols of their country and creed. Instead of education, his goal was evocation. As a second-generation reverend, he knew well that people hold noble ideals but don't always live up to them. Ideals become buried in our minds under the clutter of everyday tasks and selfish concerns. Part of a minister's role is to rouse people's higher selves and lift their ideals to the fore of their minds. King decided it was time to preach—and not just to the "converted" activists who gathered before him, but also to the larger "unconverted" public who watched from their homes. By evoking the ideal through tribal symbols of equality, King described a dream rooted in the audience's political and religious allegiances. It was a call to act on the hero codes that they already shared.

While peer codes are evoked by the signs of a tribe, hero codes are evoked by a tribe's *symbols.* Tribal symbols are the special signs that a community uses to stand for itself. A group's symbols tend to be associated with its core ideals. When King's audience saw Old Glory and Honest Abe and heard phrases like "unalienable rights" and "the American Dream," it called up the political ideal of equal opportunity. When they heard Old Testament proverbs and New Testament parables, it called up the Judeo-Christian ideal of souls equal before God. Iconic symbols are like magnets of meaning; they lift latent ideals from the recesses of memory to the fore of the mind.

The word "icon" first referred to religious paintings and statues that help believers call up spiritual states. Icons can be so moving that worshippers start to venerate them as if they were the deity or saint that they represent (iconophilia, which often incites iconoclasm). The Christian cross is an icon associated with the faith's ideal of sacrifice. A field study in a French town found that pedestrians were 15 percent more likely to enroll as organ donors when the canvasser who stopped them wore a cross necklace. Christians who have just passed by a church (or Muslims who have just heard the call to prayer) become more likely to give to charity than otherwise. Even in experiments when icons (e.g., an angel) are merely flashed on a screen subliminally, participants' religious concepts like "charity" activate in their minds, their physiology shifts into a challenge mode, and they make corresponding prosocial choices like volunteering for a food bank. That said, religious symbols don't bring out benevolence toward everyone; for some groups they heighten opposition to same-sex marriage and abortion. Symbols trigger a tribe's ideals and the aspiration to uphold them, but this can play out as charity or as condemnation.

National icons are potent in parallel ways. For centuries, soldiers have followed flags into battle, often defending them to the death. Even today, Americans pledge allegiance *to the flag* (just as Orthodox Christians pray to icons). Flags on the battlefield trigger patriotism, while American flags in a classroom or courtroom evoke our civic ideals. The equal stars (for fifty states) and stripes (for the thirteen founding colonies) represent egalitarian ideals. As Reverend King hoped, the sight of the flag activates egalitarian concepts and promotes inclusive choices for Americans, especially those who strongly identify with the nation. France's *tricolore* represents the three estates of the ancien régime and remains associated with ideals of French culture such as eating for epicurean pleasure rather than practicality. A recent study found that for French students the *tricolore* triggers an epicurean mindset, so they are flummoxed by a presentation of detailed nutritional information. It reduces their enjoyment and evaluation of food, to the extent that their French identity is activated. Meanwhile, a shop in Brittany found that replacing the *tricolore* with the black-and-white Breton flag spurs shoppers to buy local cheeses such as Saint-Paulin rather than those like Brie from other provinces. Flags call forth the society's ideals, but precisely which ideals depends on the context and the judgments being made.

Before flags and crosses, the first group symbols were totem animals.

For the Huns of Mongolia, it was the wolf; for the Bai people of the Yunnan rainforest, the tiger; for the nomadic Daur clan, the horse. The animals chosen had attributes that each group idealized. In the Ojibwe nation of eastern Canada, the virtue of each clan can be guessed from their totems. For instance, defending settlements was the job of the Nooke (or bear) clan. Many of the animals chosen as totems—characterized by fierceness, strength, and speed—reappear in coats of arms (e.g., heraldic lions and roosters), corporate logos (MGM's lion, Ferrari's horse, or Twitter's bird), and sports team insignias (Detroit's Lions, Chicago's Bulls, South Africa's Springboks). The power of totems lives on when a mascot in a furry costume sends fans into a frenzy of cheers for their side and jeers for the other.

When symbols trigger our group identities and ideals, we tend to see the world in terms of "Us" and "Them." It starts at the level of evaluations. Fans are awed by the virtuosity of their team and disgusted by the fouls committed by the opponent. But it also guides our prosocial actions. In a study of Manchester United soccer fans, a researcher posing as a jogger tripped and clutched his ankle. Fans went out of their way to provide help if he was wearing the bee-logo Manchester jersey—more than if he was wearing a bird-logo Liverpool jersey or if he was wearing an unbranded shirt. This is not too surprising—the urge to help one of "Us" is stronger than the urge to help one of "Them" or to help an uncategorizable person. A more remarkable finding came in the next study when participants were first asked about their experience as soccer buffs, enthusiasts of "the beautiful game." When this more inclusive "soccer fan" identity was salient, they were then likely to help a fallen jogger in either team's jersey, more than one in the unbranded shirt. This "superordinate identity" effect shows the mutability of tribal thinking. A stranger who is "Them" at one moment can become "Us" when a broader identity is triggered.

Leaders who are adept at triggering tribal identities can build coalitions to overcome long odds. Consider the example of Ukrainian President Volodymyr Zelenskyy, a former actor who united the country's factions in part by becoming an icon of Ukrainian resolve. Taking selfies in the Kyiv streets while Russian rockets fell, he steeled his compatriots to stay and fight. Just as artfully, he has pulled in allies by wielding their national symbols for the cause. To Parliament, he echoed Churchill's iconic speech during the Blitz about "fighting for our land" against aggressors. To Congress, he invoked Pearl Harbor and 9/11 and echoed the line "I have a dream." While it's hard to know how the conflict will end, Zelenskyy has led a resistance far stronger than the "realist" political scientists deemed possible. Like Reverend King, he has relied on tribal symbols more than on rational arguments.

In 1991 North Carolina National Bank acquired a regional rival to become the dominant player in the Southeast. In 1998 the Charlotte-based bank took advantage of a financial crisis to acquire the San Francisco–based Bank of America and, in an unusual move, took on its broadly encompassing name. Then the acquisitions accelerated: New England's Fleet, the DC area's MBNA, Chicago's LaSalle, and LA's Countrywide.

Prioritizing size, standardization, and cost cutting, CEO Ken Lewis called it the "Wal-Mart of banking." Employees even dressed the part. Branches were strictly business casual. Executives at headquarters eschewed fine tailoring for unfussy off-the-rack suits. American flag lapel pins completed the look.

Most managers of acquired firms transitioned smoothly. Bank of America's name and flag logo were an easy fit. Its core ideals, like equal treatment and broad access, aligned with the central mission of the consumer banking industry. Moreover, Bank of America consolidated the transition by bringing managers from the two sides together at off-site team-building events to identify common aspirations. At one retreat, employees composed and performed a heartfelt adaptation of U2's "One":

It is even better
Now that we're the same
Two great companies come together, now
MBNA is B of A
And it's One Bank! One Card! . . .

It may seem a stretch to turn an anthem about creative unity into a paean to bank amalgamation. But if you've seen the leaked video from this event, the buttoned-down bankers belt out these lyrics with genuine passion and the audience tap their wingtips in time. The iconic bank acronyms and slogans in the lyrics were symbols that meant a lot to them, and the melding of corporate symbols motivated them for the challenge of integrating business operations.

By assimilating former rivals, Bank of America grew into a nationwide brand befitting its name. In 2007 Lewis's bank counted one in five Americans as its customers. Still, he was unsatisfied. He wanted to expand beyond the safe consumer banking industry of checking accounts and credit cards to investment banking, with its headline deals and high-stakes returns. It would be the final act in his storied career. The financial crisis presented a sudden opportunity; blue-chip Wall Street banks were struggling to stay afloat under the weight of troubled assets.

In September, Lewis flew to New York and met with the century-old firm Merrill Lynch. Its sonorous name and charging bull logo were synonymous with Wall Street in the popular imagination. In wealth management offices across the country, the firm's thousands of brokers (the "thundering herd") offered stocks, bonds, and investment advice, "bringing Wall Street to Main Street." The far-flung herd converged frequently to meet with leaders, share tips, and collaborate on deals. Brokers were independent but called on each other's expertise to find the best solutions for their clients, and those who were most helpful gained clout and rose into leadership roles. They called the firm "Mother Merrill" because of the loyalty it inspired. This unparalleled network enabled the firm to do more underwriting than any other bank in the twentieth century.

After two days of secret negotiations, Lewis and the Merrill Lynch CEO held a press conference to announce the world-shaking news: Bank of America would acquire Merrill for fifty billion dollars. At first this seemed like a stroke of strategic brilliance. It would steady Merrill against the crisis and open Bank of America to new kinds of business. But the euphoria did not last long. After the merger, Merrill paid out generous executive bonuses and then announced devastating losses that substantially eroded the value of the combined firm. As a result, Bank of America executives had to cut their comparatively much smaller bonuses in response. Executives in Charlotte seethed that Lewis had bought a lemon.

When the post-merger branding appeared, signs and business cards prominently featured the Bank of America name and flag, with "Merrill Lynch" in a faint font below. The iconic charging bull—the best-known logo in banking—was nowhere to be seen. How, Merrill brokers wondered, could they attract clients to their high-end advisory service if it was branded like a retail bank branch? Many offices decided to continue answering their phone with "Merrill Lynch" and giving out their old Merrill business cards. They missed the Merrill conferences of old, and they scoffed at the training sessions and off-site retreats meant to "Bank of Americanize" them (run by people whose idea of client development was to "give away free toasters"). Imperatives from Charlotte to "cross-sell" investment clients on Bank of America credit cards ran afoul of the Merrill ethos that brokers should be beholden only to their clients. Some of the top brokers in the organization decamped to competitor firms like Morgan Stanley, taking their clients with them. This set off a cascade of defections. Others stayed, but hunkered down in their local offices, loath to share tips or clients with colleagues who might jump ship any day. The business was bleeding talent, declining in assets under management, and losing the collaborative culture that had been its signature strength.

As financial analysts declared the widening conflict a "merger from hell," Lewis looked around for a savior, someone who could stanch the outflow of talent and restore trust among the thundering herd. In August 2009 he found Sallie Krawcheck, formerly CEO of Citibank's wealth management business, who had gained fame for calling out conflicts of interest and supporting brokers and clients. She also happened to be a born and raised Tar Heel, as fluent in the language of Charlotte as she was in the private wealth industry.

After a listening tour with brokers and months of bargaining in Charlotte boardrooms, Krawcheck unveiled a reorganization with the words "The bull is back!" Wealth management would be a separate division named Merrill Lynch marked by the iconic charging bull and emphasizing close relationships and strong advising. Almost immediately the attrition slowed and business began to improve. A headhunter who had thrived by poaching Merrill advisers complained, "She is a recruiter's worst nightmare." Brokers were able to project that they were "bullish on America," that postcrisis lows were a buying opportunity. They became more confident in taking risks in search of higher rewards. They worked overtime and picked up the phone to call other offices to collaborate. The private wealth business became the bright spot of Bank of America's earnings statements. By 2011 revenues and balances rose to above precrisis levels. Krawcheck made other changes, too, such as toughening up noncompete clauses to harden the group boundary that had become too porous. But the restoration of the group's symbols—its name and totemic logo—was the linchpin on which the recovery turned. It not only attracted customers but served "to rally Merrill Lynch brokers and bankers." It was the small difference that incited the "herd" to stampede once again.

Like Reverend King, Krawcheck induced people to contribute by surrounding them with familiar symbols—like the charging bull that represented Merrill's entrepreneurial spirit. The Bank of America name and its flag logo went over fine when they were assimilating other consumer banks, but no amount of flag pins and motivational songs could prompt dyed-in-the-wool Merrill brokers to do Charlotte's bidding. One veteran said, "They want everyone to look the same, act the same, and wear pins the way Bank of America bankers do." Group symbols fall flat for those who don't identify with the group and its ideals. Churches and ecclesiastical images activate moral decisions and judgments for the devout but not for skeptics. Marketers who target demographics through ethnic or regional symbols find these signifiers don't sway the many members of a category who don't identify with it. Some members even respond defiantly—acting against a group's norms when its symbols are made salient—because they want to disassociate themselves from the category. The brokers who ridiculed Bank of America off-sites and railed against cross-selling initiatives may have felt that Bank of America loyalty meant Merrill betrayal. It is crucial to understand people's identifications, and even their identity conflicts, to know how they will be affected by group symbols.

This case also illustrates a condition conducive to the triggering of group ideals. Krawcheck took over after a year or so of post-merger anomie. The Merrill brokers were civic-minded people who had lost their community and lost their heroes. Part of why the momentum shifted so dramatically upon Krawcheck's restoration of boundaries and meetings is that there was a pent-up desire for contribution and recognition. This is the same dynamic seen in social experiments where participants rebound from isolation by frenetically cooperating in order to regain the feeling of esteem and status that they have missed. Deprivation of a need heightens efforts to fulfill it. Once the Merrill advisers felt like a herd again, their motivations to contribute exploded in a thunderous stampede.

In 1964, just under a year after the March on Washington, the Freedom Summer project selected one thousand young people from a pool of many more applicants to volunteer in Mississippi to register Black citizens to vote (less than 7 percent were registered at the time). Many volunteers had been inspired by Reverend King's symbol-laden speech. They were motivated to make a difference—to do the civil rights work that would move the country toward its unfulfilled ideals. Before being posted in the South, they attended a training in Ohio, where they were instructed to expect forceful resistance from white Mississippians.

In mid-June the first volunteers began work in Mississippi. Three drove to a small town to investigate the burning of a Black church where the project held classes. As they left town, their car was followed, and it was later found burned out and abandoned near a swamp. Local authorities treated it as a missing persons matter. Later, a tip to the FBI turned up their bodies. It came out that they had been beaten and shot point-blank by a Ku Klux Klan mob, abetted by local police.

As the horrifying news reached the rest of the prospective volunteers, a third of them withdrew from the program, while two thirds chose to stay and work in Mississippi nonetheless. In truth, the project didn't succeed in getting many voters registered that summer, but it succeeded in drawing national attention to the problem. Organizer Robert Moses had counted on this: "Bring the nation's children, and the parents will have to focus on Mississippi." The remaining volunteers were critical to this success, as their parents and the national media shone a spotlight on their Southern sojourn.

Two decades later, sociologist Doug McAdam wondered what, if anything, distinguished the stayers from the leavers. He was able to access their original applications to the program, which asked about values, experiences, and affiliations. Surprisingly, the two groups didn't differ in their values or level of experience. The only difference was their social affiliations: stayers were more likely to have belonged to civil rights organizations and to have had prior relationships with fellow volunteers. They were more "socially embedded" in the Civil Rights Movement.

People who take great risks for a cause are often steeled by such relationships and memberships. The soldiers who follow flags into battle are usually acting in solidarity with their platoon and their buddies from basic training. The same is true for the insurgents who step to the front of the street protest to throw stones. Even acts of terrorism are less often committed by maladjusted "lone wolves" than by well-connected members of radicalized networks. For individuals who are socially embedded in a cause, the decision of whether to act is not just political but social. They will face audiences whose good opinion they cherish and who would approve of action and disapprove of inaction.

For sacrifices of money and time as well, the approval of audiences matters. Philanthropists who write eye-popping checks to arts organizations or universities tend to do so to ones favored by their social circle. Greenpeace holds fundraising galas with celebrity guests and public auctions because their supporters will pledge more money when other environmentalists are watching. Visitors to a donation-optional park give more when they arrive in groups than when they arrive alone. Pedestrians are more likely to pledge to give blood if they are with family or friends when they are asked. A classic study even found that patrons of a public restroom are twice as likely to stop to wash their hands when others are present. Across many kinds of settings, people are more inclined to act prosocially when they are observable to others, even if these others are not fellow activists in a cause.

One reason for giving, and giving when watched, is reputation. Classical economics explained philanthropy as the self-interested seeking of reputational rewards. However, recent evidence makes it clear that this is not the only reason. Behavioral economics experiments show that people tend to share their wealth even when that act is anonymous and thus carries no reputational consequences. In games where one player receives a windfall of cash, they take opportunities to share some of it with a fellow player who received none. In 2023 the TED organization bequeathed $10,000 each to two hundred lucky applicants and found that on average they spent $6,400 on purchases to benefit others. Even in child psychology laboratories, toddlers choose to share when they have received many treats and another player has none. Toddlers share more than chimps do when put through the same procedure, suggesting that human tribal instincts are involved. Generous behavior is seen even in the "terrible twos." If there's anyone we can be sure is not calculating reputation gains and reproductive payoffs, it's a two-year-old!

Of course, the motivation for all of this anonymous giving is not such a mystery. We've all felt the "warm glow" inside from helping our community. People feel better at the end of the day when assigned to spend a $20 windfall on someone else than when assigned to spend it on themselves. This is retrospective pride, but people act prospectively by giving so that they will feel it. A study by Elizabeth Dunn found that students who passed up an opportunity to share with a classmate felt a tinge of shame. Inducing shame can increase sharing behavior. Psychopathy is a genetically determined condition characterized by a deficit in the shame response.

Serial killer Gary Gilmore put it this way: "I know I'm doing something grossly fucking wrong. I can still go ahead and do it."

Pride and shame have often been depicted as symptoms of dysfunctional self-focus. However, cross-cultural studies provide a different picture. Groups of respondents in many societies are asked to imagine many possible actions (e.g., dressing well, catching a fish, graduating from school) and for each to describe the emotions they would feel. Others from each society are asked to score each action on many attributes, including how much it is valued by the society. Analyses then investigate which emotions depend on which action attributes. The results consistently show that people feel pride or shame for actions that their society values or devalues, respectively. It's an adaptation (part of the hero instinct) that guides people toward actions that help their reputation. In doing so, it usually (but not always) also guides them toward actions that are good for the group. Given this function, we can understand why the warm glow of pride or the hot burn of shame amplifies when the eyes of the group are upon us. When we are observable to many others, our reputation is particularly on the line. This is one reason why leaders like King and Krawcheck bring members of a community together: the presence of an audience raises the pride felt in making contributions and the shame felt in failing to do so.

Even the hint of an audience can set off anticipatory pride or shame and the prosocial behavior that ensues. In an employee coffee room that had suffered from "free-riding," more employees contributed to the "honor box" to support the common good when the poster behind the coffeepot featured watchful eyes rather than flowers. Cameras deter car and bike theft but so do posters alluding to watchers. It's the same principle as swimming pool signs about "urine indicator dye" that will alert other swimmers to your antisocial lapse. It's why we lie to children about Santa Claus: "He knows if you've been bad or good / So be good for goodness' sake." We also tell them about all-seeing, judgmental, and punitive gods. These religious beliefs develop when societies grow large enough that people interact with strangers, anonymously. Hunter-gatherers, like the !Kung, believe only in animistic spirits with more limited powers and less interest in human comportment. In these communities, people are always observable to others who know them; they don't need Jehovah, Jesus, or Allah to deter bad behavior.

Let's bring this back to the embedded "stayers" who saved the Freedom Summer program. Maybe they stayed to impress their activist groups and friends, or at least to not disappoint them. But it was not necessarily a bid for reputation and status. Just because of the different audiences in their lives, they would have felt a stronger glow of pride when considering staying and a sharper burn of shame when considering leaving. They may have decided based on their inner esteem, not the esteem of others. Either way, the socially embedded stayers help us understand another rhetorical flourish of Reverend King's speech. Like many politicians and rabble-rousers before him, King addressed his audience not just as individuals, but as groups. He called out their home states ("Go back to Mississippi, go back to Alabama, go back to South Carolina, go back to Georgia, go back to Louisiana"). He mentioned their religious affiliations ("Jews and Gentiles, Protestants and Catholics"). Though his was a national cause, King understood that local groups are the audiences that weigh on people most. By referencing different regions, races, creeds, and professions, King reminded people of their embeddedness in clans—congregations, union chapters, political organizations—that would approve of and support their further contributions.

In these cases, we see that triggering prosocial contributions is an interplay of external prompts such as tribal icons and inner needs for esteem or recognition, which themselves reflect opposite forces. Just as hunger builds with reward deprivation (missing lunch) and also sharpens with reward proximity (passing a pizzeria), so, too, do appetites for esteem. Merrill brokers leaped at the chance to contribute once Krawcheck restored their tribe's boundary and iconography, as they had been *deprived* of ways to contribute to their clan. The embedded stayers stuck to their Freedom Summer work because they were more proximal to groups that cared about it—and hence more proximal to the rewards of reputation and pride. Reverend King's recitations of the many specific groups that constituted the Washington crowd similarly piqued appetites for contributing to the cause.

3

Visiting the Temple

Tradition means giving a vote to the most obscure of all
classes, our ancestors. It is the democracy of the dead.

—G. K. CHESTERTON

In Southern France, a natural stone arch called Pont d'Arc towers one
hundred feet above the waters of the Ardèche River, a tributary of the
Rhône. Nearby, rocky cliffs dotted with scrub plants rise above lush
valleys of oak forests and lavender fields. In spring and summer, vaca-
tioners congregate at the river gorge, descending the easy rapids in kayaks
and canoes.

In 1994 a park ranger named Jean-Marie Chauvet led two cavers in a
climb up the cliffs above Pont d'Arc to a recently discovered seam in the
rocks that emanated a mysterious draft. After using picks to widen the
hole opening, they crawled into it and found a narrow tunnel that eventually opened into a chamber one hundred feet high. Crystalline stalactites
and stalagmites glinted in the light like giant icicles and drip castles. After
gazing upon these geological wonders, Éliette Brunel Deschamps turned

and her headlamp illuminated the far wall, spotlighting a startling image of a mammoth. Then she saw handprints and more drawings. She cried out, "*They* were here!"

"*They*" meant prehistoric humans. Every French spelunker dreams of discovering prehistoric cave art. Not far away was Lascaux Cave with its famous seventeen-thousand-year-old murals of horses and aurochs. At the time, these paintings were the earliest known representational art. Could these sketches in the cavern above Pont D'Arc be as old? In their initial photographs, the drawings looked so sharp that some experts dismissed them as a modern forgery. Then carbon dating came back with answers that defied all expectations. Most of the drawings in Chauvet Cave (as it became known) date from around thirty-six thousand years ago—twice as old as any previously known.

Stone Age residents of the river valley must have climbed to the high cave, which likely had a more visible opening then. Torch burns along the passage reveal the path they took. Like Chauvet's friends, they would have breathed dank air, ducked screeching bats, and stepped over the bones of cave bears before arriving at the eerie chamber with its glittering limestone formations. But they didn't retreat from this otherworldly sight.

Instead, they broke off charcoal from their torches and began to draw on the chalky white walls: lines, dots, and hand stencils. They went on to sketch the awe-inspiring animals of their valley. Eventually, in the deeper chambers, they drew murals of animal scenes that expressed a close understanding of their behavior: rhinos butting horns, horses cavorting, and wary aurochs edging away from lions on the prowl.

We don't know exactly why our forebears devoted themselves to this art, but it was more than just wallpaper, we can be sure. Archaeologists can tell from its human traces that the cave was never a place of residence. From footprints and handprints, they have determined that relatively few individuals ever entered the inner chambers. When illuminated by flickering torchlight, the animals take on a phantasmagoric vitality. Some paleoanthropologists conjecture that the cave was a mystical netherworld, a place where the earliest shamans communed with animistic spirits they revered. The artistry extended for years and grew more complex in technique, until one day the cave and its ritual drawings were suddenly entombed by a cataclysmic rockslide that engulfed its entrance.

Six thousand years later, another seismic event rocked the region and resculpted the Ardèche cliffs. It exposed the cave entrance once again. Soon some valley dwellers of that era climbed up the cliffs to explore. They squeezed through the narrow passage, came upon the wondrous limestone chamber with columns that glittered in their torchlight, and then noticed the arresting images of formidable animals. But they didn't run away or seal off the cave (like Hollywood cavemen do). Instead, these late Stone Age humans stayed and studied the drawings long enough to learn the style and then continued the project by making new drawings in this style, sometimes adding to existing murals. They used shading, etching, and red ochre for color. This went on until one day, the cliff collapsed again in another landslide, sealing off the cave like a time capsule until thirty thousand years later Chauvet's friends dug their way in.

The second wave of paleo painting at Chauvet Cave is in some ways even more intriguing than the first. Late Stone Age people came upon ancient images of fearsome animals in a dark remote cavern, drawn by unknown hands. Instead of retreat, they responded with reverence: closely observing the technique and replicating it to extend this mural tribute to their animal neighbors. This compulsion to maintain ways of the past—even arcane, impractical activities—bespeaks a new layer of human psychology, distinct from peer-instinct conformity or hero-instinct prosociality. We can recognize this psychology in ourselves today—our fascination with ancient rites, antiquarian documents, and antique furniture; our deep curiosity about past generations and especially the founders of our national, religious, and organizational tribes; our zeal for religious rituals, holiday routines, and original recipes that connect us to the past ways. We are driven to learn about, maintain, and even defend group traditions. This final piece of evolved tribal psychology can be called the "ancestor instinct." Like peers and heroes, ancestors are another reference group that we take lessons from and feel motivated by.

The ancestor instinct, as best we can tell, evolved in the late Stone Age, in our own kind *Homo sapiens* ("wise man"). Despite the flattering name, this species was not always so savvy or secure. Starting three hundred thousand years ago, in the river valleys of North and East Africa, they scratched out a living in small bands and clans. By two hundred thousand years ago, they had become "anatomically modern," their bodies just like ours, but their lifeways were little advanced from that of *heidelbergensis*, hundreds of millennia earlier. As recently as one hundred thousand years ago, they were still a marginal primate species, with a population less than that of a small city today. However, by eighty thousand years ago, *sapiens* had begun to hit their stride. They multiplied in numbers and migrated in multiple directions, southward throughout Africa and eastward into the Levant. Fifty thousand years ago, they spread into Europe and Asia, not long after reaching Australia as well.

When *sapiens* migrated North to Europe, glaciers were not their only obstacle: another species of humans had long been living there—*Homo neanderthalensis*. You may picture Neanderthals as stooped clumsy brutes, the way archaeology first imagined them and pop culture still portrays. But archaeologists eventually recognized their mistake and determined from broader data that these stocky northerners had spines as straight as ours, much bigger muscles, and brains just as large. These hulky humans were physically very well adapted to Ice Age Europe. In fact, one of our forebears wouldn't have stood a chance in a physical contest against a lone Neanderthal. Yet a few millennia after *sapiens* spread throughout Europe, *neanderthalensis* went extinct.

The opposing fates of these two species may have less to do with their fitness as individuals and more to do with their fitness as groups. *Sapiens* clans at the time were rapidly developing more complex cultures. They developed specialized bone tools such as awls and needles to tailor garments. They started adorning themselves with ochre dye and donning jewelry made of seashells and mammoth ivory. Sophisticated tools and symbolic behaviors were not entirely "new under the sun." They had appeared much earlier (we have learned in the past decade) at several *sapiens* sites in Africa, but these were scattered sparks of progress that glowed briefly before sputtering out. The cultural complexity didn't last for many generations or spread widely to other nearby groups. By contrast, in late Stone Age Europe, cultural complexity took root in a lasting and widespread way. While this sea change probably reflects a combination of many factors, such as increased population density and greater likelihood of encountering artifacts from the past to learn from, the new penchant for past ways seen in Chauvet Cave likely contributed as well. This increased attention shows in the archaeological record: *sapiens* tools became more distinctive and standardized within a given group, as though craftspeople were replicating designs of their teachers. After starting his career studying the crude, irregular artifacts of Neanderthals, archaeologist Richard Klein was astounded by the refinement and standardization of their *sapiens* contemporaries: "It was as if they went to a hardware store to get special-purpose tools."

Recent digs in Spanish caves have resolved the long debate about whether art is unique to *sapiens*. A few Neanderthals made symbolic drawings on cave walls. However, cave art didn't "catch on" in the same way it did in *sapiens* communities, whose artistic activity at sites like Chauvet Cave continued and developed across great stretches of time. We can picture an eccentric Neanderthal elder who picked up a stick of charcoal to sketch a horse—only to turn around to blank stares from the younger generation. *Sapiens* became wired for curiosity and compulsive motivation to maintain ancestral ways, even those with no evident practical purpose. As a result, they learned practices from found artifacts, clan elders, and other clans they interacted with. All across Europe, groups carved ivory into fecund female figurines, fabricated flutes from hollow bones, and buried their dead ritually, aligned with the sun.

Another edge for *sapiens* at this time was an expansion in the radius of trust and cooperation. While Neanderthals constructed tools from local stone (quarried near their living area), *sapiens* sometimes used "exotic stone" from hundreds of miles away. No one wandered that far in those times. As with seashell jewelry found at sites far inland, it tells of the exchange of materials across different clans. Relatedly, DNA analysis at *sapiens* sites finds that residents were no more inbred than people in nearby villages today, whereas DNA from Neanderthal sites indicates highly localized mating. Consistent with this clannish picture, Neanderthal bones betray signs of frequent combat (e.g., spear scars) and of cannibalism (e.g., human toothmarks). In sum, the two species differed in "foreign policies": *neanderthalensis* fought and ate its neighboring clans, while *sapiens* traded and mated with theirs. The latter turned out to be a more winning long-term strategy.

The most eye-opening evidence for the expanded scope of cooperation, however, comes from revelations about ritual activities in the late Stone Age. Thirty-five thousand years ago, at a Russian site called Sungir, a fifty-year-old man was interred in a "princely burial," garlanded with an ornate hat and lavish strings of ivory beads. Archaeologists estimate the beadwork alone reflects ten thousand person-hours of skilled work, which suggests a collaborative effort by multiple groups. Twenty thousand years ago, many shrine-like structures were built of mammoth bones (each requiring sixty animals) along its migration path through vast stretches of Poland, Ukraine, and Russia. Starting twelve thousand years ago, nomadic groups from across present-day Turkey and Syria converged seasonally to build monumental temples at Göbekli Tepe out of ten-ton stone blocks. These stunning discoveries have upended twentieth-century orthodoxies about the human journey and highlighted the role of ritual in the development of broader social connections.

Late Stone Age *sapiens* began to reach out to other clans as stone traders, seducers, and temple builders. In so doing they gained more and more "common ground" with neighboring clans. Learning rituals of greeting and worship opened doors to greater trust and exchange, enabling outsiders to present themselves more like insiders. Gradually *sapiens* clans became nested within broader networks of shared understanding. These broad networks—connecting the clans in a region—brought them access to richer and richer stores of shared knowledge. They became more capable than Neanderthals even though their brains were no bigger. Our species became wiser thanks to our tribes.

In 1943 a band of Arrernte people in central Australia faced a devastating drought. They journeyed to all the water holes and "sinks" in their territory, only to find them dry. Facing a threat to survival, their elder Paralji reflected on the *songlines* sung in their tribal ceremonies. (These are song cycles that encode the routes of ancestral beings across the desert through descriptions of the successive landscapes they passed through.) Remembering traditional lyrics about a journey to the sea, he led his band of several families into unknown desert territory reciting the lyrics in the proper order. They walked for hundreds of miles, finding land features and sources of water near where the lyrics said they would be, until they finally reached the lush grasslands and marshes of Mandora Station on Australia's west coast. This group was saved from a deadly drought by an old man's faith in tradition.

This wasn't just luck. Tribal traditions often preserve critical lessons about environmental threats. Just as the Bible records the story of Noah, Aboriginal peoples in different parts of Australia pass down myths about a primeval flood that vary by region. In 2016 geologists ran simulations of how the post-glacial sea rise of seven thousand years ago played out in different parts of the country, finding an impressive match to local flood myths. Bringing an impressive "big data" approach, Brown University economist Stelios Michalopoulos analyzed the oral tradition corpuses of more than one thousand cultural groups and matched them to historical records about the groups' ancestors in preindustrial times. He found that present-day folklore motifs tend to match the threats that their ancestors faced—whether earthquakes, diseases, or invasions.

Traditions can preserve lessons because of the way we psychologically process them: We learn them by rote and then we replicate them compulsively. We take a different stance toward traditions than other kinds of knowledge. When anthropologists ask Navajo elders to explain the rain dance, they answer, "This is how we have always done it." This rigid replication is part of what lends meaning to a ritual. The Jewish Passover dinner is called a Seder ("order") for good reason. Six prescribed foods—bitter herbs, unleavened bread, lamb shank, and so on—must be eaten in sequence along with stipulated steps of wine sipping, singing, and praying. A routine becomes ritualized through this reverential and compulsive repetition. Anthropologist Alan Fiske showed that obsessive-compulsive disorder involves the same stance as cultural rituals (even many of the same behaviors such as washing) but often without the resulting feeling of unity that makes cultural rituals existentially comforting.

When we are taught traditions, we memorize and replicate them faithfully even though there are impractical elements. In a Seder, for example, a glass of wine is poured for the prophet Elijah (in case he should magically appear). If you were to mention at a Seder that this is a waste of time (or of wine), your hosts would look at you like you just don't get it. The fantastical or counterintuitive elements foster myths and rituals being remembered and repeated. These elements mark them as traditions to "take on faith" rather than ordinary stories or skills. On the coasts of Thailand and Myanmar, the seafaring Moken people tell tales about *laboon*, an angry wave that devours living things. They end with a moral: if the sea retracts sharply, don't be tempted by the tidal pools—run for high ground. The Moken spotted the 2004 Indian Ocean tsunami from early wave patterns and took cover, saving themselves from a disaster that killed over 230,000 others. They didn't have to understand the hydrodynamics of tsunamis for their *laboon* tales to save them. Thanks to the ancestor instinct, we can benefit from ancient lessons about threats even if the underlying science is beyond us.

This a central theme in anthropologist Joseph Henrich's superb book

The Secret of Our Success. He describes how tribal traditions work precisely *because* they are followed blindly. Divination customs (e.g., reading the cracks in a roasted caribou bone as a map) direct hunters randomly, an effective strategy because their prey can never learn from experience how to evade them. The Tukanoan people of the Amazon subsist on the local species of cassava, which contains enough cyanide that it causes paralysis if consumed cumulatively without detoxification processing. The women of the tribe follow a rigid tradition of many steps: "scraping, grating, and finally washing the roots to separate the fiber, starch, and liquid. . . . the fiber and starch must then sit for two more days, when they can then be baked and eaten." To Portuguese colonizers, this elaborate rigamarole seemed a primitive superstition. They skipped steps in preparing cassava, realizing their error far too late, when paralysis began to set in.

In many cultures, traditions are taught during gatherings that bring generations together. Adults demonstrate them to children, while elders watch to correct any missteps. You may have learned how to light religious candles or to prepare a holiday dish in this kind of setting. Children respond as learners in special ways when an adult deliberately teaches something to them, suggesting that we may have adaptations for the pedagogy by elders. Even "once upon a time" bedtime stories evoke special expectations. My young nephew went through an obsessive *Gruffalo* phase in which he would object if the reader happened to accidentally skip a page. He didn't yet know how to read, but he had memorized the "proper" sequence of this myth, down to the last detail. Ages three and four are sometimes called the "magic years" because children begin to believe in fantastical creatures like monsters and unseen forces like magic spells. A new mode of social learning unfolds in children's cognitive development at these ages. When two-year-olds in experiments see a demonstration by an adult involving unneeded steps (e.g., extracting a marshmallow from a jar by first waving a feather over the jar then twisting off the top to access the treat), they act when it's their turn by skipping the feather-waving and grabbing the marshmallow as directly as possible. Chimps and bonobos in this procedure do the same. Children older than three, however, attend to the demonstration with rapt attention and then compulsively reenact it, superfluous feather-waving and all. They take it "on faith" that the sequence should be replicated just as performed. This shift toward "over-imitation" develops at the same age for children wherever it has been tested—in California suburbs, the Kalahari Desert, and everywhere in between. Developmentalists believe that it's a special mode of high-fidelity social learning that is evoked by teaching functionally opaque practices such as symbolic rituals or complex techniques.

In addition to learning mechanisms, the ancestor instinct involves motivations for reenacting traditions faithfully. When we replicate some traditional words or actions—whether at a ballet recital, a bar mitzvah, or a baseball game—we may not understand all of it, but it's hallowed tradition, not a hollow exercise. Cooking from a heritage recipe on the holidays is a lot more work than ordering in, but it feels meaningful to maintain the continuity of practice. At the New York Stock Exchange, an opening bell is rung each morning at nine thirty to mark the start of the trading day. The physical bell once had an instrumental purpose of announcing the start of the trading session above the commotion of a busy room; while that is no longer necessary, it has taken on ritual significance—ringing the bell is now an honor for visiting dignitaries or companies making their debut. At Amazon, meetings begin with a six-page memo. At Alcoholics Anonymous, they start with the Serenity Prayer. These rituals may look to outsiders like mindless repetition, but to insiders the recurrence of a rigid sequence provides a sense of meaningful continuity. As workers have returned to the office, firms have rushed to reintroduce company rituals— whether it's Monday Meditation or Taco Tuesdays—to bolster the feelings of meaningful community that atrophied during the ritual-starved Zoom years.

Even painful rituals can be motivating. In his riveting book, *Ritual: How Seemingly Senseless Acts Make Life Worth Living*, anthropologist Dimitris Xygalatas describes people who engage in risky, aversive rites like getting nailed to a cross on Easter Sunday or walking on hot coals at a corporate retreat. These daring devotees gain feelings of renewed connection to their community, in spite of (or perhaps *because* of) the discomfort. Borrowing from evolutionary biology, the aversive ritual is a "costly signal" that proves and thereby cements one's commitment. You may have felt a milder dose of this meaningful misery when sitting through a long Easter mass, serving on a tedious professional awards committee, or standing in a two-hour line to vote in an election. It's not always fun to fulfill the obligations of group rituals, but it's satisfying to feel that doing so cements your connection to a tribe.

In the fifteenth century, a teenaged peasant girl named Jeanne tended sheep in the village of Domrémy in northeast France. Though she never learned to read or write, Jeanne grew up steeped in the traditions of the Catholic Church—its doctrine, sacraments, holy days, and stories of the saints. One day in the fields in 1425, Jeanne was transfixed by a vision of Saint Michael the Archangel who appeared in the sky and spoke to her, along with Saint Margaret and Saint Catherine. A French folk tradition held that one day a maiden bearing a religious banner would liberate France from its enemy. The saints told Jeanne that she was destined to be that savior.

France's enemy at the time was England. It was eight decades into the

Hundred Years' War. In the prior decade, King Henry V had conquered most of northern France, including the capital, Paris, as well as Reims, the site of coronations. As a result, the Dauphin Charles VII could not be crowned. Many of Jeanne's fellow villagers had fled from the English invaders. The English invaders were pressing farther southward each year. But Jeanne believed what others found preposterous: she could lead the army to victory so that the country could regain a king.

In 1428, when Jeanne was sixteen, she persuaded a relative to bring her to the nearest French garrison. She asked the commanding officer to take her to the Dauphin and was dismissed as an addled farm girl. But some ordinary soldiers were moved by her piety and conviction and agreed to help. Jeanne sheared off her hair and put on men's clothes, and they spirited her across the countryside to the Dauphin's makeshift court in the castle of Chinon. She announced herself as the long-prophesized virgin savior: if she rode in front with a white banner proclaiming alliance with Jesus and Mary, per the legend, the French troops would be invincible. This made no sense on a practical level, but the Dauphin had exhausted all practical options. The city of Orléans had been under siege for six months, and its demoralized army could not hold out much longer. If it fell, the remainder of independent France would soon follow. After his theologians confirmed that Jeanne was a good Catholic and his mother-in-law confirmed that she was a virgin, the Dauphin had her escorted to Orléans in borrowed armor, carrying the outlandish banner.

Upon arrival, Jeanne arranged for the soldiers of Orléans to cleanse their souls with Catholic sacraments. They lined up for public penance, kneeling in groups before a priest to confess their sins and hear Latin benedictions. They filled the pews for Sunday Mass—kneeling and standing on cue, reciting prayers, and singing hymns in unison to the familiar music. Then they lined up for Communion, tasting the bread and wine transubstantiated into Christ's body and blood. When Jeanne announced that she was the banner-bearing virgin of legend who would lead them to victory, the troops believed her.

Jeanne advised the French generals to change their strategy by going on the attack, making sorties against the English encampments around the city. She led the first charge with her streaming banner, and the soldiers rallied behind her. At the first fort, the astonished English troops were easily trounced. As the French army pressed onward, Jeanne was wounded by an arrow to the neck but returned to the front to lead the final assault. Her indomitable conviction, and seeming immunity to English arrows, inspired the French troops to attack further. Within days, the siege was broken, and with it the aura of English invincibility.

The tale of this miracle flew across the countryside. Recruits arrived to join the fight full of fervor. The tide of the long war turned. In battle after battle, the French army attacked, led by the charismatic mystic with her streaming banner, and the English lost city after city. In July 1429, French forces marched into Reims, and the Dauphin was coronated with Jeanne at his side. The war didn't end well for the *jeune fille* we know in English as Joan of Arc, but history nonetheless remembers her as the savior of France.

Jeanne galvanized the French troops by changing how they framed the fight. Before, they were just pawns in a real estate dispute between two royals. After Jeanne's arrival, they became crusaders in a holy war with God on their side, defenders of the French Catholic tradition. By surrounding them with sacraments, she had lulled them into this mythic mindset. She revealed herself as the savior promised by tradition and called upon them as Catholics and Frenchmen to step up to this epic moment. (Ironically, the English campaign had been ignited this same way at Agincourt, fourteen years before, when charismatic Henry V rallied his "band of brothers" on St. Crispin's Day by inviting them to become legendary figures of English tradition.)

If peer codes are prompted by tribal signs and hero codes by tribal symbols, the situational cue that summons ancestor codes is tribal ceremony. By this I mean choreographed public events that reference the collective past—a Catholic mass, a Greek wedding celebration, the GOP electoral convention, and so forth. These events have in common at least two critical features: synchrony and history. It's a tribal ceremony if people act in unison (e.g., pray, dance, vote) while being reminded of parts of their community's past, often parts that are suitable as analogies for the present.

We don't realize how much ceremonies affect us, as it happens mostly at an unconscious level. Children are most likely to engage their ritual mode of rote learning and rigid reenactment when adults demonstrate it synchronously and introduce it as collective institution (i.e., "We've always done it this way"). In many communities, extreme initiation ceremonies (e.g., rites of passage, fraternity pledges, Hell Week for Navy SEALs) break down individual identities to forge a sense of unity with and obligation to the group. Research on religiosity and its consequences started with the presumption that private faith would matter more than public participation in religious ceremonies. But surprisingly, it's the ceremonies that go along with volunteering and commitment.

In international rugby, the All Blacks of New Zealand have spent more time atop the rugby world rankings than any other team—in fact, more than all other national teams combined. For more than a century, the team has started each game with a *haka*, a martial dance that Māori warriors traditionally performed before battles to access the *mana*, or spiritual power, of their ancestors. Players stand in a wedge formation at midfield, staring across at their opponents. All at once, they begin to stomp their feet, thrust their chests, and thrash their arms in rhythmic unison while chanting, "*Ka mate, ka mate! Ka ora! Ka ora!*" ("I might die, I might die! I may live! I may live!"). These vows are punctuated with blood-curdling screams and guttural grunts; eyes bulge and tongues protrude. As players lunge, yell, and mug in unison, individual egos drop away, and players fuse into a united force, each obliged to do anything for the team's victory.

It's not just the *haka*'s deep roots in the team's (and the nation's) history that brings about this unity. Tribal ceremonies often involve rhythmic vocalizing and percussion that have a mesmerizing effect. Even exposure to ten minutes of repetitive shamanic drumming tends to induce a trance state accompanied by altered patterns of neural activity. Acting in unison with others, particularly when extended and with a large group, alters psychological processing in a more profound way. Experiments have found that participants induced to perform even simple activities synchronously with others (waving hands, rowing machines, or playing instruments) experience the effects of feeling closer to each other, cooperating more in mixed-motive tasks, and sacrificing to help collective outcomes. (In the control condition, participants do the same activities but not synchronized with each other.) After synchronous activity, participants' pain tolerance rises to higher than usual, perhaps an adaptation to support sacrifices. Neuroscientists find that synchrony induces brain activation patterns of reduced self-focused processing, attunement to others, and self-other blurring.

You probably haven't danced a *haka*, but you've undoubtedly felt the empowering shift that comes from acting in unison with a group. When running sprints at a sports team practice, you burst into action and cross the line with your teammates at your side. At a music festival, dancing with your friends as the band plays its final song, your individual self-consciousness recedes to enable a broader sense of identity. In church, as your congregation stands, kneels, and sings together during a service, a feeling of unity and joy descends upon you. Émile Durkheim called this feeling "collective effervescence." Through the resonance of your behavior with others, a feeling of unity and empowerment emerges. At a political rally, when the crowd chants as one, you start to feel capable of changing the world. Even at a baseball game, when you rise together to do "the wave," there's a sense that your side will prevail. It may seem hokey when corporations ask a new team to do warm-up exercises or sing a song together, but synchrony sets the stage for group camaraderie, identity, and efficacy. They become primed to attempt epic feats.

It's no coincidence that communities use ceremonies—weddings, matriculations, coronations—to seal people's commitments to a new social role. Promise rituals are surrounded by group processions and singing, but also by ponderous references to the collective past. Together, synchrony and history predispose people to thinking in terms of tradition. Whether a wedding is a church service or a courthouse protocol, the vow feels like an obligation of tradition. In the white coat ceremony at the start of medical school, incoming students line up on stage to be "cloaked" in white coats by their professors. Then, echoing their teacher's lead, they recite the Hippocratic oath, full of references to ancient Greek mythology. Medical students report that the ceremony imparts a sense of unity, duty, and awe. The codes of the profession are conveyed not just as normal practices or respected ideals but also as sacred traditions, so that students are driven not just by conformity or aspiration but also obligation.

On the morning of September 11, 2001, I happened to be teaching my first-ever class at Columbia University. It was a nine a.m. class on negotiation and conflict management for a group of MBA students. Like many New Yorkers, we had heard chatter about a first plane crash and hoped it was an errant Cessna. The classroom was full, so I launched into my opening spiel. I got halfway through a story about two chefs and the last orange in the kitchen when a student exclaimed that the South Tower had been hit.

Students began blurting out theories and worries, while others frantically typed on their PalmPilots and BlackBerries. The phone rang with a message from the university that classes should go on, but I couldn't return to my lesson plan about win-win solutions. This was obviously not a conflict with a win-win solution. Phones stopped working and we had to learn what we could. We walked down the avenues toward downtown, eventually meeting the dazed crowd that was heading uptown. By the end of the day, almost everyone discovered friends and neighbors missing.

The attack lasted only a few hours, but it changed the country in lasting ways: heightened airline security, prejudice against Muslims, not to mention the unending "War on Terror." The country reacted with vigilance and retribution. In New York City, where we felt an existential threat, the changes after 9/11 went beyond those elsewhere. To be sure, New Yorkers displayed the flag in every way they could—hung on pizzeria walls, mounted on cab dashboards, stuck to bodega cash registers. But the famously jaded denizens of the city began to act differently. Busy lawyers, aloof models, and surly cabbies showed up for candlelight vigils at local firehouses. They packed the pews at churches and turned out in droves for Thanksgiving parades and Christmas tree lightings. The tabloids labeled all of this "a message to Bin Laden."

But there was change in less obvious places, too, such as on our dinner plates. The trend in restaurants had been avant-garde fusion cuisine, but the mode shifted toward regional americana. Diners flocked to Craft, Bubby's, Savoy, and Blue Smoke. Kate Krader of *Food & Wine* may have been the first to draw the link: "After 9/11 . . . there is a kind of illogical need for stuff like macaroni and cheese, and fried chicken." This fresh craving for grandma's staples was not a message to Bin Laden. We weren't posturing toward Tora Bora with our fancied-up cheeseburgers; we were taking comfort in continuity. After a brush with annihilation, we clung to tradition.

In the army, they used to say, "There are no atheists in foxholes." It's an adage about situational influence. Soldiers may act sinfully when on leave, but when the threat of death looms, they revert to religion. A study of WWII soldier diaries confirmed that, indeed, the closer a diarist was to combat, the more he mentioned prayer. The war historian Cyril Falls writes of reciting his school's Latin grammar drills as battle shells fell around him: "Ante, apud, ad, adversus . . ." The exception proves the rule. Some soldiers soothe themselves with secular rituals.

Anthropologists have long observed that traditional rituals are practiced in contexts of threat. In his classic ethnography of Trobriand Islanders, Bronisław Malinowski observed that rituals were practiced before launching canoes for open-sea fishing, which was full of danger—but not before embarking to the inland lagoon, which was safe and predictable. Mary Douglas and others theorized that rituals reduce anxiety by asserting control over dangers. Communities tend to form rituals relating to the local dangers that make life precarious. Kosher and halal laws address anxieties about food poisoning, a scourge of desert societies. Ritual bathing by Hindus provides a sense of control over infectious diseases, rife in humid environments. And should such traditions fail to ward off mortal danger, virtually every culture has funeral rites that assert control over death by ushering the deceased's soul to the afterlife.

The mere awareness of mortality may trigger people to immerse themselves in tribal traditions. In *The Denial of Death*, Ernest Becker proposed that traditions serve as defense mechanisms against otherwise-crippling mortality anxiety. He argued that humans are the only animals aware that they will die, and this is relevant to our craving for tradition. While your life will be all too brief, your tribe's traditions have existed for generations and hence will likely persist many generations into the future. *You*—as part of them—can live on too! Wrapping ourselves in tradition is an existential balm that serves our need for continuity.

At the time, behavioral scientists found this to be murky philosophizing, but a decade later some began to find effects of death reminders that fit the theory. When a researcher stopped German pedestrians in front of a cemetery to answer a consumer survey, they defended Volkswagen, German cuisine, and the old Deutsche Mark more than did a control group stopped several blocks away in front of a shopping center. A similar defensive shift was seen in a US study that stopped passersby either in a spot facing a funeral home or several hundred yards away. A study in Varanasi, India, found that farmers defend Hindu tradition less than funerary workers (who are surrounded by death), but farmers express more traditional attitudes after reminders of death. Mere reminders of mortality are less triggering than actual brushes with death, but that death reminders matter at all shows that traditionalism is not just a message to external adversaries but also a means of coping with inner anxiety.

Cemeteries, funeral homes, and funeral pyres may be particularly evocative because they are sites of both death *and* ceremony. This combination—spellbinding ceremony and adrenalizing threat—incited the traditionalism of Paralji's band, Joan of Arc's troops, and New Yorkers after 9/11. A study of Palestinian youth by psychologist Hammad Sheikh and his colleagues investigated this volatile combination. Six hundred teens from across the West Bank and Gaza were surveyed repeatedly about their lives and attitudes about the peace process, in particular about the possibility of concessions on issues (e.g., giving up their "right of return," accepting Israeli control of East Jerusalem, recognizing Israel's right to exist) if they could bring great benefits and enable a peaceful and happy Palestinian state. Teens highly exposed to both threat *and* religious ceremonies were most likely to hew to the traditional party line that these concessions are unthinkable.

Threats to tribal mortality can come in many forms. Even if the community's lives are not in peril, changes can threaten the continuity of their tradition. The Crusades were not provoked by a threat to European lives but by a threat to Christian institutions in Jerusalem and Constantinople. The Pope sent around charismatic priests who sermonized about the thousand-year-old institutions, such as the Hagia Sophia cathedral, "in elaborate ceremonial settings accompanied by liturgical acts such as prayers, chants, processions, and sometimes the exposition of relics." The anguishing threat to tribal tradition and the mesmerizing spell of ceremony swayed countless Europeans to leave behind their peace to join these unrealistic foreign wars.

Another threat to tribal continuity can be demographic trends. Established majority groups, who think of a country as "their land," feel threatened by rising populations of minority cultures and immigrants. When the media celebrates increasing diversity, the majority group sometimes responds defensively with rash efforts to lock in and defend their traditions. A rising Arab population in Israel (even though just 20 percent) set off a defensive political movement that culminated in the 2018 Nationality Bill declaring Jews as the nation's only legitimate rulers and Hebrew as its only official language. In the US, the rising Hispanic population along the Southern border has long been taken as a threat by others to their way of life. When studies share projections about demographic and cultural change in coming generations (e.g., "Spanish will become the language of everyday life"), participants respond by opposing diversity policies—even those like bilingual education that would seem warranted by the demographic trends. In national surveys, when whites are shown projections that they will no longer be a majority, they react with fears about loss of cultural continuity (e.g., "I fear that in forty years' time, it won't be clear what it means to be American") and endorse exclusionary policies (e.g., English-only laws). This defensive reflex of established groups who fear displacement has contributed to the wave of populism in diversifying countries over the past decade.

While threats to tribal continuity can trigger ugly intolerance, they can also summon great acts of sacrifice and collective resolve. In 2011, a tsunami with 130-foot waves engulfed the Fukushima nuclear plant in Japan. It set off explosions, destroyed power generators, and left the reactors leaking radiation at unsafe levels while heating up toward a meltdown that would irradiate all of Tokyo, the capital and home to thirty-five million people. Evacuated by company policy to a nearby crisis center, the nuclear engineers and technicians felt terrified and ashamed. In the face of this existential threat to their nation's institutions—not to mention that of their corporation and that of their profession—they talked with each other about Japanese tradition, including the samurai code of sacrifice before surrender. A group of older employees banded together and requested a return to the stricken plant, even though doctors warned they would die from the radioactivity. They had already raised their children, so they would take the risk. Engineer Atsufumi Yoshizawa describes a spontaneous ceremony as technicians, firefighters, police officers, and soldiers lined up to solemnly salute the "suicide squad," bolstering their conviction. They felt like ancient samurai or WWII kamikaze pilots ready for sacrifice. The Fukushima 50, as they came to be known, knew the plants' layout by heart and worked in shifts to investigate the damage. They slept on their desks, grew beards, and subsisted on vending machine crackers and juice. They found old-fashioned ways to reduce the temperature in critical chambers such as by releasing steam valves by hand. Several suffered fatal burns, but most survived to tell the story. "There is a special bond between us," said Yoshizawa. "I can't put it into words—it's just a feeling we have towards one another. I guess it's the same as the camaraderie soldiers experience in wartime."

The Fukushima 50 coalesced through the power of the ancestor instinct. Their decision to return to the danger zone was guided by a time-honored cultural code that they all knew well. In the end, a meltdown was averted, and the contamination was contained. However, this rescue can't be credited to the traditionalist reflexes of the ancestor instinct *alone*; the hero and peer instincts also played a part.

During the crisis, a humble plant manager, Masao Yoshida, found himself unexpectedly the point person for a national crisis. His bosses weren't on the ground and declared the reactors as beyond rescue. The prime minister phoned him and spoke about the threat to Tokyo—the population center, capital, and site of the Imperial Palace. Looking out at the tsunami-ravaged plants, Yoshida envisioned the solution of pumping water from the sea to cool the reactors. His corporate bosses rejected the idea, but he pursued it anyway. The local fire department couldn't do it, so he called Tokyo's. Could they drive 150 miles to Fukushima, pump saltwater, and spray reactors from a great distance, he asked, with radioactivity levels that allowed each man to be exposed only ten minutes a day? Cued by national symbols and aware of the world watching, Yoshida morphed from a mundane manager to a visionary problem solver.

The fire department he called is the largest in the world, and its mission is to protect Tokyo. But its leaders saw that their equipment and protocols for fighting high-rise infernos could be adapted to this challenge. They sent convoys of trucks from firehouses across the vast city, crews who had never worked together before. But they all knew the department's procedures, so they could work together seamlessly, setting up the rigs and spraying jets of water around the clock to stabilize the temperature and ward off a meltdown. Soon crews from Yokohama, Osaka, Kyoto, and other cities arrived and joined in the tag-team effort, coordinating through standard occupational protocols. Under pressure, peer codes kicked into action.

The commendable rescue of the Fukushima plant involved all three tribal triggers: the call of traditions in times of ceremony and threat, the aspiration to heroic contributions inspired by symbols and audiences, and the empowering impulse to coordinate as a united front spurred by peers and time pressure. It took the combination of these three psychological forces to meet the challenge of a tsunami turned meltdown turned threat to the national tradition.

Likewise, for our paleo predecessors, while each instinct brought a leap forward, the real magic happened when all three instincts began to function together. As the ancestor instinct instilled new motivations about the past, tribes remembered the lessons of the past. Once people didn't have to "reinvent the wheel" each generation, hero instincts became channeled toward building on and surpassing past skills. These new innovations would then spread through peer-instinct imitation, adding to the group's stock of shared expertise. The wisdom of tribes began accumulating. They passed down more knowledge about surviving and thriving.

It was this snowballing process of cultural accumulation—not a boost of individual intelligence—that explains the noticeable uptick of cultural complexity in late Stone Age Europe. These forebears used bone tools to fish and to tailor garments. They drew on cave walls, carved Venus figurines, and played bone flutes. By twenty thousand years ago, hunter-gather groups converged to bury chiefs and build shrines and eventually design massive temples. Around ten thousand years ago, agriculture appeared, along with permanent settlements and tools like the plow for tilling soil and clay vessels for storing surplus food. By five thousand years ago, human cultures involved domesticated animals, cities, wheels, bronze, and writing. Tribes became kingdoms in Mesopotamia, Egypt, China, and elsewhere, then became linked into larger empires—tribes of tribes. By one thousand years ago, more people began to live with a balance of multiple tribes in their lives—nations, religions, guilds, armies, and businesses. A few centuries later, the Renaissance brought another revolution of teachings, technologies, and exploratory travels. By two hundred years ago, the Industrial Revolution brought railways, steamships, textile factories, telegraph communication, and colonialism. By fifty years ago, we had split the atom, made computers, flown to space, and formed international organizations like the UN. By twenty-five years ago, the internet began to link online communities and networks larger than any prior empires, nations, or organizations. This exponential growth of cultural knowledge and connection continues, through the engine of cultural accumulation. We can see far today because we stand on the shoulders of giants, though we cannot see the future.

Yet our progress also threatens our survival. Splitting the atom to unleash nuclear energy was a crossroads. At Fukushima, the tribal impulses that created the exponential growth of technology were able to rein in its danger. But the world faces an increasing number of challenges of this sort. We shall turn to them in the final chapter, in the hope that even if tribal psychology has contributed to the problems, it can also be part of the solution.

PART II

TRIBAL
SIGNALS

4

The Rise and Fall
of Prohibition

The areas of consensus shift unbelievably fast;
the bubbles of certainty are constantly exploding.

—REM KOOLHAAS

Only ten decades ago, the US shocked the world by banning alcohol sales, amending the Constitution to do so. This upended widespread routines of social life and shuttered entire industries. Then, thirteen years later, the country changed its mind and amended the Constitution again to repeal the policy. How did public opinion swing so dramatically? And then, even more swiftly, swing back?

Nowadays, Prohibition seems mainly to live on as a backdrop for gangster movies and "speakeasy" bars. It's harder to remember the fundamental cultural changes it involved. Like many ideas good and bad, the temperance movement first took root on the religious fringe. The "dry crusade" started in the nineteenth century and spread slowly through church networks. Preachers railed against "demon alcohol," but these sermons didn't convince many, just the churchy types in the front pews.

Abstinence groups tried promoting other kinds of beverages: they installed water fountains in parks and championed "soft drinks" (launching the nation's addiction to Coca-Cola in the process). Still, the public kept on imbibing. (Coke mixes well with rum, it turns out!) Alcohol was ingrained in many cultural routines: it was commonplace to drink wine with dinner, beer at the saloon, and cocktails at the club. So long as people were surrounded by these peer patterns—so long as this was their "normal"—fiery sermons and beverage alternatives wouldn't change their drinking habits.

Once temperance leaders began to see drinking as a cultural pattern rather than a personal failing, they tried to change the perceived normalcy of abstinence. Inspired by missionaries, they held conspicuous pledge events in public squares that brought parishioners sympathetic to temperance. After rousing speeches, many lined up to place their hand on a Bible, recite orotund vows of teetotalism, then sign their name to a leather-bound registry—to the approving applause of their peers. We can understand based on the foregoing chapters that this event was well-designed to trigger these avowals: the religious folk were surrounded by tribal signs, symbols, and ceremony. But pledge events also affected *outsiders*, passersby who didn't go to these churches but stopped to gawk at the spectacle—the line of pledgees, the thick registry book, the abundant applause for each new initiate. We can imagine what they surmised: "Sure looks like a lot of folks around here lean dry."

Temperance activists developed methods for using media to bolster this impression. Press releases touted the swelling ranks of teetotalers: one million pledges, then two million (never mentioning the other ten million Americans who had *not* pledged). The former ballplayer Billy Sunday drew tens of thousands to sermons from temporary "tabernacles" in city centers, events staged for newspaper coverage. The fiery preacher Mordecai Ham broadcast his revival meetings over the radio. Temperance unions bought their own printing presses and flooded the nation's mailboxes with "scientific temperance instruction" about the perils of alcohol, reaching one in five American homes. Regardless of its medical soundness, the sheer prevalence of this literature sent its own message: the abstinence attitude appeared to be everywhere.

In 1913 the Anti-Saloon League invented the technique of "pressure politics." As states prepared to vote on dry laws, Wayne Wheeler and William "Pussyfoot" Johnson orchestrated thirteen thousand members to write their representatives demanding restrictions. To legislators, who had never received such a tide of correspondence, it appeared that the entire business community was demanding a fix for public drunkenness. State after state went dry. By 1917 nationwide prohibition was proposed as the Eighteenth Amendment, and two years later, it was ratified by the requisite thirty-seven states. It banned the sale of alcohol, even beer and wine. When the Volstead Act (which provided enforcement of the amendment) came before Congress, the Anti-Saloon League flooded their telegraph wires for weeks. A crucial vote came from Senator Warren Harding of Ohio, who attested that he was personally opposed to Prohibition but felt moved by the public mandate to vote for it.

On the evening of January 16, 1920, restaurants, taverns, and nightclubs held mock funerals, laying John Barleycorn to rest. Drinkers gathered around open coffins and talked about how life would never be the same. At the stroke of midnight, mourners took their last swigs before tossing their bottles into the box.

Notice that the temperance movement didn't achieve this radical change just through tribal triggers (which we discussed in the foregoing chapters). Triggers *activate* cultural codes that are already latent inside people, but social change sometimes requires more than that—it requires *changing* people's cultural codes, reprogramming them. Temperance required changing Americans' perception of their peers, their working assumption about the public consensus. This couldn't happen overnight; it took a sustained campaign of events and messages that incrementally changed people's perception of their fellow Americans' support for abstinence.

Around the same time, a New York weekly called *Literary Digest* was gaining readership through an innovative gimmick: reader polls to measure public opinion. The *Digest* dazzled the American public by forecasting the election of President Woodrow Wilson in 1916 and of Warren Harding in 1920. Other polls probed human-interest topics. In 1922 a poll tested that women were more likely than men to support Prohibition. The results corroborated the gender difference, but it also returned a surprise: *most* respondents (regardless of sex) did not support the law—they preferred that at least some alcohol sales be allowed.

This may not seem surprising in hindsight, but at the time it was shocking. For years, the dry faction had made themselves highly visible through pledge events, revival meetings, and letter-writing campaigns. Their moralistic fervor shamed imbibers into silence. The legislative votes went strongly in favor of Prohibition. All appearances indicated that most Americans were dry. But in the privacy of a mail poll, a different reality was revealed.

Magazine polls don't create much buzz today, but at the time they were a revelation. They revealed public opinion more accurately than a reporter could by conducting interviews. Temperance leaders impugned this newfangled form of journalism and the suspicious "literary" types behind it, but many Americans who preferred evidence to ideology found it credible. It particularly moved people in the center of the divide who didn't have a settled opinion either wet or dry. These "undecideds" tend to gravitate toward the majority stance on an issue—they go with what the "average American" believes. After the news that "dry" supporters were a minority, some centrists who had leaned dry adjusted their position to lean wet.

The poll also piqued renewed public debate. Opponents of Prohibition took the occasion to express their reasons in op-eds and town halls. Congressional hearings began investigating its unintended consequences: gangsters, moonshine, and bread lines. With change in the elite discourse, ordinary people felt freer to voice opinions that might have sounded heretical and risked their reputation a year earlier. This new outspokenness pulled more fence-sitters to the wet camp. When the *Digest* repeated its poll in 1930, almost 70 percent opposed Prohibition. By 1932, it was 75 percent. Soon it was the wets circulating petitions and organizing letter-writing campaigns. A repeal amendment, the Twenty-First, was drafted and ratified in under nine months. Support for Prohibition collapsed like a punctured balloon.

A religious movement from the heartland broadened into a groundswell and changed the Constitution, then a few urban journalists researching a human interest story with a novel tool stumbled onto some news that reversed the tide of opinion—and then the law of the land. The prime movers on the opposing sides could hardly have been more different (moralistic ministers trying to suppress drinking versus innovative journalists looking for a scoop), but they each gained influence through the same psychological route: they provided information that shifted Americans' perception of their peers. Temperance events created an illusion of ubiquitous abstinence, and the illusion started to become reality as it manifested opinions, lifestyles, and ultimately votes. When polls, debates, and hearings later revealed the hidden wet majority, the illusion was dispelled, undecideds became wets, and conformity became a force for reversion to the status quo ante.

The information that shapes (and reshapes) people's cultural codes can be called tribal *signals*. Each tribal instinct updates in response to a different tribal signal. Peer codes are sensitive to *prevalence signals*: information about what groupmates do, or think, or say. These signals are sent by telling people, showing people, or (best of all) involving them in experiences. Recall how Coach Hiddink orchestrated new kinds of social interactions

at the Reds training camp to shift the team culture. Months of these egalitarian interactions with teammates reprogrammed players' sense of "the
Reds way." Temperance activists faced a parallel challenge of instilling
new cultural habits. The repeal movement faced a different challenge:
exposing the wet opinion, which was widespread but was not assumed to
be such. It had to *correct* the public's mistaken peer codes. As we shall see,
these two challenges—creating a new norm versus exposing an existing
norm—call for different strategies in sending prevalence signals.

In Victorian photographs, subjects wore a serious visage. These grim expressions were a practical necessity—slow camera shutters couldn't capture
fleeting smiles. By the early twentieth century, technology was no longer
a limiting factor, yet dour faces still prevailed. It had become a custom.
Smiling simply wasn't done in front of a camera. Portrait sitters used to say
the word "prunes" to achieve the standard pressed-lip look.

The Eastman Kodak Corporation held a near-monopoly on cameras
and film at the time, but there wasn't much popular demand for either.
Photography was regarded as an ordeal best left to professionals in their
studios. Kodak realized it needed to change the cultural assumptions
around photography. It introduced a cheap, user-friendly camera, the
Brownie, as a loss-leader product. Kodak donated cameras to schools,
Scout troops, and YMCAs to hook the youth. Magazine ads—"Save your
happy moments with a Kodak"—showed parents capturing family occasions
in "snapshots." *Kodakery*, a newsletter for "shutterbugs," held amateur
photo contests and published the resulting pictures of ordinary Americans beaming at picnics, parades, and proms. It taught tricks for evoking
smiles: squeaking toys for a baby, asking adults to say "cheese."

Largely through Kodak's efforts, early twentieth-century Americans began to see others smiling for the camera. Smiling became an acceptable practice, which gave more people license to try it, and this put more smiling photographs into circulation. Through this cycle of changed perceptions and changed behavior, smiling became the *standard* thing to do and then even the *obvious* thing to do. Nowadays we do it as a reflex, on autopilot. Even mug shots feature goofy grins. Kodak seeded this practice with inducements and ads, then helped it appear widespread by publishing the resulting pictures and coining catchy terms to facilitate conversations about it. The resulting cultural change is visible in aggregated American yearbook photos across the twentieth century—the pressed lips and dead eyes of early decades become replaced by wide smiles and sparkling eyes.

It's a familiar point that people conform to the *majority*. Our brains don't just "read minds"; they also "read the room." In the 1950s, psychologist Solomon Asch recruited college students for a study that tested their vision with obvious slides like those used by an eye doctor: *Which of the three lines is the longest? Is this color blue or green?* The students were tested in small groups. At first, everyone around the table would give the same correct answer to each of the (easy) questions. Midway through, though,

most began voicing incorrect answers, the same incorrect answers (they were fake participants, in league with the experimenter). The *real* participants reacted by whipping their heads around to stare bewilderedly at these peers. As it continued over many rounds, they began to show signs of self-doubt: cleaning their glasses, rubbing their eyes, and scratching their heads. A third of them began answering in agreement with the incorrect majority, against the evidence of their own senses.

Did they feel peer pressure to conform to the majority, or did the prevalence signal seep in to their preconceptions and ultimately their perceptions and beliefs? Many twists on the experiment failed to definitively answer this question. Recently it was run with the participants hooked up to an fMRI brain scanner. Participants who answered correctly, against the majority of their peers, were distinguished by higher activation in the caudate nuclei (which handles inhibitory self-control) and in the amygdala (the alarm system that detects social dangers). Participants who conformed to the incorrect majority were distinguished by more activation in the visual cortex (where perceptions are constructed). Both explanations seem supported: people do feel peer pressure but must actively resist to prevent peer information from insinuating itself into their perceptions.

Less familiar, but no less important, are findings that even a *minority* faction can also exert peer influence. The French social psychologist Serge Moscovici found that a minority faction consistent in its views (e.g., several participants calling a shade of blue "green") influences their peers: their behavior prompts a third of participants to see the stimulus that way at least once. People "try out" alternative beliefs and practices suggested by peers, even if they are not sure that they will embrace them permanently. Sociologist Damon Centola finds that the pressure for coordination in interactions brings groups to settle on conventions (such as shared labels or interpretations), but when "activists" firmly committed to alternative practices join the mix, their influence can disrupt and even flip the group convention. Across several studies in different settings, he finds that the "critical mass" for this is about 25 percent of the population. Less than that, and the new practice rarely gains ground. More than that, and the alternative practice often shifts the prevailing convention. We've all seen this happen as, for example, the LGBTQ+ community and its allies pressed the use of "they" as a singular pronoun. It's a "tipping point" dynamic in which the coordination incentive and conformity pressure heighten as a larger and larger share of the group adopts the new practice.

Public health NGOs that strive to change social practices in developing societies (e.g., encouraging men to use condoms or to stop hitting their wives) have found that sustained training and dialogue sessions in workshop groups can persuade individuals and build their confidence and conviction in the changed practice. However, it's not feasible to offer this experience to the whole population, so critics have questioned whether such interventions scale up to produce broader change. In some cases, however, these interventions have resulted in change that spreads outward from the small number of participants in the workshop to the broader community. A key to this is "organized diffusion" techniques that guide participants to share their new belief with close contacts in their social network. When these contacts become converted, they are encouraged to do the same. This cascade creates the critical mass of activists in the community that enables a new cultural practice to spread.

The influence of a minority opinion depends not just on frequency but also on conspicuity. Sometimes actions by a small minority stand out as a noticeable pattern. This can happen if many others are undecided or if they are divided among many distinct opinion positions—if so, a small minority may still be the plurality, the modal opinion. Or a minority practice may stand out because it is enacted dramatically and visibly: less than a tenth of Americans took temperance pledges, but they were more notice-able than non-pledgers.

Or a minority practice may be influential because it is well publicized—a big factor, as we saw, in both the campaign to promote alcohol abstinence and the one to promote amateur photography. A go-to move for government agencies and advocacy groups seeking to promote a new behavior is to incentivize and then publicize early adoption of the practice. When I read about my neighbors composting, it's no longer some far-out hippie idea; it's something that people just like me do. Another publicity trick is to focus on trends. If you hear that 20 percent of the city composts, that might not sway you to start. But if you hear that it's 20 percent, up from zero a decade ago, that makes a compelling impression. When a practice is gaining ground, we infer it is becoming the norm and want to get in on it.

The power of a few peers to exert influence is sometimes used for nefar-ious purposes. Auction houses and casinos used to rely on "shills," fake customers whose apparent interest in a product or game lured in others. Today, it's *online* shills that we are most often manipulated by. They feign enthusiasm in online forums, leave fake reviews at rating sites, and spread disinformation in political discussions. When we engage in instinctive learning from the information of peer behavior, we don't think critically and can make regrettable choices. In 2017 five thousand affluent millenni-als bought tickets to the Fyre Festival—an island music festival with VIP packages costing up to $12,000—after seeing that their Instagram and Facebook friends were going (the ticket site encouraged sharing). Event details were sketchy, but scenesters didn't want to miss out on a festival that their friends were attending. When they arrived at the site in the Bahamas, there was no music, no food, and definitely no festivity.

But contrived peer signals are not always just smoke and mirrors; at times they are the existence proof that others need to see in order to com-mit to a practice. We saw in chapter 1 that Malaysia's Cyberjaya campus failed to *trigger* startups; Silicon Valley jargon and architecture didn't suffice to ignite a tech boom. But that doesn't mean that policymakers can't foster a startup culture over the longer term by changing people's peer codes. Start-Up Chile launched in 2010 by recruiting foreign startups to move to Santiago for a six-month program with free visas, office space, funding, and publicity. Over 1,600 startups visited over the next few years, and more than half stayed on and hired locals. The impressive part, however, is what ensued. Hundreds of Chileans initiated ventures, spawning "Chilecon Valley," an ecosystem of tech companies, university labs, and VC funds that is now Latin America's largest. From the perspective of economic competition, inviting foreign startups might seem like the *worst* thing for local entrepreneurs. But from a tribal perspective, we can understand that it provided community and reprogrammed peer codes.

In 2006 a camp counselor in Alabama named Tarana Burke listened to a young woman recount a traumatic experience of sexual violence. Because Burke herself was still healing from similar experiences, she followed protocol in referring the teen to a different counselor. Afterward, though, she realized what she had really wanted to say to the young woman: "Me too."

Years later, Burke created a Myspace page named after this two-word phrase, where survivors could share their stories. If more people began to say "me too," Burke hoped, survivors would feel less alone. The page was meant as a safe space for young women of color, but soon it also began to attract women of various races, ages, and regions. They joined the chorus of survivors in this online space, building strength in numbers.

A decade later, the #MeToo movement exploded in Hollywood when dozens, then hundreds, of Hollywood actresses used this hashtag to identify themselves as survivors of sexual exploitation. As more and more survivors told their stories, it became shockingly clear just how extensive this problem was—the widespread peer pattern was just not very *observable* before. The entertainment industry's norm of silence was soon replaced by one of outspoken activism. Before this, survivors had been unable to mobilize collective action to address the problem. Sexual exploitation was highly prevalent in the industry, but this was not recognized by most of the industry because the survivors tended to keep their experiences and their anger private—fearing career repercussions. The viral #MeToo signaling on social media emboldened survivors by exposing the rampancy of the abuse. Networked online protest served to *demonstrate* the prevalence of the anger that already existed.

In his book *Private Truths, Public Lies*, political scientist Timur Kuran considered peer perceptions in the fall of the Soviet Union—an event that caught most of its citizens by surprise. Why didn't they see it coming? For decades, the Kremlin had repressed dissent. Citizens tended to praise the system in public even if they harbored doubts in private. The frequent eruptions of local discontent in the vast country were known only through vague rumors, as they were not covered in the news. Clandestine printing (samizdat) of news and opinion was a critical form of activism that was sharply repressed. When the Eastern Bloc press boldly began to cover political protests in the late 1980s, rallies in Ukraine and Eastern Europe soon cascaded into much larger demonstrations. Two million people joined arms to form a chain across the Baltic states. In February 1990, half a million Muscovite marchers converged on the Kremlin, and days later a vote ushered in a multiparty system. Street protests are called "demonstrations" because they do just that—they reveal the prevalence of a belief or practice that is otherwise unseen and unknown.

A society's understanding of itself often lags behind progressive change in its members' private attitudes, as attitudes are not directly observable. Many citizens are loath to express their liberalized attitudes in public, for fear of offending more traditional neighbors, but this reticence perpetu-ates the community's inaccurate self-understanding and its exclusionary behavior. Lagging peer codes delayed progress in whites socially integrat-ing with Blacks in the US, in Indian shopkeepers hiring from lower castes, and in Hungarian schools accepting Roma students. For definitive social change, it's not enough to change many individuals' private attitudes about an issue; there also must be change in their perception of the societal con-sensus on the issue, because this peer code is a strong determinant of their behavior.

Even when prevalence information starts to become available, people won't always abandon a long-held assumption based on the disconfirming new data. To persuade the American public that opponents of Prohibition were the majority, the *Literary Digest*'s polls had to be repeated several times and had to be supplemented by different kinds of prevalence signals, such as hearing individuals explain their wet views. Getting the public to recognize a consensus that they have long overlooked requires overcoming skepticism with multiple types of evidence. Pollsters, journalists, film-makers, podcasters, and others who shape people's social beliefs all have a critical role to play.

Promoting health practices can involve the same challenge of demon-strating that there is widespread support. "I Gave Blood" pins in company drives are not just plaudits but prevalence signals. They help the diffusion of the practice: in any group there are "laggards" who adopt a new prac-tice only once it becomes obvious that the majority has already done so. Research suggests that masks worked as a pandemic response measure not just for medical but also tribal reasons; they act as a coordination mechanism through making peers' attitudes observable. It's hard to know if your neighbors are washing their hands regularly, but you can't miss that they are wearing masks. They are taking the pandemic seriously, so you will too.

This is the same reason why fundraising drives list all the employees who gave last year. Campaigns to "get out the vote" sometimes list the residents of your block who voted in the last election (from public voting rolls). In 2010 Facebook tested an online version of this tactic on election day by displaying a banner for over sixty million users asking if they voted. Half also received peer information—a list of their Facebook friends who had already voted. The prevalence signal affected their immediate online behavior (checking polling locations) and their real-world behavior: voting rolls showed that sixty thousand more signaled users made it to the polls than in the control condition. There was also a second-order effect: their close friends (who presumably observed their voting behavior in some way) also became more likely to vote.

Prevalence signals are a time-honored way to tout a brand's popularity. For decades McDonald's displayed a running count of its total burgers served—it rose to 100 billion before the company stopped. This approach lives on in the entertainment industry: TikTok tells us it is up to 1.1 billion active users; The Weeknd has 111 million monthly listeners on Spotify; the Super Bowl is watched by 113 million people. These counts get a bit dizzying. It's easier for consumers to process comparative prevalence: *more people by far use Hertz to rent a car; British Airways is the world's favorite airline; four out of five dentists recommend Trident gum.* The democratization of data, however, has rendered these sweeping claims obsolete. With a glance at our phones we can see which airline is rated highest for a particular route, which hotel is favored by our traveler type, which restaurants have been visited by our Facebook friends. We respond more to peer information about the folks who are really our peers.

A pivotal moment in the evolution of prevalence signaling came during a hot summer of rolling blackouts in San Marcos, California. An intervention effort tested different messages to local households, starting with these pitches:

You can save $54 this month by conserving energy.

You can save the planet by conserving energy.

You can prevent local blackouts by conserving energy.

These doorknob messages centered on values that residents had expressed in prior interviews—cutting costs, saving the planet, and stopping blackouts. Each headline was substantiated by relevant facts and supplemented with actionable tips, such as substituting fans for air-conditioning. For several months, researchers left the messages and checked electricity meters at houses, but they found that *none* of them moved the needle at all. Residents cared about money, climate, and blackouts, but messages about these values didn't mend their wasteful habits, such as leaving lights on or running the AC all day.

Fortunately, the team included social psychologist Robert Cialdini, who suggested a different kind of message. Instead of referencing residents' values, this new message focused on their neighbors: "Join your neighbors in conserving energy," it began. Then it listed the average energy usage of households in residents' neighborhoods compared to their own household usage. Over the next months, the energy gluttons in town responded as hoped: signals of their neighbors' lower consumption shifted their sense of normal, and eventually, their consumption behavior. They cut their energy usage by 2 percent. However, the energy ascetics, the households who had been consuming less than average, *increased* their consumption as they learned about their neighbors—not what the conservationists wanted, but consistent with peer-code updating and conformist behavior.

Inspired by this study, a startup called OPOWER aimed to reap the benefits of peer feedback (while avoiding the problem of discouraging ascetics). Its strategy relied on the insight that people identify with multiple tribes. OPOWER provided consumers with peer benchmarks of two kinds—the overall household average and the "green" household average. Low-consuming households were invited to compare themselves to the *green* benchmark, not the overall benchmark. This way, all customers could aspire to stretch goals. In large-scale experiments across different states, this two-tiered prevalence signal reduced overall consumption by 2.5 percent and maintained the gains for years, so long as the peer information came consistently over time. OPOWER's success highlights that prevalence signals update people's sense of the norm and change their habits.

Data about peer behavior has also proved useful in contemporary temperance campaigns. On campuses, "binge drinkers" are a highly visible (and highly audible!) minority. They boast of their debauchery in exaggerated terms, which skews others' perceptions of what's normal. The University of North Carolina at Chapel Hill sought to break the cycle by objectively surveying sobriety on weekend nights with a breathalyzer. Most students blew a zero, and only a small fraction blew DUI levels. For the next two years, the campus was plastered with catchy posters relaying this news. ("It's not what they say, it's what they blow," one slogan read.) Then the breathalyzer survey was repeated at the same time of year. The DUI rate was 30 percent lower. Credible data dispelled the illusion that most students drink heavily and, thereby, reduced the number of people doing this.

If this form of prevalence signal rings a bell, it's probably because you've been targeted with peer feedback yourself lately, from more and more directions. Vanguard reminds you that your 401k is lagging below the average American your age. A text from your gym informs you that your fellow patrons worked out more last month than you did (as if Strava hadn't already broken the news). Perhaps you've been asked to use "bossware" programs such as InterGuard that compare your work-from-home productivity with that of your coworkers.

All of this peer feedback can feel exhausting at times in an already competitive world, but it does shift our habits, often because it corrects inaccurate perceptions of our peers. When the English tax agency started telling
citizens the rate of their postal code peers who file on time, this single-
sentence nudge boosted compliance by 15 percent. When Australian taxpayers were disabused of the stereotype that all their compatriots cheat
on taxes, they made fewer questionable deductions. When young Saudi
women were informed that the vast majority of their generation supports
women working outside the home, they became emboldened to take on
such jobs.

We've seen that many kinds of prevalence signals can change peer codes
and the habits that flow from them. But it is equally important to learn how
these change efforts often fail. Signals don't always get through, because
audiences have psychological defenses against being unduly influenced.
Conversely, sometimes the problem is that too many signals get through,
including unintended messages that move audiences in unwanted ways.

Doubt is a defense that is particularly relevant to prevalence signals,
whether a message, observation, or experience. When audiences question
whether the picture of prevalence portrayed reflects the behavioral reality of their group, they close their minds and resist updating their peer
codes. For instance, WeWork pitched itself as a firm that provided purpose and community, showing new employees videos of off-site events
where WeWorkers crammed into auditoriums to hear the CEO talk about
higher purpose. When it leaked that attendance at the CEO sessions was
mandatory—even monitored by wristband trackers—employees stopped
believing the firm's self-portrayal. When prevalence information is being
used deceptively, people defend themselves against being duped.

When we know that we are listening to a sales pitch or advertisement, our doubting muscles start to twitch. Ads can exaggerate product popularity in many ways—cooked statistics, cherry-picked testimonials, rigged demonstrations—so our critical thinking defenses activate in response. As a result, many firms resort to signaling their popularity covertly—through product placements and sponsored content. These sneaky prevalence signals have never been used so excessively as in "informercials": actors in a test kitchen clamor to use the grape-peeler; a tuxedoed MC reads thank-you letters from satisfied customers; sales associates at a long table await your call, their phones ringing off the hook; a sales counter ticks off the units sold every minute. You would scoff at these flimsy signals of popularity if they were in an ad, but the talk-show format of infomercials sometimes allows them to slip through. They also screen late at night when our critical thinking defenses are tired or otherwise dulled.

When our defenses are raised, ads with facile prevalence signals like testimonials fail to impress. But well-chosen ads can still work, because verifiable claims *gain* persuasiveness when critical thinking is engaged. For instance, when Ford's ads tell us that its F-Series has been the bestselling truck in the US for forty-six years, that's a claim that can be easily checked. Retailers like Nordstrom actively challenge customers to verify their lowest price claims. If there's nothing to hide, then it works best for firms to be overt in their persuasion methods.

If not blocked by defenses, change efforts sometimes fail by sending signals too well—unintended signals. Universities tried to prevent eating disorders by bringing together "restrained eaters" in support groups, but follow-up studies found this was counterproductive, increasing rates of disordered eating. Undeniably these programs create *support* that helps some participants. But they also create a *group*, one with abnormally high prevalence of the problem behavior. Recently, a friend confided that she attended a month-long retreat for women with disordered eating at a spa-like setting in Europe. Her description made it sound idyllic: morning yoga, walks in the woods, cooking classes. But, I asked, did people's eating habits change? Yes, she said, some of the bulimics became anorexic.

Comedian Norm Macdonald expressed a similar complaint about Gamblers Anonymous—hearing all the stories about gambling only made him want to gamble more.

Similar problems of mixed signals come when advocacy agencies over-dramatize the problems that they are trying to correct. The Partnership for a Drug-Free America produced many famous ads ("This is your brain on drugs") but didn't make progress on its stated goal. When behavioral scientists were brought in to precisely test how its ads affect teens, they found that some actually *increased* interest in drugs. For instance, director Ridley Scott (of *Blade Runner* fame) showed a rocker kid in a gritty club bathroom writhing in the aftermath of drug use. As the word "heroin" overwrites the scene, an upbeat jingle reaches its refrain: "It's always around / Everybody's doing it, doing it." These lyrics signal that heroin is de rigueur at nightclubs. The ad may have landed more as a *dare* than a *scare*.

Arizona's Petrified Forest used to warn park visitors: "Your heritage is being vandalized every day by theft, losses of petrified wood of 14 tons a year, mostly a small piece at a time." That's piles and piles of petrified wood! The influence expert, Cialdini, recognized that this signage might be licensing misbehavior. To understand the problem, his team placed marked pieces of wood on trails before visitors walked them and found it was very few individuals who took the "souvenirs." So Cialdini and his team produced new signage emphasizing that *almost all* visitors respect the park; only a deviant few break the rule. When visitors were exposed to this new signage, the problem of theft declined. The new message removed the inadvertent signal that normalized theft and instead highlighted the prevalence of responsible environmental behavior.

Conversely, if you want to encourage a behavior, don't emphasize how many people currently aren't doing it. Political campaigns used to try to shame voters about low turnout: "Only one in three Americans voted in the last election." But this message informs you that your peers are not bothering to vote—so why should you? In my work advising presidential campaigns, I've encouraged messages that portray widespread voting: "Hundreds of millions of Americans will be heading to polls" or "A record turnout is expected on Tuesday." Studies by Harvard behavioral scientist Todd Rogers find that everyone-is-doing-it appeals work better than don't-be-a-part-of-the-problem appeals, particularly for occasional voters.

The people leading programs for behavioral change tend to be idealistic. They like to think that their audience will be informed by facts and swayed by reason. Indeed, sometimes they can be. But too much focus on rationality can distract us from more powerful ways to change minds. They may overlook ways to convey that most peers are doing the desired behavior. Or they may send unverifiable prevalence signals that raise doubt and resistance. Or, even worse, they may inadvertently send signals that normalize the behavior they want to discourage.

Change advocates tend to be free thinkers comfortable with challenging convention. Even so, it behooves them to recognize that most of their audience is different from themselves. For most people, the inner conformist is stronger than the inner activist. Changemakers do best to work with (rather than working against) this basic human instinct. Our sensitivity to information about peer patterns is typically portrayed as a bug rather than a feature, but it's a foundation of culture *and* of cultural evolution. With the right prevalence signals nudging it along, the peer instinct can become a powerful force for adaptive change.

5

Soap Operas
and Social Change

Life doesn't imitate art, it imitates bad television.

—WOODY ALLEN

In the 1970s and '80s, an odd thing happened to Brazilian families: the average number of children fell from six to three. China had achieved a similar decrease at around the same time through its strict single-child policy, enforced through fines, abortions, and even sterilizations. Brazil's population policy, by comparison, was virtually nonexistent. Abortion was (and still is) illegal in the highly Catholic country. Contraception was available, but the government did not consistently encourage it. Many politicians were pro-natalist, arguing that Brazil needed population growth to fill its vast territory. Still, somehow, family size plummeted.

To investigate this dramatic change, economists Eliana La Ferrara and Alberto Chong, working with the Inter-American Development Bank, compiled data about birth rates and their determinants from all of Brazil over the relevant years. They noticed that the drop didn't happen everywhere at the same time: It started in the coastal metropolises, Rio de Janeiro and São Paulo, then radiated outward to smaller cities, finally spreading to outlying rural areas. None of the usual drivers of family size decline—wealth, education, and contraception access—moved in the same way. What *did* change that could have made the difference? Chong, who was from Latin America, proposed an unorthodox explanation: cable television access.

In Brazil, cable is primarily the story of the Globo network. By the early seventies, Globo had become a fixture of life in Rio and São Paulo; it expanded over that decade to provincial cities, and by the end of the eighties, it reached rural areas, too, eventually covering 98 percent of the country. Globo's programming centered on prime-time telenovelas, the souped-up Latin soap operas that make *General Hospital* look staid by comparison. The top twenty Brazilian TV shows from this era were all Globo telenovelas. Globo's market penetration was extraordinary: on average half the nation tuned in *every day* (a rate reached in the US only once a year by the Super Bowl). The lead characters of Globo's telenovelas became central figures of popular conversation. They usually included independent, worldly women. For instance, *Malu Mulher* was about an enterprising divorcee making it on her own. In sharp contrast to the average Brazilian woman at the time, these characters were unburdened by large families: 72 percent had no children, and 21 percent had only one.

When the development economists added the variable of Globo access to their giant datasets, they found that as Globo (and its charismatic heroines) expanded outward in Brazil, the family size in each new region would soon start to decline. The fertility drop was larger after years with telenovelas that featured particularly emancipated women, sending a stronger signal. And it was larger for poorer families, who were otherwise less exposed to this lifestyle. It occurred primarily for women in their late childbearing years, consistent with the aspiration to limit family size.

Still, population experts found it preposterous that a profound change could arise from soap operas. Could fictional characters be so impressive that they influenced family-related choices? When La Ferrara and Chong probed further into birth records data, they found that after Globo access arrived in a region, baby names matching those of the telenovela leads increased in frequency, even when not common names. This was undeniable evidence that these characters (and not some broader changes in society) were affecting family choices. Another study found a subsequent rise in divorce rates that followed, hinting that the family planning choices of Globo-influenced wives were coming into conflict with their partners. Globo's heroines may have been fictional, but their influence was all too real.

Brazil's drop in family size is a story of how cultural ideals evolve. Before the arrival of telenovelas, notions of women's place in society had been predominantly shaped by priests and politicians. They valorized mothers who raised many children for God and country. After Globo arrived, *brasileiras* spent an hour a day in the thrall of heroines with lives beyond childrearing. These characters were not just likable; they were *respected* by the other characters. And they also received attention and plaudits from viewers who talked about the show. Hence, despite being fictional characters, they registered intuitively as figures of status. Unwittingly, Globo sent the women of Brazil *prestige signals* that promised an alternative path to social approval. With a new telenovela each year, it became a new archetype in popular culture: the independent woman.

While no television shows today capture public attention like telenovelas used to in Brazil, we remain influenced in our choices by prestigious figures. When Pepsi hired Beyoncé as a brand ambassador for record sums, it was not because of her many Grammy Awards; it was because she was consistently found to be one of the most admired women in the world. This influence extends well beyond consumer choices to decisions about lifestyle, health, and politics. It reaches an unhealthy extreme in "look-alike" plastic surgery for those seeking to emulate Justin Bieber's hairline or Kim Kardashian's derriere. After clinics named lip-plumping procedures after Angelina Jolie, she leveraged her medical influence for good by publicizing her 2013 genetic testing for breast cancer risk and her subsequent mastectomies, leading to a 64 percent rise in testing rates and sustained increases in rates of the risk-reducing surgery. As much as pop stars and actors are admired for their talents, they also gain prestige from their fame itself. Increasingly, advertisers save money by hiring "influencers" with no talent (aside from that of self-promotion). A million followers by itself confers prestige and thereby influence. For influencers, revelations of faked accomplishments are not as damaging as those of fake followers. Some top influencers are merely CGI avatars rather than real people, but their followers are real. This attention is a source of real prestige and real influence.

The sway of telenovela heroines, celebrities, and influencers over people's aspirations is consistent with the theory of social learning from role models. This notion is so familiar today that it sounds obvious, but it wasn't always so. For much of the twentieth century, the science of learning (and psychology more generally) was dominated by behaviorists like B. F. Skinner, who maintained that humans, like rats, learn what they know from the rewards and punishments that they experience firsthand. Social psychologist Albert Bandura challenged this reductionism by documenting that children draw strong lessons about appropriate behavior from watching models in anticipated roles. For example, boys who saw a respectable-looking man smack around an inflatable clown doll went on to hit the same doll when they were given a chance. In a recent study, children in a room with adults watched two of them make a series of diverging choices (e.g., which toy to play with, which beverage to drink, which table to sit at). When given their turn, the children were *twice* as likely to emulate one of the adults than the other. What made the difference? A group of observers in the room had closely gazed at the first adult and *not* the second one. Without any words, a prestige signal was sent. The children didn't need titles or biographies to read status; they just emulated the person with more followers!

The Globo network had no idea its soap operas were changing Brazilian culture, but around the same time, a Mexican telenovela producer named Miguel Sabido began to realize how deeply these daily dramas move viewers. His leading man was assaulted at a grocery store by fellow shoppers, who were incensed by *his character's* misdeeds. Sabido wanted to harness this intense engagement by writing shows that targeted a specific behavioral change. Inspired in part by Bandura's writings, Sabido built the drama around three kinds of characters: positive models who practiced the focal virtue and were rewarded with success and status, negative models who flouted it and met with ignominious ends, and in-between transitional characters who tried at first, fell off the wagon, then finally committed for good. *Ven Conmigo* ("Come with Me") centered on an adult literacy school. This may not sound like an exciting premise, but it featured compelling characters—some struggling to better their lives and others scoffing at them while enjoying vices. During its run, a million new clients enrolled at adult schools nationwide. *Accompaname* ("Come Along") centered on family planning. In the year of its run, contraceptive sales grew 23 percent, and family planning appointments rose 33 percent—gains that far surpassed those of standard educational-format public health programs.

Development agencies around the world took notice and began inviting Sabido to work with local writers to develop "edutainment" dramas targeting local needs, mostly in the genre of radio plays. *Twende na Wakati* ("Let's Go with the Times") aired in Tanzania during the AIDS crisis and focused on safe sex. A large team of local writers conducted thousands of interviews and hundreds of focus groups to flesh out relatable characters (e.g., a tireless nurse, a promiscuous truck driver). Dozens of subplots and supporting characters enabled this radio drama to engage a large audience for two years. In a survey afterward, 82 percent of listeners reported adopting some safe-sex practice as a result, such as condom use or forgoing multiple partners. The show also fostered conversation about safe sex. The greatest change came for those who not only listened but also discussed the show with friends. To test whether this social interaction is a critical ingredient in the intervention, field experiments in Mexico varied whether a radio drama on domestic violence was played in a public setting or distributed on CDs for private listening. Results showed more changed behavior in communities that consumed the show publicly, privy to each other's reactions, than in communities that watched the show privately.

In Rwanda, ten years after the tragic Hutu-Tutsi conflict, an NGO sponsored a drama called *Musekeweya* ("New Dawn"), a Rwandan Romeo and Juliet story but with a happy ending of reconciliation between the ethnic-differing families. Social psychologist Betsy Levy Paluck randomly assigned villages either to this ethnic reconciliation drama or to a "placebo" drama about health practices. Villagers gathered in public spaces to hear the weekly episodes and then engage in group conversations. Researchers visited periodically to observe their interactions and survey their reactions. Hutus and Tutsis began to interact more cooperatively in villages watching the reconciliation-themed drama. The show didn't much change their personal attitudes, but it dramatically changed their perception of the cultural ideal, what Rwandans collectively value.

Having assumed that *Musekeweya* would change personal attitudes, the sponsoring NGO grumbled about these results. But they shouldn't have. Changing lives doesn't always mean changing hearts. People's personal attitudes are rooted in personal experiences and hence difficult to change. It's much easier to shift their perceptions of others, and for many social behaviors it's these perceptions of what "society values" that matter most. Especially in a volatile country, people don't know what their society collectively values on many issues, but they are wired to care about this and soak up signals like a sponge. Watching and discussing a radio soap opera for a year reprogrammed villagers' sense of what kinds of relationships Rwandan society approves of—and this made all the difference.

It's not just fictional characters who send signals through drama. Activists and politicians often engage in ethical theater, performing actions publicly to become role models for the kinds of sacrifices or contributions needed. When the lawyer Mohandas Gandhi emerged as a political leader in India, he made a deliberate commitment to travel only on the lowest-class trains, among the poor. Gandhi personified renunciation and anti-materialism, the virtues that he needed from Indians to break the colonial economy. At times this performative asceticism exasperated his fellow leaders, but it mobilized tens of thousands of Indians from different social strata who joined him in marches, boycotts, fasts, and other acts of resistance.

Some leaders in business have shown this same knack for leading through example. In the heyday of Madison Avenue, David Ogilvy built an eponymous agency famed for enigmatic ads: The man wearing an eye-patch in Hathaway shirts. The tonic water with "Schweppervescence." Instead of catchy jingles, these were "big idea" ads that perplexed viewers, provoked thought, and got people talking. Today, the agency still aspires to this. Its "Real Beauty" campaign for Dove showed women of widely ranging ages, shapes, and shades instead of just the usual model type; during the pandemic, these ads featured the lined faces of nurses and doctors who had been wearing protective equipment. The agency's time-lapse video "Moldy Whopper" proved dramatically that Burger King no longer uses preservatives! These provocative ads occasionally offend but more often win awards and generate buzz. But in the 1970s, Ogilvy almost lost its edge. The firm had expanded through mergers and opening new offices, and the founder could no longer personally oversee all the key hires. It's the usual trend that as firms grow larger, they become increasingly populated by people who focus on bureaucracy rather than people who focus on creativity. The firm was no longer hiring Don Draper types who ruffle feathers and take creative risks.

David Ogilvy didn't do what most CEOs do in this predicament—post a prominent mission statement or list of "core values." (Enron chiseled "integrity, communication, and respect" into its marble walls, but this failed to inscribe these values into their managers' minds.) Nor did Ogilvy fire off a bullet-pointed memo with detailed rules about hiring and creative decisions. You can't *legislate* creative risk-taking. More bureaucracy couldn't be the answer. One day, a group of senior executives arrived at a boardroom and found that the CEO was uncharacteristically missing. To add to the mystery, there was a strange object at each of their places—a wooden *matryoshka* doll. To pass the time, they began twisting open the dolls, finding smaller and smaller replicas nested within, until inside the tenth and tiniest doll they discovered a note, rolled up as if in a fortune cookie: *If you hire people who are bigger than you are, we shall become a company of giants.*

At first the dolls appeared to be leftovers from a prior pitch meeting, but the executives soon recognized their boss's bent for oblique messages. But what exactly could he mean? The room exploded with conjectures about the need for big ideas. They reminisced about the bold ideas and colorful characters of the early years. It reminded them of what made their firm special, and they vowed to keep the spirit alive. They left with arms full of wooden dolls and aspirations to big ideas.

An effective prestige signal depends not just on the message but on the *messenger* and the *medium*. It was wise for Ogilvy to absent himself physically and communicate symbolically rather than literally. It demonstrated the kind of risk-taking and flair that the firm needed, and it forced his key people to articulate the message themselves. Afterward, those who had been in the meeting (and even some who had not) put *matryoshka* dolls on their desks, eliciting informal retellings of the story (until it became an official part of new employee trainings). Ogilvy began a practice of sending dolls to every new director in the firm. The doll became a corporate icon—featured on posters, mugs, and screensavers—that reminded employees of the ideal of taking creative risks.

The challenge of signaling creative ideals arises in other industries as well. Netflix wants its executives to take big risks so that its content stays innovative. However, dictums from the C-suite won't work to sustain this ideal; shows of authority make employees feel more cautious. Netflix tries to sustain the ideal by celebrating tales of "big bets," such as when Chief Content Officer (now co-CEO) Ted Sarandos committed $100 million to

House of Cards without even informing the CEO at the time, Reed Hastings. Not only are these stories passed through the grapevine, but they are foregrounded in the firm's presentations and communications.

When Satya Nadella took the helm of Microsoft in 2014, he needed to "hit refresh" on its culture. A culture of deferring to technical experts, from the CEO on down, had resulted in ever-heavier apps (overloaded with features that few customers used) that were rapidly losing market share. In the "cloud computing" era, it had become imperative to know your customers' needs well and tailor offerings to them. However, Nadella didn't use his bully pulpit to demand managers learn customer focus. Shouting at people to become better listeners doesn't work very well. Instead, he went on a "listening tour," meeting with managers throughout the firm and quickly implementing some of the bottom-up requests (e.g., dropping the company's force-ranked performance evaluations). He also toured the firm's ecosystem, such as customers, partner firms, and universities it recruits from. After a gaffe in responding to a question at a tech conference about gender discrimination, Nadella went out of his way to apologize, drawing attention to his mistake and publicly meeting with women in tech groups to learn more. These actions modeled the managerial style that the times required—curiosity, listening, and humility. Through leading by example, Nadella updated the firm's "know-it-all" culture into a "learn-it-all" culture that helped it regain its growth and innovation.

It's hard for an executive to call for revolutionary innovation. You can't role model challenging authority if you *are* the authority. This problem came up for Indian IT firms who sought to move up the value chain after the "offshoring era" by competing on innovation. Innovating requires that frontline employees criticize current procedures and brainstorm better ways. At HCL Technologies, CEO Vineet Nayar tried holding sessions at different worksites to hear employees' ideas, but the auditorium would fall silent the moment he stepped on stage. To a demigod of Indian industry, employees would only express praise for the firm. One time, as the curtains opened with a blast of music, Nayar tried breaking into a Bollywood dance routine. Seeing employees' astonished expressions, he kept bouncing and wiggling to the bhangra beat, moving his way up the aisles of the room and pulling young engineers to their feet to show him how. By the time the music stopped, everyone in the room was laughing. Nayar had found a way to telegraph that the executives don't know everything. He followed it up by posting executives' critical performance reviews on the intranet for employees to see. This helped to convey that the leaders really needed ideas from junior employees. This "employees first" push shifted the culture toward one in which employees shared critiques of current products and suggestions about better ways.

Their competitor Infosys faced the same challenge, and CEO Narayana Murthy decided to take himself off the stage entirely. Instead, he "spotlighted" employees who had made marketable innovations by training them to give public talks (which became videos) about their contributions. Murthy imbued them with prestige, and they became relatable heroes that employees could emulate. Their talks crystallized for other employees what it meant to contribute as an innovator at Infosys. This approach grew into Infosys Stories, a web-based collection of videos that illustrates different kinds of desired contributions.

An alternative strategy is identifying members of an organization who already have status and co-opting them into championing a new cultural ideal. On many topics employees are more influenced by coworkers with local prestige than by a far-off executive. In corporations, co-opting prestige takes the form of inviting respected employees to join a task force that develops and promotes a change plan. But it has worked to change many stubborn cultures, even that of bullying in high schools. Typically, admonitions against bullying come from vice principals, whom teens don't look up to very much (and sometimes even enjoy defying). In 2013 Princeton researchers developed a program that asked students at over fifty New Jersey high schools to design and deliver an anti-bullying message. Peer conflicts (according to school disciplinary records) declined by 30 percent in its wake. In some schools, researchers tapped students who were high status (those who get the most attention from their peers), while in other schools they selected a random cross section of students. The effect was much stronger with high-status students, as their prestige rubbed off onto the anti-bullying agenda.

▼

In the 1970s, thousands of young Americans "dropped out" of mainstream life to join cults. They shaved their heads, donned saffron robes, chanted "Hare Krishna," and begged for donations in airports. Many joined the mysterious Unification Church of Reverend Moon, which merged Christianity and Confucianism, and married partners arranged by "True Father" in mass ceremonies. Others traveled with the socialist-leaning People's Temple to rural Californian communes and then to a Guyanese jungle compound, where they submitted to the escalating commands of Reverend Jim Jones: when he instructed them to drink Kool-Aid laced with cyanide, 914 people died, including 276 children. Cults are not just "strong" cultures; they are communities that severely restrict the prestige signals their members receive, so that cult leaders acquire extreme mystique and control.

How did these sects seduce people to leave behind their comfortable lives and submit to costly and sometimes tragic sacrifices? Bereft families called it brainwashing and suspected drugs, hypnotism, or exotic mind-control tactics. But when journalists went undercover as recruits, they found a more mundane recruitment process. Unificationists, for example, approached lonely-looking people at colleges or city parks, invited them to small-group gatherings with preternaturally friendly hosts (they coined the term "love bombing" for this stage), and then invited them to extended retreats (usually in a bucolic setting that lacked phone or media access) for long days of inspiring lecturers, one-on-one counseling, and group conversations, all laden with praise for Moon and his mission. Fully 10 percent of attendees at retreats got hooked enough to take the next step of moving into Church residences. There, leaders would convince them to cease communication with their families and old friends, often using fabricated allegations (what they termed "heavenly deception"). This tended to provoke angry responses from these outsiders, providing apparent confirmation of the Church's allegations of hostility.

Cults rearrange a recruit's social life until the person is totally enveloped by ties to insiders and sealed off from outside ties. Members living at a cult residence are suffused in signals of approval for one hero—all day long, one day after another—without any balancing signals of approval for alternative heroes and countervailing ideals. This unbalanced experience destabilizes the person's identity and renders them vulnerable to unchecked adulation. In modern life, people ordinarily take part in multiple communities with differing heroes and ideals. This can create dissonance, but it empowers us to question any one of these heroes. Cults allow an escape from this tension to a bubble where everyone's values are aligned. The approval of a cult leader can affect followers like a drug. They become willing to conduct extreme actions (e.g., violence or sacrifice) to keep it. Contemporary groups like Scientology and NXIVM present themselves less like religions and more like therapy, but they follow the same playbook of network envelopment and extreme deference to leaders.

To be fair, cults didn't invent these tactics. Catholics, Muslims, Buddhists, and other religions "cloister" aspiring clerics during their indoctrination into their vocations. Their lay societies like Opus Dei and the Muslim Brotherhood similarly invite recruits to events, then retreats, and then collective residences. Some sects, like the Amish or Hasidic Jews, limit the whole community's interactions with outsiders. Studies find that religious extremism tends to occur when members have little diversity in their lives. With colleagues Yu Ding and Gita Johar, I've found across many studies that low religious diversity in a region precipitates rejection of other faiths and rejection of science as well.

The Communist Party in China developed its strength by inviting members to live in rural strongholds with highly programmed schedules reinforcing its ideals. Rural "re-education camps" were used again to reshape members' ideals during the Cultural Revolution. In *1984* George Orwell imagined a totalitarian regime where citizens cannot travel and the state-run media ubiquitously exposes them to professions of love for the regime's leader, "Big Brother." North Korea is the country that most closely approximates this: Foreign travel and media are prohibited, and the official news is largely adulation of the "Supreme Leader," Kim Jong Un. Monuments, billboards, and posters proclaim his greatness. When he appears in public, citizens applaud until their hands are raw. In *1984* the dissident Winston Smith slips into feelings of love for Big Brother in spite of himself; in North Korea dissidents report the same difficulty of resisting the monolithic prestige signals they are immersed in.

Military groups, too, control social interactions and prestige signals to inculcate their ideals. Recruits to the Marine Corps are isolated in boot camp for twelve weeks, restricted from talking to outsiders, drilled from dawn to dusk into obedience to officers and adherence to the "semper fi" ideal. Once service begins, prestige signals are sent through selecting exemplars of the designed behaviors for honors or promotions. Those who act selflessly in battle are awarded Purple Hearts or Silver Stars. It often happens posthumously, but dead heroes still live on as role models. Likewise, paramilitary groups use isolated training camps to inculcate their extremist ideals and then use recognition to spotlight exemplary members as role models to others. The Tamil Tigers encouraged the practice of suicide bombing by celebrating all prior martyrs on the anniversaries of their deaths. Chechen insurgencies commemorate their suicide bombers with personalized songs. Hamas sends its members calendars heralding the "Martyr of the Month." Just as prestige learning contributes to copycat suicides, it has been weaponized by insurgent groups to normalize the inherently repugnant act of suicide bombing.

When vulnerable people have become immersed in a cult or another extremist group, their families often respond by warning them of the group's dangers or trying to forcefully separate them from the group. These actions are understandable, but they can play into the hands of the group by seeming to corroborate its narrative of persecution by the establishment. Research suggests that the best redress for pathological prestige signals is not rational appeals or force, but more prestige signals. Indoctrinated members of a totalistic community feel most able to exit in the wake of a high-status insider; they feel psychological permission to leave if they are emulating someone who has had prestige within the group. A covert tactic against extremists is to infiltrate their group with charismatic "true believers" who can gain status before making a conspicuous exit—an exit that gives others the license to leave. It uses the cult's prestige system against itself rather than attacking it from the outside in a way that can heighten the group's solidarity.

The same principles apply when trying to rescue parts of larger organizations that have gone rogue. In 2012 Boston University faced the problem of a sports team that had drifted toward toxic ideals. A member of the hockey team was charged with sexual assault; a few months later, another was charged with rape. Rumors flew around campus about further incidents. University President Robert Brown appointed a task force to investigate, which returned a damning report, full of unsavory details: a website where sexual conquests were logged as "kills," female students reporting that groping is "just what they do," illicit late-night parties at the hockey arena. ("It was insane," one attendee said. "People were having sex in the penalty box.") Hall of Fame coach Jack Parker professed ignorance about these bashes and downplayed them as "a few guys drinking." He acknowledged hearing chatter about sex at team parties but insisted, "My job is *not* to say, 'You guys gotta be celibate.'"

But the misdeeds had escalated beyond campus jock posturing, and President Brown needed to act immediately. But how? Some called for canceling the next season. But hockey is to BU what basketball is to Duke or football to Ohio State: the marquee program that unites alumni. Or Brown could have tossed out the bad apples, expelling any players implicated in improprieties. But what if new players stepped into the same "party animal" roles? The task force blamed a bad barrel, not just bad apples. The hockey team had developed a "culture of sexual entitlement," according to the report. Even though Coach Parker was not an active part of it, his laissez-faire attitude allowed it to grow. Hockey players saw themselves as the campus studs who were allowed and expected to sexually transgress. An ideal like this can take hold in a group even without any individual explicitly endorsing it. It persists in the space between individuals: banter on the team bus, high-fives at parties, double-entendre nicknames. It was part of the glue that held the team together.

Changing the team culture required both eliminating the current prestige signals and introducing different ones. It meant easing out the longtime coach, even though he hadn't technically broken any rules. This left some large skates to fill, but BU managed to recruit one of its former stars, David Quinn, whose pro career had been cut short and who had switched to coaching. Quinn went straight to work recruiting players who were a good fit for BU, not just for the hockey team. He put an end to players attending the continuing-education school at night, requiring that they immerse themselves in the undergraduate community and its ideals, such as the policy of affirmative consent. He chose captains who were "straight arrows" like himself. Under Quinn's watch, the Terriers' disciplinary problems disappeared, but the victories kept coming: the team achieved four consecutive NCAA tournament appearances.

A few years later, in 2016, a neighboring university discovered a similar problem. Members of Harvard's league-leading men's soccer team produced a sexualized "scouting report" about the women's team recruits, rating them and describing their "positions." The document leaked outside of the intended circle of recipients and fell into the hands of the campus newspaper. The athletic department tried to suppress reporting about it, but that just added to the scandal when the story went viral. Female players were pursued by journalists with invasive questions, and some quit the team to escape the discomfort. Harvard's President, Drew Faust, condemned the document, canceled the team's season, and assigned the players to many hours of bias training. Team members who were uninvolved in the sexist document felt unfairly lumped in with the perpetrators. The coach kept his job, because the "scouting report" started before his time, but he struggled to recruit and retain players for the next few years, falling from the top of the league to the bottom. In 2019 the team went winless for the first time in its century-long history.

Harvard's response was strong—as it needed to be—but it wasn't very constructive. It left the team divided, demoralized, and damned by sins of the past. It didn't introduce a new set of ideals. Bringing in a different kind of coach, perhaps a woman (as some colleges have done), would have created fresh prestige signals that could have jump-started the process of bonding around a different ideal. An executive transition shouldn't depend only on culpability for past problems. It's one of the most powerful signals for affecting cultural change.

▼

Knowing when to use prestige signals is important, but knowing *how* to use them is equally vital. In a classic television spot from the 1970s, a stately Native American man in buckskin and feathers paddles down a sparkling river through a pristine forest. He was a familiar face from Hollywood Westerns, an actor known as Iron Eyes Cody. As the river empties into an industrial harbor, Cody's canoe comes upon soda bottles, cups, and newspaper pages. When he pulls ashore, it is strewn with more trash: broken glass, hubcaps, and candy wrappers. A car whizzes by, and a fast-food bag arcs through the air to splatter over his moccasins. The camera pans up slowly to reveal Cody's stoic stare, belied by a single tear that trickles down his high cheekbone.

Keep America Beautiful's "Crying Indian" ad screened frequently throughout the 1970s and won Clio awards, but it didn't make a dent in the problem. Thanks to the last chapter, you may have spotted one problem already: the exaggerated depiction of rampant littering—*everyone is doing it*—sent the wrong prevalence signal. A bigger issue, though, was the message source. Cody played the protagonist as a figure of great dignity. But for most viewers he was, quite literally, from a different tribe. He wasn't an in-group hero who could easily become a role model. This is another way that the right messenger matters. When approval or disapproval messages come from out-group sources, it raises the audience's suspicion. Who made this ad and *why*? Is the benefit for *us* or for *them*? Suspicion suspends automatic social inference processes that otherwise operate to update hero codes.

A decade after Cody's memorable but futile tear, another anti-littering campaign, "Don't Mess with Texas," reduced trash on the state's highways by 72 percent. These spots starred native sons and daughters, such as

Willie Nelson, LeAnn Rimes, and Matthew McConaughey, taking revenge against litterers in comical ways. Littering is portrayed in these ads as the work of lowly outsiders, such as sketchy-looking truck drivers with Arkansas plates—not something that proud Texans do. By choosing recognizable in-group heroes to deliver the message, Texans internalized it, so much so that the tagline (a faux-colloquial saying cooked up in an ad agency) became part of the Texas vernacular.

The psychological defense of suspicion also explains the mixed record of celebrity product endorsements. For every striking success (Roger Federer for Rolex, Dwayne "The Rock" Johnson for Under Armour), there's an absolute flop (Ozzy Osbourne for I Can't Believe It's Not Butter, Paris Hilton for RICH Prosecco). A recent meta-analysis uncovered key factors in audiences' impression that a star is sharing a personal conviction or just trying to make a buck. First: the product's relevance to the celebrity's expertise. The Rock clearly hits the gym, so we trust his advice about gym shorts. But it's suspicious that Ozzy, who bit off a bat's head onstage, is a margarine maven. Second: real use of the product. When Roger Federer lifted his trophies, there was always a Rolex on his wrist. But we don't see Paris Hilton sipping canned prosecco in real life, only in the RICH ads. Our hero-instinct brain is eager to emulate celebrities, but suspicion halts this process when the source doesn't fit the message.

Aside from raising suspicions that block prestige signals, another way that change initiatives can fail is by inadvertently lending prestige to the wrong message. There are many great anti-war films: *Full Metal Jacket*, *Saving Private Ryan*, *1917* (to name just a few). But they have not stopped military recruitment, and in some cases, they've helped it. The characters of Colonel Kurtz and Colonel Kilgore in *Apocalypse Now* were written to be evil maniacs, but many viewers find them to be entrancing antiheroes. No matter how damning the dialogue, leaders in battle still hold a spellbinding allure. French director François Truffaut concluded that there's no such thing as an anti-war film. It's not just that explosions look beautiful, helicopters sound cool, and your favorite leading man looks handsome in uniform and with a crew cut—it's also that army drama pushes our prestige-instinct buttons. An officer leading the charge can't help but look heroic, even if the war is unjust. At a visceral level, we aspire to be like them.

Satire is another genre prone to unintended prestige signals. Songs satirizing jingoism—Neil Young's "Rockin' in the Free World" or Bruce Springsteen's "Born in the U.S.A."—are mistaken for nationalistic anthems. Stand-up comics are troubled by "blood laughs," when part of an audience laughs along *with* the racism they caricature, not *at* it. Archie Bunker, from the sitcom *All in the Family*, was meant to caricature a blue-collar conservative railing against changing times. He browbeats his "dingbat" wife, Edith, harangues his "Polack" son-in-law, Mike, and spews slurs at African American and Jewish neighbors. Producer Norman Lear thought that the popularity of the show would discredit "law and order" conservatives. Then research revealed that the show's most loyal watchers were authoritarians who admired "Arch" for "telling it like it is." Likewise, when excerpts from *The Colbert Report* were streamed to college students in a study, it increased their support for Republican policies. Colbert's bloviating talk show host is obviously a parody to the cognoscenti, but not (it seems) to a channel surfer. Satire subtle enough to please the critics is fated to go "over the head" of the average viewer. Fan clubs for characters like Ron Swanson on *Parks and Recreation* have shocked the show's writers, who didn't intend him to be sympathetic. But to viewers' hero-instinct wiring, any widely watched TV character registers as a figure of prestige.

For similar reasons, crime-prevention programs sometimes have counterproductive effects. The 1978 documentary *Scared Straight!* followed a group of New Jersey juvenile offenders taken to a prison to meet its scariest residents. The hardened felons—pumped up from the weight room, wearing crude tattoos and sagging pants, snarling about "snitches" and "shivs"—poured all of their coiled ferocity into threatening confrontations to break the trembling teens, cracking their facades of toughness. The documentary concluded with purported proof of concept: 80 percent of the teens who had been through the program avoided recidivism. The program spread across the country and the globe. (In Germany, for instance, young skinheads were introduced to jailed neo-Nazis who had committed murder.) But sponsoring organizations rarely conducted tests that compared the recidivism of participants to control groups, and those that did often found unexpected albeit hard-to-interpret results that they then discounted. Only after twenty years were these datasets analyzed in aggregate to reveal an undeniable and sobering conclusion: Scared Straight participants become 13 percent *more* prone to recidivism (meaning that the New Jersey program alone, with 50,000 graduates over the years, has created 6,500 repeat offenders). The budding criminals in the programs do learn from the experience, but they learn from the program because they meet impressive role models. How far can one go in crime? Very far indeed! Some re-offenders were aware of the influence; they claimed their crimes were to show to the lifers that they weren't "scared straight."

"Three Strikes and You're Out" laws, an early 1990s sentencing regimen that sent repeat offenders to prison for long stretches, backfired in a similar way. Young repeat offenders, a large fraction of some urban underprivileged communities, spent their formative years in penitentiaries where hardcore felons held the highest prestige. It's no coincidence that the "prison culture" practices that were exotic to viewers of the "Scared Straight" documentary are today just familiar features of urban culture. These laws turned prison into the primary socializing institution of young men in some zip codes. Overall crime rates didn't decline, and comparison of individuals who served their time versus others whose sentences were randomly commuted (as prisons reached capacity) found that prison hardens people rather than rehabilitating them (the evidential basis for the 2018 criminal justice reform). Scared Straight programs and Three Strikes policies inadvertently exposed young people to prestige signals that increased their long-term propensity toward crime.

Prestige signals can help us understand why even highly successful change campaigns sometimes fail in some demographics. Consider the rises in teen smoking and other forms of tobacco use over the recent decades. High-profile campaigns directed at teens ("Think. Don't Smoke.") and their parents ("Talk. They'll listen.") didn't work as promised. They were particularly ineffective for teens who recognized their listed sponsor, Philip Morris International. It's more than a little suspicious when the world's largest tobacco company tells you *not* to smoke. Studies find that exposure to the "Talk. They'll listen." campaign slightly *increased* teens' intention to smoke, perhaps by associating smoking with adults. The company's recent call for a future "smoke-free world" similarly raises suspicions: Is it just a virtue-signaling pitch for vaping products?

The teen trend is notable because it's a failure set within a larger success story. The adult smoking rate in the US dropped from 43 percent in 1972 to under 12 percent today. This was accomplished largely through public health efforts to alter the media landscape of prestige signals. In Hollywood's golden years, Bogie and Bacall seduced with cigarettes, but their successors don't indulge. In early Bond films, Agent 007 suavely smoked through almost every scene, but over the films he dropped the habit, until only evil villains and their minions lit up. When the Flintstones debuted on television, it was sponsored by Winston Cigarettes, and Fred and Wilma puffed away happily after dinner, but soon their lifestyle evolved. None of this happened by chance. The surgeon general had been releasing health warnings since 1964, but it was only when health regulators leaned on Hollywood to not let its heroes smoke that the smoking rate began its dramatic decline. In 1971, President Nixon, himself a heavy smoker, signed a law banning cigarette ads from airing on television and radio. Tobacco product placement has been prohibited also. The change in the media landscape signaled a changed ideal: the cultural cachet of cigarettes fell from hero to zero. Nicotine may be physically addictive, but this was no match for our tribal need for esteem.

6

Inside the History Factory

The past is never dead. It's not even past.

—WILLIAM FAULKNER

E very American schoolchild learns the story of Thanksgiving. The details vary across each telling, but the gist of it goes like this: The Pilgrims of the Plymouth colony (wearing funny hats and large belt buckles) shared a solemn meal of turkey, cranberries, and pumpkin pie with their Native American neighbors, giving thanks to the creator for their survival through their first year. They launched an autumnal tradition of gratitude prayers, generous helpings, and intergroup harmony. Every November since, Americans have gathered for the same ritual. It's a story that we know well. At least we think we do.

In fact, our Thanksgiving tradition emerged through a far less linear process. Not to rain on your Thanksgiving Day parade, but it owes less to seventeenth-century settlers than to nineteenth-century statesmen, who instituted a national holiday (and tradition) to solve problems of their own time. The Pilgrims *did* hold a feast in the fall of 1621, but it was a "rejoicing" (an occasion of feasting, drinking, and games), not a "thanksgiving" (a day of fasting, prayer, and contemplation). The sole record of it, a letter sent home to England by Edward Winslow, describes a three-day revelry with Wampanoag guests over venison, waterfowl, and berries. Over the first century of American colonies, harvest rejoicings occurred occasionally, on dates that varied by region (like the harvest itself). There are also records of thanksgivings after the arrival of a ship from England or the safe return of an exploring party. On October 3, 1789, after victory in the War of Independence, President George Washington called for "a day of thanksgiving" on "Thursday the 26th day of November next." He spent the day at church services and then donated food and beer to a debtors' prison. It was a day of prayer and giving, not a reenactment of the Pilgrims' harvest feast.

It wasn't until nearly 250 years after the Pilgrims' party that the plan for an annual national ritual coalesced. In 1841 Reverend Alexander Young discovered Winslow's letter (which had been long-lost) and republished it as an account of "the first thanksgiving," conflating the two Puritan customs. In New England, autumn thanksgivings became customary but their timing varied. This inspired Sarah Josepha Hale, a leading poet and journalist, to lobby for a unified national holiday. She wrote to a series of presidents that it needed only "authoritative fixation" from their hand. Who would finally listen? It was the poet president who had promised the riven nation in his inauguration speech that "the mystic chords of memory . . . will yet swell the chorus of the Union."

On October 3, 1863, the same year as his more-famous Gettysburg Address, Abraham Lincoln issued a proclamation that the "blessings of fruitful fields and healthful skies . . . [from] ever-watchful providence . . . be solemnly, reverently, and gratefully acknowledged as with one heart and one voice by the whole American people." He asked citizens to "set apart and observe the last Thursday of November next as a Day of Thanksgiving." While it was not a legal holiday, the public—traumatized at the time by civil war, draft riots, and epidemics—embraced it as an autumnal routine. Northern service clubs mobilized to ship the key ingredients—turkeys, cranberries, and pumpkin pie—to Union armies across the land, institutionalizing these Yankee dishes as a national menu.

A *New York Times* editorial in 1864 marveled that the New England custom had "assumed the scope and standing of a grand national holiday." Eating the same meal on the same day helped Americans feel at one with their diverse and far-flung compatriots—Northern and Southern, in Eastern cities and Western towns—bolstering what political theorist Benedict Anderson calls the "imagined community" of the nation. As families gathered and reminisced about prior Thanksgivings, they also imagined that generations past had done the same.

Before long, Thanksgiving became a sacred tradition that cast a spell of nostalgia, belonging, and commitment. In 1939, when President Franklin Roosevelt tried to shift the holiday a week earlier to extend Christmas shopping season, outraged citizens derided this travesty as "Franksgiving." Half the states refused to go along. A political rival even compared Roosevelt to Hitler for tinkering with the (not-so-ancient) tradition.

In two different senses, the tradition of Thanksgiving began in the nineteenth century. First, in the sense that from the nineteenth century *forward*, the national ritual has taken place every year. Second, the nineteenth century was when mythmakers began tracing the ritual *backward* to the Pilgrims' first year on these shores. Young, Hale, and Lincoln did not deliberately fabricate a false history, but they exercised hindsight bias, selective memory, and wishful thinking. It was comforting at the time to think that a ritual of unifying different groups with different cultures dated back to the first settlers on American shores. Artists helped promote this myth with etchings and paintings of "the first Thanksgiving" portraying beneficent Pilgrims and Wampanoag guests giving thanks over a spread of turkey, cranberry, and pie. Statues of a grateful Massasoit, the Wampanoag leader, were erected all over the country. In the popular imagination, traditions are launched, fully formed, by prescient founders. But the reality is more complex. Many myths and rituals are passed down from ancient times, but some are shaped more recently and restrospectively by leaders who promote their agendas through activities framed as continuous with the collective past.

The "log cabin" president proved remarkably adept at introducing the new national holiday. As a lawyer, he knew the power of precedents, such as George Washington's proclamation of seven decades before and the Puritan providentialist custom of giving thanks for good fortune. A seasoned storyteller, he took on the role of national narrator-in-chief—not just a custodian of collective memory but its curator and creator, using history-speckled speeches to construe the nation's Civil War struggles in terms of its past. He sent "precedent signals" that framed Thanksgiving Day as deeply rooted in the American past, and he stamped it all with the imprimatur of his office: a presidential proclamation. It quickly took on the patina of an established institution.

Precedent signals can be used to introduce new customs or change the meaning of existing routines. They infuse present activities with connection to the tribal past, framing them as traditional and thus matters of meaningful significance, due a certain reverence. Revisionist histories may be associated with totalitarian regimes, but they don't require propaganda and suppression. People are eager to learn, and relearn, their group's history and its connections to their current practices. Anthropologists living with small-scale tribes observe dramatic changes in shared narratives about who the group is descended from and what traditions define it, noting that "genealogical dexterity is common throughout the tribal world." Two narrative attributes that make precedent signals compelling are antiquity and consistency. A particularly *ancient* precedent for a present option lends gravity to the experience and imbues the group and its leaders with heightened legitimacy. A highly *consistent* precedent creates a binding obligation and a sense of group identity. These two qualities—antiquity and consistency—are often at odds, as the more recent past tends to be more consistent with the present. Hence, institution builders often reference multiple precedents for a plan. Lincoln echoed centuries-old Puritan providentialist themes for historical gravitas, but he also referenced a more recent and consistent precedent by following Washington's terminology (Thanksgiving Day) and timing (announcing on October 3 a celebration on the last Thursday of November). As we'll see, both impressively old and impressively consistent precedents are used to shape not only traditions of nations but also those of industries, religions, and organizations.

The Champagne region bills itself as the cradle of viniculture. Signs inform oenophile tourists where Romans planted hillside vineyards two thousand years ago. The monk Dom Pérignon refined grape harvesting and pressing techniques there. Houses such as Veuve Clicquot remind us that they have bottled their bubbly since the ancien régime. When we take a sip, we taste this estimable tradition. There are many effervescent wines in the world, but the time-honored history legitimates Champagne's preeminent status—and justifies its premium prices.

But wine is much, much older than this. Recently, the Republic of Georgia sponsored archaeological digs in its wine region that discovered *qvevris* (the egg-shaped earthenware vessels they use for fermentation) with wine residue from eight thousand years ago. Georgia received a UNESCO certification for this contribution to the world's cultural heritage. Since then, its wine industry and tourism have boomed. While Georgians knew they had good wine, these signals of antiquity gave its vintners a new sense of purpose and its consumers a cause for deeper devotion. The *qvevri* method is one of humanity's oldest epicurean traditions.

It's not just wine regions that document their estimable histories. The oldest American bank, the Bank of New York Mellon, uses familiar images of its founder, Alexander Hamilton. In Paris, La Tour d'Argent prints its founding year, 1582, on menus, plates, even ashtrays. In Osaka, the temple-building company Kongō Gumi displays a ten-foot scroll listing the succession of sons at the helm since 578. These firms signal that they are fixtures on the cultural landscape, time-honored institutions.

Why are consumers drawn to a long lineage? A rationalist interpretation is that they infer quality from longevity. A business won't survive long if it loses depositors' money, serves spoiled food, or builds flimsy structures, so one that endures must be doing something right. Such inferences, no doubt, play a role in the appeal of venerable traditions, but people prefer older pedigrees even among options that have passed the test of time. Psychologists Scott Eidelman and Chris Crandall found that acupuncture treatments are evaluated 20 percent more favorably when billed as centuries-old versus decades-old. In both cases, the treatment has been thoroughly tested and allure is higher when it is associated with a deeper history. What would intrigue you more: a ritual from 1996, or one from 1669? My guess is that you'd select the time-honored treatment.

When taking part in a long-standing institution, we feel a sense of meaning that goes beyond the practical purposes accomplished. We often feel a touch of reverence and awe. Underneath this is the feeling of connection to ancient ancestors, people who took the same action in totally different eras. The persons involved need not be your ancestors in a direct genetic way; they may be *cultural ancestors*, predecessors in tribes that you identify with (whether it is Beijing residents, Buddhists, or acupuncture enthusiasts). Our existential ache for tribal continuity is well served by precedents that are many generations old, as they betoken traditions that we can believe will persist for many generations into the future.

Our ancestor-instinct penchant for perpetuating time-honored traditions brings richness into our lives, but it can also leave us credulous and vulnerable to manipulation. In a consumer study, participants who sampled a chocolate that had been sold in its home market for just a few years found it tasteless and unappealing; another group experienced the same chocolate as delicious and desirable . . . after being told it was a brand established for generations. The wine market is rife with fraud, such as new product in vintage bottles, or wine from generic grapes misattributed to ancient vines or traditional terroirs. (It's estimated that 20 percent of all wine sold is somehow phony.) One reason this persists is that oenophiles experience complex notes of flavor when they pour from a distinguished bottle, even if it contains ordinary plonk. In the same way, collectors of antique art and furniture are fooled by counterfeits; their reverence gets in the way of diligence. We are easily duped about the provenance of our pleasures for the same reason that we are swayed by stories about Pilgrim Thanksgivings.

The Gothic spires at Oxford University bespeak its twelfth-century origins. They tempt students to walk in the footsteps of past generations of scholars. Even a platitudinous lecture may be experienced as meaningful if the classroom is centuries old. The University of Chicago constructed its 1890 campus in the Gothic style to express affinity with Oxford (and perhaps to out-ancient the "Ancient Eight" campuses on the East Coast with their redbrick colonial-era architecture). Similarly, the 1878 St. Patrick's Cathedral in New York was built in this style to signal continuity with the medieval basilicas in Europe that its immigrant parishioners knew. The 1893 Salt Lake Temple might seem an exception, as there are no medieval Mormon masterpieces that its Gothic style references. But it's an exception that proves the rule. Its leaders are well aware that "Mormonism does not enjoy the authenticating quality of antiquity. Because it came of age in a modern time, its theology and saintly visitations can strike people as stranger than those of older religions shrouded by centuries." The Church of Jesus Christ of Latter-day Saints can seem a bit *too* "Latter-day" for some Americans, so it deliberately highlights its continuity with older sects in the Judeo-Christian tradition.

Signaling inspiration to the long-ago past is not just a marketing trick to bring in new customers. It's also a means of legitimation that affects loyalties of existing members to the group and its leadership. While we might think that questions about the legitimacy of presidents in the US are new, we must remember Lincoln won less than 40 percent of the popular vote and took power with nearly half of the states having seceded and many remaining states sharply divided. His invocations of a tradition from the earliest American settlers lent him the gravitas of an epic historical figure and garnered acceptance of his unifying agenda.

Few things seem more ancient on the surface than the pageantry surrounding the British monarchy. Rituals such as the changing of the guard at Buckingham Palace appear to be vestiges of age-old protocols, but in fact, many were introduced in modern times—after the displacements of industrialization created nostalgia for the past. After disruptions of continuity in the dynasty, such as the 1917 change to the name Windsor and the 1936 abdication of King Edward, the monarchy heightened the signals of ancient precedent in their rituals. Weddings were held in Westminster Abbey for the first time in five hundred years. Coronations incorporated archaic pomp such as antique swords and orbs. Historian Eric Hobsbawm called this "invented traditions"—recent solutions to recent problems that masquerade as ancient.

Invented or not, traditions are still astonishingly seductive. A Japanese myth holds that Jimmu, a descendant of the sun goddess and the storm god, arrived in ancient times to become the first emperor. The holiday of *Kigensetsu* celebrates his ascent through drum processions, attestations to his divine lineage, and ritual kowtowing to his image. Seemingly a vestige of primitive times, *Kigensetsu* didn't exist until the 1872 Meiji Restoration (when a cabal of nobles colluded to redirect public allegiance to the emperor and away from the regional shoguns, to create a constitutional monarchy that could defend the country against colonization). Previously, Jimmu's ascent had been folklore, but now affiliated historians published "evidence" to fix its exact time (February 11, 660 BC) and place (Nara). Imperialists built statues and shrines on these sites in antique styles that looked like they had been there forever. They gathered at these sites on February 11 to memorialize their earliest ancestor. Finally, it was formalized with a decree that every village must celebrate *Kigensetsu* on the prescribed day and in a prescribed way. As French sociologist Maurice Halbwachs described, collective memories can be created through "commemoration" events—often involving monuments, speeches, and group reminiscence.

It's ironic that *modernizers* promoted an ancient demigod. But they understood the tribal resonance of antiquity. The older the dynasty in the people's minds, the greater their reverence for the tradition and respect for Emperor Meiji and, by extension, for the rest of his regime. And just as planned, the Meiji Restoration catalyzed the country's rapid industrialization and militarization in the decades that followed. Notice that the *Kigensetsu* tradition was forged through the same steps as Thanksgiving—lore about ancient ancestors was historized, ritualized, and formalized as a holiday. This was around the same time that Garibaldi was forging an Italian national identity—uniting long-divided principalities—by referencing the historical memory of ancient Rome. All across the world, nineteenth-century nation-builders pitched their plans with references to ancient ancestors, real or imagined.

We saw in chapter 3 that matriculation ceremonies trigger the codes of the profession for medical students. The Greek oath hints at an unbroken tradition from the father of Western medicine, Hippocrates. But in fact, this oath was not part of medical training for most centuries since; it was adopted in modern times once physicians sought to separate themselves from bloodletters and barbers and needed a distinguished ancestor. Medical societies appropriated the white lab coat of scientists around this time too. The ceremony combining the oath and the white coat was invented only in 1993, but it spread rapidly and is now conducted in many places with a quasi-religious reverence. Traditions are often not as ancient as advertised.

Even *un*sentimental professions construct traditions in this way. International Accounting Day is an unofficial holiday promoted by societies of this profession. It's on November 10, the date in 1494 when Italian mathematician Luca de Pacioli published a tome that analyzed bookkeeping. When scholar-turned-banker Alfred Winslow Jones invented the hedge fund—with its 2 and 20 percent fee structure, he referenced the practice of Phoenician sea captains who took a fixed payment plus a fifth of the profits of a successful voyage. Clients are less likely to balk at a scalpel or a price-gouging fee if it's pitched as part of a time-honored tradition—even if the connection to the past is a bit tenuous.

Corporations, too, pitch their products as precedented by the ancients, particularly if the rationale for them would otherwise be rather weak. After unprecedented discoveries created a diamond glut in the early twentieth century, De Beers needed to radically increase demand. Before this, engagement rings had used sapphires, if any stone at all. Diamond rings were seen only on the hands of royals or robber barons. De Beers launched a full-fledged propaganda campaign to change this cultural tradition around diamonds. It involved print and radio ads, lectures at schools and fairs, and articles in magazines and newspapers. A "Diamond Information

Bureau" published historical studies, documenting (with some exaggera-
tions) that diamonds were worn by the ancient Hindus, Greeks, and
Romans; that diamond rings were symbols of marital commitment to
medieval potentates such as Charles V, the famously devoted Holy Roman
emperor; and that they were celebrated as such in the poetry of the time:
"Two wills, two hearts, two passions / Are joined in marriage by a diamond ring." This barrage of precedent symbols about diamond rings
impressed itself on post-WWII Americans. Choosing a ring became a ritual for would-be grooms, most brides began to wear one to the altar, and
after a generation, people began to assume that it had always been this
way. The campaign still lives on today: "A Diamond Is Forever."

The twisting of history to pitch products has only become more blatant
in recent years. Gwyneth Paltrow's wellness emporium, Goop, hawked its
"Jade Egg" as a "strictly guarded secret of Chinese royalty in antiquity,"
which concubines used to stimulate their hormones and tone their muscles.
Goop was fined after both the historical and medical claims were exposed
as false. Interestingly, though, customers still want more jade eggs.

Shinola is a watch company headquartered in a Detroit industrial landmark that hawks its nostalgic faith in American craftsmanship. It has won
awards for brand authenticity. But it doesn't actually manufacture watches in
the US and has no link to the long-defunct shoe polish brand immortalized
in the WWII-era saying, "*You* don't know shit from Shinola." Just as *fictional* characters can be inspiring role models, imaginary histories can be
compelling traditions. Folklorists were scandalized when it came to light
long ago that classic Paul Bunyan "folklore" was authored by a Lumber
Company copywriter ("fakelore"). But as scholars have come to appreciate
that many folktales have been molded by organizations, governments, and
even anthologists (e.g., the Brothers Grimm), they no longer draw a bright
line between folklore and fakelore.

Sometimes the provenance of a product, profession, or plan is peripheral to our reasons for choosing it, but when we're enjoying turkey and cranberries, or Georgian wine, or jade eggs, the historical backstory may be a large part of the appeal. To our ancestor-instinct brains, connections to the ancient past infuse an activity with meaning and legitimacy. While we don't always think about connections to the past consciously, we experience traditional activities as alluring, transforming, and at the same time deeply comforting. Ties to times long ago, even when tenuous, heighten our interest in an activity and our trust in associated organizations and leaders. This is why politicians, professionals, and entrepreneurs often wrap their new agendas in the mantle of the ancient past.

If one feature of powerful precedents is antiquity, another is consistency. While ancient precedents are alluring, they are often only loosely relevant to the current decision. A highly consistent precedent, on the other hand, creates a more exacting obligation because of the tight analogy to the current situation. Following a consistent precedent (as opposed to a loose inspiration from the past) also sharpens the sense of group identity, as identity is built from constancy over time. Two main ways that leaders highlight consistency are worth closely examining: selective recall and resonant framing.

The modern nation of Israel has been embattled from birth. After its UN-backed founding in 1948, it was promptly invaded by five nearby nations with larger populations. Israel's people had no shortage of tribal history, of course, but most of it did not help with this pressing problem of national defense. The founding generation descended from distinguished rabbis, scholars, and merchants—professions of the diaspora. To forge a warrior ethos, they needed to engage in selective recall and find a suitable part of their past as precedent. They seized upon a story: in 72 AD, during the Roman occupation of Judea, a community of Israelite rebels holed up in a hilltop fort called the Masada and made a stand, men and women alike, resisting a large army of invaders, ultimately choosing suicide over capture. This event was not very ancient by Old Testament standards, nor was it well documented. But the event was strikingly *consistent* with the country's current needs. An excavation by an archaeologist and general, Yigael Yadin, uncovered evidence that was mixed at best, but he held a public press conference announcing proof of the Masada stand. After this, Israelis were steeped in the story by textbooks, television shows, and political speeches, and they committed to the world's steepest military service requirements as consistent with tradition. The hilltop site was reconstructed to fit the story, and, for decades, military training culminated there with a torchlit ceremony under the desert stars, with chants of "Masada shall not fall again." Military service became the unifying institution of Israeli society, a pillar of the Sabra identity that displaced the diaspora identity in the generations born in Israel. Eventually, the Masada story was no longer needed by the army, as its own record of heroic self-defense became precedent enough.

The past speaks in many voices. Any history that we tell is very selective in its focus and thus never definitive. Official histories are strategic in what they include and what they elide. Different parts of the group's past hold different implications for present courses of action. By emphasizing parts of the past that are analogous to their favored plan, leaders rationalize it as obligated by a binding precedent, as an imperative of group identity. Group identities develop much in the same way that personal identities do—through narratives of consistency between the remembered past and present actions, intentions, and rationales. Brain-injured patients who lose their memories begin to also lose their sense of identity. Likewise for groups, memory and records of history are used to promote notions of group tradition and identity, and this has implications for future strategies. In this sense, identity is not just about the present, and strategy is not just about the future; they both have to be supported by selective recall of the past.

This hot-wiring of history isn't limited to national politics. Marketers use selective recall of a company's past to nudge purchases in the present. Levi's anchors its product line with the timeless 501 jeans, unchanged since they were designed for Gold Rush prospectors. The company's nostalgic ads show pioneers from many decades who have worn them—1950s leather-jacketed rebels, 1960s long-haired hippies, 1970s Gay Pride marchers. These durable pants have long been handed down, customized, and recycled, and current ads showcase this history as consistent with Gen Z's interest in sustainability. The more things change, the more Levi's remains the same.

Selective recall of the tribal past to create a binding tradition is a recurring theme in the 2019 *Star Wars* spin-off *The Mandalorian*. The title refers to an interstellar tribe that is not a race but a creed, bound by strong traditions. In one episode the protagonist, who works as a bounty hunter, travels to a remote planet with a rugged desert terrain, where he is attacked by horse-sized lizards called blurrgs. He is nursed back to health by a sympathetic local called Kuiil, voiced by Nick Nolte. Kuiil explains that the only way across the desert to his destination is to ride a blurrg. The bounty hunter grumbles and struggles to master the wily steed, getting thrown to the ground repeatedly and becoming frustrated. To encourage him, Kuiil draws upon his knowledge of history, involving a much larger cousin-species, the mythosaur: "You are a Mandalorian! Your ancestors rode the great mythosaur. Surely you can ride this young foal." Steeled by the sense of tradition, he gains confidence and tames the blurrg. It's his identity— even his destiny—to succeed.

While selective recall is a tactic for consistency focused on the past, resonant framing is one that focuses on the *present* activity. Entrepreneurs frame their plan to maximize its apparent consistency with familiar parts of the group's past. Lincoln appropriated Washington's terminology and timing so that his new holiday seemed warranted by this event ninety years before. It was hardly the first time that a new holiday gained traction by piggybacking on the past. Christianity spread through Europe by scheduling its holy days around prior pagan rituals (e.g., Christmas came at the time of Yule, and Easter incorporated the eggs of spring fertility rites). When new nation-states emerged in Europe, they set their civic holidays on top of age-old folk festivals (e.g., the workers' holiday on May 1, the date when countless previous generations had danced around the Maypole). Similarly, the flag and anthem of a new nation tend to be chosen to resonate with people's memories. The US kept the red, white, and blue of the Union Jack. "My Country, 'Tis of Thee" followed the tune of "God Save the Queen" (while the later "Star-Spangled Banner" followed a familiar drinking song). New rituals are constructed from familiar materials so people are drawn to them.

New policies can be framed in terms of established concepts in a group's past. When Nelson Mandela became the president of South Africa in 1994, he faced a daunting dilemma. The long reign of apartheid was over, but decades of atrocities haunted its people. Mandela realized that some reckoning with the past was needed—both for the African communities who had suffered the most and sought answers about those who disappeared, and for the European-descended communities who lived in guilt and fear of reprisals. A Nuremberg-style prosecution wouldn't foster the open cooperation between these groups that was needed for the country to move forward, but an Appomattox-style amnesty would leave too much of the past hidden. Mandela knew about the truth commission hearings after dictatorships in Bolivia and Argentina, but in his country people would not trust the judiciary to be an independent arbitrator, as it never had been one before. Mandela designed a Truth and Reconciliation Commission to be led by Anglican Archbishop Desmond Tutu, one of the few authorities in the country who had mediated between African and European communities. To persuade African communities to support immunity in exchange for testimony, Mandela pitched the plan using terms from their tribal traditions: It was in the spirit of *ubuntu*, a Zulu term for human interconnectedness, and it worked like the Xhosa tribe's truth-telling rituals that restore relationships after conflicts. To reject the plan would be a repudiation of the Xhosa ancestors and a lack of faith in *ubuntu*; the African communities strongly supported the hearings. *Ubuntu* had been appropriated by whites in the anti-apartheid movement, so veterans of that political push also felt an identity obligation to support *ubuntu* again. Hearings took place across the country for years, with tens of thousands of citizens testifying, and enabled its communities to transcend the rancor of the past.

While the Afrikaner community resisted the democratic transition, one consolation was that their rugby team, the Springboks, could play in the 1995 Rugby World Cup. Its green-and-gold jersey was for decades a symbol of apartheid. The team had taken on its first Black players, and Mandela had asked the whole country to support it. At the finals, the new national anthem was played, combining Afrikaner motifs with a pan-African hymn, as the team prepared to face the overwhelming favorite, New Zealand. Then, astonishingly, Mandela stepped out on the field wearing a Springbok jersey and cap, greeting all the players. The sixty-three thousand fans in attendance at the finals were 99 percent Afrikaners who had bitterly opposed his election. How did they respond? They rose as if one and chanted his name again and again. This scene replicated itself at viewing events across the country, and the team realized that they had the support of the whole nation. No serious commentator had given the Springboks a chance, but they met the All Blacks with unyielding defense and pulled off a narrow victory. It was through masterstrokes of tradition-building like this that Mandela forged a common identity for the rainbow nation.

For corporations, resonant framing is critical to cultivating brand identities. The art is to develop new designs resonant of past classics. We see these reincarnations on the roads: Volkswagen's New Beetle, BMW's Mini Cooper, and Fiat's 500. In fashion or cinema, it takes a generation before an old style can be "retro" rather than simply "dated." Athletics brands like Adidas and Puma have "retro" divisions that release special-edition products reprising designs from decades earlier. In a similar spirit, sports teams don uniforms from the past for special games—for example, the Boston Red Sox playing a game in the team's kit from 1908. The NBA's throwback jerseys were such a hit that expansion franchises (e.g., Dallas Mavericks) had to come up with "fauxback" jerseys—designers dreamed up what a past uniform would have looked like!

Framing current products to resonate with classics is also a way to restore brand identities that have lost their way. Harley-Davidson dominated the motorcycle market for most of the twentieth century with its distinctive heavyweight bikes. As sleeker Japanese imports caught on, Harley tried to follow the trend but in doing so just alienated its employees and customers. No one wanted a Harley that looked and sounded like a Honda. They missed the massive "hogs" with their deep-throated "*potato-potato-potato*" roar. To the rescue came designer Willie Davidson, who was a rider and collector of vintage bikes (and also a grandson of the founder). Willie dreamed up the Super Glide, a conspicuously large and loud cruiser reminiscent of the mid-century mainstays. Along with this pivot, the firm dropped standard advertising in favor of sponsoring a newsletter and rallies for Harley fans that juxtaposed the classics and new models, selling the tradition. Market share improved, and more and more customers arrived at dealerships wearing Harley patches on their jackets and even Harley tattoos on their arms. A rider sporting Harley ink was unlikely to switch to Honda. The brand had become a tribal identity.

The National Football League made a recent recovery of this sort after nearly fumbling its hard-won image of good, clean fun. Starting in 2016, the NFL suffered a tidal wave of bad press: domestic violence, brain injuries, and national anthem protests. America's game, it seemed, was now played by unpatriotic, dangerous thugs. Average viewership was down 16 percent. The league turned to the History Factory, a consultancy that helps organizations mine their heritage to support present strategies. They planned the league's 2019 centennial as an occasion for recalling the past and reframing the present to restore a consistent tradition and a favorable identity. It began with a Super Bowl ad showing current NFL stars mingling with admirable players of the past (e.g., Jim Brown, Franco Harris, and Joe Montana) at a black-tie reception celebrating the centennial. Then, during a stuffy speech, a football slips from the top of a fancy tiered cake and bounces on the floor in its unpredictable way, eliciting reflexive shouts of "FUMBLE!" and diving for the ball, then passing, rushing, and tackling, all done with big grins and extraordinary athleticism—flattening the formal waiters, banquet tables, and champagne pyramids in slapstick fashion. This spontaneous rumble conveyed that today's stars (despite their fancy clothes and haircuts) are just like the heroes of past generations (and, really, just the same as kids roughhousing on playgrounds across America—just a lot bigger and stronger). It was the first year that the top-rated Super Bowl ad was the NFL's own. Over the season that followed, each team held a "Fantennial" weekend to commemorate its local tradition, such as halftime weddings on the fifty-yard line in Buffalo. The "Huddle for 100" initiative brought fans and players to volunteer for the league's perennial charities. All of this showed football fans that the NFL had not lost its identity. By the time the league closed out its hundredth year, viewership had rebounded 12 percent to largely regain its popularity—a stunning comeback for the league. The seasons since have set all-time viewership records.

▼

In 2000, Starbucks opened a branch in the Forbidden City. The emperor's walled enclave in the center of Beijing was once "forbidden" in the sense that no commoners—and certainly no foreigners—could enter. For the past few decades it has teemed with tourists, both domestic and foreign, who visit palaces, plazas, and museums and enjoy antique-style teahouses and restaurants. Starbucks styled its site, next to the Hall of Preserving Harmony, to look like an ancient Chinese teahouse, the corporate logo barely visible. It portrayed itself as part of the time-honored Chinese tradition of serving caffeinated drinks.

This Western café with Chinese characteristics operated without controversy until 2007. That was when a popular TV journalist ranted online

that the café "tramples" on Chinese tradition. These fighting words were reposted on countless blogs and websites. Within days, half a million netizens had signed a petition railing against Starbucks' offense. The controversy spread to television and newspapers, then crowds began to picket the building. Before long, the authorities revoked Starbucks's permit, and Frappuccinos in the Forbidden City were no more.

The problem wasn't coffee—a domestic-brand coffee bar opened at the site soon afterward. Nor was a foreign brand in a historic site anathema (KFC has operated in traditional sites, including the adjacent Winter Palace). Perhaps what irked the Beijing clicktivists was Starbucks's teahouse schtick. What gave this American company the right to appropriate an ancient Chinese trope?

Incorporation of local traditions when marketing abroad is often well-intended, but it can also deeply offend. Complaints of "cultural appropriation" are sometimes dismissed as oversensitivity, but they shouldn't be. People guard their traditions vigilantly because, as we've seen, traditions are quite malleable and hence vulnerable. "Champagne" is protected by the French government as a "designation of origin," because otherwise, vintners elsewhere would appropriate the term with the eventual effect of changing its meaning, devaluing the currency. In recent years, activists have judged many acts of cultural borrowing as theft-like "cultural appropriation." Studies find that these accusations follow a coherent logic: they generally hinge on relevant factors such as the degree of misrepresentation, displacement of local entrepreneurs, and the relative power of the two groups. Cultural groups with less power over global media and discourse are particularly vulnerable to distortion of their tradition by outsiders. Antonio Gramsci coined the term "cultural hegemony" to describe how powerful societies impose their frameworks upon other groups. Even a less powerful group's self-conception—and understanding of its own traditions—can be bastardized when a hegemonic groups starts incorporating those traditions into widely marketed products. So it's not a double standard that some acts of cultural borrowing are protested and others are not; the traditions of some groups are more vulnerable.

Understanding this can save a lot of pain. When Yoplait began losing market shares to Fage and Chobani, it rolled out its own version of a strained-style yogurt, Yoplait Greek. Consumers liked the taste, but the firm came under ferocious attack from activists. How could a French corporation (partly American) call its product Greek? Food bloggers and critics nitpicked its ingredients to charge it as inauthentic. Yoplait's product gurus went back to the drawing board. French farmers had long made old-style *yaourt*, setting aside milk in little glass jars. So it developed a "French-style" yogurt, Oui. It was thick and tart like Greek yogurt, but critics raved about its authenticity, and sales topped $100 million a year. This was a tradition it had a right to mine. Yogurt is a *cultured* milk product, after all!

Resistance is not the only way precedent signals can fail. Sometimes they forge a sense of tradition so strong that it has unintended consequences. Arguably, this happened with the *Kigensetsu* holiday, which harnessed emperor worship to modernize Japan so it could defend itself. It worked a bit *too well*, as industrialization turned into militarization then imperialism. By the early twentieth century, Japan was on the attack—and it took on more battles than it could win. After Japan's surrender in World War II, *Kigensetsu* was abolished as a dangerous tradition.

Another example is UNESCO certifications. The organization was founded to recognize and preserve the world's cultural heritage sites and bring people together, but it hasn't always worked out that way. The first problem is that UNESCO's stamp puts a site on every tourist's "bucket list." Foot traffic is "ruining the ruins" at Peru's Machu Picchu, bringing tour operators into conflict with preservationists. On the George Town jetties of Malaysia, it saved decaying buildings but displaced their inhabitants, centuries-old homes becoming postcard shops. In Laos's old capital, Luang Prabang, historic (but nondescript) buildings are being replaced by "hyper-traditionalist" edifices that attract tourists (to the chagrin of residents who don't want to live in a theme park). Deeper problems arise from the politics of the certifications process. Wealthy regimes succeed in lobbying for certification more often than poor nations, leading to a highly Eurocentric representation of the world's cultural heritage. A regime's fit to UN politics also matters: Canada has more world heritage sites than Israel, the cradle of several world religions! Arbitrating the importance of ancient heritage sites is a dangerous game; it sends signals about which traditions in a region are primary and hence which occupants are more legitimate. It can unwittingly support the oppression of minority groups. It can spur aggressive moves by the group validated or by the group threatened. After Serbia secured recognition of medieval Orthodox monasteries in Kosovo, this majority Muslim province voted to secede. To its credit, UNESCO has been proactive in studying these problems and has transitioned away from recognizing historic sites and toward recognizing contributions in a less territorialized way.

▽

The counterintuitive lesson of this chapter is that leading change is not all about the future—it also requires a hands-on relationship with the perceived past. Nor is leadership primarily rational—it touches on myth-making, ritual, and nostalgia. Like Abraham Lincoln, leaders who want to create changes or avoid changes have to craft narratives of continuity between the past and the present. History is not destiny, as the malleability of perceived traditions reveals. A group's sense of its past is constantly being reconstructed and reconfigured. Traditionalism—like conformity and adulation of heroes—can be an obstacle to change, but it can also be a changemaker's secret weapon.

Few of us are called like Nelson Mandela to forge traditions and institutions that unite a formerly divided nation. But most of us will live in communities, pray in congregations, and work in organizations that are more diverse than ever and prone to conflict. We can play a part in the continual process of reconstructing traditions for greater inclusiveness. These days even national sports teams like the one Hiddink coached encompass ever more diversity as coaches draw on their countries' global diasporas. In the 2018 men's soccer World Cup, three fourths of the players for some teams, like Morocco, were born and raised elsewhere. In the 2018 Winter Olympics, host South Korea fielded a women's hockey team despite its limited development in their country by incorporating Korean Americans and then also bringing in a dozen North Korean players. This "Unified Korea" team contended with differences in language, culture, political ideology, and hockey tactics. But during their training together, they forged syncretic traditions. At the start of a game, they would skate in a circle around their goal (choreography that would not be out of place in North Korea), then "unfurl" by high-fiving the goalie before peeling off toward their position (a cultural change-up). After games, they assembled in a line and tapped their sticks to their opponent (as Western players do to show respect), then they turned to bow (Korean-style) to the opposing coaches. As the team gelled, they saw that their similarities were more important than their differences—they were all Korean, all hockey players, and all willing to defy expectations by joining this hybrid team. By the end of the tournament, they were referring to each other as "sister" and "family." They didn't win. Nor did they dissolve all differences among the two Koreas. But through recognizing plural precedents, they forged traditions both inclusive and unifying, showing the world that tribal lines can be redrawn.

PART III

TRIBAL
RIPPLES

7

When Change Spreads,
and When It Fizzles Out

The central conservative truth is that it is
culture, not politics, that determines the success
of a society. The central liberal truth is that politics
can change a culture and save it from itself.

—Daniel Patrick Moynihan

I n the sun-dappled streets of Ecuador, life seems to saunter rather than sprint. Visitors often marvel at the unhurried pace of life—lunch breaks stretching languidly, meetings commencing without regard for the clock. Locals fondly joke about the difference between *hora gringa* (when foreigners arrive) and *hora local* (a half hour later, when locals roll in). This cultural divide is captured in a popular saying: in English, the watch "runs," but in Spanish, it "walks" ("*el reloj camina*"). As if to underscore the point, Jefferson Pérez, the country's only Olympic medalist for many years, won his accolades in race*walking*. Within Ecuador's government, too, tardiness is an unwritten rule. Government officials are assertively late—the higher their status, the longer the wait. In the early aughties, an estimated two out of every three meetings started late. But foreign investors often stumbled over this cultural hurdle. The cost of the lost business was an estimated 10 percent of GDP.

In 2003, President Lucio Gutiérrez (himself notorious for arriving late) announced an initiative to eradicate unpunctuality. Supported by international corporations and NGOs, it launched with much fanfare in Quito's picturesque historic center. Posters of Pérez, the face of the campaign, were plastered everywhere, with the catchy slogan, "A second makes a difference." Several local celebrities were scheduled to speak. Government employees passed out slickly produced swag, including hotel-style embossed doorknob signs—"Do not enter! The meeting began on time."—for citizens to use at their workplace. A brass band, balloons, and *bebidas* brought out a crowd of curious citizens. They greeted the MC with warm applause but were bemused by the group activity he announced of synchronizing their watches, like military operatives before a mission. For a long time, Gutiérrez himself was nowhere to be seen, until he arrived at the last possible moment. With the crowd thinning and trash bins overflowing, the president called on citizens "to be on time for the sake of God, the country, our people and our consciences," and promised that his administration would be scrupulously so. Then Pérez took the stage to fire a starter's pistol precisely at noon, marking the start of the punctual era.

It started right on time, but you can probably guess how it worked out. While its launch drew a crowd, the campaign didn't create cultural change. The city newspaper, called *La Hora* (of all things), published the times of government officials' arrival at public events, exposing that they continued to show up late. The push had failed to change even its own sponsors, not to mention quickening the pace of *Quiteños* in general.

A society's relationship to time is a deeply entrenched cultural pattern. Psychologist Robert Levine studied the pace of life in communities all around the world, finding that it is encoded at many different cultural levels: in shared habits like a brisk walking speed, in collective ideals like administrative efficiency, and in traditions like relying on public clocks. In other words, it involves peer codes, hero codes, and ancestor codes. This means that changing the tempo of society requires levers for three different kinds of tribal codes.

The organizers of the Quito campaign understood this much. They planned different kinds of tribal signals: they drew a crowd (prevalence), involved famous athletes and politicians (prestige), and invoked time-related military and hospitality traditions (precedent). However, they didn't consider how heavy-handed tactics can raise the audience's defenses. People resent precedents plucked from extraneous domains (e.g., hotel rooms or military missions). They are suspicious of celebrities preaching what they don't practice personally. They doubt that a crowd implies a cause's popularity if it's fast dwindling and discarding the swag. These signals were even more prone to raising defenses because they were sent all at the same time. The punctuality push failed, ironically, because it was so *rushed*.

President Gutiérrez could have taken a lesson from elsewhere in Ecuador. In the small but industrious Andean city of Ambato, a group of concerned citizens had come together around the same issue. Lateness was endemic at schools and factories, in some areas delaying the start of sessions and shifts. The group committed to enforcing punctuality in their own workplaces and reached out to neighbors to do the same. In so doing, they learned about some root causes such as public transportation bottlenecks, which they lobbied to fix. This allayed some of the worst problems in visible ways. It improved residents' perceptions of their fellow citizens, and accordingly increased their efforts to be on time as well.

After this small win—a slowly widening shift toward punctual habits—the campaign turned its focus to the city's public ideals about timeliness, using their connections to the schools and to the local media. Primary schools began to stress punctuality as a civic virtue, a form of responsibility and respect for other people. Local newspapers published editorials linking this theme to municipal pride: Ambateños (unlike some *other* Ecuadorans) show up on time! Former Ecuadorean president Osvaldo Hurtado noted that the campaign appropriated "the civic mystique of Ambato with frequent references to *la hora ambateña*" (versus *la hora local*). High schools featured oratory contests called "*Somos la hora ambateña*" ("We are Ambato time"). These actions all sent prestige signals, making timeliness a central ideal in the city's identity.

Finally, the local government got involved. In speeches, officials extolled the temporal discipline of Ambato's founding fathers. The mayor announced that all city events would begin precisely on the hour. Before long, officials' lateness no longer signaled status, because the meeting would start without them. Ordinary citizens felt pressure to arrive at their seats on time too—their peers were doing it, their leaders were expecting it, and the public tolling of the old clock seemed to solemnly require it. Just as tardiness can be contagious, so, too, can punctuality.

Unlike the high-powered campaign in Quito, the homegrown Ambato movement achieved its goal. It helped that it acted gradually over time rather than bombarding people with many messages on the same day. But equally important was the sequence of steps. First they sent prevalence signals to shift habits, next prestige signals to instill new ideals, then precedent signals to forge traditions and institutions. In this sequence, each change paves the way for the next one. Once punctuality was seen as normal, *Ambateños* were ready to embrace it as normative as well. And once it was idealized, they didn't resent it being institutionalized to "lock in" the change. Changing a deeply encoded cultural pattern often requires a campaign of steps in that sequence to produce this sort of chain reaction.

This bottom-up progression of change—from ordinary people's daily habits to collective ideals shared in the media and finally to public traditions and institutions—is called a "grassroots" movement. Some of the change tactics we've viewed in the past six chapters were embedded within broader campaigns or movements of this type. Temperance activists first induced their neighbors to pledge teetotalism, then they shaped media images, and finally they lobbied to change laws. The Me Too movement started with posts that spread person-to-person before it leaped into media stories and then into changes in industry policies and legal standards.

But the grassroots model isn't the only sequential strategy we've encountered. The cultural militarization in Israel occurred first through institutions (linking the Masada story to military training), then collective ideals (the emergence of military heroes and the Sabra identity), then habits of ordinary life (military service is a shared experience and reference point that unites Israelis). Likewise, in Singapore, abrupt institutional changes (independence and stiff anti-corruption laws) set the stage for the signaling of ideals (Lee Kuan Yew's modeling of austerity and incorruptibility) and then the triggering of "free port" habits (through English and white uniforms). These are top-down progressions from institutions to ideals to habits. This strategy is often called "shock therapy" because institutional change disrupts a group's equilibrium, allowing for the coalescence of new ideals and habits.

The grassroots and shock-wave strategies each work well in the right conditions. They are different kinds of ripple effects in which the first change creates momentum for the steps that follow. But in the wrong conditions, each strategy fails. The momentum fizzles out or even backfires. Our understanding of tribal instincts can help us understand why some conditions enable grassroots momentum and different conditions enable shock-wave momentum. Understanding how these tribal chain reactions occur can help us choose the sequential strategy that fits best in a given set of conditions.

Successful grassroots movements get romanticized as victories of virtuous underdogs over corrupt establishments. A canonical case is Gandhi's independence movement, which influenced Reverend Martin Luther King Jr., Cesar Chavez, Nelson Mandela, and many others. It started in the 1920s with activists changing their daily habits so as to stop cooperating with mercantile colonialism (rejecting Western clothes, cuisine, and housing). They spread these habits through holding bonfires, organizing fasts, and establishing communes. It escalated in the 1930s into more public actions like the sixty-thousand-protester-strong Salt March that provoked brutal repression, exposing the facade of British civility in India. Gandhi increasingly led by example as the head of the Congress Party, personifying renunciation (as we saw in chapter 5). By the 1940s, boycotts and strikes had broken the mercantile system, and the war-strapped British needed to negotiate with Gandhi's party and acquiesced to independence demands.

While it's tempting to interpret this victory as karma, there was nothing inevitable about it. Gandhi had been steeped in political organizing in South Africa and had gained mastery of the levers of tribal psychology. Gandhi and his supporters started by ceasing to consume Western goods. Wearing dhotis and eating dal makhani were acts of noncooperation with the colonizers' economy, but they were particularly well-chosen acts given that attire and cuisine are potent triggers of cultural habits. And as the movement widened, these visible behaviors sent a prevalence signal to the rest of the nation. When larger-scale protests required greater sacrifice from his followers, he mobilized commitment with symbols like salt (a necessity of life that the Raj cruelly taxed) and the spinning wheel (a tool of resistance to the English textile industry). These icons inspired his *satyagrahis* to march many miles and to endure police beatings. Gandhi accepted the elevated title of "Mahatma" because he understood that the movement needed heroes. To build support for demanding an end to the Raj, the century-old institution that had made many influential Indians wealthy, he framed the changes as a return to more ancient and long-standing Indian traditions.

Psychology can also help us understand how grassroots movements gain momentum—why change that starts with minor behaviors of ordinary people can build and spread and then rise to the level of ideals represented in the group's discourse and then elevate further to the level of group traditions and institutions. When canvassers from Greenpeace stop you on the sidewalk to ask you to sign a petition, it's because that act affects your subsequent choices. Their follow-up request for a small donation to protect the oceans is hard to decline. After taking this action, you may feel inclined to avoid ordering tuna at lunch. And you'll be more likely to notice ocean-related news articles and to raise the topic in conversations with others. When we take action for a cause, especially in public, we feel *commitment* to the cause and feel inclined to act and speak consistently with it. Seeing that a given opinion or activity is widespread in our group also evokes commitment; we feel some identification with it and feel inclined to defend it. If most nurses are women, we jump to the value judgment that most nurses *should* be women. Consider how parents move from "We don't do X" to "You shouldn't do X." Eventually, they may also imply a tradition: "We have always done X." Through the escalating psychology of commitment, conventions become injunctions, and then injunctions become traditions.

Movements that start with shifts to the daily habits of ordinary people disarm the psychological defenses that can otherwise block influence attempts. These movements send prevalence signals that are credible (visible behaviors), rather than raising doubts. When a popular groundswell precedes them, prestige signals (like media stories and celebrity comments) raise fewer suspicions than if they come "out of the blue." Similarly, myth-making and institution-building by authorities that echo the vox populi are less likely to raise resentments about inappropriate meddling in tradi-tions. This is why politicians across the spectrum from Donald Trump to Bernie Sanders cast their campaigns as grassroots movements. They hide the role of political consultants and partisan think tanks and portray the campaign as a popular front. This is one reason that campaigns often exaggerate the crowd size at their events.

Especially for the traditions that a group holds sacred, impositions by political elites are resented, so the gradual buildup of a grassroots move-ment is crucial. In 2015 the Supreme Court's ruling in *Obergefell v. Hodges* made marriage equality the law of the land, citing the "equal protection" clause of the Fourteenth Amendment as a legal precedent for this change. But it wasn't an initiative by a few enlightened judges and lawyers. A long campaign had chosen the frame of "marriage equality" to resonate with this principle. And other important events were precedent signals at a psy-chological level even if they were not federal precedents. In the decade before the decision, thirty-seven states had recognized same-sex marriage, as had most Fortune 500 corporations and the Presbyterian and Method-ist churches, among others. Before this wave of institutional change, the nation's collective ideals on the matter had dramatically changed—television shows like *Will & Grace* portrayed same-sex partnerships as mature bonds between admired characters, not the caricatures of previous decades. Hol-lywood could make this update because of a deeper shift among ordinary Americans before that: in polls, the percentage of Americans who reported knowing someone openly gay grew from 30 percent in 1983 to 73 percent in 2000. Did the gay population double? No—but there was an exodus from the closet, ushered by activism around "coming out." A Pew survey found that among Americans who know "a lot" of gay people, 73 percent were in favor of allowing same-sex marriage, but among those with "none" only 32 percent were in favor. Once same-sex partnerships were visible in their everyday lives, Americans became more ready to valorize and institutionalize these commitments.

But this took decades. Could top-down initiatives by politicians have produced change faster? In 2004 then-mayor of San Francisco Gavin Newsom decided to begin marrying same-sex couples at City Hall. In the city, same-sex relationships were widespread and well-regarded, hence this move was heartily welcomed. But marriage is a matter of *state* law, not city law, and conservative areas of California saw a politician meddling in sacred matters, overstepping his authority. Sacramento courts nullified the marriages, and a movement grew against same-sex marriage, culminating in a 2008 proposition banning it in the state. The blowback was fierce, even though Newsom wasn't imposing this change outside of the city that supported it.

Guns are a sacred issue to many Americans, given the Second Amendment promise of a "right to bear arms" and rifles passed down in families for generations. For half a century, well-funded and well-connected gun control groups—the Brady Campaign and the Coalition to Stop Gun Violence—have pushed for sensible changes. But this movement has been an abject failure, without any notable accomplishments. The problem, as Kristin Goss demonstrated in *Disarmed: The Missing Movement for Gun Control in America*, is that these groups targeted "elite politics at the national level, rather than mass political or social change at the grassroots." By contrast, the opposing "gun rights" movement is grounded in its members' everyday lives. The NRA interacts with people at gun shows, supports candidates in local politics, and sponsors events related to gun owners' concerns: hunting, sport shooting, and self-defense. For gun rights supporters, this has always been an issue grounded in their lives and their political ideals, not just policy preferences. Fifty-six percent of US adults favor stricter gun control and only 31 percent believe that laws should be kept as they are now. But the gun rights contingent is more committed. They are more likely to lobby their representatives and donate to advocacy groups. Gun rights has been a stronger movement because of its grassroots foundation. As the majority group begins to reformulate as a grassroots movement, the tables may eventually turn.

The critical value of starting a movement with ordinary people does not imply, however, that there is no role for elite actors. They often play a behind-the-scenes role in grassroots movements by funding, facilitating, and publicizing protests. Sometimes this includes the deceptive practice of hiring actors to join a march or picket a building, to boost the apparent size of the movement. When corporations do this, critics call it "astroturfing." Oil companies have hired citizens to write letters to the editor and set up "think tanks" with well-paid experts who spread misinformation about climate change. Some corporate-founded "sock puppet" groups have been outed by investigative journalists (e.g., Working Families for Walmart), but it's harder to detect when corporations merely facilitate activist groups that serve their interests. "Astroturf" may be a misleading metaphor because these groups have the potential to take on a life of their own. The anti-tax Tea Party movement was seeded by the billionaire Koch brothers, or rather their dark-money foundation, Americans for Prosperity. But the organizers they trained went back to their communities and held meetings of concerned taxpayers that tapped into authentic anxieties. Their rallies provided prevalence signals, and Tea Party groups spontaneously spread to other communities. Endorsements from pundits like Glenn Beck added prestige signals. The movement adopted the colonial-era "Don't Tread on Me" flag to add the luster of tradition, and the Boston Tea Party references turned into ritual reenactments (e.g., tossing teabags into the town duck pond). While its origins were engineered by elites, the Tea Party movement gained traction through escalating commitment to accomplish significant electoral and legislative victories.

In reality, most successful grassroots movements are aided in one way or another by outside actors. Even Gandhi's ascetic activists relied on funding from sympathetic industrialists. The "people power" color revolutions in post-Soviet states like Georgia's Rose Revolution, Kyrgyzstan's Tulip Revolution, and Ukraine's Orange Revolution were fostered by Western NGOs who trained democracy organizers. These movements followed a bottom-up playbook: massive street marches, followed by a wave of sympathetic blogging, journalism, and speeches by public figures, then occupation of government buildings and clashes with police that create a crisis. They varied in their long-term success. Whether the foreign NGOs merely assisted a homegrown movement or spearheaded the destabilizing protests is still debated, but the "cultivation" of grassroots movements has unquestionably become a central part of soft-power politics.

Cultivation of grassroots movements has also become a key strategy for promoting public health in the developing world. Few cultural practices have generated more concern—and controversy—than the custom in Africa (and elsewhere) of female circumcision, which causes health complications. Parents put their daughters through the "cutting" ceremony so that they will be socially accepted and marriageable. In the past, Western missionaries tried preaching against the practice, but locals resented their trespass into tribal matters and left the church. The practice of cutting spread more widely as a result. More recently, African governments, like that of Senegal, declared it a crime, but rural villages resented these dictates from the far-off capital about a sacred tradition and continued to hold their ceremonies. A Dakar-based NGO called Tostan (meaning "breakthrough") developed a different strategy. It trains development workers (from the local ethnic group) to live in a village for three years. They hold regular workshops with local women about health practices and human rights, using the heritage language and pedagogical methods. The villagers shape the agenda toward issues of local relevance and take leadership in the process, all of which heightens their commitment toward the plans that they agree upon. Much of the time is dedicated to open dialogue about the issues, which builds women's conviction in their plans and their confidence that the group of peers shares their beliefs.

In an early rendition of the program in a village called Malicounda Bambara, the workshop participants read a play about a woman weighing the medical and social implications of "cutting" her daughter. It was an engaging way to convey the health risks, and it served as a springboard for a spirited group discussion of topics not otherwise publicly discussed. After this deliberation about the issues, the women decided that the protagonist should not do it, and this led them to the decision that perhaps they shouldn't practice cutting anymore either. They worried, however, that this was unholy, so they went to talk with the respected local imam, and they were surprised to learn that the Koran does not advocate cutting. When they shared news of the plan to stop cutting, the neighboring villages that traditionally intermarried with theirs reacted with anger. If Malicounda Bambara stopped the custom, then who would their sons be able to marry? And who would want to marry their daughters? The controversy helped the diffusion of these beliefs from the women in the workshop to the rest of the community. The process halted as Tostan offered workshops to the other villages with the help of the imam. When the women of those villages came to the same consensus, the NGO helped organize a "declaration day" led by elders of the villages where women pledged that their daughters would remain uncut and their sons would marry uncut women. In this way, a new institution was created. Since, Tostan has run its program in over nine thousand communities in Senegal and neighboring countries, leading them to abandon cutting (and the related practice of child marriage).

Asking people to reconsider the sacred traditions of their culture is a delicate process. When outsiders try to demand change, it can easily end in backlash. But this doesn't mean that it can't be done responsibly and effectively. NGOs like Tostan have learned that they can facilitate the conversations that produce change, so long as they don't lead decision-making. It has to start with ordinary people who feel empowered to consider new practices, talk about them with peers, and decide on changes; the commitment felt toward these habits can then set off changes in the community's discourse about values and ultimately even in informal and formal institutions. As Tostan shared its discovery, it found that similar processes have worked in other times and places, such as in the early-twentieth-century "natural foot" movement by Chinese progressives (and, behind the scenes, Western missionaries) that eliminated foot-binding, a thousand-year-old tradition that vanished within one generation.

We've seen from these diverse examples that the grassroots strategy, which builds gradually from below, can transform even the most sacrosanct cultural patterns. When a group of ordinary people commits to a new behavior, this can snowball into a bigger change, rising from the level of habits to ideals to institutions. As the new way spreads and gets endorsed by high-status opinion leaders, it becomes idealized and often institutionalized. But this culmination is not inevitable. Occupy Wall Street drew thousands of protesters across the country to sleep in parks and practice participatory democracy, but this direct action didn't escalate into changed cultural ideals or changed institutions. It sent prevalence signals effectively but not prestige signals or precedent signals, perhaps because of its refusal to name leaders and its rejection of comparisons to previous movements. Conversely, while Gandhi, King, and many other activists infused their movements with religious ideals, they also depended on money, connections, and expertise from outside their group. Success requires judicious use of triggers and signals, but it doesn't require miracles—or perfect purity of process.

At 4:50 a.m. on Sunday, September 3, 1967, every vehicle on the roads of Sweden came to a stop in the predawn darkness. Before that morning, Swedes had always driven in the *left* lane, like in England. All their neighboring countries in Europe drove in the *right* lane, like the US. Collisions on narrow Nordic highways had been rising over the years as border crossings increased. The Swedish public didn't want to change its driving policy: in a referendum, 83 percent voted to keep driving on the left. Prominent voices defended it as a better traffic rule (just as they still do in England). Like all societies, they had come to think of their traditions, particularly their distinctive customs, as somehow more sensible or distinguished than the alternatives. After all, the left-side custom dated back to the roads of ancient Rome.

Nevertheless, the Swedish parliament decided it was prudent to join their neighbors in right-hand driving. They announced the switch day well in advance. A government commission promoted the right-lane driving with milk cartons, novelty underwear, and a song contest. Swedes knew (from holidays) how to do it. Still many skeptics expected chaos: driving on the left was a lifelong habit, a distinctive national custom, and a historic tradition—how could that all change overnight?

On this fateful morning, drivers pulled over at the designated time and waited for government instructions on the radio. Road workers and volunteers worked to unveil new signs and painted lines for right-hand driving. When the go-ahead came, drivers cautiously crossed to the opposite lane and continued their journeys. As good citizens, they followed instructions. In part because of the collective caution, accidents dropped by 40 percent. In the months that followed, public opinion swung sharply in favor of the

new policy. Media voices that had been skeptical became advocates. By year-end, driving on the right became a habit that people followed automatically and took for granted. Within a few years, sticking to the right became the norm on escalators and sidewalks as well. What started as an institutional change became a change in cultural ideals and cultural habits.

"Never doubt that a small group of thoughtful, committed citizens can change the world," anthropologist Margaret Mead said, adding, "Indeed, it is the only thing that ever has." But this final clause goes too far: some deep cultural changes start with the elites in positions of power, such as the parliament, not with ordinary people. This is a top-down sequence: an abrupt institutional change shocks the community, disrupting the settled equilibrium of behavior, precipitating changes in ideals and habits. Not only political elites, but executives, principals, and coaches can galvanize change in this top-down way through interventions to group policies and traditions.

When the switch day in Sweden was announced, critics called it drastic and dictatorial. Wouldn't it be easier to proceed more gradually? Shouldn't citizens be able to choose when to join? An incremental approach works with many kinds of changes, but not with traffic rules. It wouldn't work to allow early adopters to switch in August and laggards to wait until October. It wouldn't work to impose the change one week for motorcycles, then the next week for cars, and finally the next week also for trucks. In a domain of behavior where people are so interdependent, everyone has to switch at once. An imposed institutional change forces everyone to comply (at least when watched). The hope is that this experience gives rise to, or at least paves the way for, changes in ideals and habits.

Another example of top-down change is smoking bans. When Mayor Michael Bloomberg announced a smoking ban in New York City bars in 2002, the tabloids called him naive (and a lot of other names). Bartenders assembled outside City Hall and greeted him with a one-finger salute. But after the first smoke-free night came and went, many bar workers and patrons found themselves surprised by how much they enjoyed fresher air. Smokers developed new habits like stepping out onto the sidewalk to light up. Within a few months, smoke-free bars became the new normal, and Bloomberg recovered politically.

While Gothamites had grumbled at the ban, they didn't widely resist. Like driving, smoking outcomes are interdependent: one person's smoke winds up in another's eyes, lungs, and clothes. The problem of second-hand smoke makes it a legitimate domain for regulation. Not long after, Bloomberg proposed a ban on large-sized "sugary beverages" to address the problem of obesity and diabetes plaguing some neighborhoods. This time, New Yorkers were not having it. Vendors pressed for exceptions (smoothies, diet sodas, Frappuccinos, etc.). Neighborhood leaders argued that it had a disparate impact on poorer communities. Ultimately a judge struck down the ban for giving the health department "limitless authority." Sugar can be as dangerous to one's health as smoke, but there is no such thing as secondhand soda. Government can stop us from harming others, but only a "nanny state" stops us from harming ourselves.

People's resistance to authorities tampering with cultural institutions is the key obstacle to top-down change. In 2014 the online bulletin board Reddit realized it desperately needed an "adult in the room." It consists of millions of discussion threads that are posted and then voted up or down by its users (who skew young, male, and libertarian). This openness gives the site an unfiltered authenticity, but by 2014 it had brought two major scandals within a year: "Gamergate," which threatened female coders, and "the Fappening," which posted hacked celebrity nudes. Reddit's valuation was dropping because of advertiser wariness. Ellen Pao, a lawyer and investor who had recently joined the company, was appointed interim CEO and tasked with setting some limits. Her first policy change was a ban on posts of involuntarily shared nudes, consistent with the emerging laws against revenge porn. After this was accepted with no pushback, she issued a policy against posts that harass specific individuals, in order to foster "safe discussion," and, following from this, announced the cancelation of several offending threads (such as the 170,000-subscriber r/fatpeoplehate, which ridiculed overweight people). While this cancellation may not strike you as problematic, it was unthinkable to Redditors. Her announcement received fifteen thousand comments, mostly negative, within a few hours. They called it "censorship" by "Chairman Pao" (among other racist and sexist names). Like a CEO should in a crisis, she posted an immediate apology to users for not communicating more clearly. But this post was down-voted into oblivion by the angry online mob. Meanwhile, a change.org petition demanding her resignation quickly topped two hundred thousand signatures, and the popular groundswell forced her exit.

Pao proposed changes that looked eminently reasonable to an outsider, but to Redditors they trampled on tribal traditions. For nine years, users had created threads and voted on them to shape Reddit in a bottom-up democratic way; a new executive wasn't allowed to just cancel a thread that 170,000 Redditors read. It also sounded like their new CEO was spouting the rhetoric of "safe spaces," not that of "free speech." Corporations often hire external CEOs to "shake things up," but large-scale studies of CEO succession show that outsiders underperform precisely because they can't adeptly read the cultural nuances and avoid blowback from the firm's stakeholders. At Reddit the users are a very entitled stakeholder group because they, more than employees, build the site.

If Reddit's culture suffered from too few rules, General Motors' culture suffered from too many. For the better part of a century, GM was the world's largest automaker, and it had acquired a stultifying bureaucracy. Headquarters involved itself in the most minor decisions (e.g., the lease for a Buick office in St. Louis), reducing innovation and slowing execution. No one understood this better than Mary Barra, who came from a GM family and began working there at age eighteen, inspecting fenders at a Pontiac plant. In a long career there, she had seen that managers were not innovating because they were mired in hierarchical directives. She entered the C-suite as the firm faced its 2009 bankruptcy, but her first move didn't tackle spin-offs or downsizing. It concerned, of all things, GM's dress policy, a hodgepodge of outmoded decrees that had bloated into a ten-page booklet. It was handed to each new employee, usually with a shrug that conveyed *I don't like it either, but it comes from upstairs.* Barra replaced it with a new code that read, in full, "Dress appropriately." The immediate reaction was a wave of emails from panicked middle managers: *Can you define "appropriately"? What will stop workers from wearing offensive T-shirts?* Barra wrote back to every person but insisted that managers work with their people to agree on answers that made sense for their unit. A buzz went through the organization as GMers brainstormed about what fit their departments, and she received another wave of emails explaining the solutions they reached.

The dress code was a well-chosen target for reasons that an insider could understand. The change affected every employee, but it didn't alter operations. The old dress code was universally derided as emblematic of the broader inertia. It was refreshing for employees to make decisions about what "appropriate" meant for their role. Her gesture served notice about how the firm would be changing: It needed to drive decision-making downward. It also changed employees' daily experience. From the C-suite to the assembly line, GMers showed up in a greater diversity of styles, bringing their more authentic selves to work. It wasn't a change that started from below, but it invigorated managers and employees, and they actively partnered to implement the change.

Over the next year, the firm rose from the ashes of bankruptcy and restructuring, and there was a feeling of a fresh start. To capture this new ethos, Barra formed a task force to interview fast-rising employees about the ideals of the new GM. The recurring themes became pithy maxims like "Be Bold," "Innovate Now," and "It's on Me." The force of these new ideals became evident when a safety scandal broke out not long after she was elevated to CEO. The firm responded with greater transparency and speed than ever before. Employees committed to changed work habits such as using clearer language and preserving meeting transcripts to increase accountability. Since then have come even larger changes: GM has spun off overseas divisions and pivoted toward electric and autonomous vehicles. Barra has committed to a radically different future in a six-word statement: "Zero crashes, zero emissions, zero congestion." It's longer than the dress policy, but by only four words.

Behavioral scientists have long sought to understand the kind of ripple effects that happened among Swedish drivers, New York smokers, and GM employees. It's not the same dynamic of escalating commitment that gives grassroots sequences their momentum; that psychology doesn't operate in the same way when an authority figure has imposed a change. In classic research on authority, social psychologist Stanley Milgram recruited New Haven townspeople for studies that were ostensibly about learning from negative reinforcement—studies that became notorious. Participants, playing the teacher, were instructed to deliver electric shocks to a fellow participant, the learner, upon any incorrect answers using a control panel. (Secretly, the other participant was an actor and was merely pretending to receive painful shocks.) As the study progressed, the experimenter instructed the participant to raise the voltage of the shock, higher and higher. Most participants complied all the way up to 450 volts, a level indicated on the panel as potentially fatal. In variations of the study, Milgram found that the rate of obedience was lower if the session was held off of the Yale campus, if the experimenter was not presented as a professional scientist, and if there were two experimenters who didn't always agree. Only when participants perceived the experimenter as a *legitimate* scientific authority did they zealously comply to the level indicated as very harmful.

Milgram, and the many journalists who wrote about his findings, described this as blind obedience: participants submit and transfer their agency to the authority figure. But several recent studies reveal that participants' experience was somewhat different than that. A reanalysis of Milgram's lab records found that in exit interviews, 84 percent of participants reported feeling "glad" or "very glad" to have participated, and 77 percent felt engaged with the goal of the research. These results suggest that their response was not passive submission. It was more like active compliance or followership. They were working with the experimenter, despite their unfamiliar role as shock-delivering teachers, to support an important scientific study. Follow-up studies varied the phrases used to prod participants to deliver higher and higher shocks. Appeals to the importance of the research ("The experiment requires that you continue") succeeded more than heavy-handed assertions of authority ("You have no other choice, you must go on"). This suggests that participants were motivated to contribute to the project and trusted in the instructions of the scientist leading it.

These insights about the psychology of compliance to authority can help us understand when people accept new and unfamiliar policies and how this paves the way for other changes. People engage with an imposed change to traditions or institutions when they feel that they are acting in league with a legitimate authority, a leader with the right to rule on the matter. Most Swedes personally disfavored right-side driving, but they complied when asked by their parliament to take part in the historical change, and they came to endorse it and to do it habitually. New York's nicotine addicts grumbled about the smoking ban, but they came to see it as collectively valued and they became accustomed to sidewalk smoking breaks. GM managers fretted about the end of the established dress code, but they went along with the rethink and came to appreciate and participate in the change. Top-down momentum doesn't come from bludgeoning people into submission; it comes from activating their motivations for collaboration with legitimate authorities, contribution to the community, and coordination with those around them.

Economist Jeffrey Sachs became interested in top-down change when he noticed that historical periods of hyperinflation (e.g., in Weimar Germany) ended through a sudden stroke of policy change. Perhaps, he theorized, an economy racing out of control is like a cardiac patient with an accelerated heartbeat—it can be reset by an abrupt shock, not by a gradual intervention. Sachs had an opportunity to test this in 1989, when the new Solidarity government of Poland recruited him to help cure their country's chronic inflation. Together they designed a suite of changed policies—allowing imports and exports, floating their currency on the exchange market, ending economic protection for state-owned enterprises—to jump-start a return to a market system after decades of a command economy. When this "shock" was imposed, it stopped inflation in its tracks, but it also produced massive unemployment and disorientation. However, the Polish people didn't question the instructions from President Lech Wałęsa and his economic experts, as the pain was sold to them as the price of independence and a "return to Europe." They rallied as if in a war effort to support the fledgling market economy. Entrepreneurs were hailed as heroes, displaced workers gamely learned new skills, and consumers patronized privatized businesses. Before long, employment recovered, and the GDP climbed 80 percent higher than before liberalization. The bracing jolt of different policies and traditions galvanized the formation of new ideals and behaviors.

Boris Yeltsin's government called a few years later and Sachs consulted on another round of sweeping free-market reforms. But shock therapy didn't "take" in post-Soviet Russia in the same way. When the country's valuable natural-resource enterprises were privatized, workers received valuable shares, but most of them immediately sold them to oligarchs for ready rubles. There wasn't much admiration for those who started businesses or eagerness to learn new trades. Public opinion soon swung sharply against free-market reforms and there was nostalgia for communist central planning. Unemployment soared and a devastating depression ensued. GDP dropped by 40 percent; average life expectancy dropped by six years. It was a humanitarian disaster far worse than the Great Depression.

This experience showed economists that shock therapy for countries shouldn't be prescribed as universally as that for cardiac patients. Success of the treatment depends on some critical psychological intangibles: perceived legitimacy of the leaders and their perceived dominion over the domain. Boris Yeltsin was popular but didn't carry the same moral authority as Lech Wałęsa. It helped greatly that in Poland there was still a living memory of the needed behaviors; markets had been gone for only forty years and they had lingered in some sectors like agriculture. And the return to the market institutions was associated with independence. In Russia, there had been no markets for seventy years, and the return to them felt like capitulation to an enemy system. It didn't help that the change coincided with the loss of an empire. Government and business leaders can't *force* people to engage with and enact a new strategy. Top-down shock therapy works only when people have "buy-in" to the authority and its initiative as well as "know-how" to engage in the new behaviors.

A few years ago, LEGO overtook Ferrari in a ranking of the world's most powerful brands. But LEGO wasn't always in the fast lane. The family-run toy maker from Billund, Denmark, plodded along steadily for its first sixty years, never posting a loss. It transitioned from handmade wooden blocks to mass-produced plastic bricks in Mondrian-inspired colors that gradually found a global audience. But by the turn of the twenty-first century, kids raised on PlayStation and Nintendo were not so dazzled by bright plastic bricks. Taking inspiration from how Mattel had diversified beyond Barbie, LEGO launched theme parks, jewelry, and clothing divisions. They retired the firm's aging design staff and hired graduates of Europe's top design schools, who produced sets that were centered on new TV shows and included idiosyncratic (and expensive) pieces like illuminated fiber optic cables. These complicated LEGO sets piled up unsold in warehouses and losses deepened.

In 2003 a young executive named Jørgen Vig Knudstorp surprised LEGO's board with numbers that showed the firm was fast heading for bankruptcy. A former McKinsey consultant, Knudstorp had been hired as a director of strategy two years before to provide an outsider's view.

Half-expecting to be fired, Knudstorp was instead given a larger team to continue his analysis. A year later, at age thirty-five, Knudstorp was appointed the new CEO, the first outside the founding family. He called for a return to the company's tradition of simple sets that can build a wide variety of structures, reducing the inventory (and thereby manufacturing costs) of the sets. He sold off the parks, jewelry, and attire divisions. He required his new designers to live, like anthropologists, with families that had small children—to observe how children play, how they build things, and how they unbuild and recombine things. It was a humbling time, but employees understood the need for cost-cutting and course corrections.

The experience of change prompted new insights and new work habits. Designers learned that many parents are LEGO fans, as much as their kids. The firm started interacting with adult users through their website— and before long these superfans were proposing product ideas and evaluating the proposals of others. The firm was among the first to realize how online crowdsourcing and "co-creation" could save on design, market research, and marketing costs. From this LEGO noticed how easily their pixel-like product lent itself to digital rendering, and they began producing mobile games and digital apps that simulated physical building as well as animated shorts that won awards. This led to the surprisingly successful *LEGO Movie*, a postmodern toy story (which Mattel mirrored in their recent Barbie movie). LEGO has become not just the world's most valuable toy company but something beyond that. Block by block, the Danish company remade itself into a pioneer of products spanning the actual and virtual realms.

LEGO's decade-long drama of reinvention involved more twists and turns than either the bottom-up or the top-down strategy. But there is an arc to this change story that may seem somewhat familiar and that involves the tribal ripple effects we've explored in this chapter. Long-term transformational change often incorporates both the commitment-based momentum of the grassroots strategy and the compliance-based momentum of the shock-wave strategy. Knudstorp was a semi-outsider who came from the consulting industry. Consulting firms offer guided change management as a multiyear engagement, not unlike psychoanalysis for a corporation. Firms that offer this service—whether generalists like McKinsey or specialists on change like Kotter—conceptualize transformation as a sequence of steps. While they vary in number (there are seven-, eight-, ten-, and twelve-step models) and nomenclature (every firm needs its own!), most are elaborations of Kurt Lewin's classic insight that a cultural transition requires an "unfreezing" of the old pattern before the development and "refreezing" of the new pattern. The component steps within the unfreezing stage roughly correspond to the shock-wave strategy. The steps within the development and refreezing stage roughly correspond to a grassroots strategy. In other words, killing the old culture happens top-down, then building the new culture happens bottom-up.

The process of a guided transformation tends to start with a top-down dynamic. Detaching from the old order is painful, requiring the speed of the shock-wave strategy. Change management models include steps with labels like "create dissatisfaction," "form a guiding coalition," and "communicate the change vision." Some consultants favor analogies to a "burning platform," lighting a fire under employees so they are willing to leap into the unknown, as offshore oil rig workers do when the platform catches fire. No one likes change, but when it's "jump or fry," employees become more willing to make a leap of faith. Knudstorp emphasized that LEGO's current way of doing things meant bankruptcy. This created an incentive for the company to consider his proposal of radical reduction of products and businesses to cut costs.

The second half of transformational change is the bottom-up process of building and locking in the new culture. In the labels for these steps—"remove barriers," find short-term wins," "build on the change," and "institute the change"—we can recognize the grassroots sequence that we've seen in examples like Ambato's punctuality campaign and Gandhi's independence movement. After the top-down dismantling of the diversification strategy that had led the company astray, LEGO began a bottom-up process of escalating commitment to digital approaches. The process started with new habits (using crowdsourcing to develop new ideas), then produced new ideals (reaffirming that LEGO was a company devoted to building things, in both physical and virtual realms). Eventually, the company even institutionalized its digital transformation by partnering with a potential competitor, Fortnite developer Epic Games, to build a metaverse of block structures. This is quite a journey for a family firm from a small town in Denmark that made its name selling wooden blocks. But it is the culmination of a long process of top-down, and then bottom-up, transformation.

The arc of the LEGO story illustrates how two different momentum dynamics can be marshaled in one extended metamorphisis. If the story arc feels familiar, that's because it echoes an archetypal tale about a tribe's transition. In Exodus, the second book of the Bible, Moses is a semi-outsider who is sent to guide the Israelites on a physical journey out of Egypt and a spiritual transition from slavery to self-mastery. His challenge at first is to "unfreeze" the normative order in Egypt. No matter how meager their life in Egypt, the Israelites had become accustomed to it and were reluctant to leave it for something completely unknown. And the Pharaoh felt highly resistant to letting the Israelites go. So Moses called down plagues to disrupt the institutions of life and make the status quo intolerable. Then he talked to the Israelite elders about the promise made to their ancestors, and they shared a vision of a land flowing with milk and honey.

The Israelites agreed to prepare for a short journey, and the Pharaoh agreed to let them visit the desert temporarily. The journey began with a few steps and became a daily trek. The Red Sea posed a barrier, so Moses parted the waters for them to pass; when the sea rushed back in, a pursuing army was engulfed and the path of retreat was removed, increasing the tribe's commitment to continue. Still, there was murmuring in the ranks: *Are we there yet? What do we eat? What was so bad about Egypt anyway?* Decades of slavery had degraded them, so Moses taught them the virtues of gathering manna and honoring the Sabbath. He appointed respected men as judges to teach ideals to others. Then, citing the precedent of the ancient covenant, he climbed Mount Sinai to receive the ten commandments that would structure their society. The new desert culture started with changed habits, then fresh ideals, and ultimately new institutions. It takes only a few days to walk from Egypt to Israel, but Moses kept them on the journey for four decades until the group was ready for its promised land.

The point is not that Moses was the original management consultant. His initial pitch referred to a burning *bush*, not a burning platform! Rather, the point is that the Exodus story—a forceful break from the ossified accustomed order, then the slow cultivation of a new community—reflects how age-old tribal psychology structures a group's transformation. This myth has inspired countless generations of changemakers for a reason. It teaches a simple lesson about the recurrent dynamics of tribal change. Leaders can transform a tribe, but it requires breaking the old culture before nurturing the growth of something new.

8

Toxic Tribalism
and Its Antidotes

Maybe we pushed too far. Maybe people
just want to fall back into their tribe.

—Barack Obama

illary Clinton's 2016 election-night bash was at the Jacob Javits
Convention Center, chosen for the symbolism of its glass ceil-
ings. After working as a behavioral science consultant for her
campaign, I was excited to be there for its historic culmination. She had
held a commanding lead in the polls for months. We all thought the election had been sewn up since the summer, and we looked forward to an
inspiring victory speech.

The room rippled with excitement as prominent politicos arrived—
advisers, politicians, and fundraisers—some of whom I'd met before and
many of whom I recognized only from television. Millennial staffers wearing "The Future Is Female" T-shirts greeted them excitedly. Some of
Clinton's contemporaries wore bright blue pantsuits, in homage to her
campaign uniform.

Early in the evening, the giant overhead screens showed CNN "calling" East Coast states like Maryland and Connecticut. As Wolf Blitzer turned each state blue on the color-coded map, the crowd cheered and clinked glasses. I could hear in their voices that it meant more than other elections, especially for the women in blue. Finally, it was their turn!

As hours passed, though, the festive mood began to lose some of its fizz. Ohio, Florida, and North Carolina were called red. The celebratory buzz was replaced by increasingly nervous chatter. No one was talking about a Clinton landslide anymore. Some people took phone calls and others fiddled with their devices in search of reassuring news. My own phone buzzed with texts from friends:

> Should I be worried?
> Is it going to be ok?
> WTF?

The room grew quieter still as more states on the election map turned red, including Pennsylvania, which had polled blue. What the hell was going on? As paths to victory narrowed, the gathered Democrats reassured each other by tallying up the electoral votes of the remaining states expected to be blue. There was an ominous delay in the news about Wisconsin and Michigan. Some people looked at their phones and began quietly sobbing. Others swore aloud in anger. Septuagenarians in front of me shook arthritic fists. I looked up at the giant screen to see a smugly smiling photograph of "President-elect Donald J. Trump."

It was like a bad dream. I felt blindsided: I had been *sure* Clinton would win. Everyone I knew had thought so too. I couldn't help but suspect some kind of foul play, even though I had no evidence for any. I felt a visceral anger rising in me and thought it better to leave. I worked my way out through crowd after crowd in the labyrinthine building and then in cordoned sections outside in the parking lot and the street—everyone staring at screens, dazed and distraught. I walked for many blocks, unable to find a cab.

Finally, I hopped into the back of an Uber Pool. The other rider, a thirty-something blonde in a silk gown and pearls, waved hello with a relaxed smile (the first I'd seen in hours).

"Coming from *the* event?" she trilled.

"At the Javits Center?" I asked.

"*No*, the Midtown Hilton . . ."

The pieces fell abruptly into place. She was one of *them*—a Trump supporter!

After several minutes of awkward silence, curiosity overcame me. "Were the folks at *your* event surprised at the outcome?" I asked.

"Not a bit," she answered. "He's been surging in the Midwest, and no one *likes* her!" She then reeled off some factoids about Trump's campaign momentum, none of which I'd heard before.

I hadn't expected to meet a Trump supporter that night. But even less had I expected to meet one so utterly unsurprised. All the evidence I had seen pointed to a Clinton landslide. But this apparently evidence-based Republican had been equally sure that *her* candidate would prevail. We shared a ride but didn't share the same reality.

How, I wondered, could this parallel reality possibly exist? And if half of the country lived in that reality, how could I have been so utterly unaware of its existence?

The rift between the "realities" of Republicans and Democrats has continued to grow—and, along with it, mutual mistrust. Red and blue voters don't socialize with each other anymore—even on dating sites. Cell phone location data reveals, sadly, that politically mixed families have cut short their Thanksgiving dinners in recent years. In the 2018 midterms, the Democratic defeat in Georgia was greeted with denial and lawsuits. Come

2020, after the "red wave" turned into a "blue shift," the Stop the Steal movement filed lawsuits and pressured state officials in an effort to halt the transfer of power, culminating in the January 6 march on the Capitol—to Democrats, an insurrection; to many Republicans, true patriotism. Americans now say they expect violence from the losing side in future elections, a large fraction adding that they might support that violence if it comes from their side.

And, of course, the rift is as pronounced *inside* the Capitol as it is outside. As congresspeople of the two parties have come to inhabit increasingly separate realities, they've lost the ability to "reach across the aisle" to pass legislation. Our democracy depends on legislative negotiation, the ability to see just what concession is needed to make a bill acceptable to the other side. But bipartisan legislation, which is needed for lasting programs, hardly happens anymore. Legislative gridlock has become the rule, with recent congresses failing to come to agreements on almost every issue they've faced. This gives rise to more executive unilateralism that further inflames partisan resentments.

These breakdowns in the functioning of our two-party system—election denial and congressional gridlock—don't merely hinder government performance; they also undermine public faith in democratic institutions. Experts worry that they could bring about the demise of our democracy. An account for all of this is "tribalism," sometimes "toxic tribalism." It's a phrase increasingly heard in debates, tweets, and call-in radio rants. Political journalists have tried to spell out what it means. Thomas Friedman mused that the US has caught a "virus of tribalism" from our Middle East adventuring, a mentality of seeing political opponents as mortal enemies rather than fellow citizens, implying that elections not won must be denied. Andrew Sullivan described the reawakening of a long-buried urge for blind allegiance and primal hate for outsiders, somehow stirred by this historical moment. Alex Altman of *Time* attributed the change to an inimicable "tribal warrior" who entered our presidential politics and forced others to respond in kind. The pundits differ about the inciting cause, but these accounts all describe toxic tribalism as the unlocking of a primal fear and loathing, a genie escaped from the bottle that we can't put back again.

This trope of toxic tribalism makes for colorful journalism but not necessarily for accurate understanding or practical solutions. It is true, as we have seen in the foregoing chapters, that our species evolved psychological systems that distinguish "Us" from "Them," and the resulting cognitive biases and motivational drives guide our behavior in politics and many other realms of life. But the tribal instincts we have reviewed do not include blind hate for outsiders. Evolution focused its group-related motives on "Us," the in-groups that kept our forebears alive day-to-day, not "Them," the out-groups that our forebears encountered only occasionally. Humans evolved solidaristic instincts to unify, help, and preserve their groups that involve different kinds of shared knowledge. Although these instincts can indirectly contribute to conflicts with other groups, solidarity within the group does not directly entail hostility toward other groups. Conflicts can escalate to hostility, but assuming that they start from hostility is inaccurate and unhelpful.

For a better understanding of the partisan conflict straining US democracy and the role of our evolved group psychology within it, we can do better by focusing on the three tribal instincts that we have come to know in this book. These are psychological systems for meshing with peers, helping the clan, and maintaining the tribe. These drives have helped human groups survive from the Stone Age to today because they guide constructive collaboration. If we were wired to obsess about outsiders and reflexively hate them, we would never have come so far as a species. That said, however, these solidaristic processes can ripple out of the healthy range at times. Each tribal instinct can spin out of control under certain conditions due to chain reactions and feedback loops.

A first step in understanding a group conflict, then, is to look for signs of an out-of-range "Us" instinct. Has peer-instinct meshing metastasized into delusional groupthink? Has hero-instinct helping become clannish favoritism that undermines broader justice? Has ancestor-instinct traditionalism turned into attacks on another tribe's institutions and legitimacy? The next step is to look for the chain reactions and feedback loops involved. If we can spot which tribal instinct is at fault, then we infer which kinds of triggers and signals are involved in the problem—and also what kinds can be involved in remediating it. This is not to say that thinking in terms of the three basic tribal instincts will enable you to solve all of the group conflicts in the world, but I promise you you'll have better responses than if you assume that conflicts start from primal hate for outsiders.

In the case of the troubles afflicting the US two-party system, it's not hard to spot a central role of peer-instinct conformity. Recall Asch's experiment in which participants conformed to the incorrect majority over the evidence of their own eyes. Further studies found that participants carry their conformist judgments into new interactions and influence those people. Political parties these days have become like Asch experiments on steroids. Most partisans take in a steady stream of similar opinions all day long—from their neighbors, news shows, and online networks. More than ever before, they have opportunities to express partisan views and gain validation and admiration for doing so. This cycle of conformist learning and conformist expression has produced ideologically inbred communities. When all of the other villagers attest to the beauty of the emperor's new clothes, it's hard *not* to see them.

Historically, in the US, institutions such as the free press and public debates helped citizens get exposure to diverse viewpoints on political questions. These institutions, and the First Amendment that safeguards them, are founded on the premise that free speech should be allowed so that truth can prevail. Supreme Court decisions reduced this premise to the metaphor that true ideas win out in the "competition of the market." This competition helps the advancement of ideas, though it can be stressful for the individuals involved (especially those with certainty-seeking personalities). Fortunately, Americans could take solace in like-minded communities (religious congregations, ethnic neighborhoods, union chapters, veterans' halls, etc.) where they could experience consensus and epistemic security. Political parties did not play this psychological role in the old days because they were heterogeneous categories. Through most of the twentieth century, both parties had a more liberal wing and a more conservative wing. Also, party membership didn't carry with it particular visible ways of life. Aside from those few zealots who planted signs on their lawns every few years, it wasn't easy to know who of your acquaintances was a Republican and who was a Democrat.

By the late twentieth century, however, these structures of belonging were in flux. Participation in religious congregations dramatically diminished. "None" became the most common answer to survey questions about religious affiliation. In his 2000 book *Bowling Alone*, sociologist Robert Putnam reported the waning of community associations: Americans bowled more than ever but didn't bowl in leagues anymore. For better or worse (but mostly for better), fewer Americans lived in ethnically homogenous neighborhoods. Instead, people of the same partisan feather increasingly "flocked together": Democrats relocated to coastal cities and college towns, while Republicans gravitated to the heartland and the countryside. Political party membership increasingly overlapped with other divides such as old/young, white/non-white, and straight/queer. As the like-minded groups of past generations waned, party leanings became increasingly visible and filled the vacuum.

At the same time, the news media landscape was splintering. The politically balanced newspapers and TV networks that had served Americans across the spectrum became increasingly supplanted by ever-more-partisan cable channels, websites, and social media networks. While Americans consume more news than ever (and hence feel highly confident), most see only a subset of the full range of political news and opinion. It's not the technology's fault; a more rational species could use the increased choice to challenge and refine their understandings, but we the tribal species use it to wallow in news with a congenial slant. We surround ourselves with a like-minded media community and we acquire incomplete, inaccurate understandings as a result.

Social media also greatly facilitates the expression of political beliefs to gain peer acceptance and validation. We don't have to talk at a political meeting. We don't even have to call in to a talk radio show. We just type a phrase or paste a link from a news site and the "likes" and approving comments from our partisan peers roll in. Social media platforms tweaked their algorithms to become more viral, and a powerful new wave of conformist signals came into our lives.

Our peer instinct (and the withering of the groups that traditionally accommodated it) gave rise to partisan "bubbles" in our residential communities and in our online communities. These bubbles surround us with peers bearing confirmatory news and opinions, insulating us from opposing viewpoints. But beyond that, they also become echo chambers: they facilitate conformist expression and provide supportive peer responses. This cycle of conformist learning and conformist behavior has tightened the consensus within the red and blue parties and broadened the gap between them.

Increasingly, it's also produced divergent views of reality. The red and blue factions always disagreed in subjective evaluations (*Is the president doing a good job?*) but increasingly they disagree about objective facts (*Is the president a Muslim?*). By the 2016 election, the two camps held different factual beliefs about global warming, fracking, Clinton's emails, Trump's ties to Russia, and many other matters. Because we are not conscious of reaching conclusions through peer-instinct conformist learning, we (naively) regard our beliefs about these matters as direct reflections of reality. The combination of partisan falsehoods and our "naive realism" gives rise to flawed predictions. Both Republicans and Democrats predict that Independents share their take on any given issue (*How could they not see it in this "reality-based" way?*). Hence both sides expect to win in a close election. They may make campaign errors as a result. The losing side feels genuinely surprised at the returns on election night.

We also form warped perceptions of the opposing party. Because we are unaware that our own beliefs are politically filtered, the other side's beliefs appear highly distorted; "they" must be blinded by ideology or self-interest. Republicans believe that 38 percent of Democrats are gay, lesbian, or bisexual, when it's actually 6 percent. Democrats believe that 44 percent of Republicans earn over $250,000 per year, when in fact it's 2 percent. Republicans estimate that 50 percent of Democrats endorse the statement "Most police are bad people"; it's really only 15 percent. Democrats estimate that only half of Republicans accept that "racism is still a problem in America"; in reality, 79 percent do.

This is "epistemic tribalism." Through runaway peer-instinct processing, tribal conformity increasingly comes before truth. Americans increasingly acquired their political beliefs through conformity—accelerated by residential and online bubbles—until their worldviews diverged. As a result, they feel surprised by, and distrusting of, the election returns. They find the opposite party baffling, impossible to communicate or cooperate with, and hence sometimes infuriating, frightening, or disgusting. Previous generations held strong stereotypes and animosities across the lines of religion or ethnicity, but nowadays, surveys show that political party is the divide where social prejudice is strongest. To be sure, Democrats and Republicans feel negatively toward each other, but this arises from the rift in worldviews—not from a primordial hate for outsiders.

When I look back on 2016, part of me finds it a little depressing that, even as a psychologist studying cultural biases, I was so susceptible to epistemic tribalism. I eagerly assimilated the blue tribe verities of my surrounding communities. I was overconfident, felt blindsided, and reacted with distrust. I'm glad, in any case, that the chance event of a shared ride home started a process of talking to the other side more. Exposing oneself to a new situation or a new piece of information can be the first step toward breaking the cycle of epistemic tribalism.

▼

You can probably guess whether a neighborhood skews red or blue by the way its residents talk: "God-given prosperity" or "white privilege"? Or by the music you hear: country or hip hop? Or by their rides: pickups or Priuses? Political analyst Dave Wasserman calculated that 78 percent of all Whole Foods, but only 27 percent of all Cracker Barrels, are sited within Democratic districts. A Brooks Brothers tells of the red tribe, Lululemon the blue.

These red or blue clues, of course, are *signs* of the partisan tribes. When a Democrat passes a Whole Foods or Lululemon on the way to work, it triggers blue-tribe habits like using "they" as a singular pronoun. When a Republican sees a Cracker Barrel or a Brooks Brothers, it readies red-tribe reflexes like greeting veterans with "Thank you for your service." Having your partisan mindset cued is a mixed blessing: it eases the process of meshing and bonding with locals, but it can set your mind on the trajectory to conventional liberal (or conventional conservative) answers. If you are working on a local problem, this may work. But if you are continually thinking this way, your imagination will be limited; you won't come up with solutions that integrate different kinds of concerns and find acceptance on a broader scale.

One way to escape limiting partisan triggers is by planting yourself in a different political culture. When your partisan identity is not constantly triggered, you will more easily develop understandings of other worldviews and be able to imagine ideas that span partisan divides. A fascinating example is the performer Lil Nas X, who grew up in the projects of Atlanta, steeped in hip hop culture. During his high school years, he decamped to live with his father in the suburbs and became immersed in "meme culture," and then chose a college in rural western Georgia where he heard a lot of country music. All these influences came together in "Old Town Road," a hit on both blue-tribe and red-tribe charts. Similarly, Pete Buttigieg took a leave in 2014 from serving as mayor of his college town—South Bend, Indiana—to deploy with the Navy to Afghanistan. This change of setting and associates no doubt helped him formulate the talking points that played well in the 2016 purple-state primaries. Perhaps if Hillary Clinton's campaign had been based outside of a blue bubble, everyone involved would have noticed the disconnects with voters in Michigan and Wisconsin. Its Brooklyn headquarters was ringed by signs of the blue tribe—vegan cafés, progressive schools, acupuncture clinics—that kept blue tribe preconceptions top of mind.

A related point about partisan signs is that we should mind our tribal language when trying to persuade the other side. Stanford's Matthew Feinberg and Robb Willer found that political advocates tend to use their own party's habitual rhetoric. But when trying to persuade the other political tribe, it works better to employ *their* tribal lexicon (for example, instead of environmentalists invoking social justice, they could invoke the "sanctity of the earth" to persuade conservatives). The right tribal signs can be critical in making a plan palatable: Republicans reject a "carbon tax" but accept a "carbon offset." Increasingly, environmentalists have used clerics and faith-based language to lobby conservative-leaning politicians.

A longer-term remediation strategy looks beyond immediate triggers to the signals that inform and update people's blue-tribe or red-tribe preconceptions. After concerns about the role of media in the 2016 election, many technologists devised tools to allay media bias. FlipFeed, for instance, is a plug-in that sends you a Twitter (now X) feed from the political camp opposite to your own. In 2017, Duke's Chris Bail tested the underlying concept by paying partisan Twitter users to follow a bot that retweeted twenty-four messages a day for a month from the other side's opinion leaders: Republicans were piped posts from sources like Barack Obama, while Democrats received updates from the likes of Donald Trump. Before and after surveys about political issues revealed an effect opposite than intended: Republicans grew significantly more conservative and Democrats became slightly more liberal.

This backfire effect reflects that people have defenses against signals that strike them as suspicious, such as out-group sources imposed upon them to correct them. After Obama publicized his long-form birth certificate in 2011, the share of Republicans who believed he was foreign-born *increased* rather than decreased. Social psychologists have long observed that partisans dismiss evidence that weighs against their side's cherished beliefs but embrace the same kinds of evidence when it weighs in favor. Dan Kahan of Yale Law School finds that this selectivity in scrutiny occurs most for those with high education levels. People use their educations to defend themselves against evidence from outsiders that challenges their beliefs.

But partisans *can* listen to people from the other side, so long as they come across as *people*, rather than as *from the other side*. University of Pennsylvania sociologist Damon Centola asked red and blue partisans to play a climate forecasting game: they predicted a climate-relevant metric before and after sharing views with a bipartisan group. Participants saw a NASA chart of Arctic ice thickness over recent decades with a down-sloping, but zigzagging, line; they were asked to extrapolate from this to predict the thickness in 2025. Consistent with partisan peer codes, Democrats tended to guess a big drop while Republicans forecasted little change. After communicating with a politically diverse group of peers (without knowing these peers' party affiliations), participants made second-round estimates. For the most part, these updated estimates moved in the direction of greater accuracy. The prevalence signal that came from exposure to a broad set of opinions worked to allay their initial partisan biases. Meanwhile, in a different condition that highlighted the peers' Democratic or Republican affiliations, the second-round forecasts didn't become more accurate. The lesson is that when political affiliations are highly salient, people's defenses spring up to block their learning from the other side.

Perhaps this is why we haven't seen dramatic progress from the wave of red-blue dialogue programs that have rolled out in recent years, such as Bridge the Divide, Hi From The Other Side, and Urban Rural Action. By emphasizing to participants that they are conversing with "the other side," programs like these may raise people's defenses. Perhaps counterintuitively, experiments by Columbia University's Erik Santoro and UC Berkeley's David Broockman found that interparty conversations on a *non*political topic ("a perfect day") worked better than on a politicized topic. Another kind of program puts people into interparty conversations about nonpolitical interests like food, coffee, or faith (e.g., Make America Dinner Again, Coffee Party USA, Civic Spirit). These may work better to launch conversations that are nonconfrontational and that continue beyond the session to exert long-term effects.

People are also pliable when a prevalence signal comes from the behavior of their own party. Psychologist Geoffrey Cohen presented Yale undergraduates with a faked newspaper article about a congressional vote on a welfare plan and asked them whether they personally favor the plan. In different versions of the article, the policy was either generous or stringent in its provisions to the needy. Information about the voting was another factor that varied in the experiment: either Republicans predominantly supported the plan or Democrats predominantly supported it. Strikingly, students' evaluations of the plan were affected by the party information more than by the policy information. When informed that most of the congresspeople from their party voted for the plan, they evaluated it positively—regardless of whether the welfare benefits were generous or stringent! When asked the basis for their evaluation, they denied that the prevalence signal affected them; instead, they rationalized why the policy details—a generous (or stringent) policy—fit their "philosophy of government." We are not usually aware of how tribal signals affect us, and we are very good at inventing post hoc explanations for our behaviors.

When the pundits proposed that partisan conflicts arise from a toxic tribalism of primal hostility, they were close but not on target. The conflict involves tribal psychology and there are hostilities, to be sure. But hostility is not where the problem starts, and thinking so yields no useful solutions. We've seen that by recognizing the "Us" instinct at the heart of the problem (peer-instinct conformity), we can understand how it escalated in the past decade and we can identify interventions related to peer-instinct triggers (red and blue signs) and signals (prevalence signals from media exposure, interactions, messages). There are no instant solutions, but politicians and citizen groups employing these tactics have been making progress.

Unfortunately, partisan conflict is hardly the only contemporary chauvinism to be chalked up to resurgent tribal hostilities. Racial inequity has risen to the center of the public discourse in the past few years, and pundits like Tucker Carlson believe that schools are "creating tribalism" in the way they teach about race. Additionally, terrorist attacks and military attacks on people of different religions are explained as a reversion to tribal rage. However, we should be wary of an all-purpose explanation, especially one that invokes an instinct that few evolutionists would recognize. Tempting though it may be to distance these ugly conflicts from our everyday psychology, doing so prevents us from seeing the best ways to remediate them.

▼

When attorneys Morris Seligman Dees and Joseph Levin founded the Southern Poverty Law Center (SPLC) in 1971, their office was a humble one-story building in an old residential neighborhood of Montgomery, Alabama. They started with classic civil rights cases against racial discrimination in workplaces, prisons, and other settings. In the 1980s, however, Dees began to shift the focus to suing the Ku Klux Klan for damages on behalf of victims. Little was ever collected, as the Klan was by then economically moribund, but Dees's courtroom takedowns of Klan "soldiers" and "imperial wizards" consistently won national press. When Klan affiliates firebombed the office one night, he looked like a present-day Atticus Finch. The SPLC's direct-mail fundraising operation flourished.

When the Center's legal team departed en masse to pursue more standard civil rights work elsewhere, Dees found an associate of Levin's, Richard Cohen, to take over as legal director, and Cohen in turn brought on a former student, Rhonda Brownstein. Together they developed the center's influential hate group list and its popular *Hatewatch* newsletter. By the turn of the millennium, the SPLC had a nine-figure endowment, a new building, and a national profile as a bastion against racial oppression.

Writer Bob Moser reflected on his experience driving down to Montgomery around this time to join the good fight, "self-righteous about the work before I'd even begun it." Expecting to join a scrappy band of lawyers tirelessly defending clients under difficult conditions, he instead arrived at a gleaming postmodern steel-and-cement tower, which locals had dubbed "the Poverty Palace." He was perplexed by the organization's overwhelming focus on direct-mail fundraising, and even more by its lack of racial equity. The executive layer was almost all white, while the administrative staff, who sarcastically called themselves "the help," were mostly Black.

Skeptical journalists had called out this discrepancy, but Dees demurred that if anything their recruitment bias was "reverse discrimination": "It is not easy to find black lawyers. Any organization will tell you that." He and other white executives sometimes offended African American employees in everyday comments, such as by casually comparing work to slavery. One of the few lawyers of color recounted that during a racial bias training, Brownstein, the newly appointed legal director (following Cohen's ascent to the presidency), asked during the Q and A sessions: "What if people are . . . saying things are racism but they're just wrong?" It's a question that must be asked at times, but in the context, it seemed to signal that leadership doubted there was racial bias in the organization.

Nevertheless, the rise of alt-right groups over the past decade made Dees's focus look prescient, especially after the 2017 white supremacist Unite the Right rally in Charlottesville. The center's endowment ballooned to nearly half a billion dollars, exceeding that of the ACLU and that of most universities. The abundance funded several new initiatives, such as the interactive *Hate Map* website and the *Sounds Like Hate* podcast. Yet the racial inequity within the organization became increasingly unbearable.

Tensions reached a flashpoint when Deputy Legal Director Meredith Horton, one of the highest-ranking African American employees, resigned, stating that the center was not a place "where the values we are committed to pursuing externally are also being practiced internally." An employee group presented a list of concerns to the board, and several days later, Dees was terminated. Within a matter of weeks, Cohen and Brownstein had also resigned.

The implosion at the SPLC is a paradox. How could lawyers and thought leaders who dedicated their careers to fighting discrimination have perpetrated it in their own backyard? Some contributing factors are obvious. Leaders like Dees were confident in their virtue, casual in their hiring practices, and not very conscious of how their words came across. But there is also a lesson here about two kinds of discrimination: the hostility toward ethnic minorities that the SPLC monitored in extremist groups, and a more innocuous-seeming favoritism toward one's own kind that may actually be a bigger problem.

While the failings of inclusion and equity at SPLC were egregious, they are not uncommon. Despite the proliferation of diversity programs by organizations in the past decade, the incomes of Black and white Americans have stopped converging and by some metrics have started to diverge again. When Obama was first elected, some optimists hailed a "post-racial" America. Instead, the year 2020 brought the largest protests of racial injustice in history. Non-whites report ethnic discrimination in particular settings. Mistreatment by the police was experienced in the past year by 18 percent of Black, 11 percent of Hispanic, and 3 percent of white Americans. Meanwhile, workplace mistreatment was even more common, experienced by 21 percent of Black, 16 percent of Hispanic, and 4 percent of white Americans.

Other evidence proves that differential treatment is real, not just a matter of perception. Suppose an entry-level job listing receives applications from Greg Smith, Jamal Jones, and José Cruz. Who is more likely to get called for an interview? Researchers test this by sending off fake résumés with equivalent qualifications but different (implied) ethnicities. A recent meta-analysis of thirty years of these field experiments found that white applicants receive on average 36 percent more callbacks than Black applicants and 24 percent more callbacks than Hispanic applicants—rates of discrimination that remained largely unchanged over this period.

As the trope of toxic tribalism has come into vogue, many business journalists and consultants have explained ethnic discrimination in the workplace this way. These accounts posit that executives and managers, who are mostly white, negatively evaluate non-white applicants and employees based on ethnic animus. There can be no doubt that the white gatekeepers of organizations acted on this motive a century or half a century ago. However, national surveys reveal that ethnic hostilities have declined steeply since then while unequal treatment is still rampant. It's perplexing that discrimination remains despite reduced ethnic hostility (whether rooted in tribal rage or otherwise), given the conventional wisdom that discrimination follows from animosities. How can we have the former without the latter?

In response to this conundrum, behavioral scientists have considered whether discrimination and inequality can arise in a different way. White employers may feel ethnic animosity upon seeing the names Jamal or José on a résumé, but they also may feel ethnic *affinity* upon seeing the name Greg. The motive to lift up one's in-group is psychologically distinct from the motive to hold down an out-group. It's a positive impulse toward "Us," not a negative reflex toward "Them." Surveys of social attitudes find that positive feelings toward one's own race are *ten times* more frequent than strongly negative feelings toward other races. While this could reflect that survey-takers are loath to admit racial animosities, the same pattern shows in behavioral evidence from children—they express ethnic in-group positivity from age three but don't develop ethnic out-group aversion until age six. (There are methodological challenges in studying preschoolers, but political correctness is not one of them.) The primacy of the in-group motive makes evolutionary sense, given that toddlers would have depended for survival on in-group bonds and rarely interacted with out-groups.

In his second inaugural in March 1865, President Lincoln called upon Americans to act "with malice toward none, and with charity towards all." For managers, charity involves allocating discretionary attention and resources: giving an unusual résumé the benefit of the doubt or offering a tongue-tied interviewee a second chance to answer a question. Hence, discrimination can come from both the malice that Lincoln renounced and the *charity* he requested, if the charity is not extended to all. But charity toward *all* is a difficult, if not impossible, standard. We all act charitably at times, often impulsively, but not all day long, if only because our time and resources are limited. Generosity comes from hero-instinct impulses, but they don't operate in every interaction. We are wired to give to our clan or community—not to all of humanity. (Evolutionary biologists call this selectivity "parochial altruism.") Although we belong to many communities, the old saying "Blood is thicker than water" conveys an undeniable truth. Shared race or ethnicity triggers the impulse of generosity more powerfully than shared profession or shared organization. Hence, job applicants of the same "blood" as most hiring managers stand to benefit from these hero-instinct impulses. This is particularly problematic in societies like ours, where one ethnic group controls most economic opportunities; their unconscious in-group favoritism can work to reproduce the ethnic inequality.

A rare study of workplace discrimination that distinguishes in-group generosity from out-group hostility supports in-group favoritism's primary role. Researchers trained aspiring actors to interview for jobs as waiters (not a big stretch for most of them). Pairs of actors—one white and one racial minority—presented equally qualified résumés and gave similar scripted answers during interviews with hiring managers (who were predominantly white). After the interviews, the interviewees tallied the acts of generosity (e.g., spent extra time with them) and of impoliteness (e.g., failed to greet them by name) that they experienced. On average, minorities did not experience *more impoliteness*, but they did experience *less generosity*. In the end, minorities were only half as likely to receive a job offer.

This kind of selective helping during hiring occurs in immigrant communities, where sociologists call it "ethnic opportunity hoarding." But the biggest opportunity hoarders are whites. Interviews by Nancy DiTomaso of Rutgers Business School found that 70 percent of US whites found their current job through the help of people they knew, usually other whites. (Whites tend to have networks that are 90 percent white.) Organizations have HR procedures to prevent nepotism and to promote diversity, but informal network-based processes operate in tandem. Hiring managers "send out feelers" to their contacts, and candidates enlist their connections to "put in a good word" for them. The SPLC was typical in this respect: it had committed to the goal of hiring Black lawyers, but it filled critical slots with white candidates sourced from personal networks, like Cohen and Brownstein.

Candidates hired through connections onboard more quickly and stay longer. Firms have increasingly adopted hiring policies to facilitate this kind of fit. Policies of selecting for "cultural fit," for instance, allow hiring managers to weigh intangible factors. A study of several "white-shoe" consulting firms observed a surprising focus on lacrosse, crew, and squash backgrounds (sports that may fit the corporate culture but are also undeniably WASPy). Another trend is formalized referral programs that ask employees to nominate people they know for open positions. At accounting firm Ernst & Young, fully half of all non-rookie hires are now referrals. At Sodexo, a facilities management firm, referral candidates are ten times more likely to be hired than external applicants. The downside, again, is diversity. A study by economist Giorgio Topa found that 72 percent of managers refer associates of the same race and ethnicity.

If ethnic in-group generosity has always been a source of discrimination in hiring, the HR trends of the past decade have turbocharged the process. The motivation of in-group generosity has drawn firms toward employee-referral systems and "culture fit" selection. In turn, these programs have legitimated favoritism in hiring. This metastasis of hero-instinct giving can be termed "ethical tribalism," in that tribal generosity gets in the way of broader justice. Ethical tribalism—bending a rule or giving the benefit of the doubt to someone from your clan—doesn't *feel* like discrimination. It feels like kindness. It involves no anger, malice, or ill regard. It's certainly a world away from torchlight marches and racist chants. But it perpetuates inequality nonetheless.

That it might be motivated by good intentions doesn't make this kind of discrimination any less harmful. But recognizing that the problem starts with in-group generosity does elucidate an alternative set of solutions. Specifically, because ethical tribalism is driven by the hero instinct, we can use the triggers and signals of hero codes to mitigate its most toxic effects.

After the firebombing, the Southern Poverty Law Center built its new headquarters across from the first White House of the Confederacy. Down the block is the Alabama State Capitol, with its eighty-eight-foot pillar memorializing Confederate veterans, its statue of Jefferson Davis, and (until recently) the Confederate flag flying overhead. When SPLC employees were not at the headquarters, they sometimes attended events held at Morris Dees's 210-acre country estate, complete with tennis courts, servants, and armed security. Although ideologically against "the Old South," SPLC employees were almost constantly exposed to symbols of it.

Dees would argue that living and working in the cradle of the Confederacy was a *statement*. Indeed, the SPLC's imposing fortress may be an intimidating sight to white nationalist pilgrims visiting Montgomery's memorials of the Southern secession.

Yet, might the influence also run in the other direction? Could the surrounding Confederate symbols have affected the executives and employees of the SPLC? Some of the insensitive acts and statements by white executives may well have come from the triggering of latent Old South ways. Black employees, for their part, may have been "triggered" in a different sense—the sights that surrounded them at work may have triggered traumatic memories, personal and collective. It's worth imagining an alternative history in which the SPLC had chosen a less loaded location. Might its executives and employees have interacted more equally and trustingly?

A bolder intervention is eliminating Confederate symbols from public spaces. When young activists in some cities began advocating for this agenda a decade ago, the older generation of the political left dismissed it as overly provocative identity politics: deep change comes only from changing underlying economic and legal structures—from changing statutes, not statues. Through a tribal psychology perspective, however, we understand why monuments can matter as much as budgets and ordinances. Public symbols are icons that trigger latent ideals and channel aspirations to glory. The 2015 Charleston church massacre was committed by a white supremacist obsessed with the Confederate battle flag. In 2017 right-wing groups converged on Charlottesville to protest the removal of a statue of Robert E. Lee, and the Confederate banners and Klan-style torches they carried inflamed conflict with counterprotesters that culminated in deadly violence.

Triggering by Confederate symbols may also contribute to the broader problem of discrimination in hiring. A 2008 study at Florida State University found that a fifteen-millisecond subliminal flash of the Confederate flag pushed white, but not Black, undergraduates toward voting for Hillary Clinton rather than Barack Obama. Even when the flag was plainly visible, it affected white students generally, not just the few who held negative attitudes toward Blacks. While this study couldn't distinguish the precise motivations that the flag activated, the breadth of the effect suggests that it triggers in-group favoritism and not just out-group hostility as is generally assumed.

In addition to reducing triggers of white-favoring codes, a longer-term strategy is to retrain the codes so that generosity is directed more inclusively. Organizations that sense a problem with racial discrimination, like the SPLC, have typically tried to redress it through racial bias training. The typical session tends to spell out what *not* to do, providing participants with examples ranging from blatantly hostile words and deeds to "microaggressions" that may not be meant as slights but come across that way.

Unfortunately, the evidence suggests that bias training does not usually achieve its goals. Meta-analyses find that these sessions produce temporary improvement in expressed attitudes, but the gains fade within days and fail to change relevant behaviors. Some white employees feel falsely accused and resentful. Others leave worried they must "walk on eggshells" and become loath to interact with minority coworkers. Sociologists Frank Dobbin and Alexandra Kalev tracked over 830 US corporations and found that minority representation in management fails to rise in the years after bias training, and in some categories even falls.

Bias training, with its emphasis on the problem of out-group hostility, may unwittingly *exacerbate* the less recognized problem of in-group favoritism. Perhaps most tellingly, employees complain that these sessions heighten the salience of race and ethnicity as opposed to other identity dimensions, such as occupation. If loyalty to one's own "clan" is not already dictating employees' generosity to coworkers, bias training sessions that make racial categories hypersalient risk making it so.

The poor record of this widely used intervention is tragic given that other kinds of group activities *do* promote cross-group cooperation. Research generally supports psychologist Gordon Allport's "contact" hypothesis, which holds that intergroup interactions that involve common goals and minimized status differences help reduce prejudice and discrimination. Laboratory studies of sports teams find that race fades as a basis of social categorization once cross-cutting team memberships are introduced. A recent field experiment tested the power of optimal contact in Iraq, where mutually mistrustful ethnic groups share a passion for soccer. Political scientist Salma Mousa assembled a new amateur soccer league, with half of the teams recruited from the majority community and the other half also incorporating the minority group. Across many practices and games, prestige signals—the behavior of role models, the coach's approval—impressed upon the players the ideal of teamwork across ethnicities. After just a single season, majority-group participants who played on a mixed team became more inclusive toward players from the other group—more likely to give them a sportsmanship award, and more willing to train and play with them in the future.

Some corporations have adopted a similar approach to cultivating generosity across racial and ethnic lines. Instead of mandatory bias trainings, these efforts are voluntary programs for developing "inclusive leadership." For instance, Coca-Cola reached a target of 25 percent minorities in upper management, up from almost zero a decade earlier, by inviting senior managers to participate in a long-term mentorship program that paired them with high-potential young employees who were predominantly minorities. Programs like this look for heroes rather than villains.

Just as hiring policies have contributed to the problem, they can also contribute to solutions. Referral programs can be tweaked so that employees are asked to nominate candidates from underrepresented groups. Intel achieved a 20 percent increase in minority hiring this way and hit their diversity targets years ahead of schedule. Pinterest held challenges across divisions in making the most minority referrals. Programs like this harness employees' knowledge and commitment to their nominees toward the goal of broader inclusion.

Likewise, a "culture fit" policy can be changed into a "culture add" ethos. Organizations look for intangible qualities that move beyond the current culture rather than matching it. In 2007 the Los Angeles Philhar-monic wooed twenty-six-year-old conductor Gustavo Dudamel, a Venezu-elan prodigy with uncommon exuberance, to take over as music director. Most major US orchestras are declining in audiences and community support, in part because they haven't kept pace with the changing demo-graphics of their cities. In 2018 African Americans were just 1.8 percent of their musicians, and Hispanics just 2.5 percent. Only 5 percent of works performed in a 2015 analysis were not composed by white men. But "the Dude" (as Angelenos called Dudamel) set out to diversify the LA Phil's ranks and its repertory. He included more Latin American composers and launched genre-blurring concerts such as celebrations of Duke Ellington and collaborations with Café Tacvba (the Mexican rock band) as well as local pop stars Gwen Stefani and Billie Eilish. The LA Phil has begun to look and sound more like the public it serves. For this progress, it has been deemed "America's most important orchestra."

In Montgomery, Alabama, three blocks from the SPLC offices, a 2018 project repurposed a landmark, the Kress department store. In the Jim Crow era, Kress restricted Blacks to its basement and became a promi-nent target of civil rights protests. The long-vacant edifice now houses co-working spaces, cafés, small businesses, and exhibits about the city's evolution of race relations. A "story booth" invites residents to record their personal narratives about transcending racial barriers, many of which describe the role of cross-ethnic friendships, families, and workplaces. Visitors listen for hours to these relatable stories by fellow Montgomerians who overcame prejudice and distrust. The Kress building has become an icon of inclusiveness instead of a symbol of segregation. It signals the pres-tige of collaborating across ethnic lines, and it showcases the heroes of racial reconciliation.

All of these efforts—Coke's inclusive leadership program, the Dude's galvanizing impact, the reincarnation of the Kress building—catalyze change through prestige signals. When people are shown new heroes, they learn new bases for esteem and new ways to contribute.

▼

When the 1984 Winter Olympics were held in Sarajevo, Yugoslavia, the world marveled at its religious diversity: it was the capital of the Bosnian province, but its Muslim majority intermingled with Orthodox Serbs, Catholic Croats, and Sephardic Jews. To be sure, the Balkan peoples had not always lived harmoniously (hence the term "balkanize"), but the Yugoslav Federation, the twentieth-century union of Southern Slavic peoples, smoothed over the historic divisions. Neighboring republics spoke a common language, even if they wrote it in different alphabets.

Not long after, an aspiring politician in Serbia named Slobodan Milošević began beating the drum of populism. He rhapsodized about Serbia's vast medieval kingdom and the recent injustice of losing Kosovo, a province granted partial autonomy by the federation on account of its Albanian Muslim majority. Most Serbs listened to these rantings about "Greater Serbia" with indifference. They were socialists who looked down on nationalism, and the federation had thrived throughout the Cold War—diverse and nonaligned as it was, it benefited from ties to all sides. What use was there in dredging up ancient history?

In the years that followed, however, fault lines began to appear in the federation. Cheap imports and expensive international loans combined to undercut its command-economy manufacturing, shuttering factories that provided a quarter of all jobs. Demographics shifted as citizens migrated to more prosperous republics. As the recession darkened, the 30 percent of Serbs who lived in other republics found themselves increasingly excluded from jobs. Serbia was the province with the largest population, but it had only one vote in federation decisions and couldn't push through new federation laws to protect its diaspora from discrimination.

A bellwether of change was Milošević's rise to the presidency of Serbia in 1989 on a platform of reasserting control over Kosovo. Shortly after his election, he sent troops there to pressure the Albanian Muslim leadership into concessions. At the same time, he partnered with the Serbian Orthodox Church in celebrations of the six-hundredth anniversary of the 1389 Battle of Kosovo, when Prince Lazar died resisting the Ottoman invaders. A year of processions and vigils culminated in a daylong ceremony at the battle site. Milošević mesmerized the crowd by fusing Serbs' historical grievances about insufficient help from allies in 1389 with their contemporary frustrations about neighboring provinces. Using selective memory about 1389, he painted it as a Serbian sacrifice: "Six centuries ago, Serbia heroically defended itself in the field of Kosovo, but it also defended . . . European culture, religion, and European society in general." He framed the current challenges to resonate with this past: "Six centuries later, now, we are being again engaged in battles. . . . They are not armed battles, although such things cannot be excluded yet." This was a sharp departure from Yugoslavia's anti-nationalist ideology. Representatives of Slovenia and Croatia in attendance "looked nervous and uncomfortable" and commented that the nationalist sentiment had perhaps destroyed the possibility of a peaceful settlement in Kosovo.

Over the next year the Berlin Wall fell, the Warsaw Pact disintegrated, and the thirst for sovereignty spread to the Balkans. First alpine Slovenia and then coastal Croatia declared themselves independent, despite protests from Belgrade. As conditions for the Serb minority in these breakaway republics worsened, Milošević's rhetoric about "Greater Serbia" began to find a broader audience. Citizens who as socialists had rejected religious identities began wearing Serbian Orthodox crosses and dwelling on the injustices suffered by their co-believers, past and present. Militias in Serb border regions were goaded into killings by media stories about Croatian atrocities, and the reprisals on both sides escalated into an irregular sectarian conflict with ethnic cleansing and the slaughter of civilians.

In 1992 Bosnia declared its independence and became the next target of the Belgrade propaganda machine. Scientists "proved" that the Muslim Bosniaks were migrants to Europe, not original inhabitants of the land. News stories reported Serb children being fed to lions at the Sarajevo zoo, evil not seen since the medieval Turks. Not long after, Serb paramilitaries began a siege of Sarajevo from the surrounding hills. Artillery blasts chipped away at historic mosques and Islamic libraries; sniper fire picked off civilians in line to buy bread. In the countryside, Bosniaks were driven out of ethnically Serb regions and vice versa. In Srebrenica, as many as thirty thousand Bosniak women and children were displaced, some tortured and raped, while more than eight thousand men were massacred.

A few years later, Milošević's troops marched south to Kosovo, where an insurgency was resisting Serbian control, sometimes violently. Hundreds of thousands of Albanian Muslims were forced from their homes. In villages like Meja and Vučitrn, thousands were executed without trial, including many civilians. Fairly or unfairly, NATO intervened with airstrikes on Belgrade and military targets. Milošević's troops withdrew from Kosovo, most ethnic Serbs emigrated, and UN peacekeepers guarded the minority province's autonomy.

How had peaceful Yugoslavia descended so quickly into sectarian slaughter?

The mass killing of civilians shocks us as inhumane and horrifying, but it has been part of human history from the start. The Greeks slaughtered the Trojans, tossing infants from city walls. The Israelites annihilated the Canaanites. Europeans settled the "New World" by decimating its Indigenous peoples. In the twentieth century, the Nazi regime carried out genocidal massacres of Jewish and Romani peoples. Despite the "Never Again" measures after the Holocaust, mass killings of "others" continued apace—not just in Yugoslavia but in Rwanda, Darfur, and Myanmar (under the watch of a Nobel Peace laureate, no less). A widening array of non-state groups, like Al Qaeda, ISIS, and Wagner Group, similarly resort to mass slaughter.

Perhaps more than any other kind of conflict, this extremist violence is often chalked up to hate, sometimes to a hardwired hostility from our primal evolutionary past. But laying this ugliness at the door of our ape precursors doesn't stand up to scrutiny. Chimpanzees are very violent creatures, to be sure, but when they gang up on wanderers from a neighboring troop, they kill only enough to eat; they don't kill a whole group at once. As best we can tell, the same is true of archaic human species. Early cave art features many scenes of hunting, but no scenes of massacre; the boneyards that bespeak of massacres appear in the archaeological record near the end of the Stone Age. Only once our forebears had evolved the ancestor instinct did the elimination of whole communities enter their behavioral repertoire. Military tribunals sometimes trace atrocities to bloodlust, but biologists find that our species does not react to the smell of blood in the way that sharks or wolves do. Journalist Arthur Koestler, who exposed the atrocities of the Holocaust, described them as less id than superego, less uncontrolled lust than excessive sublimation. "War is a ritual," he concluded. "A deadly ritual."

The ancestor instinct to maintain tradition propels some of humanity's noblest endeavors—cathedrals, courthouses, and colleges—but this "best instinct" is also, at times, our worst instinct. The danger of traditionalism is absolutism, black-and-white thinking. It yields moral certainties and excuses collateral damage. Cautious cost-benefit decision-making is overridden by identity imperatives. During times of threat, we worry that our tribal traditions could be interrupted or eroded. We start to worry about people of different traditions: the "other tribe" across the border, visitors and immigrants of different creeds, even minority faiths who have long lived among us. In Nazi Germany, Jews were less than 1 percent of the population, and not the source of Weimar's economic strains, but as a visible and successful minority, they possibly challenged the narrative of Aryan Christian supremacy. Likewise, as Yugoslavia began to fracture under globalizing pressures, Milošević focused his Orthodox warriors on the Muslims next door. Different traditions are implicit threats.

The critical role of defending tradition may explain why religions—which primarily espouse peace, love, and harmony—so often spur the bloodiest violence. Religions are the oldest tribal traditions we have. Psychology studies find that the older a tradition of ours, the more positive we feel about it, but the older the traditions of a rival group, the more we feel threatened. When a minority group doesn't share religion or ideology with a society's majority, the chances of violent conflict multiply. The persistence of sectarian extremism, while other forms of violence decline, may reflect the forces of globalization pushing disparate tribes into uncomfortable proximity. For instance, the largest source of immigrants to Sweden used to be Finland, but in recent years it has been Syria. Across Europe in the past decade, there is growing anxiety that an increase in Muslim populations will change the way of life—mosques replacing churches, burkas replacing bikinis. These sectarian anxieties have grown in the US as well and promoted exclusionary policies and violent extremism. It has reached paranoid heights in the "great replacement theory" screeds posted online before massacres of religious out-groups: the 2012 slaughter at a Sikh temple in Wisconsin, the 2018 shooting at a Pennsylvania synagogue, the 2019 carnage at a New Zealand mosque, and so forth. Troublingly, this paranoia is not limited to the lunatic fringe. Fully a third of Americans worry that increased immigration has caused a threat to the nation's identity, and almost as many suspect a conspiracy is involved.

Standard accounts of genocidal violence posit that it ensues from dehumanizing victims. That is, when out-group members are recategorized as animals or insects, eliminating them is housecleaning, not a holocaust. But this obviously can't be the whole story. In sectarian extremism, perpetrators treat their victims far worse than they ever treat animals. In particular, they humiliate victims. The Nazis forced communities to watch while they burned their Torahs. Relatedly, sectarian strife often features rhetoric denying the other group's historical claims. For instance, some Israeli voices trumpet their ancestral society in biblical times while asserting that Palestinians as a distinct group do not appear in these historical records. From their side, Palestinians dismiss biblical records as chauvinistic lore and provide legal documents of family residence in Jerusalem and elsewhere for generations before their 1948 displacement, the Nakba. This is "detribalizing" the other group, destroying or denigrating its traditions.

The dramatic changes in the religious landscape of many countries as a result of globalization have brought the ugly consequence of sectarian extremism. To some extent, this reflects "existential tribalism"—impulses to defend one's own tradition become directed toward destroying a different group's tradition. To say that this sectarian strife wells up out of traditionalism rather than out of tribal hate doesn't make it any less abhorrent. But it does, once again, illuminate some possible approaches to preventing it.

While many factors set the stage for violence in the breakup of Yugoslavia, one key trigger was ceremony. The Orthodox Church's processions of relics of the martyr Lazar brought Serbs together for stirring vigils that often transmuted into impassioned political rallies. A million of the faithful traveled to Kosovo for the sexcentenary commemoration, where Milošević spoke in front of the Gazimestan monument on a broad stage backed by a giant gold cross emblazoned with the battle cry "*Samo sloga Srbina spasava*" ("Only unity saves the Serbs"), garlanded with an image of red peonies, symbolizing the blood Lazar shed, and embossed with the years 1389 and 1989. For their part, the crowd carried signs comparing Milošević to Prince Lazar. At the mention of Serb warriors taking up arms, emotion swept over the crowd. They chanted, "Kosovo is Serbia. Kosovo is Serbia. Kosovo is Serbia." The air was thick with ceremony, traditionalism, and its galvanizing effects.

The use of ceremony to inflame passions about tradition is hardly unique to either Milošević or the Serbs. We see crowds mesmerized, filled with mythic purpose, in religious ceremonies from Delhi, Tehran, Jerusalem, and all around the world. The film *Triumph of the Will* shows a Nuremberg crowd transformed by a political rally. Ceremonies combine mesmerizing synchrony of behavior with resonant historical symbols. They guide people to construe a present challenge in terms of group tradition. Just as ceremonies could mobilize a community to work together to preserve a historic church, they could also rouse a population to destroy a minority faith's houses of worship. Rallies calling on right-wing groups to

fight preceded the political violence in Charlottesville in 2017 and at the Capitol in 2021.

All of this raises the question of whether political ceremonies are worth the trouble they cause. Freedom of speech and assembly is central to the American tradition, so we are loath to restrict it. We have many specific exceptions for reasons of safety, but we want to allow all ideas—even wrong ideas—in a bookstore or a classroom because processing bad ideas can help in refining the best ideas. But ceremonies are a different kind of gathering. They don't work toward the refinement of ideas. They do the opposite: they lock in absolutist commitments. That's also important, but not for refining ideas. In the US, extremists are allowed to march through cities with Nazi flags or menacing chants that offend and intimidate vulnerable groups. But in other democracies, ceremonies that risk inflaming sectarian conflicts are not allowed. In Germany and Austria, the *Volksverhetzung* law forbids any speech—even in print—that invites oppression or offends the dignity of a religious, racial, or national group. The legal test for incitement in the US used to be "clear and present danger," but since the 1960s it has been "imminent lawless action." Courts could broaden the rule to restrict inflammatory political marches without appreciably reducing the marketplace of ideas. A parallel issue arises on campuses. By permitting more political events that foster the exchange of perspectives (debates and panel discussions) than ceremonial events (vigils and rallies), we could encourage critical thinking rather than ceremonial absolutism. Students should feel safe from physical threats to their group, but not safe from ideas that challenge their community's preconceptions.

In addition to limiting the ceremonies that incite extremist violence, longer-term strategies can target the signals that indoctrinate people into divisive ancestor codes. Take Milošević, who spent years shaping his people's understanding of their history before mobilizing this narrative for violence. The battle of a medieval prince does not itself motivate modern soldiers; it moves them only when framed as a sacred group tradition to defend. Through political speeches and media propaganda, the popular understanding of the 1389 battle and its relevance to the present was gradually reframed: Serbs are the defenders of European Christianity against Islamic invaders. The narrative became a legitimizing myth, a justification for aggression toward Muslim republics and provinces.

Humans instinctively crave tradition, so we eagerly absorb information about the ways of our ancestors. The best way to counter precedent signals of intolerance, then, is with more compelling precedent signals of inclusion. In the aftermath of the 9/11 attacks, studies found that American Christians, when under the condition of threat, became more likely to support extreme military measures that risked killing many Muslim civilians. However, in an experiment that first exposed them to biblical passages calling for forgiveness, Christian participants under threat became *less* likely to support the military measures. Likewise, an experiment in Iran found that fundamentalist Muslims became less likely to support jihad against the US when reminded of precedents for tolerance in the Koran. Importantly, neither group's aggressive impulse was muted by messages of tolerance from other sources—precedent signals had to emerge from the group's own traditions. In times of threat, it may be easier to reshape a group's perceived tradition than to try to dissuade it from acting on tradition.

Societies also send precedent signals via their cultural policies toward minority communities. In the late twentieth century, most Western nations adopted the policy of multiculturalism (first developed in Canada to prevent French secession). While the word "multiculturalism" means many things to many people, as a government policy it means that resources such as schools and arts centers are provided to minority groups to help preserve their traditions against assimilatory pressures. One problem with this policy, however, is that it has tended to empower separatists, who indoctrinate the rising generations into divisive views of tradition. Tragically, their alienation from the mainstream culture has escalated in some places to "homegrown" jihadist violence, like the killing of filmmaker Theo van Gogh in the Netherlands in 2004. In the Netherlands, Germany, the UK, and elsewhere, leaders have declared multiculturalism policies a failure.

Other regions have embraced a variant policy called "interculturalism," which sees cultural traditions as intertwined and evolving. In Catalonia, policies toward immigrant communities don't prioritize preservation as much as dialogue, something that comes naturally to the cosmopolitan province between Spain and France. When I lived there a few years back, I paid a visit to Catalonia's director of cultural policy, Ramon Sanahuja, who showed me a selection of cultural program proposals on his desk. A soccer club had proposed sponsoring a tournament of teams from different immigrant neighborhoods: Ecuadorean, Moroccan, Italian, and so forth. A dance organization had proposed a festival juxtaposing Spanish flamenco, Argentinian tango, and Cuban salsa. Ramon declined to fund the soccer tournament, thinking that it might reinforce group boundaries; he sponsored the dance festival because it showcased that the genres developed by borrowing elements from other cultural traditions. Showing that cultures have influenced each other in the past makes their contemporary mixing less existentially threatening.

During Carnival, people in Catalonia typically celebrate with *butifarra*, a savory pork sausage, but the growing Pakistani Muslim community couldn't engage in this fun. Ramon's agency investigated Catalan history and discovered that some areas historically included cheeses in the celebration. His office publicized this and sponsored Carnival booths with these traditional cheeses, making the celebration more inclusive. When a group of businesspeople from Barcelona's Chinatown area asked for permission to hold a Chinese New Year parade, Ramon requested that the celebration reference other local customs as well, like the dragons in the city's La Mercè festival parade, and the firecrackers in the Catalan Corre-foc ("fire run"). A preservationist might grouse that his Carnival or the parade are not historically authentic. But Ramon and other Catalans would counter that it's *more* authentic to practice unique rituals that reflect their distinctive province than to worry about matching what is done in Madrid or Beijing or what was done there a century ago.

Catalonia has largely avoided the twin horrors of existential tribalism—right-wing shootings at mosques and homegrown jihadist bombings—that have plagued other parts of Europe. Some credit for this no doubt goes to the interculturalism policies that create a united meta-tribe of Catalonia. By sending the right signals about precedents, they have cultivated a tradition of Catalonia as a colloquy among different languages, religions, and ideologies.

▼

Astra inclinant, sed non obligant.
(The stars incline us, they do not bind us.)

—Latin saying

We've seen that the pressing political, ethnic, and sectarian conflicts of our time do involve tribalism. But this tribalism is not an atavistic primal rage against outsiders. While these conflicts can flare into hostilities, they don't start with hostility. They arise from the three basic tribal instincts that we have come to know well in this book. Partisan blindness arises from peer-code conformity put into overdrive by residential sorting and online echo chambers, a case of *epistemic tribalism* where tribe comes before truth. Ethnic inequity arises from the impulse to give to one's own kind and from hiring procedures that accelerate this impulse, a case of *ethical tribalism* where tribal loyalties interfere with broader justice. Sectarian extremism arises from indoctrination into traditions, perceived threats, and the incitement of mesmerizing ceremonies, a case of *existential tribalism* where people lash out at other tribes' traditions. Just as there is not just one psychological system that evolved to support tribal psychology, there is not just one way that tribal instincts can get caught in feedback loops that become dysfunctional.

While each diagnosis calls for different remedies, there are some common themes. Curbing a pattern in the short term involves understanding how it is triggered—both the environmental cues that bring a tribal code to mind and the inner needs that catalyze its enactment. Changing the code in a more enduring way involves signals. People may need to find new peers to develop better habits, find new heroes to develop better aspirations, or find new ancestors to develop better traditions.

My recommendations are not the typical tips from an academic about how to encourage more rational decisions. I think that rationality is not the strong suit of our species. We are *Homo tributus*, not *Homo economicus*. Certainly, tribal instincts are part of the problem in many pressing conflicts, but they also can be—and, I think, *have to be*—part of the solution.

For our predecessors struggling to survive in the Stone Age, tribal interaction was a way to expand the bounds of social cohesion, to work in coordination as a united force, to cooperate in ways that were not immediately rewarded, and to sustain and build upon the wisdom of the past. Tribal psychology helped our species replace aggression against neighbors with in-group cooperation, but our capacities for collaboration and single-minded defense of traditions can play out into group conflicts. Our evolutionary blessing of "Us" does not fate us to violence against "Them," but we need awareness of our tribal psychology to guard ourselves against this possibility.

Tribal psychology helped our forebears develop new ways of life to adapt to the Arctic steppe and the Australian desert. It helped them survive through the last Ice Age, a climate change of ten degrees. We are now facing another climate challenge, among many others, and I believe that help can again come from our tribal instincts. For some rationalistic economists, it has been easier to imagine the end of the planet than to imagine the end of carbon fuels. The "tragedy of the commons" holds that shared natural resources will be overexploited because it's individually rational to do so. If we are truly motivated by nothing more than rational self-interest, then this tragedy may be inevitable.

But as tribal animals, we are bound to our peers, heroes, and ancestors—not just to our own interests. Some of this happens unconsciously, but it can be even more powerful if we become aware of it. Peer codes tend to lag social change, so we underestimate popular support for climate change action by nearly half. We shouldn't despair people's slowness to act because it comes from lack of knowledge not lack of concern. Educators can make a key difference by explaining the benefits of climate actions. When we install rooftop solar panels, our neighbors become much more likely to adopt them in the next few years. It plants the idea in their head (*People just like me are doing this*). If the public was more aware of these powerful peer effects, they'd understand that investing in panels doesn't just shrink one's own carbon footprint—it convinces the rest of the community to shrink theirs too. Understanding ourselves as tribal helps us see the ripple effects of our actions.

When we interact as communities, our actions bend toward the common good. Political scientist Elinor Ostrom studied local communities around the world—like Maine lobstermen and Nepali loggers—and found that they respond to scarcity not by taking all they can for themselves, but by establishing rules for sustainable consumption. These rules are likely related to our evolved capacities for coordinating, cooperating, and maintaining traditions in groups. In my classes, when I run resource dilemma games, the students tend to reenact the tragedy of the commons—that is, unless I give them time to talk to each other before they make their choices. In that case, they tend to establish a shared ideal of collective gain and make their choices public to sustain group cooperation.

In Bali, an intricate network of irrigation channels originates in the volcanic lakes of the highlands and winds through layers and layers of rice paddies on its way to the ocean. For a thousand years, at junctures in this irrigation network, small groups of farmers met regularly in "water temples," ornate wooden structures with ceremonial gates and pagoda-like towers carved in floral patterns. In the temples, the farmers held rituals to facilitate collective decisions about how to distribute the water fairly. When Green Revolution agronomists arrived from the West in the 1970s, they replaced all this superstitious nonsense with irrigation schedules based on their calculations. The scientific approach proved disastrous— the optimization problem was too complex. When farmers were allowed to revert to their sacred tradition, a sustainable pattern of water distribution returned. Rationality was simply no match for tribal thinking.

I don't have blind faith that tribal intuitions will inevitably heal the earth and all of our divisions. But I see lots of evidence that they can help. Our long pasts are resources for future flexibility. Our capacity to evolve new cultural codes in response to new environments is endlessly surprising and should be a source of hope even in the most difficult times. One thing is certain: we will not overcome the present challenges as individuals. As even our earliest ancestors knew, we can thrive only together—in tribes.

ACKNOWLEDGMENTS

This book owes so much to so many people that it is impossible to thank them all. It took a tribe—indeed, several tribes—to raise this child.

Tribal was conceived in conversations with my agent Richard Pine, who read some of my scientific journal articles about cultural priming and polyculturalist dynamics and posed deep questions about their broader relevance. His gifted colleague at InkWell Management, William Callahan, took time to show me ways to transform my initial drafts into more accessible, story-driven prose. The book proposal was fortunate to land at Penguin Random House in the capable hands of editors Niki Papadopoulos and Merry Sun. I'm grateful for Niki's strategic brilliance, and I owe Merry the world for steady support and apt advice through the long writing journey. Finally, I thank Gareth Cook at Verto Literary for editorial consultation when paring the manuscript down to a streamlined shape.

Before the project started, my ambition to write for a broad audience had been cultivated by conversations with the book-writing vanguard of behavioral science, including Robert Cialdini, Daniel Gilbert, Max Bazerman, Jeffrey Pfeffer, Phillip Tetlock, Chip Heath, Jonathan Haidt, Adam Grant, and others. It was an interest inspired by books I've loved for expressing scientific ideas in engaging everyday language—from Charles Darwin, William James, and Margaret Mead to Richard Dawkins, Steven Pinker, and Jared Diamond.

Aside from these bookish clans, the project owes a debt to the academic tribes who raised me a researcher. My mission to investigate cultural differences in social cognition coalesced in graduate school at the University of Michigan, where I was mentored chiefly by Richard Nisbett and Edward Smith. In the egalitarian environment of Ann Arbor, I had the privilege to interact with other tribal elders like Robert Zajonc, Hazel Markus, Claude Steele, David Buss, Larry Hirschfeld, Scott Atran, Richard Shweder, and Daniel Sperber. These interdisciplinary conversations became its Culture and Cognition program. I was prepared for this only because patient professors like Gregory Murphy, William Warren, George Morgan, Barret Hazeltine, and Michael Harper took the time to help me as an undergraduate at Brown University. I'm also grateful to many other academic benefactors not mentioned.

In addition to my teachers, I want to thank the collaborators and colleagues who coauthored, critiqued, or clarified the ideas that make up this thesis, including: at Michigan, Shinobu Kitayama, Kaiping Peng, Richard Larrick, and Alejandro López-Rousseau; at Stanford, Amos Tversky, Lee Ross, Jim March, Joanne Martin, Rod Kramer, Itamar Simonson, Joel Podolny, Jennifer Aaker, Sonja Lyubomirsky, Donnel Briley, Kathy Phillips, Tanya Menon, Yuriko Zemba, Maia Young, and Bilaine Sullivan; at Chinese University of Hong Kong, Kwok Leung, Michael Bond, and

Darius Chan; at Berkeley, Verónica Benet-Martínez, Daniel Ames, and Eric Knowles; at University of Hong Kong, Chi-yue Chiu, Ying-yi Hong, and Ho-ying (Jeanne) Fu; at Columbia, Joel Brockner, Sheena Iyengar, Elke Weber, Adam Galinsky, Malia Mason, Craig Fox, Emily Amanatullah, Roy Chua, Canny Zou, Aurelia Mok, Krishna Savani, Zhi Lui, Shu Zhang, Andy Yap, Jaee Cho, Katrina Fincher, Jackson Lu, Zaijia Liu, Yu Ding, Gita Johar, Eric Johnson, Vickie Morwitz, Namrata Goyal, Shilpa Madan, Minhee Kim, and Lucy Liu.

I owe a debt to the ever-fractious tribe I work for, Columbia University, particularly Columbia Business School, the Committee for Global Thought, and the Heyman Center for Humanities. Thanks also to my former home, Stanford University, especially its Graduate School of Business, Center on International Conflict and Negotiation, and Center for Comparative Studies in Race and Ethnicity. Some of my research breakthroughs came during sabbaticals at the Chinese University of Hong Kong and University of Hong Kong. This book culminated during a recent sabbatical, visiting INSEAD-Europe (along with Institut Jean Nicod in Paris) in the fall of 2022 and then INSEAD-Asia in Singapore (along with PolyU in Hong Kong) in the spring of 2023. Thanks to Roderick Swaab, Li Huang, Frederic Godart, Andy Yap, Ko Kuwabara, Hugo Mercier, Krishna Savani, and others for arranging these delightful stays.

My family clan was foundational in making this book a reality. I could not have begun this project without an obsessive curiosity instilled by my book-loving parents, Thomas and Sharon Morris. My sister Margaret showed me the way by writing her book first, while her husband, Doug, has versed me in tech-industry myths and rituals. My sister Kathleen and her husband, Brad, were confidants, consultants, and consummate hosts. My sister Beth and her husband, Klaus, shared their beltway wisdom and shouldered family tasks when I was unavailable. My brother, Tom, and his wife, Dori, kept me in check with a Texas perspective. My nephews and nieces provided Gen-Z focus groups. My wife, Tatjana Gall, offered her keen ear, nimble mind, and deep heart to guide me from the first word to the last.

Finally, I thank the crew of companions who rallied my spirits through this long march: Allison, Andy, Gordon, Ernie, Brian, Shira, Shela, Lexi, David, Emanuele, Zhana, Zuzi, Paula, Malia, Modupe, Adam, Dan, Stephan, Sam, Sadie, Nina, Konstantino, Maureen, James, Natalie, Kiwi, Ellen, Katrina, Anna, Melanie, Jessica, and many unmentioned. Thanks, squad, for tolerating my absences, oversights, and addled moods. After Yeats: "Think where man's glory most begins and ends / And say my glory was I had such friends."

NOTES

Introduction: The Riddle of Hiddink

x **Guus Hiddink, a graying Dutch coach:** Daniel Taylor, "Sweat and Self-Belief Are the Secrets of Hiddink's Korea," *Guardian*, June 23, 2002, https://www.theguardian.com /football/2002/jun/24/worldcupfootball2002.sport2.

x **"I don't know much about Korea":** Nammi Lee, Steven J. Jackson, and Keunmo Lee, "South Korea's 'Glocal' Hero: The Hiddink Syndrome and the Rearticulation of National Citizenship and Identity," *Sociology of Sport Journal* 24, no. 3 (2007): 283–301.

x **famous names didn't make the cut:** Simon Kuper, "The Miracles of Guus," *The Monthly*, October 2005, https://www.themonthly.com.au/monthly-essays-simon-kuper -miracles-guus-can-thoughtful-dutchman-who-worshipped-korea-take-socceroos.

xii **"can adapt quicker than you think":** Rob Hughes, "Transmitting a Gift That Goes Beyond Words," *New York Times*, March 23, 2010, https://www.nytimes.com/2010 /03/24/sports/soccer/24iht-soccer.html.

xii **Korean press branded Hiddink "Oh Dae Young":** "A Revolution of Korea Soccer from Zurich to Sang-Am," *Moonhwa Ilbo Press*, July 18, 2002, 17.

xiii **150-to-1 no-hopers:** Taylor, "Sweat and Self-Belief Are the Secrets of Hiddink's Korea."

xv **others tried bringing the "Dutch style":** In Barcelona, thanks to other Dutch soccer missionaries, it morphed into the world-beating *tiki-taka* style.

xv **Hiddink repeated the trick:** Simon Kuper and Stefan Szymanski, *Soccernomics* (New York: Bold Type Books, 2018).

xv **He sold them on the *totaalvoetbal*:** "Viktor Maslov: Soviet Pioneer of the 4-4-2 Formation and the Inventor of Pressing," *Sports Illustrated*, June 28, 2019.

xvi **best coaching record in the English Premier:** Adrian Bell, Chris Brooks, and Tom Markham, "The Performance of Football Club Managers: Skill or Luck?," *Economics & Finance Research* 1, no. 1 (2013): 19–30.

xvi **the Haida people hold *potlatch* feasts:** John Reed Swanton, *Contributions to the Ethnology of the Haida* (Leiden: E. J. Brill, 1905): 294–97.

xvi **achievement-oriented personalities:** David C. McClelland, *The Achieving Society* (New York: Free Press, 1961).

xvi **Individuals were migrating:** Ulf Hannerz, *Transnational Connections: Culture, People, Places* (New York: Routledge, 1996).

xvii **Culture and psyche are inexorably intertwined:** Richard A. Shweder, *Thinking Through Cultures: Expeditions in Cultural Psychology* (Cambridge, MA: Harvard University Press, 1991).

xvii **some of the pathbreaking studies:** My work has received many recognitions of such, including the 2023 "career" contribution award for advancing cultural psychology.

xvii **Appalachia's "culture of poverty":** Ever since anthropologist Oscar Lewis described in 1962 a "culture of poverty" in overseas slums, conservative politicians have referenced the concept to caution against economic aid to the poor (e.g., Senator Joe Manchin expressed concern that the Child Tax Credit would be misused by the poor in West Virginia to buy drugs, worsening their problems). Conversely, this theory has been anathema in liberal academic fields such as sociology. Only recently have scholars found compelling ways to portray that cultural norms contribute to a group's economic profile—but not exclusively or intransigently. W. J. Wilson, "Why Both Social Structure and Culture Matter in a Holistic Analysis of Inner-City Poverty," *Annals of the American Academy of Political and Social Science* 629 (2010): 200–219.

xvii **posit an underlying essence:** Deborah A. Prentice, and Dale T. Miller, "Psychological Essentialism of Human Categories," *Current Directions in Psychological Science* 16, no. 4 (2007): 202–6.

xviii **US hawks targeted madrassas:** Peter Bergen and Swati Pandey, "The Madrassa Myth," *New York Times*, June 14, 2005, http://www.nytimes.com/2005/06/14/opinion /the-madrassa-myth.html.

xviii **a product of resentment:** C. Christine Fair, Neil Malhotra, and Jacob N. Shapiro, "Faith or Doctrine? Religion and Support for Political Violence in Pakistan," *Public Opinion Quarterly* 76, no. 4 (2012): 688–720; Mark Tessler and Michael D. H. Robbins, "What Leads Some Ordinary Arab Men and Women to Approve of Terrorist Acts against the United States?," *Journal of Conflict Resolution* 51, no. 2 (2007): 305–28.

xviii **Its breeding grounds were not madrassas:** Isabel Coles and Ned Parker, "How Saddam's Men Help Islamic State Rule," Reuters, December 11, 2015, https://www .reuters.com/investigates/special-report/mideast-crisis-iraq-islamicstate; Milan Obaidi et al., "Cultural Threat Perceptions Predict Violent Extremism via Need for Cognitive Closure," *Proceedings of the National Academy of Sciences* 120, no. 20 (2023): e2213874120.

xviii **London flat:** *Islam for Dummies***:** Aya Batrawy, Paisley Dodds, and Lori Hinnant, "'Islam for Dummies': IS Recruits Have Poor Grasp of Faith," Associated Press, August 15, 2016, https://apnews.com/article/lifestyle-middle-east-africa-europe-reli gion-9f94ff7f1e294118956b049a51548b33.

xviii **Counterterrorism measures that target:** Joby Warrick, "Jihadist Groups Hail Trump's Travel Ban as a Victory," *Washington Post*, January 29, 2017, https://www .washingtonpost.com/world/national-security/jihadist-groups-hail-trumps-travel -ban-as-a-victory/2017/01/29/50908986-e66d-11e6-b82f-687d6e6a3e7c_story.html.

xix **"I am large, I contain":** Walt Whitman, *Leaves of Grass* (Philadelphia: David McKay, 1891–1892).

xix **worked with military leaders:** At a conference for Defense personnel I conducted an interview (via satellite phone) with a general admired for his success in Afghanistan— Michael T. Flynn. Flynn's struggles soon afterward with the rituals of politics remind me that occupational cultures are as hard to cross as national cultures. National Research Council, *Sociocultural Data to Accomplish Department of Defense Missions: Toward a Unified Social Framework: Workshop Summary* (Washington, DC: National Academies Press, 2011).

xix **cultural biases of hackers:** Catherine Stupp, "U.S. Intelligence Wants to Use Psychology to Avert Cyberattack: IARPA Scientists Are Taking Up the Nascent Field of Cyber Psychology to Predict and Counter Hacker Behavior," *Wall Street Journal*, January 25, 2023, https://www.wsj.com/articles/u-s-intelligence-wants-to-use-psychology -to-avert-cyberattacks-11674670443.

xix **in the developing world:** Cislaghi, Ben, Karima Manji, and Lori Heise, "Social Norms and Gender-Related Harmful Practices: Theory in Support of Better Practice," *Learning Report* 2 (2018), London School of Hygiene & Tropical Medicine.

xix **campaigns about culture-relevant policies:** Benedict Carey, "Academic 'Dream Team' Helped Obama's Effort," *New York Times* November 12, 2012, https://www .nytimes.com/2012/11/13/health/dream-team-of-behavioral-scientists-advised -obama-campaign.html.

xx **outjump defender Paolo Maldini:** Maldini is three inches taller than Ahn and rated the greatest defender in soccer history. The Italians knew Ahn because he was a bench-sitter for Perugia, but fitness had never been his forte. Perugia promptly fired him for ruining Italy's chance in the Cup. George Vecsey, "South Korea Stuns Italy in World Cup," *New York Times*, June 18, 2002, https://www.nytimes.com/2002/06/18 /sports/south-korea-stuns-italy-in-world-cup.html.

xxi **"When Ahn scored the golden goal":** Hee-Kyung Hwang and Sang-Hee Kim, "Korea-Italy Match Notes: Celebration in Apartments, Residential Complex," *Yonhap News*, June 18, 2002.

xxii **"the greatest moment since the end":** Nam-Kwon Kim and Sang-Hoon Lee, "Biggest Tae-Guk Parade since March 1st Liberation Movement," *Yonhap News*, June 14, 2002.

xxii **"the greatest day since Dangun":** Jin-Hong Kim, Kyung-Hwan Maeng, "President Kim's Tears of Victory after Winning against Spain," *Kookmin Ilbo*, June 23, 2002.

xxii **This transformed team was trumpeted:** More than two hundred books appeared in the next five years applying lessons from the team to other kinds of organizations. Lee, Jackson, and Lee. "South Korea's 'Glocal' Hero."

xxii **"conquest of blood-lineage nationalism":** "The Light and Shadow Side of the Hiddink Phenomenon," *Hankyoreh Newspaper*, July 8, 2002, 9.

xxii **a critical step toward the confident:** Rachael Miyung Joo, "Consuming Visions: The Crowds of the Korean World Cup," *Journal of Korean Studies* 11, no. 1 (2006): 41–67.

xxiii **Ants, bees, and termites:** Edward O. Wilson, *The Insect Societies* (Cambridge, MA: Harvard University Press, 1971).

xxiv **a chimp needs to bond:** Robin I. M. Dunbar and Susanne Shultz, "Evolution in the Social Brain," *Science* 317, no. 5843 (2007): 1344–47.

xxv **broad networks of sharing in mates:** Chimpanzees, dolphins, orcas, and some other brainy mammal species share simple learned behaviors in their living groups, so they are also cultural animals. But they don't create rich cultures that become the glue for more complex social structures.

xxv **By Shakespeare's time:** Shylock says "sufferance is the badge of all our tribe."

xxv **"savage" or "barbaric" tribes rather than civilized:** Henry Sumner Maine, *Ancient Law: Its Connection with the Early History of Society and Its Relation to Modern Ideas* (London: John Murray, 1897); Lewis Henry Morgan and Eleanor Burke Leacock, *Ancient Society: Or Researches in the Lines of Human Progress from Savagery through Barbarism to Civilization* (New York: Henry Holt, 1877).

xxv **civilizing influence of European armies:** Malcolm Yapp, "Tribes and States in the Khyber, 1838–42," in *The Conflict of Tribe and State in Iran and Afghanistan*, ed. Richard L. Tapper (London: Croom Helm, 1983), 150–91.

xxv **These categories were politics:** Some of these non-Western societies rivaled European nations in their scale, and many had attained sophisticated engineering, astronomy, medicine, agriculture, and arts. The impression of primitive, close-minded, suspicious savages came in part because these groups were reeling from Western invasions, diseases, and the slave trade, influences that Western scholarship has been slow to fully recognize. Alexander Koch, Chris Brierley, Mark M. Maslin, and Simon L. Lewis, "Earth System Impacts of the European Arrival and Great Dying in the Americas after 1492," *Quaternary Science Reviews* 207 (2019): 13–36; Nathan Nunn and Leonard Wantchekon, "The Slave Trade and the Origins of Mistrust in Africa," *American Economic Review* 101, no. 7 (2011): 3221–52.

xxv **clarify the concept structurally:** Meyer Fortes and Edward E. Evans-Pritchard, *African Political Systems* (Oxford: Oxford University Press, 1940); Marshall Sahlins, *Tribesmen* (Englewood Cliffs, NJ: Prentice-Hall, 1968).

xxvi **explaining India's "sacred cows":** Marvin Harris, "India's Sacred Cow," *Human Nature* 1, no. 2 (1978): 28–36.

xxvi **new strain of theory and research:** That said, anthropology's self-questioning continues to occupy much of its energy. Akhil Gupta and Jessie Stoolman, "Decolonizing US Anthropology," *American Anthropologist* 124, no. 4 (2022): 778–99.

xxvi **As early humans learned more:** Michael Tomasello, "The Human Adaptation for Culture," *Annual Review of Anthropology* 28, 1 (1999): 509–29.

xxvi **upward spiral of co-evolution:** Joseph Henrich, *The Secret of Our Success: How Culture Is Driving Human Evolution, Domesticating Our Species, and Making Us Smarter* (Princeton, NJ: Princeton University Press, 2017).

xxvi **cultural evolution also sheds light:** Peter J. Richerson and Robert Boyd, *Not by Genes Alone: How Culture Transformed Human Evolution* (Chicago: University of Chicago Press, 2008).

xxvii "**capabilities that allow them to adapt**": Lawrence Rosen, "'Tribalism' Gets a Bum Rap," *Anthropology Today* 32, no. 5 (2016): 3.

xxvii **McLuhan's term of "re-tribalization"**: Akbar Ahmed, Frankie Martin, and Amineh Ahmed Hoti, "Re-Tribalization in the 21st Century, Part 1," *Anthropology Today* 39, no. 5 (2023): 3–6.

xxvii **three layers of "tribal instincts"**: By "instinct" I mean an evolved *system* of capacities and responses. I adapt the terminology of evolutionary anthropologists Robert Boyd and Peter Richerson, who distinguished human-specific "tribal instincts" from preexisting primate instincts like kin selection. Peter J. Richerson and Robert Boyd, "The Evolution of Subjective Commitment to Groups: A Tribal Instincts Hypothesis," *Evolution and the Capacity for Commitment* 3 (2001): 186–220.

xxvii **part of the *ancestor instinct***: Behavioral scientists often refer to these, respectively, as descriptive norms, injunctive norms, and institutional norms. But the jargon varies widely across fields, so I tried for simpler terms. Michael W. Morris, Ying-Yi Hong, Chi-Yue Chiu, and Zhi Liu, "Normology: Integrating Insights about Social Norms to Understand Cultural Dynamics," *Organizational Behavior and Human Decision Processes* 129 (2015): 1–13. Evolutionary anthropologists have made the case previously that norm psychology evolved in waves: Maciej Chudek and Joseph Henrich, "Culture-Gene Coevolution, Norm-Psychology and the Emergence of Human Prosociality," *Trends in Cognitive Sciences* 15, no. 5 (2011): 218–26.

xxviii **The term and its cognates are used**: Sebastian Junger, *Tribe: On Homecoming and Belonging* (New York: Twelve, 2016). For peoples who have who suffered colonialism, the word "tribe" can carry painful memories. I often refer to these groups as peoples, nations, or societies for that reason. Some activists suggest permitting the word "tribe" only to these peoples. But most of the world's population qualifies (e.g., my own family descends from one of the twelve tribes of Galway in Ireland). Also it hardly seems fair to groups like Jews who called themselves tribes for many centuries before colonialism. Broader usage may be the best cure for lingering pejorative connotations.

xxviii **Companies chose the term to honor**: Seth Godin, *Tribes: We Need You to Lead Us* (New York: Portfolio, 2008).

xxviii **applied it to partisan factions**: Amy Chua, *Political Tribes: Group Instinct and the Fate of Nations* (New York: Penguin Books, 2019); Stephen Hawkins, Daniel Yudkin, Miriam Juan-Torres, and Tim Dixon, *Hidden Tribes: A Study of America's Polarized Landscape* (New York: More in Common, 2019).

xxix **saw neo-tribes in consumer communities**: Bernard Cova, Robert V. Kozinets, and Avi Shankar, eds., *Consumer Tribes* (New York: Routledge, 2007).

xxix **Professions, occupations, and vocations found the term:** Dale C. Spencer and Kevin Walby, "Neo-Tribalism, Epistemic Cultures, and the Emotions of Scientific Knowledge Construction," *Emotion, Space and Society* 7 (2013): 54–61.

xxix **communities formed around shared tastes:** Michel Maffesoli, *The Time of the Tribes* (London: Sage Publications, 1995); Michel Maffesoli, "From Society to Tribal Communities," *Sociological Review* 64, no. 4 (2016): 739–47; Andy Bennett, "Subcultures or Neo-Tribes? Rethinking the Relationship between Youth, Style and Musical Taste," *Sociology* 33, no. 3 (1999): 599–617.

xxxi **primal hate for out-groups has somehow:** Andrew Sullivan, "Can Our Democracy Survive Tribalism?," *New York Magazine* 105, September 18, 2017. Thomas L. Friedman, "Have We Reshaped Middle East Politics or Started to Mimic It," *New York Times*, September 14, 2021.

xxxi **it doesn't square with evolutionary:** Dominic Packer and Jay Van Bavel, "The Myth of Tribalism," *Atlantic*, January 3, 2002.

Chapter 1: Syncing Up

3 **"Alone we can do so little":** Joseph P. Lash, *Helen and Teacher: The Story of Helen Keller and Anne Sullivan Macy* (New York: Delacorte Press/Seymour Lawrence, 1980).

3 **oldest human footprints ever:** Matthew R. Bennett et al., "Early Hominin Foot Morphology Based on 1.5-Million-Year-Old Footprints from Ileret, Kenya," *Science* 323, no. 5918 (2009): 1197–1201.

5 **human sex-segregated group activity:** Kevin G. Hatala et al., "Footprints Reveal Direct Evidence of Group Behavior and Locomotion in Homo Erectus," *Scientific Reports* 6 (2016): 28766.

5 **a hunting party stalking:** Ewen Callaway, "*Homo erectus* Footprints Hint at an Ancient Hunting Party," *Nature* (2015).

5 **collaborated this way to hunt antelopes:** Louis Liebenberg, "The Relevance of Persistence Hunting to Human Evolution," *Journal of Human Evolution* 55 (2008): 1156–59.

6 **Nor do they ever point to inform:** Michael Tomasello, "Why Don't Apes Point?," in *Roots of Human Sociality*, eds. N. J. Enfield and Stephen C. Levinson (New York: Routledge, 2006), 506–24.

6 **foraging of fifty-five different plant species:** Yoel Melamed et al., "The Plant Component of an Acheulian Diet at Gesher Benot Ya'aqov, Israel," *Proceedings of the National Academy of Sciences* 113, no. 51 (2016): 14674–79.

6 **they discovered "phantom hearths":** Nira Alperson-Afil, Daniel Richter, and Naama Goren-Inbar, "Phantom Hearths and the Use of Fire at Gesher Benot Ya'aqov,

Israel," *PaleoAnthropology* 2007 (2007): 1–15. So much for today's "paleo diet" purists who strive to subsist on raw meat. Our paleo progenitors in the Hula Valley— with their vegetables, nuts, smoked fish, and roasted venison—would look upon this diet with disdain.

6 **cooking could be the explanation:** Cooking raises the calories that we absorb from food while dramatically reducing the caloric energy needed to chew and digest it. Without cooking, chimps must spend up to eight hours a day chewing to extract nutrition from the raw plant stems, lizards, and the like. This is another example of how cultural evolution influences genetic evolution: cooking changed the selection pressures, rendering ape-like jaws and guts obsolete and enabling bigger brains. Richard W. Wrangham et al., "The Raw and the Stolen: Cooking and the Ecology of Human Origins," *Current Anthropology* 40, no. 5 (1999): 567–94; Richard Wrangham, *Catching Fire: How Cooking Made Us Human* (New York: Basic Books, 2009).

7 **Goren-Inbar's microscope revealed:** The perennial challenge of archaeology is that *absence* of evidence is not evidence of absence. Emerging methods are revealing more evidence for control of fire in a wide array of sites from this era. Katharine MacDonald et al., "Middle Pleistocene Fire Use: The First Signal of Widespread Cultural Diffusion in Human Evolution," *Proceedings of the National Academy of Sciences* 118, no. 31 (2021): e2101108118.

7 **Chimps use gestural signals:** Herbert S. Terrace, Laura Ann Petitto, Richard Jay Sanders, and Thomas G. Bever, "Can an Ape Create a Sentence?," *Science* 206, no. 4421 (1979): 891–902.

7 **90 percent of humans are right-handed:** Michael C. Corballis, "From Mouth to Hand: Gesture, Speech, and the Evolution of Right-Handedness," *Behavioral and Brain Sciences* 26, no. 2 (2003): 199–208; Marina Lozano et al., "Right-Handed Fossil Humans," *Evolutionary Anthropology: Issues, News, and Reviews* 26, no. 6 (2017): 313–24.

7 **emergence of syntactic circuitry and capacity:** Chimp gestures are guessed correctly by untrained humans and overlap highly with gestures of human toddlers. Ingrid Wickelgren, "Humans Can Correctly Guess the Meaning of Chimp Gestures," *Scientific American*, January 24, 2023, https://www.scientificamerican.com/article/humans -can-correctly-guess-the-meaning-of-chimp-gestures/.

7 **Contrary to linguist Noam Chomsky's:** Robert C. Berwick, and Noam Chomsky. *Why Only Us: Language and Evolution* (Cambridge, MA: MIT Press, 2016).

8 *The March of Progress:* This image of linear succession belies a complex family tree. Evolution is not tidy. It creates overlapping species and offshoots that get left by the wayside. Hominins were as physically diverse as the slope-browed *erectus*, the stout

neanderthalensis, and the hobbit-like *florensienis*. Even more surprising, these three distinct human species all walked the earth at the same time! The journey from apes to us was less a relay race in which each archaic species passed on the baton (or granite club) than a wrestling rumble in which many competed, some got knocked out cold, and others managed to tag a successor.

8 **Apes were already brainiacs:** Proportional to body size, humans are the brainiest and chimpanzees and bonobos tie for third, with dolphins and orcas sliding into second place! Then more "Great Apes"—orangutans and gorillas—followed by many kinds of monkeys. Next come other large-headed species such as elephants, dogs, and squirrels. Cats, some may be disappointed to learn, are a little farther back in line.

9 **But they *do* mate more judiciously:** Robin I. M. Dunbar, "The Social Brain Hypothesis," *Evolutionary Anthropology* 6, no. 5 (1998): 178–190.

9 **This "social brain hypothesis":** Matthew D. Lieberman, *Social: Why Our Brains Are Wired to Connect* (Oxford: Oxford University Press, 2013).

9 **The forebrain regions that handle:** Ralph Adolphs, "The Social Brain: Neural Basis of Social Knowledge," *Annual Review of Psychology* 60 (2009): 693–716.

10 **But on tests of social cognitive capacities:** Esther Herrmann et al., "Humans Have Evolved Specialized Skills of Social Cognition: The Cultural Intelligence Hypothesis," *Science* 317, no. 5843 (2007): 1360–66.

10 **Our innate wiring for social cognition:** Peter J. Richerson, and Robert Boyd, "The Evolution of Subjective Commitment to Groups: A Tribal Instincts Hypothesis," *Evolution and the Capacity for Commitment* 3 (2001): 186–220. Mark Van Vugt, Robert Hogan, and Robert B. Kaiser, "Leadership, Followership, and Evolution: Some Lessons from the Past," *American Psychologist* 63, no. 3 (2008): 182; Mark Van Vugt and J. Park, "Guns, Germs, and Tribal Social Identities: Evolutionary Perspectives on the Social Psychology of Intergroup Relations," *Social and Personality Psychology Compass* 3 (2009): 927–38; Daniel R. Kelly, "Moral Disgust and the Tribal Instincts Hypothesis," *Cooperation and Its Evolution* (2013): 503–24.

11 **As a practice becomes common:** Julian De Freitas, Kyle Thomas, Peter DeScioli, and Steven Pinker, "Common Knowledge, Coordination, and Strategic Mentalizing in Human Social Life," *Proceedings of the National Academy of Sciences* 116, no. 28 (2019): 13751–58.

11 **This transformative tribal wiring:** Jared Diamond, *The World Until Yesterday: What Can We Learn from Traditional Societies?* (New York: Penguin Books, 2013). Some past scholars have been more generous in their estimates, seeing the action

begin fifty thousand years ago in Europe or one hundred thousand years ago in East Africa. However, even these estimates miss the first stirrings of broader collaboration.

12 **upended this story of social development:** David Graeber and David Wengrow, *The Dawn of Everything: A New History of Humanity* (New York: Farrar, Straus & Giroux, 2021).

12 **began encoding how the others:** Collective foraging has a higher caloric return and is particularly advantageous when the supply is scarce or clumpy. Working jointly with others is an insurance policy against bad luck as a hunter or gatherer. Mathieu Lihoreau et al., "Collective Foraging in Spatially Complex Nutritional Environments," *Philosophical Transactions of the Royal Society B: Biological Sciences* 372, no. 1727 (2017): 20160238.

13 **sensitive to the others around:** Daniel B. M. Haun, Yvonne Rekers, and Michael Tomasello, "Children Conform to the Behavior of Peers; Other Great Apes Stick with What They Know," *Psychological science* 25, no. 12 (2014): 2160–67.

13 **humans who are the chief copycats:** Monkeys adeptly mimic motor movements because they have "mirror neurons." Despite the hype about them, mirror neurons do not explain empathy, therapy, or diplomacy (monkeys, last I checked, can't do these things). These more advanced social behaviors require the more complex sharing capacities of the tribal instincts.

13 **"readable" anatomy of our eyes:** Hiromi Kobayashi and Shiro Kohshima, "Unique Morphology of the Human Eye and Its Adaptive Meaning: Comparative Studies on External Morphology of the Primate Eye," *Journal of Human Evolution* 40, no. 5 (2001): 419–35; Michael Tomasello, Brian Hare, Hagen Lehmann, and Josep Call, "Reliance on Head versus Eyes in the Gaze Following of Great Apes and Human Infants: The Cooperative Eye Hypothesis," *Journal of Human Evolution* 52, no. 3 (2007): 314–20. Interestingly, dogs also have light-colored sclera, perhaps because our progenitors bred them for "readability" and communication. Consistent with this, dogs can follow human gaze and follow pointing better than apes can. Sarah C. P. Williams, "In the Eyes of a Dog," *Science*, January 5, 2012, https://www.science .org/content/article/eyes-dog.

14 **underappreciated foundation of human culture:** The selective impairment of this suite of processes in autism supports the notion that they have an evolved and interconnected basis. Parents tend to notice autism first in underdeveloped eye contact and social interactions at around age three, but earlier symptoms are infants' lower gaze tracking. Rachael Bedford et al., "Precursors to Social and Communication

Difficulties in Infants At-Risk for Autism: Gaze Following and Attentional Engage-ment," *Journal of Autism and Developmental Disorders* 42 (2012): 2208–18.

14 **original or optimal choices:** The word "autism" comes from the Greek word for "alone," but another hinted meaning is autonomy. People with this neurological con-dition can infer intentions, coordinate, and conform, but not as easily and automati-cally as most people do. Some of our greatest innovators, such as Albert Einstein and Elon Musk, are thought to have mild autism. Freedom from the constant pull to think like one's peers may help in thinking clearly about technical problems. Simon Baron-Cohen, Sally Wheelwright, Amy Burtenshaw, and Esther Hobson, "Mathe-matical Talent Is Linked to Autism," *Human Nature* 18 (2007): 125–31. A strategy of many innovators, from Warren Buffett to Georgia O'Keeffe, is exiling themselves from the settings where most of their occupational peers reside, protecting against peer influence.

14 **"Work from home" is ending:** At Microsoft, a six-month study of sixty thousand employees tracked emails, messages, calls, and calendar notices to measure changes in the company's workflow. It found that work from home became more siloed, with 25 percent less time spent coordinating across groups, and communication became less synchronous. A lesson of peer instinct: it's harder to get on the *same page* with coworkers if you are not working from the same place. The tech industry is rushing to solve this problem through metaverse meeting tools, though it remains to be seen whether culture and coordination can be cued via plastic devices strapped to our faces. Longqi Yang et al., "The Effects of Remote Work on Collaboration among Information Workers," *Nature Human Behaviour* 6, no. 1 (2022): 43–54.

15 **Singapore was founded in the early:** C. M. Turnbull, *A History of Singapore 1819–1975* (Oxford: Oxford University Press, 1977).

15 **eventually threw off British dominion:** Christopher Bayly and Tim Harper, *Forgot-ten Wars: The End of Britain's Asian Empire* (London: Allen Lane, 2007).

16 **"if we were just like our neighbors":** "Excerpts from an Interview with Lee Kuan Yew," *New York Times*, August 29, 2007, https://www.nytimes.com/2007/08/29/world/asia/29iht-lee-excerpts.html.

16 **"I was trying to create":** Katie Hunt and Susannah Cullinane, "Lee Kuan Yew: Sin-gapore's Founding Father Divided Opinion," CNN, August 9, 2015, https://www.cnn.com/2015/03/22/asia/singapore-lee-kuan-yew-obit/index.html.

16 **anti-corruption laws would not suffice:** Nina Mazar and Pankaj Aggarwal, "Greas-ing the Palm: Can Collectivism Promote Bribery?," *Psychological Science* 22, no. 7 (2011): 843–48.

16 **"the best bloody Englishman"**: "Lee Kuan Yew," *The Economist*, Obituary, March 22, 2015, https://www.economist.com/obituary/2015/03/22/lee-kuan-yew.

16 **Southeast Asian relationship-based approach**: Importantly, this is not a claim that colonial Singapore was free of corruption, or that their "free port" was motivated by high principles. Raffles wanted to legitimize English naval presence in a region where the Dutch had been the dominant colonial power. Free trade was a means to this end, so all ships were treated equally.

17 **party donned white cotton uniforms**: White uniforms were not a Chinese cultural reference (if anything, white is the color of funerals). The Party promised efficiency and order, as the English Navy had in the past. Over time, the white uniforms also came to symbolize incorruptibility.

17 **a twenty-foot statue of Raffles**: While many political leaders appeal to the group's past, it's exceedingly rare for an independence leader to install reminders of the colonial past. Most emancipators tear statues of colonizers from their plinths. They revel in removing colonialist names (Rhodesia becomes Zimbabwe) and customs (dashikis replace Savile Row suits). Lee explained that Singapore was relatively free of the "xenophobic hangover," so he could appropriate habits from the colonial past by rigging the port with reminders of it. Lee Kuan Yew, Extrapolating from the Singapore Experience (Singapore: Publicity Division, Ministry of Culture, 1978). Lee Kuan Yew, *The Singapore Story: Memoirs of Lee Kuan Yew*, vol. 1 (New York: Times Editions, 1998).

17 **Transparency International's index**: The Transparency International Corruption Perceptions Index measures the pervasiveness of graft in each country. Singapore consistently ranks in the ten least corrupt economies, an Asian outlier among primarily Scandinavian and Commonwealth countries. "Corruption Perceptions Index," Transparency International, www.transparency.org/cpi.

17 **Lee's use of biculturalism and tribal triggers**: Lee was neither pro-Western nor anti-Western. He was a pragmatic cultural engineer who understood the levers for triggering latent cultural codes. He elicited the cultural capital that best supported his current trade strategies.

18 **Merging UN personnel records with NYPD**: Raymond Fisman and Edward Miguel, "Corruption, Norms, and Legal Enforcement: Evidence from Diplomatic Parking Tickets," *Journal of Political Economy* 115, no. 6 (2007): 1020–48. Fisman is now at Boston University.

18 **In a paper entitled "Who Doesn't?"**: Nils C. Köbis, Jan-Willem Van Prooijen, Francesca Righetti, and Paul A. M. van Lange, "'Who Doesn't?'—The Impact of

Descriptive Norms on Corruption," *PloS one* 10, no. 6 (2015): e0131830; Klaus Abbink, Esteban Freidin, Lata Gangadharan, and Rodrigo Moro, "The Effect of Social Norms on Bribe Offers," *Journal of Law, Economics, and Organization* 34, no. 3, August 2018, 457–74.

18 **recruited international students from countries:** Abigail Barr and Danila Serra, "Corruption and Culture: An Experimental Analysis," *Journal of Public Economics* 94, no. 11–12 (2010): 862–69.

19 **"sprang into being" in his mind:** Marcel Proust, *Swann's Way: In Search of Lost Time*, vol. 1 (New Haven, CT: Yale University Press, 2013).

19 **Signs of a tribe are powerfully evocative:** Research studies have tested this prediction about insiders and outsiders. Jeanne Ho-Ying Fu, Chi-Yue Chiu, Michael W. Morris, and Maia J. Young, "Spontaneous Inferences from Cultural Cues: Varying Responses of Cultural Insiders and Outsiders," *Journal of Cross-Cultural Psychology* 38, no. 1 (2007): 58–75.

19 **no tech boom was evoked:** Nicole Kobie, "Inside Cyberjaya, Malaysia's Failed Silicon Valley," *Wired*, April 5, 2016, https://www.wired.co.uk/article/malaysia-cyberjaya -silicon-valley-smart-cities.

20 **limiting internet freedoms for years:** Jeremy Malcolm, "Malaysian Internet Censorship Is Going from Bad to Worse," Electronic Frontier Foundation, March 7, 2016, https://www.eff.org/deeplinks/2016/03/malaysian-internet-censorship-going-bad -worse.

21 **cartoons of fish swimming:** Michael W. Morris and Kaiping Peng, "Culture and Cause: American and Chinese Attributions for Social and Physical Events," *Journal of Personality and Social Psychology* 67, no. 6 (1994): 949. In subsequent studies we developed analogous questions about penguins, horses, and martians just to check that the divergence in interpretations was not something specific to fish. Tanya Menon, Michael W. Morris, Chi-Yue Chiu, and Ying-Yi Hong, "Culture and the Construal of Agency: Attribution to Individual versus Group Dispositions," *Journal of Personality and Social Psychology* 76, no. 5 (1999): 701.

21 **made quite a splash:** This work received the Society of Experimental Social Psychology's Dissertation Award, which attracted interest and helped to launch my career. Kaiping went on to become one of China's best-known psychologists and a dean at the leading Tsinghua University.

22 **perception of their peers' beliefs:** Xi Zou et al., "Culture as Common Sense: Perceived Consensus versus Personal Beliefs as Mechanisms of Cultural Influence," *Journal of Personality and Social Psychology* 97, no. 4 (2009): 579.

22 **code-switching among bilinguals:** John Joseph Gumpertz and Dell H. Hymes, *Directions in Sociolinguistics: The Ethnography of Communication* (Oxford: Basil Blackwell, 1986).

23 **Japanese American "war brides":** Susan Ervin-Tripp, "An Issei Learns English," *Journal of Social Issues* 23, no. 2 (1967): 78–90.

23 **a "get acquainted" chat in their native language:** Nan M. Sussman and Howard M. Rosenfeld, "Influence of Culture, Language, and Sex on Conversational Distance," *Journal of Personality and Social Psychology* 42, no. 1 (1982): 66; Edward T. Hall, *Beyond Culture* (New York: Anchor Books/Doubleday, 1976).

23 **be Mexican again:** Armando M. Padilla, "Bicultural Development: A Theoretical and Empirical Examination," in R. G. Malgady and O. Rodriguez, eds., *Theoretical and Conceptual Issues in Hispanic Mental Health* (Malabar, Florida: Robert E. Krieger Publishing Co., 1994), 30.

23 **becomes automatized in response:** This means that peer codes from the given culture spring (from memory) to the fore of their minds, where they become more likely to guide inferences and actions. Sometimes triggered cultural codes break into our conscious thoughts and we deliberate about cultural customs reflectively, but more often they operate from the "preconscious," the mental processing that occurs just below the level of awareness.

24 **They were adept at both logics:** I also ran the parallel experiments on bicultural Asian Americans in California, working with another cultural chameleon, Veronica Benet-Martinez. Ying-Yi Hong, Michael W. Morris, Chi-Yue Chiu, and Veronica Benet-Martinez, "Multicultural Minds: A Dynamic Constructivist Approach to Culture and Cognition," *American Psychologist* 55, no. 7 (2000): 709–20.

24 **judgment tasks and different bicultural populations:** Donnel A. Briley, Michael W. Morris, and Itamar Simonson, "Cultural Chameleons: Biculturals, Conformity Motives, and Decision Making," *Journal of Consumer Psychology* 15, no. 4 (2005): 351–62; Maykel Verkuyten and Katerina Pouliasi, "Biculturalism among Older Children: Cultural Frame Switching, Attributions, Self-Identification, and Attitudes," *Journal of Cross-Cultural Psychology* 33, no. 6 (2002): 596–609; Michael J. Halloran and Emiko S. Kashima, "Social Identity and Worldview Validation: The Effects of Ingroup Identity Primes and Mortality Salience on Value Endorsement," *Personality and Social Psychology Bulletin* 30, no. 7 (2004): 915–25; David Matsumoto, Ana Maria Anguas-Wong, and Elena Martinez, "Priming Effects of Language on Emotion Judgments in Spanish-English Bilinguals," *Journal of Cross-Cultural Psychology* 39, no. 3 (2008): 335–42. Other research teams have tested more direct links: situational cues of individualism/independence or of collectivism/interdependence produce

corresponding shifts in participants' judgments. Shinobu Kitayama, Hazel Rose Markus, Hisaya Matsumoto, and Vinai Norasakkunkit, "Individual and Collective Processes in the Construction of the Self: Self-Enhancement in the United States and Self-Criticism in Japan," *Journal of Personality and Social Psychology* 72, no. 6 (1997): 1245; Daphna Oyserman and Spike W. S. Lee, "Does Culture Influence What and How We Think? Effects of Priming Individualism and Collectivism," *Psychological Bulletin* 134, no. 2 (2008): 311.

24 **switching occurs automatically and unconsciously:** My lab drilled deep on this critical point. In some studies, we've presented cultural cues by subliminally flashing the word "Asian" or "American" (displaying it too quickly for them to consciously notice but long enough for their minds to unconsciously register). Aurelia Mok and Michael W. Morris, "Managing Two Cultural Identities: The Malleability of Bicultural Identity Integration as a Function of Induced Global or Local Processing," *Personality and Social Psychology Bulletin* 38, no. 2 (2012): 233–46. Likewise, we've found that switching doesn't require that participants are conscious of making social judgments. Without asking for explanations of behavior, the same attributional biases can be assessed through errors made in recalling the story. Social judgments shift with cultural cues even without ever asking participants to make judgments. Michael W. Morris and Aurelia Mok, "Isolating Effects of Cultural Schemas: Cultural Priming Shifts Asian-Americans' Biases in Social Description and Memory," *Journal of Experimental Social Psychology* 47, no. 1 (2011): 117–26.

24 **peer codes associated with different identities:** First, we measured each participant's peer codes and found that they didn't change as a function of the cue presented. Second, we tested that the extremity of participants' attributions correlated with that their peer code. Xi Zou et al., "Culture as Common Sense," 579.

24 **dwelling halfway between two cultures:** Veronica Benet-Martinez, Janxin Leu, Fiona Lee, and Michael W. Morris, "Negotiating Biculturalism: Cultural Frame Switching in Biculturals with Oppositional versus Compatible Cultural Identities," *Journal of Cross-Cultural Psychology* 33, no. 5 (2002): 492–516; Aurelia Mok and Michael W. Morris, "An Upside to Bicultural Identity Conflict: Resisting Groupthink in Cultural Ingroups," *Journal of Experimental Social Psychology* 46, no. 6 (2010): 1114–17; Andy Molinsky, *Global Dexterity: How to Adapt Your Behavior across Cultures without Losing Yourself in the Process* (Cambridge, MA: Harvard Business Review Press, 2013).

25 **Obama chalked up his adaptability:** He put it to journalist Jennifer Senior like this: "There's a level of self-consciousness about these issues the previous generation had to negotiate that I don't feel I have to." Jennifer Senior, "Dreaming of Obama," *New*

York Magazine, September 22, 2006, https://nymag.com/news/politics/21681/; Aurelia Mok and Michael W. Morris, "Bicultural Self-Defense in Consumer Contexts: Self-Protection Motives Are the Basis for Contrast versus Assimilation to Cultural Cues," *Journal of Consumer Psychology 23,* no. 2 (2013): 175–88.

25 *Key & Peele* sketch: BallIsLife, "Barack Obama Handshake: White Guy vs Kevin Durant," Facebook, August 4, 2017, https://www.facebook.com/watch/?v=1597294 740312917; Comedy Central, "Key & Peele – Obama Meet & Greet," YouTube, September 24, 2014, https://www.youtube.com/watch?v=nopWOC4SRm4.

25 difficulty speaking English fluently: Shu Zhang, Michael W. Morris, Chi-Ying Cheng, and Andy J. Yap, "Heritage-Culture Images Disrupt Immigrants' Second-Language Processing through Triggering First-Language Interference," *Proceedings of the National Academy of Sciences 110,* no. 28 (2013): 11272–77.

26 race is trumped by language: Katherine D. Kinzler, Kristin Shutts, Jasmine DeJesus, and Elizabeth S. Spelke, "Accent Trumps Race in Guiding Children's Social Preferences," *Social Cognition 27,* no. 4 (2009): 623; Danielle Labotka and Susan A. Gelman, "The Development of Children's Identification of Foreigner Talk," *Developmental Psychology 56,* no. 9 (2020): 1657.

26 preverbal infants are oblivious: Katherine D. Kinzler, Emmanuel Dupoux, and Elizabeth S. Spelke, "The Native Language of Social Cognition," *Proceedings of the National Academy of Sciences 104,* no. 30 (2007): 12577–80.

26 notice what people eat: Zoe Liberman, Amanda L. Woodward, Kathleen R. Sullivan, and Katherine D. Kinzler, "Early Emerging System for Reasoning about the Social Nature of Food," *Proceedings of the National Academy of Sciences 113,* no. 34 (2016): 9480–85.

26 skin color affects many judgments: Tamara Rakić, Melanie C. Steffens, and Amélie Mummendey, "Blinded by the Accent! The Minor Role of Looks in Ethnic Categorization," *Journal of Personality and Social Psychology 100,* no. 1 (2011): 16; Jim A. C. Everett et al., "Covered in Stigma? The Impact of Differing Levels of Islamic Head-Covering on Explicit and Implicit Biases toward Muslim Women," *Journal of Applied Social Psychology 45,* no. 2 (2015): 90–104.

26 Lee Kuan Yew declared English: Lee Kuan Yew, *My Lifelong Challenge: Singapore's Bilingual Journey* (Singapore: Straits Times Press, 2012).

26 A corporate example of language policies: Boeing had found a striking correlation across countries between crash rates and hierarchical norms. The National Transportation Safety Board noted related deficits in the cockpit conversations leading up to some of Korean Air's crashes. Malcolm Gladwell brought these kinds of evidence

together in a captivating chapter on the problem. But the most striking fact is the change since. It was indeed a strong cultural influence but an entirely malleable one. Boeing Airplane Company, *Accident Prevention Strategies: Removing Links in the Accident Chain* (Seattle, WA: Boeing Commercial Airplane Group, 1993); National Transportation Safety Board, *Aircraft Accident Report: Controlled Flight into Terrain, Korean Air, Flight 801, Boeing 747-300, HL7468, Nimitz Hill, Guam, August 6, 1997* (Washington, DC: 1999); Malcolm Gladwell, *Outliers: The Story of Success* (New York: Little, Brown, 2008).

27 **Rakuten gave a speech (in English):** "Rakuten's Decision on English Not Welcomed by Everyone," *Japan Today*, July 19, 2010.

27 **premeds who put on a doctor's white coat:** Claude M. Steele, "The Psychology of Self-Affirmation: Sustaining the Integrity of the Self," *Advances in Experimental Social Psychology* 21 (1988): 261–302; Adam Hajo and Adam D. Galinsky, "Enclothed Cognition," *Journal of Experimental Social Psychology* 48, no. 4 (2012): 918–25.

27 **Undercover agents instead adopt the attire:** Laurence Miller, "Undercover Policing: A Psychological and Operational Guide," *Journal of Police and Criminal Psychology* 21, no. 2 (2006): 1–24.

29 **Yearning for certainty attracts us:** Arie W. Kruglanski and Tallie Freund, "The Freezing and Unfreezing of Lay-Inferences: Effects on Impressional Primacy, Ethnic Stereotyping, and Numerical Anchoring," *Journal of Experimental Social Psychology* 19, no. 5 (1983): 448–68.

29 **When Chinese students are put under:** Chi-Yue Chiu, Michael W. Morris, Ying-Yi Hong, and Tanya Menon, "Motivated Cultural Cognition: The Impact of Implicit Cultural Theories on Dispositional Attribution Varies as a Function of Need for Closure," *Journal of Personality and Social Psychology* 78, no. 2 (2000): 247.

30 **personality scale that measures certainty-seeking:** Donna M. Webster and Arie W. Kruglanski, "Individual Differences in Need for Cognitive Closure," *Journal of Personality and Social Psychology* 67, no. 6 (1994): 1049.

30 **A study of immigrants to Italy:** Ankica Kosic, Arie W. Kruglanski, Antonio Pierro, and Lucia Mannetti, "The Social Cognition of Immigrants' Acculturation: Effects of the Need for Closure and the Reference Group at Entry," *Journal of Personality and Social Psychology* 86, no. 6 (2004): 796.

30 **studies of bicultural MBA students:** Jeanne Ho-Ying Fu et al., "Epistemic Motives and Cultural Conformity: Need for Closure, Culture, and Context as Determinants of Conflict Judgments," *Journal of Personality and Social Psychology* 92, no. 2 (2007): 191; Melody Manchi Chao, Zhi-Xue Zhang, and Chi-Yue Chiu, "Adherence to

Perceived Norms across Cultural Boundaries: The Role of Need for Cognitive Closure and Ingroup Identification," *Group Processes & Intergroup Relations* 13, no. 1 (2010): 69–89.

30 **Israeli intelligence officers who missed clues:** Uri Bar-Joseph and Arie W. Kruglanski, "Intelligence Failure and Need for Cognitive Closure: On the Psychology of the Yom Kippur Surprise," *Political Psycho*logy 24, no. 1 (2003): 75–99. Ronen Bergman and Adam Goldman, "Israel Knew Hamas's Attack Plan More than a Year Ago," *New York Times*, November 30, 2023, https://www.nytimes.com/2023/11/30/world /middleeast/israel-hamas-attack-intelligence.html.

31 **success comes when he "turns his brain off":** James Boyd, Zak Keefer, and Alec Lewis, "Vikings Overcome 33-Point Deficit to Defeat Colts, Complete Largest Comeback in NFL History," *The Athletic*, December 17, 2022, https://theathletic.com /4011868/2022/12/17/colts-vikings-comeback; Dan Pompei, "Overlooked Kirk Cousins Has Studied His Way to the Top of the Game," Bleacher Report, January 7, 2016, https://bleacherreport.com/articles/2605673-overlooked-kirk-cousins-has-studied -his-way-to-the-top-of-the-game.ss.

Chapter 2: Slaying Giants

33 **"Reputation, reputation, reputation":** William Shakespeare, *The Plays of William Shakespeare*, vol. 1 (Philadelphia: Charles Willliams, 1813).

33 **the leg of a woolly mammoth:** This particular specimen met its demise in the late Stone Age, but evidence for the hunting of giant pachyderms and the use of stone-tip spears dates back to the middle Stone Age, a half a million years ago. Vladimir V. Pitulko et al., "Early Human Presence in the Arctic: Evidence from 45,000 -Year-Old Mammoth Remains," *Science* 351, no. 6270 (2016): 260–63; University of Southampton, "Giant Prehistoric Elephant Slaughtered by Early Humans," Science-Daily, September 19, 2013, www.sciencedaily.com/releases/2013/09/130919085710 .htm.

34 **This cultural forgetting suggests:** Kim Sterelny, *The Evolved Apprentice: How Evolution Made Humans Unique* (Cambridge, MA: MIT Press, 2012).

35 **start of clan-level cooperation:** Nicholas J. Conard et al., "Excavations at Schöningen and Paradigm Shifts in Human Evolution," *Journal of Human Evolution* 89 (2015): 1–17; Jordi Serangeli, Utz Böhner, Thijs Van Kolfschoten, and Nicholas J. Conard," Overview and New Results from Large-Scale Excavations in Schöningen," *Journal of Human Evolution* 89 (2015): 27–45.

35 **I call the "hero instinct":** William J. Goode, *The Celebration of Heroes: Prestige as a Social Control System* (Berkeley: University of California Press, 2022).

35 **simpler term is "hero codes":** Maciej Chudek and Joseph Henrich, "Culture-Gene Coevolution, Norm-Psychology and the Emergence of Human Prosociality," *Trends in Cognitive Sciences* 15, no. 5 (2011): 218–26; Ryan P. Jacobson, Chad R. Mortensen, and Robert B. Cialdini, "Bodies Obliged and Unbound: Differentiated Response Tendencies for Injunctive and Descriptive Social Norms," *Journal of Personality and Social Psychology* 100, no. 3 (2011): 433.

36 **prosociality pays off:** This is termed "indirect reciprocity" because your beneficiaries are not the same people who reward you. The dynamic is well captured by Yogi Berra's observation that "if you don't go to their funeral, they won't come to yours." Martin A. Nowak and Karl Sigmund, "Evolution of Indirect Reciprocity," *Nature* 437, no. 7063 (2005): 1291–98.

36 **people *today* think about reputations:** Robb Willer, "Groups Reward Individual Sacrifice: The Status Solution to the Collective Action Problem," *American Sociological Review* 74, no. 1 (2009): 23–43.

36 **people's moral evaluations:** Jonathan Haidt, *The Righteous Mind: Why Good People Are Divided by Politics and Religion* (New York: Vintage Books, 2012).

36 **elicits the same feelings:** Paul Rozin, Jonathan Haidt, and Katrina Fincher, "From Oral to Moral," *Science* 323, no. 5918 (2009): 1179–80; Hanah A. Chapman and Adam K. Anderson, "Things Rank and Gross in Nature: A Review and Synthesis of Moral Disgust," *Psychological Bulletin* 139, no. 2 (2013): 300.

36 **Disgust originated as a primate reflex:** Disgust is not the only emotion elicited by observed ethical violations. It often combines with anger, another primal emotional reflex adapted socially in humans. But if anger impels punishment, disgust impels banishment. On social media today, which lends itself to denunciations of others' moral lapses, this knee-jerk distancing impulse has become "cancel culture." Molly J. Crockett, "Moral Outrage in the Digital Age," *Nature Human Behaviour* 1, no. 11 (2017): 769–71.

37 **people feel awe in response:** Dacher Keltner and Jonathan Haidt, "Approaching Awe, a Moral, Spiritual, and Aesthetic Emotion," *Cognition and Emotion* 17, no. 2 (2003): 297–314; Dacher Keltner, *Awe: The New Science of Everyday Wonder and How It Can Transform Your Life* (New York: Penguin Press, 2023).

37 **Dunbar posits that gossip emerged:** Robin I. M. Dunbar, *Grooming, Gossip, and the Evolution of Language* (Cambridge, MA: Harvard University Press, 1998).

37 **in order to earn hero status:** While in the early Greek society only warriors could become heros, later citizens of means "could earn heroic status by acting in the

public interest" through the institution of liturgy, akin to philanthropy today. Dominic Frisby, "Voluntary Taxation: A Lesson from the Ancient Greeks," Aeon, June 2, 2017, https://aeon.co/ideas/voluntary-taxation-a-lesson-from-the-ancient-greeks.

37 **earned the status of "Big Man":** Marshall D. Sahlins, "Poor Man, Rich Man, Big-Man, Chief: Political Types in Melanesia and Polynesia," *Comparative Studies in Society and History* 5, no. 3 (1963): 285–303.

37 **ways of rewarding high contributors:** Michael Gurven, "To Give and to Give Not: The Behavioral Ecology of Human Food Transfers," *Behavioral and Brain Sciences* 27, no. 4 (2004): 543–60.

38 **"insulting the meat":** If they truly felt demeaned rather than just teased, there would be a serious incentive problem—they wouldn't try as hard next time to make a kill and bring home meat! Christopher R. Von Rueden and Adrian V. Jaeggi, "Men's Status and Reproductive Success in 33 Nonindustrial Societies: Effects of Subsistence, Marriage System, and Reproductive Strategy," *Proceedings of the National Academy of Sciences* 113, no. 39 (2016): 10824–29.

38 **without anticipation of rewards:** George E. Newman and Daylian M. Cain, "Tainted Altruism: When Doing Some Good Is Evaluated as Worse Than Doing No Good at All," *Psychological Science* 25, no. 3 (2014): 648–55.

39 **saying "I have a dream":** Gary Younge, *The Speech: The Story behind Dr. Martin Luther King Jr.'s Dream* (Chicago: Haymarket Books, 2023).

41 **invited King and others over:** Gary Younge, "Martin Luther King: The Story behind His 'I Have a Dream' Speech," *Guardian*, August 9, 2013, https://www.theguardian.com/world/2013/aug/09/martin-luther-king-dream-speech-history.

42 **start to venerate them:** Calvinists rioted to tear down church paintings and statues, but icons have been neutralized in many ways throughout history. The Sphinx suffers from a missing nose, as Sufis merely *defaced* icons. In Istanbul, the Ottomans whitewashed over Byzantine mosaics (unwittingly conserving them).

42 **The Christian cross is an icon:** In linguistics, icons are symbols that perceptually resemble the thing they represent (e.g., onomatopoetic words like "hiss" as opposed to arbitrary words like "night" versus "day"). Likewise for icons in design. The perceptual association makes iconic symbols particularly evocative. This is true for religious icons (e.g., the cross evokes the story of the Crucifixion and the ideal of Christian sacrifice). In popular discourse, "icon" emphasizes a highly familiar, evocative symbol.

42 **when the canvasser who stopped them:** Nicolas Guéguen, Christine Bougeard-Delfosse, and Céline Jacob, "The Positive Effect of the Mere Presence of a Religious

Symbol on Compliance with an Organ Donation Request," *Social Marketing Quarterly* 21, no. 2 (2015): 92–99.

43 **more likely to give to charity:** Azim F. Shariff, Aiyana K. Willard, Teresa Andersen, and Ara Norenzayan, "Religious Priming: A Meta-Analysis with a Focus on Prosociality," *Personality and Social Psychology Review* 20, no. 1 (2016): 27–48.

43 **concepts like "charity" activate:** Isabelle Pichon, Giulio Boccato, and Vassilis Saroglou, "Nonconscious Influences of Religion on Prosociality: A Priming Study," *European Journal of Social Psychology* 37, no. 5 (2007): 1032–45; Max Weisbuch-Remington, Wendy Berry Mendes, Mark D. Seery, and Jim Blascovich, "The Nonconscious Influence of Religious Symbols in Motivated Performance Situations," *Personality and Social Psychology Bulletin* 31, no. 9 (2005): 1203–16.

43 **opposition to same-sex marriage and abortion:** Annetta Snell, Miron Zuckerman, and Bonnie M. Le, "Does Religious Priming Induce Greater Prejudice? A Meta-Analytic Review," *Personality and Social Psychology Bulletin* (2022): 0146167222 1135956.

43 **National icons are potent:** Rome's armies—and Napoleon's—marched behind standards topped with an iconic bronze eagle. Often blood was shed to recapture an eagle or a flag rather than recapturing territory. Carrying the standard was a great honor but a risky role. In the Battle of Sunken Road at Antietam, for instance, eight successive bearers of the 69th New York Infantry's flag were shot down in a few hours, each time a new soldier picking it up to lead the regiment onward.

43 **evoke our civic ideals:** Michael Billig, *Banal Nationalism* (London: Sage Publications, 1995).

43 **egalitarian concepts and promotes inclusive choices:** David A. Butz, E. Ashby Plant, and Celeste E. Doerr, "Liberty and Justice for All? Implications of Exposure to the US Flag for Intergroup Relations," *Personality and Social Psychology Bulletin* 33, no. 3 (2007): 396–408. A related (and much debated) question is whether flags cue people to vote more conservatively than otherwise. A study found this before the 2008 election, but it hasn't held to the same extent in elections since. Travis J. Carter et al., "Has the Effect of the American Flag on Political Attitudes Declined over Time? A Case Study of the Historical Context of American Flag Priming," *Social Cognition* 38, no. 6 (2020): 489–520. The difference may depend on "rally 'round the flag" effects, the surges in support of incumbents during military crises (related to the effects of threats that we discuss in chapter 3). William D. Baker and John R. Oneal, "Patriotism or Opinion Leadership? The Nature and Origins of the 'Rally 'Round the Flag' Effect," *Journal of Conflict Resolution* 45, no. 5 (2001): 661–87.

43 *tricolore* **triggers an epicurean mindset:** Pierrick Gomez and Carlos J. Torelli, "It's Not Just Numbers: Cultural Identities Influence How Nutrition Information Influences the Valuation of Foods," *Journal of Consumer Psychology* 25, no. 3 (2015): 404–15.

43 **Breton flag spurs shoppers:** Nicolas Guéguen, Angélique Martin, and Jordy Stefan, "Holding Your Flag: The Effects of Exposure to a Regional Symbol on People's Behavior," *European Journal of Social Psychology* 47, no. 5 (2017): 539–52.

43 **first group symbols were totem animals:** Wikipedia, s.v. "Anishinaabe Clan System," last modified December 16, 2023, https://en.wikipedia.org/wiki/Anishinaabe _clan_system.

44 **the animals chosen as totems:** Some corporate symbols pitch the product and others prod the employees. It's no coincidence that Mary Kay surrounds its itinerant "beauty consultants" with the symbol of the bumblebee, a humble creature that buzzes around busily from flower to flower helping them bloom and, along the way, making lots of honey for the queen bee. Without a shared workplace to cue the corporate ideals, this symbol triggers them and guides aspirations.

44 **When symbols trigger our group identities:** Albert H. Hastorf and Hadley Cantril, "They Saw a Game: A Case Study," *Journal of Abnormal and Social Psychology* 49, no. 1 (1954): 129.

44 **in either team's jersey:** Mark Levine, Amy Prosser, David Evans, and Stephen Reicher, "Identity and Emergency Intervention: How Social Group Membership and Inclusiveness of Group Boundaries Shape Helping Behavior," *Personality and Social Psychology Bulletin* 31, no. 4 (2005): 443–53.

44 **"superordinate identity" effect:** Samuel L. Gaertner and John F. Dovidio, *Reducing Intergroup Bias: The Common Ingroup Identity Model* (London: Psychology Press, 2014).

45 **the "Wal-Mart of banking":** Randall Smith and Dan Fitzpatrick, "Cultures Clash as Merrill Herd Meets 'Wal-Mart of Banking,'" *The Wall Street Journal*, November 14, 2008.

46 **if you've seen the leaked video:** "BoA Employee Sings A Very Heartfelt Song," You-Tube, April 9, 2014, https://www.youtube.com/watch?v=DE5QBlC4gQM.

47 **Bank of America would acquire Merrill:** William D. Cohan, "The Final Days of Merrill Lynch," *Atlantic*, September 1, 2009, http://www.theatlantic.com/magazine /archive/2009/09/the-final-days-of-merrill-lynch/307621/.

47 **the best-known logo in banking:** Alex Brownsell, "Iconic Merrill Bull Axed in Bank of America Rebrand," *Marketing Magazine*, June 18, 2009, http://www.marketing

magazine.co.uk/article/914269/iconic-merrill-lynch-bull-axed-bank-america -rebrand.

47 **"give away free toasters"**: Edward Robinson, "Brokers Disdain Toaster Salesmen in Bank of America Deal," Bloomberg, January 9, 2009.

48 **decamped to competitor firms**: David Weidner, "Another Write-Off at B of A," MarketWatch, January 6, 2009, http://www.marketwatch.com/story/mccanns-departure-a-big-blow-to-bank-of-america.

48 **he found Sallie Krawcheck**: Simon English, "Rising Star Calls Citigroup to Account," *Daily Telegraph*, September 29, 2004, https://www.telegraph.co.uk/finance/2895976/Rising-star-calls-Citigroup-to-account.html.

48 **"The bull is back!"**: Julia La Roche, "The Amazing Life of Sallie Krawcheck, the Former Banker Who Has Everyone Captivated Again" *Business Insider*, November 29, 2012, http://www.businessinsider.com/everything-you-need-to-know-about-sallie -krawcheck-2012-11?op=1.

48 **"a recruiter's worst nightmare"**: Roben Farzad, "The Bull Whisperer," *Bloomberg*, March 3, 2011.

49 **"to rally Merrill Lynch"**: "Merrill Lynch Brings Back the Bull," Mahony Partners, June 7, 2012, https://www.mahonypartners.com/2012/06/07/merrill-lynch-brings-back -the-bull/.

49 **"They want everyone to look the same"**: Linette Lopez, "The Real Reason Why High-Powered Brokers Are Leaving Merrill Lynch," *Business Insider*, December 2, 2014, https://www.businessinsider.com/merrill-lynch-brokers-tired-of-new-bac -2014-12.

49 **Group symbols fall flat for those**: D. J. Terry and M. A. Hogg, "Group Norms and the Attitude-Behavior Relationship: A Role for Group Identification," *Personality and Social Psychology Bulletin* 22 (1996): 776–93.

49 **Churches and ecclesiastical images**: Sarah E. Cavrak and Heather M. Kleider-Offutt, "Pictures Are Worth a Thousand Words and a Moral Decision or Two: Religious Symbols Prime Moral Judgments," *International Journal for the Psychology of Religion* 25, no. 3 (2015): 173–92; Mark W. Baldwin, Suzanne E. Carrell, and David F. Lopez, "Priming Relationship Schemas: My Advisor and the Pope Are Watching Me from the Back of My Mind," *Journal of Experimental Social Psychology* 26, no. 5 (1990): 435–54; Max Weisbuch-Remington, Wendy Berry Mendes, Mark D. Seery, and Jim Blascovich, "The Nonconscious Influence of Religious Symbols in Motivated Performance Situations," *Personality and Social Psychology Bulletin* 31, no. 9 (2005): 1203–16.

49   **through ethnic or regional symbols:** Amit Bhattacharjee, Jonah Berger, and Geeta Menon, "When Identity Marketing Backfires: Consumer Agency in Identity Expression," *Journal of Consumer Research* 41, no. 2 (2014): 294–309; Tiffany Barnett White, Debra L. Zahay, Helge Thorbjørnsen, and Sharon Shavitt, "Getting Too Personal: Reactance to Highly Personalized Email Solicitations," *Marketing Letters* 19 (2008): 39–50.

49   **want to disassociate themselves:** Xi Zou, Michael W. Morris, and Veronica Benet-Martinez, "Identity Motives and Cultural Priming: Cultural (Dis)Identification in Assimilative and Contrastive Responses," *Journal of Experimental Social Psychology* 44, no. 4 (2008): 1151–59; Aurelia Mok and Michael W. Morris, "Bicultural Self-Defense in Consumer Contexts: Self-Protection Motives Are the Basis for Contrast versus Assimilation to Cultural Cues," *Journal of Consumer Psychology* 23, no. 2 (2013): 175–88.

49   **same dynamic seen in social experiments:** Matthew Feinberg, Robb Willer, and Michael Schultz, "Gossip and Ostracism Promote Cooperation in Groups," *Psychological Science* 25, no. 3 (2014): 656–64.

50   **"Bring the nation's children":** Robert P. Moses, "Speech on Freedom Summer at Stanford University," April 24, 1964, American RadioWorks, transcript, https://americanradioworks.publicradio.org/features/blackspeech/bmoses.html.

51   **stayers were more likely:** Doug McAdam, "Recruitment to High-Risk Activism: The Case of Freedom Summer," *American Journal of Sociology* 92, no. 1 (1986): 64–90.

51   **soldiers who follow flags into battle:** Sebastian Junger, *Tribe: On Homecoming and Belonging* (New York: Twelve, 2016).

51   **less often committed by maladjusted:** Simon Cottee, "Jihadism as a Subcultural Response to Social Strain: Extending Marc Sageman's 'Bunch of Guys' Thesis," *Terrorism and Political Violence* 23, no. 5 (2011): 730–51.

51   **the approval of audiences matters:** Anand Giridharadas, *Winners Take All: The Elite Charade of Changing the World* (New York: Vintage Books, 2019); Teresa Jean Odendahl, *Charity Begins at Home: Generosity and Self-Interest among the Philanthropic Elite* (New York: Basic Books, 1990).

52   **when they are observable to others:** Alex Bradley, Claire Lawrence, and Eamonn Ferguson, "Does Observability Affect Prosociality?," *Proceedings of the Royal Society B: Biological Sciences* 285, no. 1875 (2018): 20180116.

52   **one player receives a windfall:** Daniel Kahneman, Jack L. Knetsch, and Richard H. Thaler, "Fairness and the Assumptions of Economics," *Journal of Business* (1986): S285–S300.

52   **spent $6,400 on purchases to benefit:** Ryan J. Dwyer, William J. Brady, Chris Anderson, and Elizabeth W. Dunn, "Are People Generous When the Financial Stakes Are High?," *Psychological Science* (2023): 09567976231184887.

52 **Toddlers share more than chimps:** Julia Ulber, Katharina Hamann, and Michael Tomasello, "Young Children, but Not Chimpanzees, Are Averse to Disadvantageous and Advantageous Inequities," *Journal of Experimental Child Psychology* 155 (2017): 48–66; Jing Li, Wen Wang, Jing Yu, and Liqi Zhu, "Young Children's Development of Fairness Preference," *Frontiers in Psychology* 7 (2016): 1274.

52 **students who passed up an opportunity:** Elizabeth Dunn and Michael Norton, *Happy Money: The Science of Happier Spending* (New York: Simon and Schuster, 2014).

52 **Inducing shame can increase:** Emmanuel Petit, Anna Tcherkassof, and Xavier Gassmann, "Sincere Giving and Shame in a Dictator Game," *Cahiers de GREThA,* no. 25 (2012).

52 **deficit in the shame response:** Just as mild autism involves selective impairment of peer-instinct processes, mild psychopathy can involve selective impairment of hero-instinct processes. The person is otherwise mentally capable, just missing this suite of psychological processes that motivates prosocial behavior and discourages anti-social behavior. Selective impairment is one form of evidence for an evolved psychological system. Robert D. Hare, *Without Conscience: The Disturbing World of the Psychopaths Among Us* (New York: Guilford Press, 1999). Gilmore and other serial killers are quoted at length in Paul Bloom, *Just Babies: The Origins of Good and Evil* (New York: Crown Publishers, 2014).

53 **Pride and shame have often been:** We hear from the pulpit: "Pride goeth before a fall." "Better to die than live in shame." Freud and his followers saw these emotions as obsessions with self-consistency. Pride blinds. Shame paralyzes—then produces explosive anger. But this lore, based on clinical cases, doesn't correspond to how these emotions operate for most people most of the time. H. Gershman, "Neurotic Pride and Self-Hatred According to Freud and Horney," *American Journal of Psycho-analysis* 7, no. 1 (1947), 53–55; June P. Tangney, Patricia Wagner, Carey Fletcher, and Richard Gramzow, "Shamed into Anger? The Relation of Shame and Guilt to Anger and Self-Reported Aggression," *Journal of Personality and Social Psychology* 62, no. 4 (1992): 669; Jeffrey Stuewig et al., "Shaming, Blaming, and Maiming: Functional Links among the Moral Emotions, Externalization of Blame, and Aggression," *Journal of Research in Personality* 44, no. 1 (2010): 91–102.

53 **people feel pride or shame for actions:** Pride correlates with societal valuation more positively than happiness or excitement do, and shame, more negatively than sadness or anger. The pride associated with a given act (e.g., "leaving home at eighteen") varies enormously across societies because of differences in how the act is valued, not much because of differing contingencies. Daniel Sznycer et al., "Cross-Cultural

245

Regularities in the Cognitive Architecture of Pride," *Proceedings of the National Academy of Sciences* 114, no. 8 (2017): 1874–79; Daniel Sznycer et al., "Cross-Cultural Invariances in the Architecture of Shame," *Proceedings of the National Academy of Sciences* 115, no. 39 (2018): 9702–7. This research also elucidates the difference between shame and guilt. Guilt is a dyadic emotion evoked by failings toward significant others and it impels actions to repair the relationship. Accordingly, the presence of audience doesn't affect the level of guilt that people feel about an action.

53 **guides them toward actions:** The expressive reflexes that are part of pride and shame also help our reputations, as they showcase our contributions while minimizing our lapses. The instinctive posture of pride (raised fists, puffed chest) attracts others' attention, whereas that of shame (slumped shoulders, bowed head) deflects it. Pride excites us to talk about our action; shame muzzles us from mentioning our misdeeds. So, this emotional system gives rise to grandstanding and cover-ups, which do not serve the greater good. This may be why in literature and life, heroes can so easily turn into villains. The motives driving heroism also drive Machiavellian acts of reputation maintenance.

53 **posters alluding to watchers:** Joel M. Caplan, Leslie W. Kennedy, and Gohar Petrossian, "Police-Monitored CCTV Cameras in Newark, NJ: A Quasi-Experimental Test of Crime Deterrence," *Journal of Experimental Criminology* 7 (2011): 255–74.

53 **"urine indicator dye":** Pool-supply companies don't sell the dye, as it doesn't exist; they only sell the signs!

54 **Hunter-gatherers, like the !Kung:** Ara Norenzayan, *Big Gods: How Religion Transformed Cooperation And Conflict* (Princeton, NJ: Princeton University Press, 2013).

Chapter 3: Visiting the Temple

56 **"Tradition means giving a vote":** G. K. Chesterton, *Orthodoxy*, vol. 12 (New York: Image, 2012).

56 **stone arch called Pont d'Arc:** "The Gorges of the Ardèche," Avignon & Provence, https://www.avignon-et-provence.com/en/natural-sites/gorges-ardeche.

57 **"They were here":** *Cave of Forgotten Dreams*, directed by Werner Herzog (London: Revolver Entertainment, 2011), film.

57 **Not far away was Lascaux Cave:** Lascaux was discovered in 1940 by teenager Marcel Ravidat, who followed his dog, Robot, down a crevasse in a rock formation in the Dordogne forest.

58 **the cave was a mystical netherworld:** In an informal study, French archaeologist Jean-Michel Geneste arranged for four elders of an Australian Aboriginal tribe, the Ngarinyins, to visit Lascaux Cave in 1994, informing them that it was a place of his own people's ancestors. Before entering, the elders insisted on purifying themselves— pulling out their body hair, burning a pile of it, and passing back and forth through the smoke. Once inside, they marveled at the murals and found them reminiscent of their own tribe's animistic myths. They pointed out geometric markings in the drawings that resemble Aboriginal clan insignia. They speculated that the cave could have been a site for ritual initiations of shamans. Judith Thurman, "First Impressions: What Does the World's Oldest Art Say about Us?," *New Yorker*, June 16, 2008, https://www.newyorker.com/magazine/2008/06/23/first-impressions.

58 **Six thousand years later:** Gregory Curtis, *The Cave Painters: Probing the Mysteries of the World's First Artists* (New York: Anchor Books, 2007).

58 **adding to existing murals:** The same charcoal techniques were used an epoch later at Lascaux Cave. The vivid bestiaries on its walls similarly reflect drawings added to scenes started many centuries before. And similar charcoal drawing techniques are still used today. When Picasso visited Lascaux, he observed that they had already "invented everything."

58 **They used shading, etching:** Deborah Netburn, "Chauvet Cave: The Most Accurate Timeline Yet of Who Used the Cave and When," *Los Angeles Times*, April 12, 2016, https://www.latimes.com/science/sciencenow/la-sci-sn-chauvet-caves-time line-20160412-story.html; Anita Quiles et al., "A High-Precision Chronological Model for the Decorated Upper Paleolithic Cave of Chauvet-Pont d'Arc, Ardèche, France," *Proceedings of the National Academy of Sciences* 113, no. 17 (2016): 4670–75.

59 **even defend group traditions:** Edward Shils, *Tradition* (Chicago: University of Chicago Press, 1981).

59 **their bodies just like ours:** If a melting glacier uncovered a frozen family from that time, they wouldn't look like people of a different species, just people of a very different lifestyle, physically fit but highly weathered and hygiene-challenged.

59 **they were still a marginal primate species:** The low genetic diversity of our species (relative to other primates) implies "genetic bottlenecks," moments when the total population fell to just a few thousand breeding pairs, and the species teetered on the brink of extinction. Geologists long pointed to the eruption of super-volcano Toba approximately seventy-five thousand years ago, which created a decade-long winter. However, drilling studies to investigate did not show the signature of a mass extinction at this time. Lily J. Jackson, Jeffery R. Stone, Andrew S. Cohen, and Chad L. Yost, "High-Resolution

Paleoecological Records from Lake Malawi Show No Significant Cooling Associated with the Mount Toba Supereruption at ca. 75 ka.," *Geology* 43, no. 9 (2015): 823–26.

60 **they spread into Europe and Asia:** This migration in the last hundred thousand years is the one that all non-Africans today are primarily descended from. However, recent evidence suggests that there were smaller, earlier migrations. Our picture of the past deepens as science advances.

60 **stooped clumsy brutes:** The first Neanderthal skeleton discovered happened to be of an aged man with scoliosis; the image of a hunched-over species has been corrected by archaeology long ago. Its persistence, particularly in popular culture, seems to reflect *sapiens* supremacism. Martin Haeusler et al., "Morphology, Pathology, and the Vertebral Posture of the La Chapelle-aux-Saints Neandertal," *Proceedings of the National Academy of Sciences* 116, no. 11 (2019): 4923–27.

60 *neanderthalensis* **went extinct:** Until recently, archaeologists weren't sure that the two species ever met, as their remains are found at different sites. But the innovation of ancient DNA analysis put the question to rest—they not only met but mated. Most people today are about 2 percent Neanderthal (and some redheads like myself are up to 4 percent). The only people today free of Neanderthal genes are Africans. Bruce Bower, "Europe's Oldest Known Humans Mated with Neandertals Surprisingly Often," ScienceNews, April 7, 2021, https://www.sciencenews.org/article/europe -oldest-known-humans-mated-neandertals-dna-fossils.

60 **developing more complex cultures:** Classical European archaeologists called these Stone Age sophisticates Cro Magnons and posited that their cultural complexity relative to older sites in Europe must have come from an IQ-boosting mutation. Then they discovered that the real reason was migration. In Africa they found outbreaks of cultural complexity much earlier. Eleanor M. L. Scerri and Manuel Will, "The Revolution That Still Isn't: The Origins of Behavioral Complexity in Homo Sapiens," *Journal of Human Evolution* 179 (2023): 103358.

60 **cultural complexity took root:** Kim Sterelny, *The Evolved Apprentice: How Evolution Made Humans Unique* (Cambridge, MA: MIT Press, 2012).

61 **"as if they went to a hardware store":** Erica Klarreich, "Biography of Richard G. Klein," *Proceedings of the National Academy of Sciences* 101, no. 16 (2004): 5705–7.

61 **Neanderthals made symbolic drawings:** Dirk L. Hoffmann et al., "U-Th Dating of Carbonate Crusts Reveals Neandertal Origin of Iberian Cave Art," *Science* 359, no. 6378 (2018): 912–15. The emerging evidence finds a few sites where simple cave art persisted across generations but didn't expand and accumulate like it did with *sapiens*. Neanderthals may have been as intelligent but less traditionalist and hence didn't accumulate the same level of cultural complexity.

61 *sapiens* **sometimes used "exotic stone":** Alison S. Brooks et al., "Long-Distance Stone Transport and Pigment Use in the Earliest Middle Stone Age," *Science* 360, no. 6384 (2018): 90–94.

61 **DNA from Neanderthal sites:** Martin Sikora et al., "Ancient Genomes Show Social and Reproductive Behavior of Early Upper Paleolithic Foragers," *Science* 358, no. 6363 (2017): 659–62.

61 **Neanderthal bones betray:** Stanley H. Ambrose, "Coevolution of Compo site-Tool Technology, Constructive Memory, and Language: Implications for the Evolution of Modern Human Behavior," *Current Anthropology* 51, no. S1 (2010): S135–S147.

62 **lavish strings of ivory beads:** It's estimated the strings of ivory beads alone took over ten thousand person-hours of skilled work, which suggests the work of many artisans, perhaps tribute to a leader respected across several groups. Erik Trinkaus, Alexandra P. Buzhilova, Maria B. Mednikova, and Maria V. Dobrovolskaya, *The People of Sunghir: Burials, Bodies, and Behavior in the Earlier Upper Paleolithic* (New York: Oxford University Press, 2014).

62 **shrine-like structures were built:** Mikhail Sablin, Natasha Reynolds, Karina Iltsevich, and Mietje Germonpré, "The Epigravettian Site of Yudinovo, Russia: Mammoth Bone Structures as Ritualised Midden," *Environmental Archaeology* (2023): 1–21.

62 **monumental temples at Göbekli Tepe:** Tracy B. Henley, "Introducing Göbekli Tepe to Psychology," *Review of General Psychology* 22, no. 4 (2018): 477–84; Oliver Dietrich et al., "The Role of Cult and Feasting in the Emergence of Neolithic Communities. New Evidence from Göbekli Tepe, South-Eastern Turkey," *Antiquity* 86, no. 333 (2012): 674–95.

62 **"common ground" with neighboring clans:** Contemporary hunter-gatherer groups were traditionally portrayed as isolated bands or clans. New ways of mapping connections, however, have revealed their embeddedness in larger-scale networks with shared institutions—in short, tribes. Douglas W. Bird, Rebecca Bliege Bird, Brian F. Codding, and David W. Zeanah, "Variability in the Organization and Size of Hunter-Gatherer Groups: Foragers Do Not Live in Small-Scale Societies," *Journal of Human Evolution* 131 (2019): 96–108; Peter Richerson and Joseph Henrich, "Tribal Social Instincts and the Cultural Evolution of Institutions to Solve Collective Action Problems," *Cliodynamics: The Journal of Theoretical & Mathematical History* 3, no. 1 (2012).

63 **journeyed to all the water:** Joseph B. Birdsell, "Ecological Influences on Australian Aboriginal Social Organization," in *Primate Ecology and Human Origins*, eds. I. S. Bernstein and E. O. Smith (New York: Garland, 1979), 117–51.

63 **match to local flood myths:** Patrick D. Nunn and Nicholas J. Reid, "Aboriginal Memories of Inundation of the Australian Coast Dating from More than 7000 Years Ago," *Australian Geographer* 47, no. 1 (2016): 11–47.

63 **folklore motifs tend to match:** Stelios Michalopoulos and Melanie Meng Xue, "Folklore," *Quarterly Journal of Economics* 136, no. 4 (2021): 1993–2046.

64 **This rigid replication is part:** Daniel H. Stein et al., "When Alterations Are Violations: Moral Outrage and Punishment in Response to (Even Minor) Alterations to Rituals," *Journal of Personality and Social Psychology* 123, no. 1 (2022): 123.

64 **A routine becomes ritualized:** Historians say that the Exodus events never happened— it's not mentioned in the Pharaohs' detailed records—but the Seder's deep meaning doesn't depend on factuality; it comes from repetition. Jews have held Seders from the time of the Babylonian Captivity of 600 BC, through Roman Judea (Jesus's "Last Supper" was a Seder), through the centuries of diasporic groups in Spain, Russia, Morocco, Yemen, North Africa, and even India and China, and into the modern era.

64 **showed that obsessive-compulsive disorder:** As with the peer and hero instinct, ancestor-instinct processes map onto a genetically determined condition. Judith L. Rapoport and Alan Fiske, "The New Biology of Obsessive-Compulsive Disorder: Implications for Evolutionary Psychology," *Perspectives in Biology and Medicine* 41, no. 2 (1998): 159–75.

64 **counterintuitive elements foster myths and rituals:** Pascal Boyer and Charles Ramble, "Cognitive Templates for Religious Concepts: Cross-Cultural Evidence for Recall of Counter-Intuitive Representations," *Cognitive Science* 25, no. 4 (2001): 535–64; Ara Norenzayan, Scott Atran, Jason Faulkner, and Mark Schaller, "Memory and Mystery: The Cultural Selection of Minimally Counterintuitive Narratives," *Cognitive Science* 30, no. 3 (2006): 531–55.

64 **Moken people tell tales about *laboon*:** Monika Bauerlein, "Sea Change: They Outsmarted the Tsunami, but Thailand's *Sea Gypsies* Could Be Swept Away by an Even Greater Force," *Mother Jones* 30, no. 6 (November 2005): 56–61.

65 **tribal traditions work precisely:** Joseph Henrich, *The Secret of Our Success: How Culture Is Driving Human Evolution, Domesticating Our Species, and Making Us Smarter* (Princeton, NJ: Princeton University Press, 2017).

65 **adaptations for the pedagogy by elders:** György Gergely, "Ostensive Communication and Cultural Learning: The Natural Pedagogy Hypothesis," *Agency and Joint Attention* (2013): 139–51.

66 **Chimps and bonobos in this procedure:** Zanna Clay and Claudio Tennie, "Is Overimitation a Uniquely Human Phenomenon? Insights from Human Children as Compared to Bonobos," *Child Development* 89, no. 5 (2018): 1535–44.

66 **compulsively reenact it:** Derek E. Lyons, Andrew G. Young, and Frank C. Keil, "The Hidden Structure of Overimitation," *Proceedings of the National Academy of Sciences* 104, no. 50 (2007): 19751–56; Ben Kenward, Markus Karlsson, and Joanna Persson, "Over-Imitation Is Better Explained by Norm Learning than by Distorted Causal Learning," *Proceedings of the Royal Society B: Biological Sciences* 278, no. 1709 (2010): 1239–46.

66 **This shift toward "over-imitation":** Mark Nielsen, Ilana Mushin, Keyan Tomaselli, and Andrew Whiten, "Where Culture Takes Hold: 'Overimitation' and Its Flexible Deployment in Western, Aboriginal, and Bushmen Children," *Child Development* 85, no. 6 (2014): 2169–84.

66 **high-fidelity social learning:** Rachel E. Watson-Jones, Nicole J. Wen, and Cristine H. Legare, "The Psychological Foundations of Ritual Learning," in *Handbook of Advances in Culture and Psychology*, eds. M. J. Gelfand, Chi-Yue Chiu, and Ying-Yi Hong (New York: Oxford University Press, 2021), 163–94; Harvey Whitehouse, *The Ritual Animal: Imitation and Cohesion in the Evolution of Social Complexity* (New York: Oxford University Press, 2021).

67 **people who engage in risky, aversive rites:** Dimitris Xygalatas, *Ritual: How Seemingly Senseless Acts Make Life Worth Living* (New York: Little, Brown Spark, 2022).

67 **a maiden bearing a religious banner:** Wikipedia, s.v. "Prophecies about Joan of Arc," https://en.wikipedia.org/wiki/Prophecies_about_Joan_of_Arc.

67 **The saints told Jeanne:** Timothy Wilson-Smith, *Joan of Arc: Maid, Myth and History* (Cheltenham, UK: History Press, 2011).

69 **The tale of this miracle:** Régine Pernoud, *Joan of Arc: By Herself and Her Witnesses* (New York: Scarborough House, 1982); M. G. A. Vale, *Charles VII* (Berkeley: University of California Press, 1974), 55.

69 **Henry V rallied his "band of brothers":** Shakespeare based the St. Crispin's Day speech in *Henry V* on firsthand accounts by soldiers present at Agincourt.

70 **choreographed public events:** In everyday parlance, the words "ceremony" and "tradition" can be used interchangeably, so it may sound circular to say that exposure to ceremony gives rise to traditionalism. But I use the terms more precisely here. By "ceremony" I mean choreographed events that people experience as part of their social environment. By "traditions" I mean the stories and practices in a group that connect people to past generations.

70 **"We've always done it this way":** Cristine H. Legare and Rachel E. Watson-Jones, "The Evolution and Ontogeny of Ritual," in *The Handbook of Evolutionary Psychology*, ed. David M. Buss (Hoboken, NJ: John Wiley, 2015), 1–19.

70 **extreme initiation ceremonies:** Harvey Whitehouse, "Dying for the Group: Towards a General Theory of Extreme Self-Sacrifice," *Behavioral and Brain Sciences* 41 (2018).

70 public participation in religious ceremonies: Robert D. Putnam and David E. Campbell, *American Grace: How Religion Divides and Unites Us* (New York: Simon and Schuster, 2012).

70 All Blacks of New Zealand: Former captain Wayne "Buck" Shelford once suffered a traumatic scrum kick to the groin, leaving him bloody and in excruciating pain, with one testicle exposed outside of his body. He insisted on returning after a few sideline stitches, and played on until he was knocked out cold. Long after his playing days, fans expressed appreciation for his ethic of sacrifice with signs saying "Bring Back Buck." "Is Wayne Shelford the Hardest Man to Play Rugby?," All Blacks, May 7, 2021, https://www.allblacks.com/news/is-wayne-shelford-the-hardest-man-to-play-rugby/.

71 repetitive shamanic drumming: Bruno Gingras, Gerald Pohler, and W. Tecumseh Fitch, "Exploring Shamanic Journeying: Repetitive Drumming with Shamanic Instructions Induces Specific Subjective Experiences but No Larger Cortisol Decrease than Instrumental Meditation Music," *PloS one* 9, no. 7 (2014): e102103; Emma R. Huels et al., "Neural Correlates of the Shamanic State of Consciousness," *Frontiers in Human Neuroscience* 15 (2021): 140.

71 perform even simple activities synchronously: Scott S. Wiltermuth and Chip Heath, "Synchrony and Cooperation," *Psychological Science* 20, no. 1 (2009): 1–5; Emma E. A. Cohen, Robin Ejsmond-Frey, Nicola Knight, and Robin I. M. Dunbar, "Rowers' High: Behavioural Synchrony Is Correlated with Elevated Pain Thresholds," *Biology Letters* 6, no. 1 (2010): 106–8.

71 self-other blurring: Kyle M. Jasmin, Carolyn McGettigan, Zarinah K. Agnew, Nadine Lavan, Oliver Josephs, Fred Cummins, and Sophie K. Scott, "Cohesion and Joint Speech: Right Hemisphere Contributions to Synchronized Vocal Production," *Journal of Neuroscience* 36, no. 17 (2016): 4669–80; Leonie Koban, Anand Ramamoorthy, and Ivana Konvalinka, "Why Do We Fall into Sync with Others? Interpersonal Synchronization and the Brain's Optimization Principle," *Social Neuroscience* 14, no. 1 (2019): 1–9; Marta Zaraska, "All Together Now," *Scientific American* 323, no. 4 (2020): 64–69, https://www.scientificamerican.com/article/moving-in-sync-creates-surprising-social-bonds-among-people/.

72 synchrony sets the stage: Aimee L. Drolet and Michael W. Morris, "Rapport in Conflict Resolution: Accounting for How Face-to-Face Contact Fosters Mutual Cooperation in Mixed-Motive Conflicts," *Journal of Experimental Social Psychology* 36, no. 1 (2000): 26–50.

72 primed to attempt epic feats: Ceremony may explain why the Olympics evokes such extraordinary performances. From the opening ceremony to the medal ceremonies,

athletes are surrounded by synchrony and references to tradition. In 1968, in Mexico City, Bob Beamon sought to uphold an American tradition in the long jump, dating back to Jesse Owens. In repeated attempts, he sprinted like a man possessed but missed his mark. On his final try, as storm clouds gathered in the sky, he launched himself from the very edge and sailed through the air for an impossibly long moment. His landing spot was out of range of the measurement device and had to be checked by tape measure. The distance was beyond belief—beyond what was regarded as humanly possible! He broke the world record by two feet (records usually move by an inch or two).

72 **recite the Hippocratic oath:** This text originated between the third and fifth century BC, written by followers of Hippocrates (460–370 BC). It does not say "Do no harm" but expresses the general principle of non-maleficence. Some medical schools have switched to modernized versions that omit references to Greek gods and some of the prejudices of the time.

72 **as sacred traditions:** The three situational cues are not exclusive categories but rather concentric sets: tribal signs are perceptual details that tell of this group's presence, tribal symbols are the subset of these that this group uses to stand for itself; and tribal ceremonies are one of the ways that symbols get displayed, in choreographed history-referencing events. This means the triggers also overlap. For a Hindu, a *puja* ceremony may trigger ancestor codes, but the symbols involved may also trigger hero codes, and the signs involved may trigger peer codes.

73 **changed the country in lasting ways:** Ida Susser, "An Anthropological Take on the Aftermath of 9/11, in New York City," *Critique of Anthropology* 24, no. 1 (2004): 5–7; Jeremy E. Uecker, "Religious and Spiritual Responses to 9/11: Evidence from the Add Health Study," *Sociological Spectrum* 28, no. 5 (2008): 477–509.

73 **"illogical need for stuff":** Brian Thomas Gallagher, "Eating Our Feelings: Finding Comfort in Comfort Food," *New York Observer*, September 7, 2011, https://observer .com/2011/09/eating-our-feelings-finding-comfort-in-food/. As testament to this reflex, the 9/11 Memorial was originally slated to have a Danny Meyer bar and grill serving Americana classics and domestic wines, until bereaved families rightly objected to "wining and dining" above the resting place of lost ones.

74 **the closer a diarist to combat:** Brian Wansink and Craig S. Wansink, "Are There Atheists in Foxholes? Combat Intensity and Religious Behavior," *Journal of Religion and Health* 52 (2013): 768–79.

74 **"Ante, apud, ad, adversus":** Cyril Falls, *The First World War* (Barnsley, UK: Pen and Sword, 2014).

74 **rituals are practiced in contexts of threat:** Bronislaw Malinowski, "Fishing in the Trobriand Islands," *Man* 18 (1918): 87–92.

74 **rituals reduce anxiety:** Mary Douglas, *Purity and Danger: An Analysis of Concepts of Pollution and Taboo* (New York: Routledge, 2003).

74 **serves our need for continuity:** Ernest Becker, *The Denial of Death* (New York: Free Press, 1973).

75 **effects of death reminders:** Inconsistent replication of some of the original experiments have convinced researchers in the area that the effect is weaker and more contingent on the political context than it initially appeared. Lihan Chen, Rachele Benjamin, Addison Lai, and Steven Heine, "Managing the Terror of Publication Bias: A Comprehensive P-Curve Analysis of the Terror Management Theory Literature," PsyArXiv, January 3, 2023, doi.org/10.31234/osf.io/kuhy6.

75 **pedestrians in front of a cemetery:** Eva Jonas, Immo Fritsche, and Jeff Greenberg, "Currencies as Cultural Symbols—An Existential Psychological Perspective on Reactions of Germans toward the Euro," *Journal of Economic Psychology* 26, no. 1 (2005): 129–46; Tom Pyszczynski et al., "Whistling in the Dark: Exaggerated Consensus Estimates in Response to Incidental Reminders of Mortality," *Psychological Science* 7, no. 6 (1996): 332–36.

75 **after reminders of death:** Silvia Fernandez, Emanuele Castano, and Indramani Singh, "Managing Death in the Burning Grounds of Varanasi, India: A Terror Management Investigation," *Journal of Cross-Cultural Psychology* 41, no. 2 (2010): 182–94. I narrated a documentary, "Die the Good Death," about this setting: https://vimeo.com/30387484

75 **spellbinding ceremony and adrenalizing threat:** Hammad Sheikh, Jeremy Ginges, Alin Coman, and Scott Atran, "Religion, Group Threat and Sacred Values," *Judgment and Decision Making* 7, no. 2 (2012): 110.

76 **The Pope sent around:** To ensure impressive crowds, the pope offered small indulgences just for attending and bigger ones for those who signed up as Crusaders. Particularly successful sermons were written down, copied, and shared as model sermons with recruiters working in other regions; Alan V. Murray, ed., *The Crusades to the Holy Land: The Essential Reference Guide* (Santa Barbara, CA: ABC-CLIO, 2015), 215.

76 **rising Hispanic population:** Michael A. Zárate, Christine Reyna, and Miriam J. Alvarez, "Cultural Inertia, Identity, and Intergroup Dynamics in a Changing Context," in *Advances in Experimental Social Psychology* 59 (Cambridge, MA: Academic Press, 2019), 175–233.

76 **fears about loss of cultural continuity:** Felix Danbold and Yuen J. Huo, "No Longer 'All-American'? Whites' Defensive Reactions to Their Numerical Decline," *Social Psychological and Personality Science* 6, no. 2 (2015): 210–18; Maureen A. Craig and Jennifer A. Richeson, "Hispanic Population Growth Engenders Conservative Shift among Non-Hispanic Racial Minorities," *Social Psychological and Personality Science* 9, no. 4 (2018): 383–92.

76 **diversifying countries over the past decade:** Arlie Russell Hochschild, *Strangers in Their Own Land: Anger and Mourning on the American Right* (New York: New Press, 2018). Populist politicians capitalize on fears about loss of continuity by blaming problems like crime and unemployment on minorities and immigrants and promise to restore the "good old days" through exclusionary measures (even some that are not actually consistent with the nation's traditions). This is a way that populists diverge from true conservatives.

77 **solemnly salute the "suicide squad":** Justin McCurry, "Fukushima 50: 'We Felt Like Kamikaze Pilots Ready to Sacrifice Everything,'" *Guardian*, January 11, 2013, https://www.theguardian.com/environment/2013/jan/11/fukushima-50-kamikaze-pilots-sacrifice.

78 **but he pursued it anyway:** "The Yoshida Testimony," Asahi-Shimbun, December 3, 2014, http://www.asahi.com/special/yoshida_report/en;), Investigation Committee on the Accident at the Fukushima Nuclear Power Stations, *Final Report* (Tokyo: ICANPS, 2012).

78 **They sent convoys of trucks:** Dan Kedmey, "Lessons in Courage, from a Team of Japanese Firefighters," ideas.ted.com, January 20, 2016, https://ideas.ted.com/lessons-in-courage-from-a-team-of-japanese-firefighters.

Chapter 4: The Rise and Fall of Prohibition

83 **"The areas of consensus shift":** Matt Tyrnauer, "Architecture in the Age of Gehry," *Vanity Fair*, June 30, 2010, https://www.vanityfair.com/culture/2010/08/architecture-survey-201008.

85 **"scientific temperance instruction":** Wikipedia, s.v. "Department of Scientific Temperance Instruction," https://en.wikipedia.org/wiki/Department_of_Scientific_Temperance_Instruction.

85 **the Eighteenth Amendment:** Joseph P. Pollard, *The Road to Repeal: Submission to Conventions* (New York: Brentano's, 1932), 107.

86 **reader polls to measure public opinion:** Jeremy Norman, "The 'Literary Digest'

Straw Poll Correctly Predicts the Election of Woodrow Wilson," historyofinforma
tion.com, https://www.historyofinformation.com/detail.php?entryid=1652.

87 **the *Digest* repeated its poll:** David Karol, "Has Polling Enhanced Representation?
Unearthing Evidence from the Literary Digest Issue Polls," *Studies in American
Political Development* 21, no. 1 (2007): 16–29.

87 **Support for Prohibition collapsed:** John C. Gebhart, "Movement against Prohibition," *Annals of the American Academy of Political and Social Science* 163, no. 1
(1932): 172–80.

89 **Largely through Kodak's efforts:** Shiry Ginosar et al., "A Century of Portraits: A
Visual Historical Record of American High School Yearbooks," in *Proceedings of the
2015 IEEE International Conference on Computer Vision Workshops.*

90 **peer pressure to conform:** Gregory S. Berns et al., "Neurobiological Correlates of
Social Conformity and Independence During Mental Rotation," *Biological psychia-
try* 58, no. 3 (2005): 245–53; Malia F. Mason, Rebecca Dyer, and Michael I. Norton,
"Neural Mechanisms of Social Influence," *Organizational Behavior and Human
Decision Processes* 110, no. 2 (2009): 152–59.

90 ***minority* faction can also exert peer influence:** Serge Moscovici, "Toward a Theory
of Conversion Behavior," in *Advances in Experimental Social Psychology* 13 (1980):
209–39.

90 **pressure for coordination in interactions:** Damon Centola, Joshua Becker, Devon
Brackbill, and Andrea Baronchelli, "Experimental Evidence for Tipping Points in
Social Convention," *Science 360*, no. 6393 (2018): 1116–19.

91 **a "tipping point" dynamic:** People differ in their thresholds of peer prevalence. A
classic framework by sociologist Everett Rodgers distinguished "early adopters,"
"majority adopters," and "laggards." Everett M. Rogers, *Diffusion of Innovations*
(New York: Free Press of Glencoe, 1962).

91 **share their new belief with close contacts:** Beniamino Cislaghi et al., "Changing
Social Norms: The Importance of 'Organized Diffusion' for Scaling Up Community
Health Promotion and Women Empowerment Interventions," *Prevention Science* 20
(2019): 936–46.

92 **When a practice is gaining ground:** Chad R. Mortensen et al., "Trending Norms: A
Lever for Encouraging Behaviors Performed by the Minority," *Social Psychological
and Personality Science* 10, no. 2 (2019): 201–10.

93 **Start-Up Chile launched:** Jonathan Moed, "Start-Up Chile's Impact 2010–2018:
Inside the Revolutionary Startup Accelerator," *Forbes*, November 19, 2018, https://
www.forbes.com/sites/jonathanmoed/2018/11/19/start-up-chiles-impact-2010-2018
-inside-the-revolutionary-startup-accelerator/?sh=70c374ed6dc5.

93 **Myspace page named after this:** Abby Ohlheiser, "The Woman behind 'Me Too' Knew the Power of the Phrase When She Created It—10 Years Ago," *Washington Post*, October 19, 2017, https://www.washingtonpost.com/news/the-intersect/wp/2017/10/19/the-woman-behind-me-too-knew-the-power-of-the-phrase-when-she-created-it-10-years-ago/.

94 **online protest served to *demonstrate*:** Zeynep Tufekci, *Twitter and Tear Gas: The Power and Fragility of Networked Protest* (New Haven, CT: Yale University Press, 2017).

94 **Citizens tended to praise the system:** Timur Kuran, *Private Truths, Public Lies: The Social Consequences of Preference Falsification* (Cambridge, MA: Harvard University Press, 1997).

95 **Lagging peer codes delayed progress:** Dale T. Miller, "A Century of Pluralistic Ignorance: What We Have Learned about Its Origins, Forms, and Consequences," *Frontiers in Social Psychology* 1 (2023): 1260896.

95 **Research suggests that masks:** Oleg Urminsky and Abigail Bergman, "The Masked Majority: Underprediction of Widespread Support for Covid-19 Safety Policies," PsyArXiv Preprints, February 4, 2021, https://doi.org/10.31234/osf.io/fhdkv.

95 **they are wearing masks:** Samantha Heiman et al., "Descriptive Social Norms Caused Increases in Mask Wearing during the COVID-19 Pandemic," *Scientific Reports* 13 (2023).

96 **why fundraising drives list:** This also involves a threat that your *non*participation will be revealed by your absence from the next list. Alan S. Gerber, Donald P. Green, and Christopher W. Larimer, "Social Pressure and Voter Turnout: Evidence from a Large-Scale Field Experiment," *American Political Science Review* 102, no. 1 (2008): 33–48.

96 **second-order effect:** Robert M. Bond et al., "A 61-Million-Person Experiment in Social Influence and Political Mobilization," *Nature* 489, no. 7415 (2012): 295–98.

96 **McDonald's displayed a running count:** The figure would be about 400 billion today. It's actually the count of patties (a Big Mac counted as two), typical of the shady accounting often used to inflate prevalence signals.

96 *more people by far use Hertz*: Hertz based its boast on (once) leading the industry in locations, cars, and transactions. British Air based its claim on (formerly) leading in passenger miles flown internationally. Where did the dentist factoid come from? Trident commissioned a market research firm to ask 1,200 dentists what they would recommend to their patients who chew gum: a) sugared gum, b) sugarless gum, or c) no gum at all. Four out of five dentists chose option b, which didn't, by the way, specifically mention Trident. The fifth chose option c, something that Trident failed to mention.

97 **You can save $54:** Thu-Hong Ha, "The psychology of saving energy: Alex Laskey at TED2013," TED Blog, February 27, 2013, https://blog.ted.com/the-psychology-of -saving-energy-alex-laskey-at-ted2013/. Mark Joseph Stern, "A Little Guilt, a Lot of Energy," *Slate*, March 1, 2013, https://slate.com/technology/2013/03/opower-using -smiley-faces-and-peer-pressure-to-save-the-planet.html.

97 **peer-code updating and conformist behavior:** P. Wesley Schultz, et al., "The Constructive, Destructive, and Reconstructive Power of Social Norms," *Psychological Science* 18, no. 5 (2007): 429–34.

97 **a startup called OPOWER:** Hunt Allcott and Todd Rogers, "The Short-Run and Long-Run Effects of Behavioral Interventions: Experimental Evidence from Energy Conservation," *American Economic Review* 104, no. 10 (2014): 3003–37.

98 **On campuses, "binge drinkers":** "University of North Carolina," Social Norms National Research & Resources, http://www.socialnormsresources.org/casestudies /unc.php. H. Wesley Perkins and Alan D. Berkowitz, "Perceiving the Community Norms of Alcohol Use Among Students: Some Research Implications for Campus Alcohol Education Programming," *International Journal of the Addictions* 21, no. 9–10 (1986): 961–976.

98 **Credible data dispelled the illusion:** For information about these interventions, see the National Social Norms Center, Michigan State University, http://socialnorms .org. Public health researchers distinguish this kind of intervention as norms correction as opposed to the norms transformation intervention that actively cultivate new practices. Beniamino Cislaghi and Alan D. Berkowitz, "The Evolution of Social Norms Interventions for Health Promotion: Distinguishing Norms Correction and Norms Transformation," *Journal of Global Health* 11 (2021).

99 **it does shift our habits:** Richard H. Thaler and Cass R. Sunstein, *Nudge: Improving Decisions about Health, Wealth, and Happiness* (New York: Penguin Books, 2009).

99 **When Australian taxpayers:** Michael Wenzel, "Misperceptions of Social Norms about Tax Compliance: From Theory to Intervention," *Journal of Economic Psychology* 26, no. 6 (2005): 862–83.

99 **When young Saudi women:** Leonardo Bursztyn, Alessandra L. González, and David Yanagizawa-Drott, "Misperceived Social Norms: Women Working Outside the Home in Saudi Arabia," *American Economic Review* 110, no. 10 (2020): 2997–3029.

99 **WeWork pitched itself:** Eliot Brown and Maureen Farrell, *The Cult of We: WeWork, Adam Neumann, and the Great Startup Delusion* (New York: Crown, 2021).

100 **listening to a sales pitch:** Marian Friestad and Peter Wright, "The Persuasion Knowledge Model: How People Cope with Persuasion Attempts," *Journal of*

Consumer Research 21, no. 1 (1994): 1–31; Margaret C. Campbell and Amna Kirmani, "I Know What You're Doing and Why You're Doing It: The Use of the Persuasion Knowledge Model in Consumer Research," *Handbook of Consumer Psychology* (2008): 549–74.

100 **verifiable claims *gain* persuasiveness:** Mathew S. Isaac and Kent Grayson, "Beyond Skepticism: Can Accessing Persuasion Knowledge Bolster Credibility?," *Journal of Consumer Research* 43, no. 6 (2017): 895–912.

100 **bringing together "restrained eaters":** Traci Mann et al., "Are Two Interventions Worse Than None? Joint Primary and Secondary Prevention of Eating Disorders in College Females," *Health Psychology* 16, no. 3 (1997): 215.

101 **Norm Macdonald expressed a similar complaint:** Dan Brooks, "Norm Macdonald, Still in Search of the Perfect Joke," *New York Times Magazine*, August 30, 2018, https://www.nytimes.com/2018/08/30/magazine/norm-macdonald-still-in -search-of-the-perfect-joke.html.

101 **some actually *increased* interest:** Martin Fishbein et al., "Avoiding the Boomerang: Testing the Relative Effectiveness of Antidrug Public Service Announcements before a National Campaign," *American Journal of Public Health* 92, no. 2 (2002): 238–45; Dan Werb et al., "The Effectiveness of Anti-Illicit-Drug Public-Service Announcements: A Systematic Review and Meta-Analysis," *Journal of Epidemiology and Community Health* 65, no. 10 (2011): 834–40.

101 **"It's always around":** "Partnership for a Drug-Free America—Everybody's Doing It," Musical PSAs, Public Information Film Wiki, https://pif.fandom.com/wiki/Part nership_for_a_Drug-Free_America_-_Everybody%27s_Doing_It.

101 **signage emphasizing that *almost all*:** Robert B. Cialdini et al., "Managing Social Norms for Persuasive Impact," *Social Influence* 1, no. 1 (2006): 3–15.

102 **"Hundreds of millions of Americans":** The final statement is true because the population expands from that of four years prior. It's why Biden could accurately boast in his acceptance speech that he got more votes than Obama. My group works confidentially but some details have become public. Michael Grunwald, "How Obama Is Using the Science of Change," *Time*, April 2, 2009, https://content.time.com/time /subscriber/article/0,33009,1889153,00.html; Benedict Carey, "Academic 'Dream Team' Helped Obama's Effort," *New York Times*, November 12, 2012, https://www .nytimes.com/2012/11/13/health/dream-team-of-behavioral-scientists-advised -obama-campaign.html.

102 **everyone-is-doing-it appeals:** Alan S. Gerber and Todd Rogers, "Descriptive Social Norms and Motivation to Vote: Everybody's Voting and So Should You," *Journal of*

Politics 71, no. 1 (2009): 178–91; Todd Rogers, Donald P. Green, John Ternovski, and Carolina Ferrerosa Young, "Social Pressure and Voting: A Field Experiment Conducted in a High-Salience Election," *Electoral Studies* 46 (2017): 87–100.

Chapter 5: Soap Operas and Social Change

103 **"Life doesn't imitate art":** "Husbands and Wives Script," Scripts on Screen, https://scripts-onscreen.com/tag/husbands-and-wives-screenplay/.

104 **they found that as Globo:** Eliana La Ferrara, Alberto Chong, and Suzanne Duryea, "Soap Operas and Fertility: Evidence from Brazil," *American Economic Journal: Applied Economics* 4, no. 4 (2012): 1–31.

105 **baby names matching those:** Many parents discover that the "unusual" name they've given their tike (e.g., Ethan for a boy or Sophia for a girl) is common in the kindergarten class. We are guided by prestige signals even when trying to be original.

105 **rise in divorce rates that followed:** Alberto Chong, and Eliana La Ferrara, "Television and Divorce: Evidence from Brazilian Novelas," *Journal of the European Economic Association* 7, no. 2–3 (2009): 458–68.

106 **those seeking to emulate Justin Bieber's:** People emulate admired celebrities and characters even in their final acts of suicide: After the death of revered comedian Robin Williams, U.S. suicide deaths rose 9.85 percent in the months that followed, largely among middle-aged white men, disproportionately by hanging. David S. Fink, Julian Santaella-Tenorio, and Katherine M. Keyes, "Increase in Suicides the Months after the Death of Robin Williams in the US," *PloS one* 13, no. 2 (2018): e0191405. Suicide spikes have been incited by fictional characters from Goethe's 1774 novel *The Sorrows of Young Werther* to that of Netflix's 2017 series *13 Reasons Why*. These are not large or enduring cultural changes, but the fact they happen at all reveals how hero-instinct can eclipse self-interest.

106 **her 2013 genetic testing for breast cancer risk:** Sunita Desai and Anupam B. Jena, "Do Celebrity Endorsements Matter? Observational Study of BRCA Gene Testing and Mastectomy Rates after Angelina Jolie's *New York Times* Editorial," *British Medical Journal* 355 (2016); Narendra Nath Basu et al., "The Angelina Jolie Effect: Contralateral Risk-Reducing Mastectomy Trends in Patients at Increased Risk of Breast Cancer," *Scientific Reports* 11, no. 1 (2021): 2847.

106 **social learning from role models:** Albert Bandura, Dorothea Ross, and Sheila A. Ross, "Transmission of Aggression through Imitation of Aggressive Models," *Journal of Abnormal and Social Psychology* 63, no. 3 (1961): 575.

107 **person with more followers:** Maciej Chudek, Sarah Heller, Susan Birch, and Joseph Henrich, "Prestige-Biased Cultural Learning: Bystander's Differential Attention to Potential Models Influences Children's Learning," *Evolution and Human Behavior* 33, no. 1 (2012): 46–56.

107 **His leading man was assaulted:** This intense identification still occurs. When actress Kate del Castillo played a narcotrafficker in a popular telenovela, the real narcotrafficker El Chapo began texting her and taking risks that led to his arrest. Juliana Jiménez Jaramillo, "'I Will Take Care of You More Than I Do My Own Eyes': El Chapo's Texts to Kate del Castillo," *Slate*, January 13, 2016, https://slate.com/news-and-politics/2016/01/el-chapos-texts-to-mexican-actress-kate-del-castillo.html.

107 **harness this intense engagement:** Deborah Smith, "The Theory Heard 'Round the World," *Monitor on Psychology* 33, no. 9 (2002): 30–32.

107 **a million new clients enrolled:** Jeff Crider, "Adult Literacy, Birth Control Addressed in Dramas: Third World Soaps Tackle Social Problems," *Los Angeles Times*, September 20, 1987.

107 **contraceptive sales grew 23 percent:** Arvind Singhal, Michael J. Cody, Everett M. Rogers, and Miguel Sabido, eds., *Entertainment-Education and Social Change: History, Research, and Practice* (New York: Routledge, 2003).

107 **aired in Tanzania during the AIDS:** Peter W. Vaughan, Everett M. Rogers, Arvind Singhal, and Ramadhan M. Swalehe, "Entertainment-Education and HIV/AIDS Prevention: A Field Experiment in Tanzania," *Journal of Health Communication* 5, no. sup1 (2000): 81–100.

108 **communities that watched the show:** Eric Arias, "How Does Media Influence Social Norms? Experimental Evidence on the Role of Common Knowledge," *Political Science Research and Methods* 7, no. 3 (2019): 561–78.

108 **People's personal attitudes are rooted:** Elizabeth Levy Paluck, "Reducing Intergroup Prejudice and Conflict Using the Media: A Field Experiment in Rwanda," *Journal of Personality and Social psychology* 96, no. 3 (2009): 574.

109 **this performative asceticism:** Fellow independence leader, Sarojini Naidu, quipped that it cost a lot of money to keep Gandhi in poverty, as it was logistically challenging to provide security on third-class trains.

109 **Its "Real Beauty" campaign for Dove:** Shannon Miller, "Dove's 'Courage Is Beautiful' Wins Cannes Print and Publishing Grand Prix," *Adweek*, June 21, 2021, https://www.adweek.com/agencies/doves-courage-is-beautiful-wins-cannes-print-and-publishing-grand-prix/.

110 **If you hire people who are bigger:** Kenneth Roman, "The House That Ogilvy Built,"

Strategy + Business, February 24, 2009, https://www.strategy-business.com/article /09103

111 **Netflix wants its executives to take:** WeAreNetflix, "Netflix Culture: Taking Risks, Making Bets," YouTube, December 10, 2018, https://www.youtube.com/watch?v= PDD5dt7GJ9I.

112 **"hit refresh" on its culture:** Satya Nadella, *Hit Refresh: The Quest to Rediscover Microsoft's Soul and Imagine a Better Future For Everyone* (New York: Harper Business, 2017).

112 **resulted in ever-heavier apps:** As applications became available as online services rather than locally installed software, customer switching costs greatly dropped, and customers paid on a per-use basis.

113 **This "employees first" push:** Vineet Nayar, "A Maverick CEO Explains How He Persuaded His Team to Leap into the Future," *IEEE Engineering Management Review* 40, no. 1 (2012): 24–29.

113 **contribute as an innovator at Infosys:** Infosys Stories, https://www.infosys.com /infosys-stories.html.

114 **those who get the most attention:** Who were these peer-admired students? Hint: They were not valedictorians. They were not even the squeaky-clean types whom teachers would have picked. Some were right in the middle of the conflicts that the bullying centered on (e.g., "drama" between the jocks and the goths). There were a few common denominators: they often played a sport, had a boyfriend or girlfriend, or had older siblings at the school. You can probably picture who they would have been in your high school class, the prom queen and king whom other students looked up to.

114 **their prestige rubbed off:** Elizabeth Levy Paluck, Hana Shepherd, and Peter M. Aronow, "Changing Climates of Conflict: A Social Network Experiment in 56 Schools," *Proceedings of the National Academy of Sciences* 113, no. 3 (2016): 566–71.

115 **10 percent of attendees at retreats:** Marc Galanter, "Engaged Members of the Unification Church: Impact of a Charismatic Large Group on Adaptation and Behavior," *Archives of General Psychiatry* 40, no. 11 (1983): 1197–1202; Eileen Barker, *The Making of a Moonie* (Oxford: Basil Blackwell, 1984).

115 **take part in multiple communities:** The Mormon Church is a strong and hierarchical culture, but a Mormon lawyer in Los Angeles doesn't live in a bubble with monolithic prestige signals: at Temple, the priest or bishop has palpable prestige; at work, senior partners and judges loom large; and out on the town, she gets to feel the mystique of Hollywood stars. The competing ideals enable her to question any one of them.

116 **Studies find that religious extremism:** Douglas Pratt, *Religion and Extremism: Rejecting Diversity* (London: Bloomsbury Publishing, 2017).

116 **With colleagues Yu Ding and Gita Johar:** Yu Ding, Gita V. Johar, and Michael W. Morris, "When the One True Faith Trumps All: Low Religious Diversity, Religious Intolerance, and Science Denial," *PNAS nexus* 3, no. 4 (2024): 144.

116 **Rural "re-education camps":** The word "brainwash" was coined in relation to prisoners in Chinese thought reform camps—primarily teachers and missionaries—who praised Chairman Mao even after their release. Psychiatrists who studied them learned that the camps did not use an exotic method of indoctrination, just long days of charismatic lectures, confession sessions, and group discussions. Several of the missionaries even noted that the camp reminded them of their seminary training. Robert J. Lifton, "'Thought Reform' of Western Civilians in Chinese Communist Prisons," *Psychiatry* 19, no. 2 (1956): 173–95.

117 **"Martyr of the Month":** Assaf Moghadam, *The Globalization of Martyrdom: Al Qaeda, Salafi Jihad, and the Diffusion of Suicide Attacks* (Baltimore, MD: Johns Hopkins University Press, 2008); Ariel Glucklich, *Dying for Heaven: Holy Pleasure and Suicide Bombers—Why the Best Qualities of Religion Are Also Its Most Dangerous* (New York: HarperCollins, 2009); Paul Gill, "A Multi-Dimensional Approach to Suicide Bombing," *International Journal of Conflict and Violence* 1, no. 2 (2007): 142–59.

117 **"true believers" who can gain status:** Matthew DeMichele, Peter Simi, and Kathleen Blee, *Research and Evaluation on Domestic Radicalization to Violent Extremism: Research to Support Exit USA* (Washington, DC: Office of Justice Programs (2021).

118 **"My job is *not* to say":** Mary Carmichael, "Graphic Details Emerge from BU Hockey Panel Reports: Sex, Drinking Escapades by Hockey Players," *Boston Globe*, September 6, 2012, https://www.boston.com/news/local-news/2012/09/06/graphic-details-emerge-from-bu-hockey-panel-reports/.

118 **eliminating the current prestige signals:** Leon Neyfakh, "How to Change a Culture," *Boston Globe*, September 23, 2012, https://www.bostonglobe.com/ideas/2012/09/22/how-change-culture/HitMpC95xPFidEjEl2cx9J/story.html.

119 **team produced a sexualized "scouting report":** Hannah Natanson, "The Ways Things Linger," Harvard Crimson, December 10, 2018, https://www.thecrimson.com/article/2018/12/10/consequences/.

119 **Harvard's response was strong:** Draconian measures often produce unintended consequences. When all Ba'ath Party members were fired from the Iraq army, it created a bitter, disenfranchised faction of skilled soldiers. Many went on to lend their

expertise to ISIS. Liz Sly, "The Hidden Hand behind the Islamic State Militants? Saddam Hussein's," *Washington Post*, April 4, 2015, https://www.washingtonpost .com/world/middle_east/the-hidden-hand-behind-the-islamic-state-militants -saddam-husseins/2015/04/04/aa97676c-cc32-11e4-8730-4f473416e759_story.html.

119 **a new set of ideals:** For example, Jill Ellis, repeat winner of the World Cup, has indicated interest in coaching a men's team. Women have coached men's college teams and club teams successfully.

120 **known as Iron Eyes Cody:** Cody was Hollywood's "go-to Indian" for decades, notorious for wearing his moccasins, fringed buckskin, and braided wig even when off set.

120 **"Crying Indian" ad:** See "The Crying Indian—Full Commercial—Keep America Beautiful," YouTube, uploaded May 1, 2007, https://www.youtube.com/watch?v= j7OHG7tHrNM.

120 **exaggerated depiction of rampant littering:** The campaign portrayed pollution as a problem of "litterbugs" rather than as a problem of wasteful industry practices, probably because it was funded by an industry consortium.

120 **he wasn't an in-group hero:** The character and the actor presented as a traditional Native American, hence not in-group to the target audience. Oddly enough, Cody was later outed as a "pretendian," the son of Sicilian immigrants to New Orleans. Angela Aleiss, "Iron Eyes Cody: Wannabe Indian," *Cineaste* 25, no. 1 (1999): 30–31.

120 **Suspicion suspends automatic social inference processes:** Geoffrey D. Munro, Carrie Weih, and Jeffrey Tsai, "Motivated Suspicion: Asymmetrical Attributions of the Behavior of Political Ingroup and Outgroup Members," *Basic and Applied Social Psychology* 32, no. 2 (2010): 173–84.

120 **Don't Mess with Texas:** This was a novel tagline written to sound like a vernacular Texan saying. It has become just that, another indication of the impulse to emulate in-group heroes.

120 **starred native sons and daughters:** See "Don't Mess with Texas commercial (1987)," YouTube, uploaded January 10, 2014, https://www.youtube.com/watch?v=V2qIF-3PL7lQ.

121 **mixed record of celebrity product endorsements:** Johannes Knoll and Jörg Matthes, "The Effectiveness of Celebrity Endorsements: A Meta-Analysis," *Journal of the Academy of Marketing Science* 45 (2017): 55–75.

121 **it's suspicious that Ozzy:** Relevance matters the same way for brand extensions. Customers followed when Planters launched a peanut butter, when *Playboy* opened nightclubs, and when Clorox made a toilet cleaner. But incongruous extensions raise

suspicions that firms are just trading on their name to make a quick buck. Colgate's Frozen Lasagna? *Cosmopolitan's* Yogurt? Reddi-Wip's Reddi-Bacon?

121 **suspicion halts this process:** Suspicion has been a chief obstacle to persuading some communities to take a COVID vaccine. In a recent experiment, unvaccinated Republicans became more likely to get a stab after hearing an endorsement from Donald Trump and *less* likely after one from Joe Biden. Unvaccinated Christians were more likely to follow vaccination advice from medical experts who revealed themselves to be Christians than from those who didn't. Again, the *messenger* matters. The practical implication is that public health campaigns should search for cultural heroes of vaccine-resistant communities who are willing to be advocates. Sophia L. Pink et al., "Elite Party Cues Increase Vaccination Intentions among Republicans," *Proceedings of the National Academy of Sciences* 118, no. 32 (2021): e2106559118; James Chu, Sophia L. Pink, and Robb Willer, "Religious Identity Cues Increase Vaccination Intentions and Trust in Medical Experts among American Christians," *Proceedings of the National Academy of Sciences* 118, no. 49 (2021): e2106481118.

121 **many great anti-war films:** Anthony Swofford, "'Full Metal Jacket' Seduced My Generation and Sent Us to War," *New York Times Magazine*, April 18, 2018, https://www.nytimes.com/2018/04/18/magazine/full-metal-jacket-ermey-marine-corps.html; Max Hauptman, "How 'Saving Private Ryan,' 'Black Hawk Down' and Other Films Inspired a Generation to Join the Military," Task & Purpose, July 8, 2022, https://taskandpurpose.com/culture/movies-television-joining-us-military/.

122 **no such thing as an anti-war film:** Gene Siskel, "The Touch That Transcends Violence and Death," *Chicago Tribune*, November 11, 1973, 2.

122 **show's most loyal watchers:** Neil Vidmar and Milton Rokeach, "Archie Bunker's Bigotry: A Study in Selective Perception and Exposure," *Journal of Communication* 24, no. 1 (1974): 36–47.

122 **excerpts from *The Colbert Report*:** Jody C. Baumgartner and Jonathan S. Morris, "One 'Nation,' under Stephen? The Effects of *The Colbert Report* on American Youth," *Journal of Broadcasting & Electronic Media* 52, no. 4 (2008): 622–43.

122 **Satire subtle enough to please:** Satire backfires in other genres as well. Stand-up comics call it a "blood laugh" when audience members laugh along *with* the racist character they are parodying not *at* the character. Songs satiring jingoism—Neil Young's "Rockin' in the Free World" or Bruce Springsteen's "Born in the U.S.A."—are mistaken for nationalistic anthems and appropriated by hawkish politicians.

122 **1978 documentary *Scared Straight!*:** It won an Academy Award for opening a window into the world (then-little-known) of prison culture.

123 **13 percent *more* prone to recidivism:** Anthony Petrosino, Carolyn Turpin-Petrosino, and James O. Finckenauer, "Well-Meaning Programs Can Have Harmful Effects! Lessons from Experiments of Programs Such as Scared Straight," *Crime & Delinquency* 46, no. 3 (2000): 354–79; Timothy Wilson, *Redirect: The Surprising New Science of Psychological Change* (London: Allen Lane, 2011).

123 **found that prison hardens:** John L. Worrall, "The Effect of Three-Strikes Legislation on Serious Crime in California," *Journal of Criminal Justice* 32, no. 4 (February 2004): 283–96, doi:10.1016/j.jcrimjus.2004.04.001; David J. Harding et al., "A Natural Experiment Study of the Effects of Imprisonment on Violence in the Community," *Nature Human Behaviour* 3, no. 7 (2019): 671–77; David L. Weisburd, David P. Farrington, and Charlotte Gill, "What Works in Crime Prevention and Rehabilitation: An Assessment of Systematic Reviews," *Criminology & Public Policy* 16, no. 2 (2017): 415–49.

124 **long-term propensity toward crime:** This is not the first anti-crime program to run aground on errant prestige signals. The mid-twentieth-century Cambridge-Somerville Youth Study recruited a mix of delinquent and nondelinquent kids from poor neighborhoods to attend an enriching summer camp together for multiple years. A decade later, its participants' rate of criminality was compared to a control group and found to be significantly higher. From records of the camp counselors, researchers concluded that the program became a forum for the more delinquents kids to boast of their misadventures and become role models to the rest. Joan McCord, "Cures That Harm: Unanticipated Outcomes of Crime Prevention Programs," *Annals of the American Academy of Political and Social Science* 587, no. 1 (2003): 16–30.

124 **recognized their listed sponsor:** Melanie Wakefield et al., "Effect of Televised, Tobacco Company–Funded Smoking Prevention Advertising on Youth Smoking-Related Beliefs, Intentions, and Behavior," *American Journal of Public Health* 96, no. 12 (2006): 2154–60.

124 **slightly *increased* teens' intention to smoke:** Editorial, "When Don't Smoke Means Do," *New York Times*, November 27, 2006, 22; Zoe Wood, "Tobacco Firm Philip Morris Calls for Ban on Cigarettes within Decade," *Guardian*, July 25, 2021, https://www.theguardian.com/business/2021/jul/25/tobacco-firm-philip-morris-calls-for-ban-on-cigarettes-within-decade.

124 **evil villains and their minions:** Sara G. Miller, "Live and Let Die: James Bond's Smoking Habits over the Years," LiveScience, January 17, 2017, https://www.livescience.com/57519-james-bond-smoking-habits.html.

125 **Tobacco product placement:** "It's All about the Evidence," Smoke Free Media,

University of California San Francisco, https://smokefreemedia.ucsf.edu/research
/evidence.

125 **change in the media landscape:** Another reason for the rise in youth smoking and
tobacco use may be access to a wider range of films and shows given streaming media
platforms, not all from mainstream studios that abide the policy. "Smoking in the
Movies," CDC, November 10, 2020, https://www.cdc.gov/tobacco/data_statistics
/fact_sheets/youth_data/movies/index.htm.

Chapter 6: Inside the History Factory

126 **"It's not even past":** William Faulkner, *Requiem for a Nun* (New York: Vintage, 2011).

127 **letter sent home to England:** The letter was directed to the investors financing the
colony, so it likely exaggerated the Pilgrims' efficacy and generosity. Other records
make it clear that only the help of Native Americans enabled them to survive their
difficult first year. One of them, Tisquantum, who spoke English and Spanish in
addition to several local languages, taught them how to plant native crops and bro-
kered peaceable relations. These helpers were repaid with fatal diseases and eventually
with hostile attacks. David J. Silverman, *This Land Is Their Land: The Wampanoag
Indians, Plymouth Colony, and the Troubled History of Thanksgiving* (New York:
Bloomsbury, 2019).

127 **account of "the first thanksgiving":** Arthur George, "Thanksgiving: Our American
Mythmaking in Action," in *The Mythology of America's Seasonal Holidays: The
Dance of the Horae* (London: Palgrave Macmillan, 2020), 175–91.

127 **Sarah Josepha Hale, a leading poet:** "Sarah J. Hale to Abraham Lincoln, Monday,
September 28, 1863 (Thanksgiving)," Abraham Lincoln Papers at the Library of
Congress, https://www.loc.gov/static/classroom-materials/thanksgiving/documents
/sarah_hale.pdf.

127 **"the mystic chords of memory":** Abraham Lincoln, "First Inaugural Address," in
Emily Mofield and Tamra Stambaugh, *Finding Freedom* (New York: Routledge,
2021), 79–89.

127 **He asked citizens:** Abraham Lincoln, "Proclamation 118," Thanksgiving Day, 1864,
https://obamawhitehouse.archives.gov/sites/default/files/docs/transcript_for
_abraham_lincoln_thanksgiving_proclamation_1863.pdf.

128 **"a grand national holiday":** David S. Reynolds, "How Lincoln Turned Regional Holidays into National Celebrations," *Atlantic*, November 24, 2021, https://www.theat
lantic.com/ideas/archive/2021/11/how-lincoln-redefined-thanksgiving-and
-christmas/620800/.

128 **the "imagined community":** Benedict Anderson, *Imagined Communities: Reflections on the Origin and Spread of Nationalism* (New York: Verso, 2006).

128 **derided this travesty as "Franksgiving":** In a lapse of his usually keen sensibilities, FDR announced to reporters that Thanksgiving was a "perfectly moveable feast. . . . There is nothing sacred about it." Abram Brown, "When President Roosevelt Tried to Save Christmas—And America Ended Up with Two Thanksgivings," *Forbes*, November 28, 2019, https://www.forbes.com/sites/abrambrown/2019/11/28/when-president-roose velt-tried-to-save-christmas-and-america-ended-up-with-two-thanksgivings/?sh= 672b2c3f53fe.

128 **compared Roosevelt to Hitler:** Thereby launching another American tradition: equating those that you disagree with to Hitler!

129 **Statues of a grateful Massasoit:** Lisa Blee and Jean M. O'Brien, *Monumental Mobility: The Memory Work of Massasoit* (Chapel Hill: University of North Carolina Press, 2019).

129 **"genealogical dexterity is common":** Lawrence Rosen, "'Tribalism' Gets a Bum Rap," *Anthropology Today* 32, no. 5 (2016): 3–4.

130 **antiquity and consistency:** These dual goals of legitimacy and identity are discussed in business research on organizational rhetorics about firm history. Roy Suddaby and Peter Jaskiewicz, "Managing Traditions: A Critical Capability for Family Business Success," *Family Business Review* 33, no. 3 (2020): 234–43; Roy Suddaby and Royston Greenwood, "Rhetorical Strategies of Legitimacy," *Administrative Science Quarterly* 50, no. 1 (2005): 35–67.

130 **since the ancien régime:** As the yellow label says, "Maison Fondée en 1772."

131 **wine industry and tourism have boomed:** Sarah Hucal, "Why the World Is Talking about Georgian Wine," *DW*, October 15, 2019, https://www.dw.com/en/why-the -world-is-talking-about-georgian-wine/a-50798532; Dimitri Avaliani, Magda Gugu- lashvili, and Mikhail Shevelev Jr., "All You Need to Know about Georgian Wine Boom," *JAM News*, December 11, 2021, https://jam-news.net/all-you-need-to-know -about-georgian-wine-boom/.

131 **acupuncture treatments are evaluated:** Scott Eidelman, Jennifer Pattershall, and Christian S. Crandall, "Longer Is Better," *Journal of Experimental Social Psychology* 46, no. 6 (2010): 993; Scott Eidelman and Christian S. Crandall, "The Intuitive Traditionalist: How Biases for Existence and Longevity Promote the Status Quo," *Advances in Experimental Social Psychology* 50 (2014): 53–104.

132 **wine market is rife with fraud:** Donato Romano et al., "A SAM-Based Analysis of the Economic Impact of Frauds in the Italian Wine Value Chain," *Italian Economic*

Journal 7 (2021): 297–321; Peter Hellman, "Color-shifting Ink and Secret Wafer-Thin Security Tags: How Top-End Wineries Are Fighting Back against the New Age of Scammers," *Business Insider*, September 16, 2021, https://www.businessinsider.com /winemakers-use-ultraviolet-ink-and-microprinting-to-deter-scammers-2021-9?r= US&IR=T.

132 **oenophiles experience complex notes:** Hilke Plassmann, John O'Doherty, Baba Shiv, and Antonio Rangel, "Marketing Actions Can Modulate Neural Representations of Experienced Pleasantness," *Proceedings of the National Academy of Sciences* 105, no. 3 (2008): 1050–54.

132 **University of Chicago constructed its 1890 campus:** This faux-antique style became all the rage in the Gilded-era expansion of US universities. In this era, the newer a campus building in the United States, the older it looked!

133 **"Mormonism does not enjoy":** Jason Horowitz, "Is Mitt Romney's Mormonism Fair Game?," *Washington Post*, June 1, 2012, https://www.washingtonpost.com/opinions /is-mitt-romneys-mormonism-fair-game/2012/06/01/gJQAhDo56U_story.html.

133 **seem a bit *too* "Latter-day":** Ruth H. Warner and Kristin L. Kiddoo, "Are the Latter-Day Saints Too Latter Day? Perceived Age of the Mormon Church and Attitudes toward Mormons," *Group Processes & Intergroup Relations* 17, no. 1 (2014): 67–78.

133 **many were introduced in modern times:** David Carradine, "The Context, Performance and Meaning of Ritual," in *The Invention of Tradition*, eds. Eric Hobsbawm and Terence Ranger (Cambridge: Cambridge University Press, 1983), 101–64.

133 **"invented traditions"—recent solutions:** Eric Hobsbawm, "Introduction: Inventing Traditions," in *The Invention of Tradition*, eds. Hobsbawm and Ranger.

134 **every village must celebrate:** Alan Cheng, "National Foundation Day: Japan's Forgotten Holiday," Unseen Japan, February 19, 2020, https://unseen-japan.com/national -foundation-day-japan/#The_%E2%80%9CFounding%E2%80%9D_of_a_Nation.

134 **created through "commemoration" events:** Maurice Halbwachs, *On Collective Memory* (Chicago: University of Chicago Press, 2020).

135 **white lab coat of scientists:** Raphael Hulkower, "The History of the Hippocratic Oath: Outdated, Inauthentic, and Yet Still Relevant," *Einstein Journal of Biology and Medicine* 25, no. 1 (2016): 41–44.

135 **The ceremony combining the oath:** Drs. Linda Lewis and Arnold Gold designed the first white-coat ceremony at Columbia Medical School in 1993.

135 **Alfred Winslow Jones invented the hedge fund:** *His* clients fared well because he had an edge in investing techniques. Most hedge funds today do not beat the market, but they still take the well-institutionalized 20 percent fee.

136 **precedent symbols about diamond rings:** Uri Friedman, "How an Ad Campaign Invented the Diamond Engagement Ring," *Atlantic*, February 13, 2015, https://www .theatlantic.com/international/archive/2015/02/how-an-ad-campaign-invented-the -diamond-engagement-ring/385376/.

136 **hawked its "Jade Egg":** "Better Sex: Jade Eggs for Your Yoni," Goop, January 17, 2007.

136 **Goop was fined:** Jennifer Gunter and Sarah Parcak, "Vaginal Jade Eggs: Ancient Chinese Practice or Modern Marketing Myth?," *Urogynecology* 25, no. 1 (2019): 1–2; Dorson, Richard M. *Folklore and Fakelore: Essays Toward a Discipline of Folk Studies* (Cambridge: Harvard University Press, 1976); Wang, Amy, "Gwyneth Paltrow's Goop Touted the 'Benefits' of Putting a Jade Egg in Your Vagina. Now It Must Pay," *Washington Post* 5 (2018).

136 **"don't know shit from Shinola":** J. C. Reindl, "FTC Tells Shinola: Stop Saying 'Where American Is Made,'" *Detroit Free Press*, June 17, 2016.

138 **hilltop fort called the Masada:** In all the extensive records from this period, the sole mention of what would seem a newsworthy story was by Flavius Josephus, a Jewish-Roman writer regarded by historians as questionable source.

138 **"Masada shall not fall again":** Nachman Ben-Yehuda, *The Masada Myth: Collective Memory and Mythmaking in Israel* (Madison: University of Wisconsin Press, 1996).

138 **Brain-injured patients who lose their memories:** Endel Tulving, "Memory and Consciousness," *Canadian Psychology/Psychologie Canadienne* 26, no. 1 (1985): 1.

139 **tames the blurrg:** Ashkhan, "Taming a Blurrg—The Mandalorian Season One (2019)," YouTube, https://www.youtube.com/watch?v=Tq2u3dhdxJA.

140 **"Star-Spangled Banner":** "The Star-Spangled Banner," Smithsonian, audio, https:// amhistory.si.edu/starspangledbanner/mp3/song.anac.dsl.mp3.

141 **Truth and Reconciliation Commission:** Jay A. Vora and Erika Vora, "The Effectiveness of South Africa's Truth and Reconciliation Commission: Perceptions of Xhosa, Afrikaner, and English South Africans," *Journal of Black Studies* 34, no. 3 (2004): 301–2; James L. Gibson, "Overcoming Apartheid: Can Truth Reconcile a Divided Nation?," *Annals of the American Academy of Political and Social Science* 603, no. 1 (2006): 82–110.

141 **Ubuntu had been appropriated:** Stanlake John Thompson Samkange and Tommie Marie Samkange, *Hunhuism or Ubuntuism: A Zimbabwe Indigenous Political Philosophy* (Salisbury, UK: Graham Publishing, 1980); Desmond Tutu, *No Future without Forgiveness* (New York: Image Books, 2009).

141 **Mandela stepped out on the field:** John Carlin, "Nelson Mandela Unites a Nation with His Choice of Jersey," *Guardian*, January 6, 2007, https://www.theguardian.com/sport /2007/jan/07/rugbyunion.features1.

142 **We see these reincarnations:** Stephen Brown, Robert V. Kozinets, and John F. Sherry, Jr., "Teaching Old Brands New Tricks: Retro Branding and the Revival of Brand Meaning," *Journal of Marketing* 67, no. 3 (2003): 19–33.

142 **a generation before an old style:** Paul Grainge, "Nostalgia and Style in Retro America: Moods, Modes, and Media Recycling," *Journal of American Culture* 23, no. 1 (2000).

143 **The brand had become a tribal identity:** Arpita Agnihotri, "Turnaround of Harley Davidson—Cult Brand or Strategic Fit Approach?," *Journal of Strategic Marketing* 21, no. 3 (2013): 292–301; Douglas B. Holt, *How Brands Become Icons: The Principles of Cultural Branding* (Cambridge, MA: Harvard Business School Press, 2004).

143 **began with a Super Bowl ad:** Tim Rohan, "NFL 100 Commercial Succeeds in Making Fans Forget the League's Many Issues," *Sports Illustrated*, February 7, 2019, https://www.si.com/nfl/2019/02/07/nfl-100-commercial-roger-goodell-colin-kaepernick-boycott; "NFL 100 Super Bowl Commercial," YouTube, uploaded February 9, 2019, https://www.youtube.com/watch?v=E6JjyRhfjOE.

143 **"Huddle for 100":** "Celebrating 100 Years of Football," NFL, https://www.nfl.com/100/.

143 **viewership had rebounded 12 percent:** "Average Television Viewership of the NFL Regular Season from 2010 to 2023," Statista, January 2023, https://www.statista.com/statistics/289979/nfl-number-of-tv-viewers-usa/. "NFL Playoffs and Conference Championship Games Draw Highest Viewership Average on Record," AP News, January 30, 2024, https://apnews.com/article/nfl-playoffs-tv-ratings-bf435642324a34a69e6b258e033d249d.

145 **Starbucks's teahouse schtick:** Chi-Yue Chiu et al., "Culture and Consumer Behavior," *Foundations and Trends in Marketing* 7, no. 2 (2014): 109–79.

145 **Complaints of "cultural appropriation":** Rui Zhang, Melody Manchi Chao, Jaee Cho, and Michael W. Morris, "Appropriate or Appropriative? Diversity Ideologies, Judgment Factors, and Condemnation of Cultural Borrowing," PsyArXiv Preprints, November 8, 2023, doi.org/10.31234/osf.io/qpzsh; Ariel J. Mosley, Larisa Heiphetz, Mark H. White, and Monica Biernat, "Perceptions of Harm and Benefit Predict Judgments of Cultural Appropriation," *Social Psychological and Personality Science* (2023): 19485506231162401.

145 **Gramsci coined the term "cultural hegemony":** James O. Young, *Cultural Appropriation and the Arts* (Hoboken, NJ: John Wiley & Sons, 2010).

146 **a "French-style" yogurt, Oui:** Charles Duhigg, "Yoplait Learns to Manufacture Authenticity to Go with Its Yogurt," *New York Times*, June 26, 2017, https://www

.nytimes.com/2017/06/26/business/yoplait-learns-to-manufacture-authenticity-to
-go-with-its-yogurt.html.

146 **Sometimes they forge a sense:** Robert K. Merton, "The Unanticipated Consequences of Purposive Social Action," *American Sociological Review* 1, no. 6 (1936): 894–904.

146 **Another example is UNESCO certifications:** Elizabeth Betsy Keough, "Heritage in Peril: A Critique of UNESCO's World Heritage Program," *Washington University Global Studies Law Review* 10 (2011): 593; Lior Bear, Jackie Feldman, and Nir Avieli, "The Politics of Authentication in a UNESCO World Heritage Site: Luang Prabang, Laos," *Journal of Tourism and Cultural Change* 18, no. 4 (2020): 404–20.

147 **UNESCO has been proactive:** "Global Strategy," UNESCO World Heritage Convention, https://whc.unesco.org/en/globalstrategy/.

148 **In the 2018 men's soccer World Cup:** Stephen Osserman and Youyou Zhou, "How Migration Has Shaped the World Cup," *Vox*, December 8, 2022, https://www.vox .com/c/world/2022/12/8/23471181/how-migration-has-shaped-the-world-cup.

148 **South Korea fielded a women's hockey team:** Seth Berkman, *A Team of Their Own: How an International Sisterhood Made Olympic History* (Toronto: Hanover Square Press, 2019).

Chapter 7: When Change Spreads, and When It Fizzles Out

151 **"The central conservative truth":** Joe Klein, "Daniel Patrick Moynihan Was Often Right," *New York Times*, May, 24, 2021, https://www.nytimes.com/2021/05/15 /books/review/daniel-patrick-moynihan-was-often-right-joe-klein-on-why-it-still -matters.html.

151 **Jefferson Pérez, the country's only:** "Jefferson Perez—Reaching for Olympic Gold," Ecuador.com, https://www.ecuador.com/blog/jefferson-perez-reaching-for-olympic -gold/.

152 **The cost of the lost business:** James Surowiecki, "Punctuality Pays," *New Yorker*, March 28, 2004, https://www.newyorker.com/magazine/2004/04/05/punctuality-pays.

152 **"Do not enter! The meeting began":** Scott Wilson, "In Ecuador, a Timeout for Tardiness," *Washington Post*, November 4, 2003, https://www.washingtonpost.com /archive/politics/2003/11/04/in-ecuador-a-timeout-for-tardiness/2a911269-f223 -45a0-977e-e120188bb9c3/.

152 **synchronizing their watches:** Veronica Davidov, "Time and the NGOther: Development and Temporalities in an Ecuadorian Coastal Village," *Critique of Anthropology* 36, no. 1 (2016): 27–43.

152 **arrived at the last possible moment:** "Ecuadorean Time—The Price of Lateness," *The Economist,* November 22, 2003, 38.

152 **"to be on time for the sake":** Surowiecki, "Punctuality Pays."

152 **The push had failed:** Surowiecki, "Punctuality Pays."

152 **Levine studied the pace of life:** Robert N. Levine, *A Geography of Time: On Tempo, Culture, and the Pace of Life* (New York: Basic Books, 2008).

153 **raise the audience's defenses:** At a subsequent event, the businessmen slated to speak showed up late for the event. Reuters, "World Briefing | Americas: Ecuador: With Punctuality For All," *New York Times,* October 2, 2003, https://www.nytimes.com /2003/10/02/world/world-briefing-americas-ecuador-with-punctuality-for-all.html.

154 **"the civic mystique of Ambato":** Lawrence E. Harrison, *The Central Liberal Truth: How Politics Can Change a Culture and Save It from Itself* (New York: Oxford University Press, 2008), 192.

154 **discipline of Ambato's founding fathers:** Patricio Durán, "La Hora Ambateña," *La Hora,* February 10, 2020, https://www.lahora.com.ec/opinion/la-hora-ambatena/.

154 **Changing a deeply encoded cultural pattern:** In the past few years, a national campaign has been launched following the Ambato model. "'La Hora Ecuatoriana,' Una Campaña Que Nace para Combatir la Impuntualidad en Ecuador," ¡Mucho Mejor! Ecuador, March 10, 2022, https://muchomejorecuador.org.ec/la-hora-ecuatoriana -una-campana-que-nace-para-combatir-la-impuntualidad-en-ecuador.

154 **bottom-up progression of change:** Like informal traditions, laws and policies are shaped on precedents. We say "possession is nine tenths of the law," because common law favors preexisting arrangements, especially those "since time immemorial." Practices such as habeas corpus started as informal traditions then became codified as law. The word "institution" is used to refer to traditions, policies, and laws, and captures the common role of ancestor-instinct psychology. "Institutionalizing" a practice is another way of saying that a sense of tradition is being constructed around it.

156 **Gandhi's independence movement:** John C. Hammerback and Richard J. Jensen, *The Rhetorical Career of César Chávez* (College Station: Texas A&M University Press, 2003).

156 **cooperating with mercantile colonialism:** In this model the colony serves as a source of raw materials (e.g., cotton) and market for manufactured goods (fabrics).

157 **we feel *commitment* to the cause:** Aaron C. Kay et al., "Inequality, Discrimination, and the Power of the Status Quo: Direct Evidence for a Motivation to See the Way Things Are as the Way They Should Be," *Journal of Personality and Social Psychology*

97, no. 3 (2009): 421; Björn Lindström, Simon Jangard, Ida Selbing, and Andreas Olsson, "The Role of a 'Common Is Moral' Heuristic in the Stability and Change of Moral Norms," *Journal of Experimental Psychology: General* 147, no. 2 (2018): 228.

158 **Hollywood could make this update:** Alissa J. Rubin, "Public More Accepting of Gays, Poll Finds," *Los Angeles Times*, June 18, 2000, https://www.latimes.com/archives/la-xpm-2000-jun-18-mn-42265-story.html.

158 **A Pew survey found:** "Support for Same-Sex Marriage at Record High, but Key Segments Remain Opposed," Pew Research Center, June 8, 2015, https://www.pewresearch.org/politics/2015/06/08/support-for-same-sex-marriage-at-record-high-but-key-segments-remain-opposed/.

159 **Americans became more ready:** Maura Dolan and Jessica Garrison, "Knowing Gay Person a Key Factor in Rising Support for Gay Marriage," *Los Angeles Times*, March 26, 2013, https://www.latimes.com/local/la-xpm-2013-mar-26-la-me-gay-marriage-close-20130326-story.html.

159 **targeted "elite politics at the national":** Kristin A. Goss, *Disarmed: The Missing Movement for Gun Control in America* (Princeton, NJ: Princeton University Press, 2010).

159 **Fifty-six percent:** "Guns," Gallup, https://news.gallup.com/poll/1645/guns.aspx.

160 **the gun rights contingent:** Recently, the top-down Mayors Against Illegal Guns group reconfigured itself into Everytown for Gun Safety, incorporating Moms Demand Action to gain a "visible constituency that had passion, energy, and moral authority," akin to iconic grassroots group Mothers Against Drunk Driving. It has helped pass gun safety laws at the state level and President Biden's Safer Communities Act, which supports state and local efforts. Drew Lindsay, "The New Gun-Control Movement," *Chronicle of Philanthropy*, October 4, 2022, https://www.philanthropy.com/article/the-new-gun-control-movement.

160 **Oil companies have hired citizens:** Peter C. Frumhoff and Naomi Oreskes, "Fossil Fuel Firms Are Still Bankrolling Climate Denial Lobby Groups," *Guardian*, March 25, 2015, https://www.theguardian.com/environment/2015/mar/25/fossil-fuel-firms-are-still-bankrolling-climate-denial-lobby-groups.

160 **"Astroturf" may be a misleading metaphor:** Caroline W. Lee, "The Roots of Astroturfing," *Contexts* 9 (Winter 2010): 73–75; Kate Shaw Yoshida, "Astroturfing Works, and It's a Major Challenge to Climate Change," Ars Technica, July 18, 2011, https://arstechnica.com/science/2011/07/astroturfing-a-major-challenge-to-climate-change/.

160 **anti-tax Tea Party movement:** Jeff Nesbit, *Poison Tea: How Big Oil and Big Tobacco Invented the Tea Party and Captured the GOP* (New York: St. Martin's Press, 2016).

161 **"people power" color revolutions:** Lincoln A. Mitchell, "The Color Revolutions. Successes and Limitations of Non-violent Protest," in *Handbook of Revolutions in the 21st Century: The New Waves of Revolutions, and the Causes and Effects of Disruptive Political Change*, eds. Jack A. Goldstone, Leonid Grinin, and Andrey Korotayev (Cham: Springer International Publishing, 2022), 435–45.

161 **central part of soft-power politics:** No one believes this more than the Russian and Chinese governments (who manipulate public opinion so extensively that they may doubt that any political movement arises organically). Putin's perception of the 2014 Maidan Revolution as an illegal, Western-fueled coup is part of the background of his 2022 aggression toward Ukraine. Ben Sohl, "Discolored Revolutions: Information Warfare in Russia's Grand Strategy," *Washington Quarterly* 45, no. 1 (2022): 97–111.

161 **rural villages resented these dictates:** Bettina Shell-Duncan, Katherine Wander, Ylva Hernlund, and Amadou Moreau, "Legislating Change? Responses to Criminalizing Female Genital Cutting in Senegal," *Law & Society Review* 47, no. 4 (2013): 803–35.

163 **eliminated foot-binding:** Gerry Mackie, "Ending Footbinding and Infibulation: A Convention Account," *American Sociological Review* (1996): 999–1017.

164 **the left-side custom dated back:** Historians say this equilibrium formed because most people found horses easier to mount from the left.

164 **join their neighbors in right-hand driving:** Elizabeth Flock, "Dagen H: The Day Sweden Switched Sides of the Road," *Washington Post*, February 17, 2012, https://www.washingtonpost.com/blogs/blogpost/post/dagen-h-the-day-sweden-switchedsides-of-the-road-photo/2012/02/17/gIQAOwFVKR_blog.html.

164 **public opinion swung sharply in favor:** "Swedish Elevator Etiquette," *A Swedish American in Sweden* (blog), August 29, 2014, http://welcometosweden.blogspot.com/2014/08/swedish-escalator-etiquette_29.html.

165 **"Never doubt that a small group":** This, her most famous quote, is not from her published works, but from her conversation. "Frequently Asked Questions about Mead/Bateson," Institute for Intercultural Studies, http://www.interculturalstudies.org/faq.html#quote.

167 **"nanny state" stops us from harming:** This has been a barrier for the gun control effort as well. Gun safety researchers are pushing back with evidence that cohabitants of handgun owners are at elevated risk of dying from homicide and suicide.

167 **unthinkable to Redditors:** Brady Robards, "Belonging and Neo-Tribalism on Social Media Site Reddit," *Neo-Tribes: Consumption, Leisure and Tourism* (2018): 187–206; Adrienne Massanari, "#Gamergate and The Fappening: How Reddit's Algorithm,

Governance, and Culture Support Toxic Technocultures," *New Media & Society* 19, no. 3 (2017): 329–46.

168 **studies of CEO succession:** Thomas Keil, Dovev Lavie, and Stevo Pavićević, "When Do Outside CEOs Underperform? From a CEO-Centric to a Stakeholder-Centric Perspective of Post-Succession Performance," *Academy of Management Journal* 65, no. 5 (2022): 1424–49.

168 **it had acquired a stultifying bureaucracy:** John De Lorean described the legendary fourteenth floor of GM headquarters: "There were literally 600 to 700 pages a day to be read and processed. Some of it was important material, such as performance reports from the divisions. Most of it, however, was unimportant to this level of management—like a lease agreement to be signed for a new Buick zone office in St. Louis." J. Patrick Wright, *On a Clear Day You Can See General Motors: John Z. De Lorean's Look inside the Automotive Giant* (Grosse Pointe, MI: Wright Enterprises, 1979).

169 **drive decision-making downward:** Rick Tetzeli, "Mary Barra Is Remaking GM's Culture—And the Company Itself," Fast Company, October 17, 2016, https://www .fastcompany.com/3064064/mary-barra-is-remaking-gms-culture-and-the -company-itself.

169 **The firm responded with greater transparency:** James L. LaReau, "GM CEO Mary Barra's Rare, Behind-the-Scenes Interview: Who She Relies on in 'Lonely Job,'" *Detroit Free Press*, June 3, 2022, https://www.freep.com/in-depth/money/cars/gen eral-motors/2022/06/03/gm-ceo-mary-barra-reveals-personal-details-rare -interview/9705679002/; Peter Valdes-Dapena, "'Deathtrap' on GM's Naughty Words List," CNN Business, May 17, 2014, https://money.cnn.com/2014/05/17/autos/gm -words-not-to-use/index.html.

169 **"Zero crashes, zero emissions, zero congestion":** Julie Cooper, "Mary Barra Shares Her Winning Solution to Battling Climate Change," CEO Magazine, July 20, 2021, https://www.theceomagazine.com/business/coverstory/mary-barra-general -motors/.

170 **"glad" or "very glad" to have participated:** S. Alexander Haslam, Stephen D. Reicher, Kathryn Millard, and Rachel McDonald, "'Happy to Have Been of Service': The Yale Archive as a Window into the Engaged Followership of Participants in Milgram's 'Obedience' Experiments," *British Journal of Social Psychology* 54, no. 1 (2015): 55–83.

170 **more like active compliance:** Jerry M. Burger, Zackary M. Girgis, and Caroline C. Manning, "In Their Own Words: Explaining Obedience to Authority through an Examination of Participants' Comments," *Social Psychological and Personality*

Science 2, no. 5 (2011): 460–66; S. Alexander Haslam, Stephen D. Reicher, and Megan E. Birney, "Nothing by Mere Authority: Evidence That in an Experimental Analogue of the Milgram Paradigm Participants Are Motivated Not by Orders but by Appeals to Science," *Journal of Social Issues* 70, no. 3 (September 1, 2014): 473–88.

170 **varied the phrases used:** S. Alexander Haslam and Stephen D. Reicher "50 Years of 'Obedience to Authority': From Blind Conformity to Engaged Followership," *Annual Review of Law and Social Science* 13, no. 1 (October 13, 2017): 59–78.

171 **reset by an abrupt shock:** In medicine, this means a defibrillator that resets the heart rhythm back to normal. In economics, a "shock" is an exogenous change that resets supply and demand into a new equilibrium.

172 **When this "shock" was imposed:** Jeffrey D. Sachs, "Shock Therapy in Poland: Perspectives of Five Years," April 6 and 7, 1994, Tanner Lectures, University of Utah, transcript, https://tannerlectures.utah.edu/_resources/documents/a-to-z/s/sachs95 .pdf, 265–90; Taylor Marvin, "Shock Therapy: What We Can Learn from Poland," *Prospect: Journal of International Affairs at UCSD* (2010).

173 **coincided with the loss of an empire:** Whereas Poles had familiarity with markets from pre-1947 memories and experiences in sectors like agriculture that never were fully collectivized, Russians (after seventy years of sweeping socialism) had no living memory of markets. Trying to spark a capitalist economy overnight was like trying to jump-start a car that didn't have an engine. Thomas W. Hall and John E. Elliott, "Poland and Russia One Decade after Shock Therapy," *Journal of Economic Issues* 33, no. 2 (1999): 305–14.

174 **world's most valuable toy company:** Paul Skeldon, "LEGO Builds Sales 36% as Digital Transformation Starts to Click," Internet Retailing, September 29, 2021, https:// internetretailing.net/lego-builds-sales-36-as-digital-transformation-starts-to-clcik -23771/.

175 **conceptualize transformation as a sequence:** Julien R. Phillips, "Enhancing the Effectiveness of Organizational Change Management," *Human Resource Management* 22, no. 1–2 (1983): 183–99.

175 **"unfreezing" of the old pattern:** Bernard Burnes, "The Origins of Lewin's Three-Step Model of Change," *Journal of Applied Behavioral Science* 56, no. 1 (March 2020): 32–59.

175 **Change management models include steps:** John P. Kotter, *Leading Change* (Cambridge, MA: Harvard Business School Press, 1996).

175 **analogies to a "burning platform":** When the rig caught fire, workers jumped a five-story distance into the North Sea to escape. Daryl R. Conner, *Managing at the Speed of Change: How Resilient Managers Succeed and Prosper Where Others Fail* (New York: Random House, 1993).

177 **ready for its promised land:** Robert Carroll and Stephen Prickett, eds., *The Bible: Authorized King James Version* (Oxford: Oxford University Press, 2008).

Chapter 8: Toxic Tribalism and Its Antidotes

178 **"Maybe we pushed too far":** Ben Rhodes, *The World as It Is: A Memoir of the Obama White House* (New York: Random House, 2019).

180 **Red and blue voters don't socialize:** Anna Brown, "Most Democrats Who Are Looking for a Relationship Would Not Consider Dating a Trump Voter," Pew Research Center, April 24, 2020, https://www.pewresearch.org/short-reads/2020/04/24/most -democrats-who-are-looking-for-a-relationship-would-not-consider-dating-a -trump-voter; Gregory A. Huber and Neil Malhotra, "Political Homophily in Social Relationships: Evidence from Online Dating Behavior," *Journal of Politics* 79, no. 1 (2017): 269–83.

180 **cut short their Thanksgiving dinners:** M. Keith Chen and Ryne Rohla, "The Effect of Partisanship and Political Advertising on Close Family Ties," *Science* 360, no. 6392 (2018): 1020–24.

181 **they expect violence:** David Lauter, "The Year Political Tribalism Proved Toxic," *Los Angeles Times*, January 7, 2022, https://www.latimes.com/politics/newsletter/2022 -01-07/the-year-political-tribalism-proved-toxic-essential-politics.

181 **Legislative gridlock has become the rule:** Sarah Binder, "The Dysfunctional Congress," *Annual Review of Political Science* 18 (2015): 85–101.

181 **undermine public faith:** Shaun Bowler and Todd Donovan, "Confidence in US Elections after the Big Lie," *Political Research Quarterly* (2023): 10659129231206179.

181 **the demise of our democracy:** Vanessa Williamson, "Understanding Democratic Decline in the United States," Brookings, October 17 2023, https://www.brookings .edu/articles/understanding-democratic-decline-in-the-united-states/.

181 **sometimes "toxic tribalism":** It may have been President Obama, whose mother was an anthropologist and whose father belonged to the Luo people of Kenya, who first voiced the political tribalism trope. But he was soon joined by many others from both parties, even those, like Senator Ben Sasse, who don't agree with him on many topics. See "Remarks by President Obama to the United Nations General Assembly," The White House Office of the Press Secretary, September 28, 2015; Ben Sasse, *Them: Why We Hate Each Other—and How to Heal* (New York: St. Martin's Press, 2018).

181 **Political journalists have tried:** Lauter, "The Year Political Tribalism Proved Toxic."

181 **"virus of tribalism":** Thomas L. Friedman, "Have We Reshaped Middle East Politics or Started to Mimic It?," *New York Times*, September 14, 2021, https://www.nytimes .com/2021/09/14/opinion/america-democracy-middle-east-tribalism.html.

181 **a long-buried urge for blind allegiance:** Andrew Sullivan, "Can Our Democracy Survive Tribalism?," *New York*, September 19, 2017, https://nymag.com/intelligencer /2017/09/can-democracy-survive-tribalism.html.

182 **inimicable "tribal warrior":** Alex Altman, "Donald Trump: Tribal Warrior," *Time*, March 3, 2016, https://time.com/4246080/tribal-warrior/.

182 **tribal instincts we have reviewed:** Anthropologist Lawrence Rosen adds another objection: calling close-minded, exclusionary, quarrelsome behavior "tribalistic" is an inaccurate stereotype. Ethnographers observe that Indigenous tribes survive through shape-shifting, exchange, and collaboration with other groups—not close-mindedness and conflict. The "toxic tribalism" trope is misleading and injurious to the thousands of Indigenous peoples around the world. Lawrence Rosen, "'Tribalism' Gets a Bum Rap," *Anthropology Today* 32, no. 5 (2016): 3–4.

183 **carry their conformist judgments:** Robert C. Jacobs and Donald T. Campbell, "The Perpetuation of an Arbitrary Tradition through Several Generations of a Laboratory Microculture," *Journal of Abnormal and Social Psychology* 62, no. 3 (1961): 649; Mark K. MacNeil and Muzafer Sherif, "Norm Change over Subject Generations as a Function of Arbitrariness of Prescribed Norms," *Journal of Personality and Social Psychology* 34, no. 5 (1976): 762.

184 **so that truth can prevail:** John Stuart Mill, *"On Liberty" and Other Writings* (Cambridge: Cambridge University Press, 1989).

184 **"competition of the market":** Wonnell, Christopher T., "Truth and the Marketplace of Ideas," *UC Davis Law Review*, 19 (1985): 669.

184 **Political parties did not play:** Ezra Klein, *Why We're Polarized* (New York: Simon and Schuster, 2020).

184 **same partisan feather increasingly "flocked together":** Bill Bishop, *The Big Sort: Why the Clustering of Like-Minded America Is Tearing Us Apart* (Boston: Houghton Mifflin Harcourt, 2009). We have become so accustomed lately to the map of red and blue states that it can be hard to remember it wasn't always this way. The "blue" states for George McGovern from South Dakota in 1972 were not the same as those for Jimmy Carter from Georgia in 1976. The swing in blue support from one election to the next in that time was almost 8 percentage points, whereas in recent decades it's been less than 2 points. Alan I. Abramowitz, *The Great Alignment: Race, Party Transformation, and the Rise of Donald Trump* (New Haven, CT: Yale University Press, 2018).

184 **party membership increasingly overlapped:** Lilliana Mason, *Uncivil Agreement: How Politics Became Our Identity* (Chicago: University of Chicago Press, 2018); Emily A. West and Shanto Iyengar, "Partisanship as a Social Identity: Implications for Polarization," *Political Behavior* 44, no. 2 (2022): 807–38.

185 **news with a congenial slant:** Erik Peterson and Shanto Iyengar, "Partisan Gaps in Political Information and Information-Seeking Behavior: Motivated Reasoning or Cheerleading?," *American Journal of Political Science* 65, no. 1 (2021): 133–47.

185 **Social media also greatly facilitates:** Jonathan Haidt, "Why the Past 10 Years of American Life Have Been Uniquely Stupid," *Atlantic*, April 11, 2022, https://www.theatlantic.com/magazine/archive/2022/05/social-media-democracy-trust-babel/629369/.

186 **two camps held different factual beliefs:** Cory J. Clark, Brittany S. Liu, Bo M. Winegard, and Peter H. Ditto, "Tribalism Is Human Nature," *Current Directions in Psychological Science* 28, no. 6 (2019): 587–92.

186 **direct reflections of reality:** Robert J. Robinson, Dacher Keltner, Andrew Ward, and Lee Ross, "Actual Versus Assumed Differences in Construal: 'Naive Realism' in Intergroup Perception and Conflict," *Journal of Personality and Social Psychology* 68, no. 3 (1995): 404.

186 **when in fact it's 2 percent:** Douglas J. Ahler and Gaurav Sood, "The Parties in Our Heads: Misperceptions about Party Composition and Their Consequences," *Journal of Politics* 80, no. 3 (2018): 964–81; Arlie Hochschild, "Think Republicans Are Disconnected from Reality? It's Even Worse among Liberals," *Guardian*, July 21, 2019, https://www.theguardian.com/commentisfree/2019/jul/21/democrats-republicans-political-beliefs-national-survey-poll.

186 **79 percent do:** Leaf Van Boven, Charles M. Judd, and David K. Sherman, "Political Polarization Projection: Social Projection of Partisan Attitude Extremity and Attitudinal Processes," *Journal of Personality and Social Psychology* 103, no. 1 (2012): 84; Jacob E. Rothschild, Adam J. Howat, Richard M. Shafranek, and Ethan C. Busby, "Pigeonholing Partisans: Stereotypes of Party Supporters and Partisan Polarization," *Political Behavior* 41 (2019): 423–43.

186 **This is "epistemic tribalism":** Shanto Iyengar and Masha Krupenkin, "Partisanship as Social Identity; Implications for the Study of Party Polarization," *The Forum* 16, no. 1 (2018): 23–45.

187 **78 percent of all Whole Foods:** Klein, *Why We're Polarized.*

187 *signs* **of the partisan tribes:** Dan Hiaeshutter-Rice, Fabian G. Neuner, and Stuart Soroka, "Cued by Culture: Political Imagery and Partisan Evaluations," *Political Behavior* 45, no. 2 (2023): 741–59.

188   **the performer Lil Nas X:** Josh Eels, "Lil Nas X: Inside the Rise of a Hip-Hop Cowboy," *Rolling Stone,* May 20, 2019, https://www.rollingstone.com/music/music-features/lil-nas-x-old-town-road-interview-new-album-836393/.

188   **when trying to persuade the other political tribe:** Matthew Feinberg and Robb Willer, "The Moral Roots of Environmental Attitudes," *Psychological Science* 24, no. 1 (2013): 56–62; Matthew Feinberg and Robb Willer, "Moral Reframing: A Technique for Effective and Persuasive Communication across Political Divides," *Social and Personality Psychology Compass* 13, no. 12 (2019): e12501.

188   **Republicans reject a "carbon tax":** David J. Hardisty, Eric J. Johnson, and Elke U. Weber, "A Dirty Word or a Dirty World? Attribute Framing, Political Affiliation, and Query Theory," *Psychological Science* 21, no. 1 (2010): 86–92.

189   **clerics and faith-based language:** Guthrie Graves-Fitzsimmons and Maggie Siddiqi, "Religious Americans Demand Climate Action," American Progress, July 21, 2021, https://www.americanprogress.org/article/religious-americans-demand-climate-action/.

189   **tools to allay media bias:** The tech fixes tended to presume bubbles were just a matter of information supply and not also of demand. Neither cable news, blogs, or social media inherently force users to consume news that corroborates their tribe's biases; we used the technology to do this because we crave consensus, albeit at a largely unconscious level. Even those curious about bursting their bubble found reasons to be suspicious of many of these tools. Amanda Hess, "How to Escape Your Political Bubble for a Clearer View," *New York Times,* March 3, 2017, https://www.nytimes.com/2017/03/03/arts/the-battle-over-your-political-bubble.html.

189   **an effect opposite than intended:** Christopher A. Bail et al., "Exposure to Opposing Views on Social Media Can Increase Political Polarization," *Proceedings of the National Academy of Sciences* 115, no. 37 (2018): 9216–21.

189   **people have defenses against signals:** Twitter feed from another tribe does work, at least anecdotally, for people who organize it themselves. Having chosen whom from the other camp to follow, they can overcome doubts and suspicions about jarring ideas. B. J. May, "How 26 Tweets Broke My Filter Bubble," Medium, January 18, 2016, https://medium.com/@bjmay/how-26-tweets-broke-my-filter-bubble-88c1527517f3.

189   **Republicans who believed he was foreign-born:** John Clinton and Carrie Roush, "Poll: Persistent Partisan Divide over 'Birther' Question," NBC News, August 10, 2016, https://www.nbcnews.com/politics/2016-election/poll-persistent-partisan-divide-over-birther-question-n627446.

189   **partisans dismiss evidence:** Lee Ross and Richard E. Nisbett, *The Person and the Situation: Perspectives of Social Psychology* (London: Pinter & Martin Publishers, 2011).

189 **selectivity in scrutiny:** Dan M. Kahan et al., "The Polarizing Impact of Science Literacy and Numeracy on Perceived Climate Change Risks," *Nature Climate Change* 2,
no. 10 (2012): 732–35; Dan M. Kahan, Ellen Peters, Erica Cantrell Dawson, and Paul
Slovic, "Motivated Numeracy and Enlightened Self-Government," *Behavioural Public Policy* 1, no. 1 (2017): 54–86.

189 **rather than as *from the other side*:** Douglas Guilbeault, Joshua Becker, and Damon
Centola, "Social Learning and Partisan Bias in the Interpretation of Climate Trends,"
Proceedings of the National Academy of Sciences 115, no. 39 (2018): 9714–19; Michele
W. Berger, "Can Social Media Networks Reduce Political Polarization on Climate
Change?," Penn Today, September 3, 2018, https://penntoday.upenn.edu/news/cli
mate-change-political-polarization-disappears-social-networks.

190 **found that interparty conversations:** Erik Santoro and David E. Broockman, "The
Promise and Pitfalls of Cross-Partisan Conversations for Reducing Affective Polarization: Evidence from Randomized Experiments," *Science Advances* 8, no. 25 (2022):
eabn5515. Similarly, Lees and Cikara found that partisans overestimate the other
camp's opposition and correcting the presumed hostility reduces negative perceptions, an intervention that replicates in twenty-six countries with similar partisan
divides. Jeffrey Lees and Mina Cikara, "Inaccurate Group Meta-Perceptions Drive
Negative Out-Group Attributions in Competitive Contexts," *Nature Human Behaviour* 4, no. 3 (2020): 279–86; Kai Ruggeri et al., "The General Fault in Our Fault
Lines," *Nature Human Behaviour* 5, no. 10 (2021): 1369–80.

190 **interparty conversations about nonpolitical interests:** While political theorists like
Francis Fukuyama advocate healing partisan divides with strengthened national identities, psychologist Jennifer Richeson makes a compelling case for more specific identities
that afford distinctiveness. Francis Fukuyama, "Against Identity Politics: The New Tribalism and the Crisis of Democracy," *Foreign Affairs* 97 (2018): 90; Stacey Y. Abrams
et al., "E Pluribus Unum: The Fight over Identity Politics," *Foreign Affairs* 98 (2019): 160.

191 **affected by the party information:** Geoffrey L. Cohen, "Party over Policy: The
Dominating Impact of Group Influence on Political Beliefs," *Journal of Personality
and Social Psychology* 85, no. 5 (2003): 808.

191 **hostility is not where:** Dampening negative feelings is possible but it doesn't reduce
the deeper dysfunctions. Jan G. Voelkel et al., "Interventions Reducing Affective
Polarization Do Not Necessarily Improve Anti-Democratic Attitudes," *Nature
human behaviour* 7, no. 1 (2023): 55–64.

191 **schools are "creating tribalism":** Tucker Carlson, "Schools Are Creating Tribalism
in Our Kids," Fox News, August 12, 2021, https://www.foxnews.com/opinion/tucker
-carlson-schools-are-creating-tribalism-in-our-kids.

191 **terrorist attacks and military attacks:** Elihu D. Richter, Dror Kris Markus, and Casey Tait, "Incitement, Genocide, Genocidal Terror, and the Upstream Role of Indoctrination: Can Epidemiologic Models Predict and Prevent?," *Public Health Reviews* 39, no. 1 (2018): 1–22.

193 **lack of racial equity:** Bob Moser, "The Reckoning of Morris Dees and the Southern Poverty Law Center," *New Yorker*, March 21, 2019, https://www.newyorker.com /news/news-desk/the-reckoning-of-morris-dees-and-the-southern-poverty-law -center.

193 **recruitment bias was "reverse discrimination":** Dan Morse, "Does Center Practice What It Preaches?," *Tampa Bay Times*, April 3, 1994, updated October 6, 2005, https://www.tampabay.com/archive/1994/04/03/does-center-practice-what-it -preaches.

193 **leadership doubted there was racial bias:** Audra D. S. Burch, Alan Blinder, and John Eligon, "Roiled by Staff Uproar, Civil Rights Group Looks at Intolerance Within," *New York Times*, March 25, 2019, https://www.nytimes.com/2019/03/25/us/morris -dees-leaves-splc.html.

193 **"where the values we are committed to":** Alan Blinder, "Southern Poverty Law Center President Plans Exit amid Turmoil," *New York Times*, March 22, 2019, https:// www.nytimes.com/2019/03/22/us/splc-richard-cohen-resigns.html.

194 **workplace mistreatment was even more common:** "On Views of Race and Inequality, Blacks and Whites Are Worlds Apart: Personal Experiences with Discrimination," Pew Research Center, June 27, 2016, https://www.pewresearch.org/social-trends /2016/06/27/5-personal-experiences-with-discrimination/.

194 **white applicants receive on average 36 percent:** Lincoln Quillian, Devah Pager, Ole Hexel, and Arnfinn H. Midtbøen, "Meta-Analysis of Field Experiments Shows No Change in Racial Discrimination in Hiring over Time," *Proceedings of the National Academy of Sciences* 114, no. 41 (2017): 10870–75.

195 **toxic tribalism has come into vogue:** Thomas Kochman and Jean Mavrelis, *Corporate Tribalism: White Men/White Women and Cultural Diversity at Work* (Chicago: University of Chicago Press, 2019); Puja Mehta and Christopher D. Buckley, "'Your People Have Always Been Servants': Internalised Racism in Academic Medicine," *The Lancet* 400, no. 10368 (2022): 2045–46.

195 **ethnic hostilities have declined steeply:** Howard Schuman, Charlotte Steeh, and Lawrence Bobo, *Racial Attitudes in America: Trends and Interpretations*, vol. 2 (Cambridge, MA: Harvard University Press, 1985); Sarah Patton Moberg, Maria Krysan, and Deanna Christianson, "Racial Attitudes in America," *Public Opinion Quarterly* 83, no. 2 (2019): 450–71.

195 **motive to lift up one's in-group:** Marilynn B. Brewer, "Intergroup Discrimination: Ingroup Love or Outgroup Hate?," in *The Cambridge Handbook of the Psychology of Prejudice*, eds. Chris G. Sibley and Fiona Kate Barlow (Cambridge: Cambridge University Press, 2017); Anthony G. Greenwald and Thomas F. Pettigrew, "With Malice toward None and Charity for Some: Ingroup Favoritism Enables Discrimination," *American Psychologist* 69, no. 7 (2014): 669.

195 **positive feelings toward one's own race:** S. A. Ziegler, T. A. Kirby, K. Xu, and A. G. Greenwald, "Implicit Race Attitudes Predict Vote in the 2012 Presidential Election," Political Psychology Preconference of the Annual Meeting of the Society for Personality and Social Psychology, New Orleans, Louisiana, 2013.

195 **ethnic in-group positivity:** David Buttelmann and Robert Böhm, "The Ontogeny of the Motivation That Underlies In-Group Bias," *Psychological Science* 25, no. 4 (2014): 921–27.

195 **to act "with malice toward none":** Abraham Lincoln, *Great Speeches* (Mineola, NY: Dover Publications, 1991).

196 **unconscious in-group favoritism:** Of course, many people conceive of their ethnicity more narrowly than white versus Black, but most narrow categories are still nested within race, so in-group favoritism (e.g., WASPs helping fellow WASPs) still contributes to racial inequality.

196 **interviewees tallied the acts of generosity:** Marc Bendick, Rekha Eanni Rodriguez, and Sarumathi Jayaraman, "Employment Discrimination in Upscale Restaurants: Evidence from Matched Pair Testing," *Social Science Journal* 47, no. 4 (2010): 802–18.

197 **"ethnic opportunity hoarding":** Charles Tilly, *Durable Inequality* (Berkeley: University of California Press, 1998).

197 **70 percent of US whites:** Nancy DiTomaso, *The American Non-Dilemma: Racial Inequality without Racism* (New York: Russell Sage Foundation, 2013).

197 **Whites tend to have networks:** Daniel Cox, Juhem Navarro-Rivera, Robert P. Jones, "Race, Religion, and Political Affiliation of Americans' Core Social Networks," PRRI, August 3, 2016, https://www.prri.org/research/poll-race-religion-politics-americans-social-networks/.

197 **selecting for "cultural fit":** One interviewing manager admitted that a recruit who passes the "airport test" (someone he would have interests in common to talk about if stuck at an airport) might get grilled less hard about the numbers in a case-analysis question. Lauren A. Rivera, "Hiring as Cultural Matching: The Case of Elite Professional Service Firms," in *Working in America*, ed. Amy S. Wharton (New York: Routledge, 2015), 157–68.

197 **half of all non-rookie hires:** Nelson D. Schwartz, "In Hiring, a Friend in Need Is a Prospect, Indeed," *New York Times* January 27, 2013. Burks, Stephen V., Bo Cowgill, Mitchell Hoffman, and Michael Housman. "The Value of Hiring Through Employee Referrals," *The Quarterly Journal of Economics* 130, no. 2 (2015): 805–839.

197 **refer associates of the same race:** Meta Brown, Elizabeth Setren, and Giorgio Topa, "Do Informal Referrals Lead to Better Matches? Evidence from a Firm's Employee Referral System," *Journal of Labor Economics* 34, no. 1 (2016): 161–209.

199 **Public symbols are icons that trigger:** Hawes Spencer and Michael Levenson, "Charlottesville Removes Robert E. Lee Statue at Center of White Nationalist Rally," *New York Times*, updated November 8, 2021.

199 **subliminal flash of the Confederate flag:** Joyce E. Ehrlinger et al., "How Exposure to the Confederate Flag Affects Willingness to Vote for Barack Obama," *Political Psychology* 32, no. 1 (2011): 131–46.

200 **bias training does not usually achieve:** Patricia G. Devine and Tory L. Ash, "Diversity Training Goals, Limitations, and Promise: A Review of the Multidisciplinary Literature," *Annual Review of Psychology* 73 (2022): 403–29; Elizabeth Levy Paluck, Roni Porat, Chelsey S. Clark, and Donald P. Green, "Prejudice Reduction: Progress and Challenges," *Annual Review of Psychology* 72 (2021): 533–60; Elizabeth Levy Paluck and Donald P. Green, "Prejudice Reduction: What Works? A Review and Assessment of Research and Practice," *Annual Review of Psychology* 60 (2009): 339–67.

200 **minority representation in management fails:** Frank Dobbin and Alexandra Kalev, "Why Diversity Programs Fail," *Harvard Business Review* 94, no. 7 (2016): 1, https://hbr.org/2016/07/why-diversity-programs-fail; Jesse Singal, "What If Diversity Training Is Doing More Harm than Good?," *New York Times*, January 17, 2023, https://www.nytimes.com/2023/01/17/opinion/dei-trainings-effective.html.

200 **may unwittingly *exacerbate*:** Rohini Anand and Mary-Frances Winters, "A Retrospective View of Corporate Diversity Training from 1964 to the Present," *Academy of Management Learning & Education* 7, no. 3 (2008): 356–72.

200 **Allport's "contact" hypothesis:** Elizabeth Levy Paluck, Seth A. Green, and Donald P. Green, "The Contact Hypothesis Re-Evaluated," *Behavioural Public Policy* 3, no. 2 (2019): 129–58.

200 **studies of sports teams:** Robert Kurzban, John Tooby, and Leda Cosmides, "Can Race Be Erased? Coalitional Computation and Social Categorization," *Proceedings of the National Academy of Sciences 98*, no. 26 (2001): 15387–92.

201 **teamwork across ethnicities:** Salma Mousa, "Building Social Cohesion between Christians and Muslims through Soccer in Post-ISIS Iraq," *Science* 369, no. 6505 (2020): 866–70.

201 **developing "inclusive leadership":** Alexandra Kalev, Frank Dobbin, and Erin Kelly, "Best Practices or Best Guesses? Assessing the Efficacy of Corporate Affirmative Action and Diversity Policies," *American Sociological Review* 71, no. 4 (2006): 589–617.

201 **long-term mentorship program:** Lauryn Burnett and Herman Aguinis, "How to Prevent and Minimize DEI Backfire," *Business Horizons* (2023); Dobbin and Kalev, "Why Diversity Programs Fail."

201 **candidates from underrepresented groups:** John Sullivan and Kimberly N. Do, "Instantly Improve Diversity Recruiting Results with a Bonus for Diversity Referrals," ERE, September 14, 2015, https://www.ere.net/instantly-improve-diversity-recruiting-results-with-a-bonus-for-diversity-referrals/.

201 **Intel achieved a 20 percent increase:** Grace Donnelly, "Intel CEO in New Diversity Report: 'Let's Turn This Tragedy into Action,'" *Fortune*, August 15, 2017, https://fortune.com/2017/08/15/intel-ceo-in-new-diversity-report-lets-turn-this-tragedy-into-action.

201 **Pinterest held challenges across divisions:** Abby Maldonado, "Diversifying Engineering Referrals at Pinterest," LinkedIn, January 15, 2016, https://www.linkedin.com/pulse/diversifying-engineering-referrals-pinterest-abby-maldonado/.

202 **major US orchestras are declining:** Michael Cooper, "Seeking Orchestras in Tune With Their Diverse Communities," *New York Times*, April 18, 2018, https://www.nytimes.com/2018/04/18/arts/music/symphony-orchestra-diversity.html.

202 **5 percent of works performed:** Javier C. Hernández, "U.S. Orchestras Playing More Works by Women and Minorities, Report Says," *New York Times*, June 21, 2022, https://www.nytimes.com/2022/06/21/arts/music/american-orchestras-women-minorities.html.

202 **diversify the LA Phil's ranks:** These sold-out events at the Hollywood Bowl have funded the Youth Orchestra Los Angeles (YOLA), which gives 1,500 children, many of them Latin American immigrants, instruments, lessons, and a stage. With "The Dude" as their role model, 100 percent are attending college, 90 percent as first-generation. "YOLA 2023 Donor Impact Report," La Phil, https://www.laphil.com/about/watch-and-listen/yola-2023-donor-impact-report.

202 **deemed "America's most important orchestra":** Zachary Woolfe, "Los Angeles Has America's Most Important Orchestra. Period," *New York Times*, April 18, 2017, https://www.nytimes.com/2017/04/18/arts/music/los-angeles-has-americas-most-important-orchestra-period.html.

202 **Kress department store:** Keith Schneider, "Revitalizing Montgomery as It Embraces Its Past," *New York Times*, May 21, 2019, https://www.nytimes.com/2019/05/21/business/montgomery-museums-civil-rights.html.

202 A "story booth" invites residents: "Bernice: March 12, 2020," StoryBooth Montgomery, https://storybooth.us/stories/kress-20200312144644.

204 "Six centuries ago": Slobodan Milošević, "1989 St. Vitus Day Speech," June 28, 1989, transcript, Slobodan-Milosevic.org, http://www.slobodan-milosevic.org/spch-kosovo 1989.htm

204 This was a sharp departure: Marcus Tanner, "Milosevic Carries off the Battle Honours," *The Independent*, June 29, 1989.

204 wearing Serbian Orthodox crosses: Timur Kuran, "Ethnic Norms and Their Transformation through Reputational Cascades," *Journal of Legal Studies* 27, no. S2 (1998): 623–59.

206 resort to mass slaughter: Ervin Staub, *Overcoming Evil: Genocide, Violent Conflict, and Terrorism* (New York: Oxford University Press, 2013); Natalie Impraim, "Russian Wagner Mercenaries Commit War Crimes in C.A.R.," Genocide Watch, March 28, 2023, https://www.genocidewatch.com/single-post/russian-wagner-mercenaries -commit-war-crimes-in-c-a-r.

206 evolved the ancestor instinct: Lawrence H. Keeley, *War before Civilization* (New York: Oxford University Press, 1996); Marc Kissel and Nam C. Kim, "The Emergence of Human Warfare: Current Perspectives," *American Journal of Physical Anthropology* 168 (2019): 141–63.

206 Journalist Arthur Koestler: Arthur Koestler, *The Ghost in the Machine* (New York: Macmillan, 1968).

207 Different traditions are implicit threats: Jeremy Ginges, "The Moral Logic of Political Violence," *Trends in Cognitive Sciences* 23, no. 1 (2019): 1–3.

207 the older the traditions of a rival group: Ruth H. Warner, Ana H. Kent, and Kristin L. Kiddoo, "Perceived Collective Continuity and Attitudes toward Outgroups," *European Journal of Social Psychology* 46, no. 5 (2016): 595–608.

207 When a minority group doesn't share: Joshua R. Gubler and Joel Sawat Selway, "Horizontal Inequality, Crosscutting Cleavages, and Civil War," *Journal of Conflict Resolution* 56, no. 2 (2012): 206–32.

207 other forms of violence decline: Steven Pinker, *The Better Angels of Our Nature: Why Violence Has Declined* (New York: Penguin Books, 2012); Robert Muggah and Ali Velshi, "Religious Violence Is on the Rise. What Can Faith-Based Communities Do about It?," *World Economic Forum* 25 (2019); Jonas Baumann, Daniel Finnbogason, and Isak Svensson, "Rethinking Mediation: Resolving Religious Conflicts," *CSS Policy Perspectives* 6, no. 1 (2018).

207 These sectarian anxieties have grown: Milan Obaidi, Jonas Kunst, Simon Ozer, and

Sasha Y. Kimel, "The 'Great Replacement' Conspiracy: How the Perceived Ousting of Whites Can Evoke Violent Extremism and Islamophobia," *Group Processes & Intergroup Relations* 25, no. 7 (2022): 1675–95.

207 **"great replacement theory":** Michael Feola, "'You Will Not Replace Us': The Melancholic Nationalism of Whiteness," *Political Theory* 49, no. 4 (2020): 528–53.

207 **a third of Americans worry:** Nik Popli, "How the 'Great Replacement Theory' Has Fueled Racist Violence," *Time*, May 16, 2022, https://time.com/6177282/great-replacement-theory-buffalo-racist-attacks/.

209 ***Triumph of the Will:*** Filmmaker Leni Riefenstahl captured the 1934 rally with a crowd of seven hundred thousand people lining the streets of the city, saluting goosestepping soldiers in crisp uniforms and listening to the Führer speak from a stage bedecked with swastikas and war eagles about the past glory of their tribe, its recent humiliation, and its future reign.

210 **"imminent lawless action":** David L. Hudson, Jr., "Does the First Amendment Protect Trump on Incitement to Riot?," First Amendment Watch, January 8, 2021, https://firstamendmentwatch.org/does-the-first-amendment-protect-trump-on-incitement-to-riot/.

210 **ceremonial events (vigils and rallies):** Elihu D. Richter, Dror Kris Markus, and Casey Tait, "Incitement, Genocide, Genocidal Terror, and the Upstream Role of Indoctrination: Can Epidemiologic Models Predict and Prevent?," *Public Health Reviews* 39, no. 1 (2018): 1–22.

211 **support extreme military measures:** Tom Pyszczynski et al., "Mortality Salience, Martyrdom, and Military Might: The Great Satan versus the Axis of Evil," *Personality and Social Psychology Bulletin* 32, no. 4 (2006): 525–37.

211 **precedent signals had to emerge:** Zachary K. Rothschild, Abdolhossein Abdollahi, and Tom Pyszczynski, "Does Peace Have a Prayer? The Effect of Mortality Salience, Compassionate Values, and Religious Fundamentalism on Hostility toward Out-Groups," *Journal of Experimental Social Psychology* 45, no. 4 (2009): 816–27. Behavioral scientists debate whether political judgment effects like this depend on the historical moment, but a recent preregistered replication of the study found the same fascinating effect. Kenneth E. Vail III, Emily Courtney, and Jamie Arndt, "The Influence of Existential Threat and Tolerance Salience on Anti-Islamic Attitudes in American Politics," *Political Psychology* 40, no. 5 (2019): 1143–62.

211 **the policy of multiculturalism:** Han Entzinger, "Changing the Rules while the Game Is On: From Multiculturalism to Assimilation in the Netherlands," in *Migration, Citizenship, Ethnos* (New York: Palgrave Macmillan, 2006), 121–44; "State Multiculturalism

Has Failed, Says David Cameron," BBC, February 5, 2011, https://www.bbc.com/news /uk-politics-12371994; "Merkel Says German Multicultural Society Has Failed," BBC, October 17, 2010, https://www.bbc.com/news/world-europe-11559451.

213 **united meta-tribe of Catalonia:** Of course, another factor is that Catalan traditionalists have been more threatened by Madrid, given the harsh crackdown on its bid for greater autonomy. There is nothing like a larger threat to make other differences recede.

215 **survive through the last Ice Age:** Denise Su, "How Many Ice Ages Has the Earth Had, and Could Humans Live through One?," Space.com, June 29, 2022, https:// www.space.com/ice-ages-on-earth-could-humans-survive.

215 **"tragedy of the commons" holds:** David Feeny, Fikret Berkes, Bonnie J. McCay, and James M. Acheson, "The Tragedy of the Commons: Twenty-Two Years Later," *Human Ecology* 18 (1990): 1–19.

215 **we underestimate popular:** Gregg Sparkman, Nathan Geiger, and Elke U. Weber, "Americans Experience a False Social Reality by Underestimating Popular Climate Policy Support by Nearly Half," *Nature Communications* 13, no. 1 (2022): 4779.

215 **We shouldn't despair people's slowness:** Eric J. Johnson, Eli Sugerman, Vicki Morwitz, Gita Johar, and Michael W. Morris, "Widespread Misestimates of Greenhouse Gas Emissions Suggest Low Carbon Competence," *Nature Climate Change* (2024).

215 **rules for sustainable consumption:** In 2009, Ostrom became the first woman to win the Nobel Prize in economics. Elinor Ostrom, "A General Framework for Analyzing Sustainability of Social-Ecological Systems," *Science* 325 (2009): 419–22.

216 **sustainable pattern of water distribution returned:** J. Stephen Lansing, *Perfect Order: Recognizing Complexity in Bali* (Princeton, NJ: Princeton University Press, 2006); Indosphere Culture, "Balinese Water Temples: Merging Religion and Science," Medium, September 15, 2019, https://indosphere.medium.com/balinese-water -temples-merging-religion-and-science-da26b5cd268b.

216 **evidence that they can help:** When British Catholics reverted to abstaining from meat on Fridays, it made an immediate environmental difference. Wes Stenzel, "Catholic Church Could Consider Resurrecting Old Practice after Successful Study: 'Pope Francis Has Already Highlighted [It],'" Yahoo News, August 30, 2023, https:// www.yahoo.com/news/catholic-church-could-consider-resurrecting-190000391 .html. Many other cultures have precedents for vegetarianism—Orthodox Lenten traditions, Buddhist belief in *ahisma* (doing no harm)—that could be similarly invoked. A sacrifice is less onerous knowing that it connects one to one's ancestors.

INDEX

Note: Italicized page numbers indicate material in tables or illustrations.

Acompáñame ("Come Along"), 107
Aché of Paraguay, 37–38
activists, influence of, 109
acupuncture treatments, 131–32
adult literacy, 107
advertisements, 100, 109–10, 120–21, 124–25
African Americans, 24, 40, 193, 199, 202
Afrikaners, 141–42
agriculture, 11, 79
AIDS crisis, 107–8
Alabama State Capitol, 198
Albanian Muslims, 204
alcohol consumption, 83–87, 92, 95, 98
Alcoholics Anonymous, 66
All Blacks of New Zealand, 70–71
Allen, Woody, 103
All in the Family (television series), 122
Allport, Gordon, 200–201
Altman, Alex, 181–82
alt-right groups, 193
altruism, 35–36

Amazon, 66
Ambato, Ecuador, 153–54, 176
American Civil Liberties Union (ACLU), 193
Americans for Prosperity, 160
Amish communities, 116
ancestor instinct/codes, 56–80
   about, xxvii, 59
   and cave art, 56–59, *57*, 61
   and comfort in continuity, 72–73
   and dangerous/threatening contexts,
      76–79
   and death/mortality, 74–75
   and early humans, 59–62, 79
   and Joan of Arc, xxx, 67–69
   and mass violence, 206, 208
   and punctuality standards, 153
   and rituals/traditions, 63–67, 70–72, 74,
      183, 211
   and tribal ceremony, 70
   triggered by cues or needs, xxx
   See also ceremonies and rituals

ancient precedents, 130–37
anthropology, xxv
anti-corruption laws, 155
Anti-Saloon League, 85
anti-war films, 121–22
anxiety, 74, 75
apes, 5, 8, 9, 13
Appalachia's "culture of poverty," xvii
Arab population in Israel, 76
architecture and signals of antiquity,
    132–33
Aristotle, xxiii, xxv
Arizona's Petrified Forest, 101
Arrernte people, 63
Aryanism, 207
Asch, Solomon, 89–90, 183
Asian Cup, 2000, ix
astroturfing, 160
Atta, Mohammed, xviii
attire/dress, 26, 27, 168–69, 171
audience approval, 52–55, 79
Austria, 210
authority, compliance to, 170–71

Bail, Chris, 189
Bali, 216
Balkans, 203–5
Bandura, Albert, 106
Bank of America, 45–50
Bank of New York Mellon, 131
Barcelona, Spain, 212–13
Barr, Abigail, 18
Barra, Mary, xxxi, 168–69
bathing, ritual, 74
Battle of Kosovo, 204
Beck, Glenn, 160
Becker, Ernest, 74
behavioral freedom of humans,
    xxiii–xxiv
Belgrade, capital of former Yugoslavia,
    204–5
Berlin Wall, fall of, 204
Beyoncé, 105
biases, cultural influence on, 20–22, 187,
    193, 200–201
Bible, 176–77, 211
bicultural individuals, 22–25, 30
Biden, Joe, xx
birtherism, 189
blackouts in California, 96–98

Black people
    and discrimination, 192–94
    and diversity programs, 194–97, 199
    and white Americans' peer codes, 95
Blitzer, Wolf, 179
Bloomberg, Michael, 166
BMW, 142
Bond films and Agent 007, 124
"Born in the U.S.A." (Springsteen), 122
Bosniaks, 205
Boston University hockey team, 117–19
bottom-up change, 175–76
Bowling Alone (Putnam), 184
Brady Campaign, 159
brain, evolution of, xxvi, 5–6, 9–15
brand identities/popularity, 96, 142
Brazil, declining family sizes in, 103–5
Bridge the Divide, 190
British monarchy, 133
Broockman, David, 190
Brown, George, 16
Brown, Robert, 117–18
Brownstein, Rhonda, 192, 193–94
Buckingham Palace, changing of the
    guard at, 133
bullying in high schools, 113–14
Bunker, Archie (character), 122
Bunyan, Paul (folklore character), 136
bureaucracy, 110, 168
Burger King's "Moldy Whopper" ad
    campaign, 109–10
Burke, Tarana, 93–94
business leaders, influence of, 109–13
butifarra, 212
Buttigieg, Pete, 188

cable television access, 104–5
California, blackouts in, 96–98
Canaanites, 205
Canada, 147
Carlson, Tucker, 191
Carnival, 212
Catalonia, 212–13
cave drawings, 56–59, 61, 79
celebrities, influence of, 105–6, 121
censorship, 167
Centola, Damon, 90, 189–90
ceremonies
    and ancestor instinct, 70–72
    and anxiety, 74

and athletic performances at Olympics, 252n72
in dangerous/threatening contexts, 74, 76–79
to facilitate water resources negotiations, 216
feelings of unity and empowerment from, 71–72
and Fukushima plant disaster, 77–79
and initiations, 70
and mass violence, 208–10
political, 204, 208–10
and resource dilemmas, 216
relationship to traditionalism, 251n70
and sectarian extremism, 214
of South Korean soccer team, xiii
synchronous activities in, 70–72
and violence in Yugoslavia, 204, 208–10
white coat ceremony of medical students, 72, 135, 253n72
certainty-seeking, 28–32
Champagne region of France, 130, 145
Change.org, 167
chanting, 72
charity, 195–96
Charleston church massacre (2015), 199
Charlottesville "Unite the Right" rally, 193, 210
Chauvet, Jean-Marie, 56
Chauvet Cave, 56–58, 57, 61
Chavez, Cesar, 156
Chechen insurgencies, 117
Chesterton, G. K., 56
children
    emulation of adults, 106–7
    and rituals/traditions, 65–66, 70
Chile, 93
chimpanzees
    brain evolution of, 9
    cooperation in troupes of, xxiv
    and gaze-tracking reflex, 13–14
    gestural signals of, 7
    low collaboration among, 6
    and massacres, 206
    and peer instincts of humans, 13
China and Chinese people, 20–22, 29, 103, 116, 144–45, 163, 212–13
Chiu, Chi-yue, 23
Chomsky, Noam, 7
Chong, Alberto, 103–4

Chung Mong-joon, x
Church of Jesus Christ of Latter-day Saints, 132–33
Cialdini, Robert, 97, 101
Civil Rights Movement, 39–42, 51, 54–55, 192, 202
climate change, 189–90, 215
Clinton, Hillary, xx, 178–80, 186, 188, 199
Coalition to Stop Gun Violence, 159
Coca-Cola, 201, 202–3
codes. See ancestor instinct/codes; hero instinct/codes; peer instinct/codes
code switching, 22–26
Cody, Iron Eyes, 120
cognitive biases, 182
Cohen, Geoffrey, 190–91, 193–94
Cohen, Richard, 192
The Colbert Report (television series), 122
Cold War, 203
collaboration, 11, 62
collective ideals, 154–55
colonialism, 16, 80, 156
Columbia University, 72, 190
commitment to causes, 157
common ground/knowledge, 11, 62
Communist Party in China, 116
Confederacy, 198–99
conformity
    bias for, xxvii
    and certainty-seeking, 28–32
    negative perceptions of, xxix
    and peer instincts of humans, 28–32, 35, 183
    and peer pressure, 89–90
    and Prohibition/temperance movement, 83–87, 88
    strength of impulse, 102
Congress Party (India), 156
conservatism, 151
consistent precedents, 130, 137–44
conspicuity of peers' preferences, 91–92
conspiracy theories, 207
consulting industry, 173, 175
"contact" hypothesis, 200–201
continuity, xxvii, 73, 147
contraceptive sales, 107
contributing, drive for, xxvii
cooking, advent of, 6–7, 8
cooperation, 39, 61–62, 215–16
coordination, 31, 79, 90

corporations
    and resonant framing, 142
    and signals of antiquity, 135–36
    See also specific corporations
corruption, 15–19, 155
cost-benefit decision-making, 206
counterterrorism, xviii
Crandall, Chris, 131
creativity, xxix
crime-prevention initiatives, 122–23
Croatia, 204
crowdsourcing, 174
The Crusades, 75–76
cues, cultural
    about, 19
    attire as, 26, 27, 28
    and code switching, 23, 24
    language as, 26–27
    and Lee's leadership in Singapore,
      16–17
    limitations, 20
    and South Korea's Reds soccer team,
      xi–xiii, xv
    and triggering of codes, xxx
cults, power of, 114–16, 117
cultural accumulation, 79–80
cultural appropriation, 144–45, *144*
cultural codes
    activated by tribal triggers, xix, xxx, 85
    conforming to, 31
    and Lee's leadership in Singapore, 16
    as shaped/reshaped by tribal signals,
      xxxi, 85, 87
    and temperance movement, 85
    See also ancestor instinct/codes; hero
      instinct/codes; peer instinct/codes
cultural complexity, xxviii, 60–61, 79
cultural evolution, xxvi–xxvii
cultural hegemony, 145–46
cultural psychology, xvii, 24
Cultural Revolution in China, 116
curiosity, 61
Cyberjaya, 19–20, 92–93

danger/threats, rituals practiced in
    contexts of, 74
Darwin, Charles, 35
Davidson, Willie, 142–43
death and mortality, 74–76
De Beers, 135–36

decision-making and certainty-seeking,
    28–32
Dees, Morris Seligman, 192–94, 198
deferential communication, 26
democracy movements, 161
Democratic Party, 179–81, 184, 186–87,
    189–91
demographic trends, 76, 203–4
The Denial of Death (Becker), 74
Deschamps, Éliette Brunel, 56–57
diamond rings, 135–36
Ding, Yu, 116
Disarmed (Goss), 159
disordered eating, 100–101
DiTomaso, Nancy, 197
diversity, 116, 169, 192–203
Dobbin, Frank, 200
"Don't Mess with Texas" campaign, 120–21
Douglas, Mary, 74
Dove's "Real Beauty" ad campaign, 109
dress/attire, 26, 27, 168–69, 171
drug use/culture, xvii, 101
Dudamel, Gustavo, 202–3
Dunbar, Robin, 9, 37
Dunn, Elizabeth, 52
Durant, Kevin, 25
Durkheim, Émile, 71

early humans
    and agriculture, 11, 79
    cave drawings of, 56–59, 61, 79
    and cultural accumulation, 79
    and cultural complexity, xxviii, 60–61, 79
    earliest fossilized footprints of, 3–4, *4*
    emergence of *Homo sapiens*, 59–62
    evolution of prosociality, 35–36
    and hero instinct/codes, 33–35, 39
    hunting practices of, 5–6, 8, 33–35
    and mass violence, 206
    and reputation mindedness, 36–38
    tools of, 60–61
    and tribal instincts, xxviii, 79, 182
    tribal interaction among, 214
Eastman Kodak Corporation, 88–89, *89*
eating disorders, 100–101
echo chambers, 185
economic policy, 171–73
Ecuador, 151–54
education levels, 15, 189
edutainment dramas, 107–8

Eidelman, Scott, 131
elections, 178–81, 186
elites, xxvii, 165, 176–77
encephalization index, 9
engagement rings, 135–36
English-only policies, 26–27
environmentalists, 188–89
Epic Games, 176
epistemic tribalism, 213
equal protection clause, 158
Ernst & Young, 197
Ervin-Tripp, Susan, 22–23
essentialism, xvii
ethical tribalism, 198
ethnic identity and tribalism, 194–99, 205, 213–14
evolution, human, 182–83
executive transitions, 117–18, 119
existential tribalism, 208, 213, 214
exits of insiders, 117–18, 119
Exodus, book of, 176–77
extremist groups, 116–17
eyes and readability of human gaze, 13–14

Falls, Cyril, 74
fame, prestige gained from, 106
family size/planning, xxxi, 103–5, 107
the Fappening, 167
Faulkner, William, 126
Faust, Drew, 119
Federer, Roger, 121
fees justified with tradition, 135
Feinberg, Matthew, 188
female circumcision, 161–63
festivals, 212
Fiat, 142
Finland, 207
First Amendment, 184
fish test, 21–22, 21
Fiske, Alan, 64
Fisman, Ray, 18
flags, 43, 140
The Flintstones (cartoon), 124
FlipFeed, 189
flood myths, 63
Florida State University, 199
folklore and fakelore, 136
food traditions, 212–13
foot-binding, 163
footprints, oldest human, 3–4

Ford's advertisements, 100
forgiveness, 211
Fourteenth Amendment, 158
France, 212
Freedom Summer in Mississippi, 50–51, 54–55
free-rider problem, 39, 53
free speech, 184
Friedman, Thomas, 181
friends, impact of discussions with, 108
"FUD" (fear, uncertainty, and doubt), 29
Fukushima plant disaster, xxx, 77–79, 80
fundamental attribution error, 20–22
funeral rites, 74
Fyre Festival, 92

Gamblers Anonymous, 101
Gamergate, 167
Gandhi, Mohandas, 109, 156–57, 161, 163, 176
Garibaldi, 134
Gaza, 75
gaze-tracking reflex, 13–14
General Motors, 168–69, 171
generosity, 51–52, 196
genetic evolution, xxvi
genocide, 205–6, 208
Georgia (country), 161
Germany, 210, 212
Gilmore, Gary, 53
globalization, 207
Globo network, 104–5, 107
glory, aspirations for, xxvii
Gogh, Theo van, 212
Goop, 136
Goren-Inbar, Naama, 6, 7
Goss, Kristin, 159
gossip, 37
Gramsci, Antonio, 145
grassroots movements, 155–61, 163, 169–70, 175–76, 274n159
Great Depression, 172
"great replacement theory," 207
Greeks, 205
Greenpeace, 157
Green Revolution, 216
Grylls, Bear, 7
guided transformation, 175–76
"gun culture," xvii, 159
Gutiérrez, Lucio, 152

habits, 157
Haidt, Jonathan, 36
haka ceremonies, 70–71
halal laws, 74
Halbwachs, Maurice, 134
Hale, Sarah Josepha, 127, 128
Ham, Mordecai, 84
Hamas, 117
Hamilton, Alexander, 131
Harding, Warren, 85
Harley-Davidson, 142–43
Harris, Jack, 3
Harvard's soccer team, 119
Hasidic Jewish communities, 116
Hastings, Reed, 112
Hatala, Kevin, 4, 5
Hate Map website, 193
Hatewatch newsletter, 192
HCL Technologies, 112–13
health practices, promotions of, 91, 95
hedge funds, 135
Henrich, Joseph, 64–65
hero instinct/codes, 33–55
    about, xxvii, 35
    and approval from communities, 52–55
    and collective ideals, 155
    in the context of national icons, 78
    and early humans, 33–35, 39, 79
    emulation of heroes, 38–39
    and evolution of prosociality, 35–39
    and Fukushima plant disaster, 78–79
    and generosity, 196, 198
    and identification with group, 45–50
    and Indian independence movement, 157
    individual sacrifices for benefit of group,
        33–35, 36, 39
    and King's "Dream" speech, 39–42
    and reputation mindedness, 36–38
    rewards/tributes to heroes, 38
    and social embeddedness, 50–52
    symbols' ability to evoke, 39–45, 49
Hiddink, Guus, x–xviii, xix–xxix, xxx, 87–88
hierarchical cultures, 26
Hi From The Other Side, 190
high-school bullying, 113–14
Hilton, Paris, 121
hindsight bias, 128
Hindu traditions/rituals, 74, 75
hip hop culture, 188
hiring practices, 194–99, 201–2, 213–14

Hispanic population in the US, 76, 202
historical records, 138
History Factory, 143
Hobsbawm, Eric, 133
Holmes, Elizabeth, 39
Holocaust, 206
Homo erectus, 3–4, *4*, 12, 31–32, 33–35.
Homo heidelbergensis, 35, 39, 59
Homo neanderthalensis, 60–62
Homo sapiens, 59–62
Hong, Ying-yi, 23
Hong Kong, 23
Horton, Meredith, 193
hostility, 191, 194–96, 199–200, 206, 213
"Huddle for 100" initiative, 143
human resources (HR) departments, 197
Hungary, 95
hunter-gatherer societies, 37–38
hunting practices of early humans, 5–6, 8,
    33–35
Hurtado, Osvaldo, 154
Hutu-Tutsi conflict, 108–9
Hwang Sun-hong, xiii
hyperinflation, 171–73

IBM, xvii
Ice Age, 215
iconic symbols, 42–43
ideals, evoking, 42–44, 50
identities, tribal/group, 44–45, 49–50,
    138–44
identity politics, 199
Iliad (Homer), 37
imitation as adaptive, xxvi
immigrant communities, 197, 207
incitement, legal test for, 210
inclusive leadership, 201
India
    independence movement, 156–57, 176
    influence of business leaders in, 112–13
    and lower castes, 95
Indigenous peoples, xvi, xxvi, 37–38, 205
indoctrination, 214
Industrial Revolution, 80
inflation, 171–73
influencers, 106
Infosys, 113
in-group/out-group dynamic, 182–83, 191,
    195, 197–98, 214
initiation ceremonies, 70

innovation, 111–13
instincts. *See* tribal instincts
institutional change
  and bottom-up change, 154–55
  and economic policy, 171–73
  General Motors' dress code, 168–69, 171
  and grassroots movements, 156–63
  and LEGO turnaround, 173–76
  Reddit moderation, 167–68
  smoking bans, 166–67
  soda bans, 166–67
  traffic laws in Sweden, 164–66
institution-building, 158
insurgent groups, influence of, 117
intentions of others, perceiving, 13
Inter-American Development Bank, 103
interculturalism, 212–13
International Accounting Day, 135
irrigation systems, 216
ISIS recruitment, xviii
isolation as part of indoctrination, 115–17
Israel
  Arab population in, 76
  detribalizing rival groups, 208
  and Exodus tale, 176–77
  intelligence community of, 30
  and Masada, 137–38, 155
  military service in, 155
  and Palestinians, 75
  UNESCO sites in, 147

Jackson, Mahalia, 40
Jacob Javits Convention Center,
  178, 180
"Jade Egg" of Goop, 136
January 6, 2021, insurrection, 181
Japanese myth of Jimmu, 133–34, 146
jerseys, throwback/fauxback, 142
Jewish people/culture, 64, 206, 207
jihadist violence, 212
Jim Crow era, 202
Jimmu, 133–34, 146
Joan of Arc, xxx, 67–69
Jobs, Steve, 39
Johar, Gita, 116
Johnson, Dwayne "The Rock," 121
Johnson, William "Pussyfoot," 85
Jolie, Angelina, 106
Jones, Alfred Winslow, 135
Jones, Jim, 114

Kahan, Dan, 189
Kalev, Alexandra, 200
Keep American Beautiful ad campaign, 120
Keller, Helen, 3
Keltner, Dacher, 37
Kennedy, John F., 41
Kigensetsu holiday in Japan, 134, 146
Kim Dae-jung, xiv
Kim Jong Un, 116
King, Martin Luther, Jr., xxx, 39–42, 43, 45,
  50, 53, 54–55, 156, 163
Klein, Richard, 61
knowledge sharing, xxiv–xxv
Knudstorp, Jørgen Vig, 173–75
Koch brothers, 160
Kodak's impact on amateur photography,
  88–89, *89*
Koestler, Arthur, 206
Kongō Gumi (temple-building company), 131
Koolhaas, Rem, 83
Koran, 162, 211
Korean Air, 26
Korean Football Association (KFA), x
kosher laws, 74
Kosovo, 147, 203–5, 208–9
Kotter International, 175
Krader, Kate, 73
Krawcheck, Sallie, 49–50, 53, 55
Kress department store, 202–3
Kruglansk, Arie, 30
Ku Klux Klan, 192
!Kung bushmen, 38, 54
Kuran, Timur, 94
Kyrgyzstan, 161

La Ferrara, Eliana, 103–4
La Hora, 152
La Mercè festival, 213
Lange, Paul van, 18
language, 7, 8, 22–27
La Tour d'Argent, 131
Lazar, Prince of Serbia, 204, 208–9
leadership changes, 119
Lear, Norman, 122
learning, science of, 106
Lee, Kuan Yew, xxx, 15–18, 26, 155
Lee, Robert E., 199
legislative gridlock, 181
LEGO, 173–76
Levin, Joseph, 192

Levine, Robert, 152
Levi's, 139
Lewin, Kurt, 175
Lewis, Ken, 46–49
LGBTQ+ community, 91
liberal attitudes, expression of, 94–95
Liebenberg, Louis, 5
Lil Nas X, 188
Lincoln, Abraham, 127–28, 129, 133, 140, 147, 195–96
littering, ad campaign fighting, 120–21
long-term transformations, 174–75
Los Angeles Philharmonic, 202

Macdonald, Norm, 101
madrassas, xviii
MaGIC (Malaysian Global Innovation and Creativity Centre), 19
Mahābhārata, 37
majority groups and "contact" hypothesis, 201
Malaysia, 19–20, 92–93
malice, 195–96
Malicounda Bambara, Senegal, 162–63
Malinowski, Bronisław, 74
Malu Mulher (soap opera), 104
Manchester United soccer fans, 44
The Mandalorian (series), 139
Mandela, Nelson, xxxi, 140–42, 148, 156
The March of Progress illustration, 8
Marine Corps, xvii, 116
marketplace of ideas, 184, 210
marriage equality, 158
Masada tradition, 138, 155
masking during pandemic, 95
mass killings, 205–6
matryoshka dolls, 110, *111*
Mattel, 173, 174
McAdam, Doug, 51
McDonald's, 96
McKinsey & Company, 173
McLuhan, Marshall, xxvii
Mead, Margaret, 165
media, 158, 185, 189
medical students, white coat ceremony of, 72, 135
Meiji Restoration, 134
meme culture, 188
memories, creation of collective, 134
Mendel, Gregor, 35

mercantile colonialism, 156
Merrill Lynch, 47–50, 55
#MeToo movement, 93–94, 155
Mexico, 107, 108
Michalopoulos, Stelios, 63
microaggressions, 200
Microsoft, xxxi, 112
Middle East, 181
Milgram, Stanley, 170–71
militaries
    and anti-war films, 121–22
    military service in Israel, 155
    use of prestige signals, 116–17
militias, 205
Milošević, Slobodan, 203–5, 207, 208–9
Mini Cooper, 142
minority groups/factions
    and "contact" hypothesis, 201
    peer influence of, 90–91
Moken people, 64
Montgomery, Alabama, 202
Moon, Sun Myung, 114–15
morality, xxix, 36–37
Mormonism, 132–33
Moscovici, Serge, 90
Moser, Bob, 192–93
Moses, biblical, 176–77
Moses, Robert, 50
Mousa, Salma, 201
Moynihan, Daniel Patrick, 151
multiculturalism, 211–12
Murthy, Narayana, 113
Musekeweya ("New Dawn"), 108–9
Muslim Bosniaks, 205
Muslim Brotherhood, 115–16
mythmaking, 158

Nadella, Satya, xxxi, 112
the Nakba, 208
National Football League (NFL), 143
nationalism, 203, 204
National Rifle Association (NRA), 159
"natural foot" movement, 163
Nayar, Vineet, 112–13
Nazism, 205–6, 207, 208–10, *209*
Neanderthals, 60–62
nepotism, 197
Netflix, 111–12
Netherlands, 212

network-based hiring, 197
New England and Thanksgiving tradition, 127, 128
Newsom, Gavin, 159
New World, 205
New York City, 166–67
New York Stock Exchange, 66
1984 (Orwell), 116
Nixon, Richard, 124–25
Nokia, 27
nongovernmental organizations (NGOs), 152, 161–63
North Atlantic Treaty Organization (NATO), 205
North Korea, 116, 148
nostalgia, xxvii
nuclear energy, 80
Nuremberg rally, 209–10, *209*
NXIVM, 115

Obama, Barack, xx, 24–25, 178, 189, 194, 199
obedience, 170–71
Obergefell v. Hodges, 158
Occupy Wall Street, 163
Ogilvy, David, 109, 110–11
Old South, 198–99
"Old Town Road" (Lil Nas X), 188
oligarchs, 172
OPOWER, 97–98
Opus Dei, 115–16
Orange Revolution, 161
orangutans, 13
Osborn, Ozzy, 121
Ostrom, Elinor, 215
Othello (Shakespeare), 33
Ottomans, 204
Oxford University, 132

Pacioli, Luca de, 135
Palestinians/Palestinian state, 75, 208
Paltrow, Gwyneth, 136
Paluck, Betsy Levy, 108
pandemic, masking during, 95
Pao, Ellen, 167
paramilitary groups, 116–17
Parker, Jack, 118
Park Ji-sung, xiv
Parks and Recreation (television series), 122
parochial altruism, 196

partisan "bubbles," 185
partisan triggers, 188
Partnership for a Drug-Free America, 101
peer instinct/codes, 3–32
    about, xxvii, 12–15
    as adaptation in early humans, 12–13
    and certainty seeking, 28–32
    and code switching, 22–26
    and conformity, 28–32, 35, 183, 213
    and conservation behaviors, 215
    and corruption, 17–19
    cultural cues triggering, xxx, 15–28
    and dress policies, 27
    and early humans, 3–8, 12, 79
    and language policies, 26
    and MeToo movement, 93–94
    and partisan "bubbles," 185
    pressure as cue for, 29–31, 78, 79
    and punctuality standards, 153
    and social development, 9–12
    and tribal signals, 69, 87
peer patterns. *See* prevalence signals
Peng, Kaiping, 21
Pepsi, 105
Pérez, Jefferson, 151–54
persistence hunting, 5
Pew Research Center, 158
philanthropy, 52
photographs, smiling in, 13, 88–89, *89*
Pilgrims and Thanksgiving day tradition, 126–29
Pinterest, 201
plastic surgery, 106
Poland, 171–73
police misconduct, 194
political culture, 178–87, 188–92, 213
politicians, influence of, 109
populism, 203
precedent signals, 126–48
    about, 129
    ancient, 130–37
    consistent, 130, 130–44
    and cultural policies, 211
    failed or unintended, 144–47
    and marriage equality, 158
    of intolerance vs. inclusion, 211
    and Occupy Wall Street, 163
    and punctuality standards, 153
    and resonant framing, 139–43
    and selective recall, 137–39

precedent signals (*cont.*)
    and success of Ambato movement, 154
    for Thanksgiving Day tradition, 126–29,
        133, 140
    See also traditions and traditionalism
prehistoric humans. *See* early humans
presidential election (2016), 178–81, 186
pressure, 29–31, 78, 79
prestige bias, xxvii
prestige signals, 103–25
    and anti-crime programs, 266n124
    and baby names, 260n105
    and business leaders' influence, 109–13
    of celebrities, 105–6
    co-opted from existing status holders,
        113–14
    of cult leaders, 114–16, 117
    exits of insiders, 117–18, 119
    failed or unintended, 120–25
    fame as, 106
    for grassroots movements, 157–58
    and grassroots movements, 160
    messenger and medium's impact on, 111,
        120–22
    military/paramilitary groups' use of,
        116–17
    nations' deployment of, 116
    and Occupy Wall Street, 163
    and punctuality standards, 153
    and role models, 106–7
    and smoking trends, 124
    and sports teams' cultures, 117–19
    and success of Ambato movement, 154
    suspicions that block, 120–21, 124
    and Tea Party groups, 160
    and television/radio, 103–9, 120–21, 123
    of working across ethnic lines, 201,
        202–3
prevalence signals, 83–102
    about, 87
    and alcohol consumption/temperance
        movement, 83–87, 88, 95, 98
    benchmarks used in, 97–98
    and brand popularity, 96
    as commonplace, 98–99
    comparative prevalence, 96
    and conformity, 102
    and conspicuity of peers' preferences,
        91–92
    defenses against, 99–100

    and early/slow adoption of new practices,
        92, 95–96
    and focus on undesired outcomes, 102
    and grassroots movements, 156, 157, 163
    and influence of minority factions, 90–91
    and Kodak's impact on amateur
        photography, 88–89, *89*
    and Occupy Wall Street, 163
    and "organized diffusion" of
        information, 91
    peer codes' sensitivity to, 87
    and peer pressure/influence, 89–91
    and political partisanship, 190–91
    and product placements, 100
    and punctuality standards, 153
    and social change, 95
    as strong determinant of behavior, 95
    and success of Ambato movement, 154
    and Tea Party groups, 160
    and tipping point dynamic, 91
    and trends focus, 92
    unintended, 100–101
    used nefariously/deceptively, 92–93,
        99–100
pride, 53–54, 55
primates
    brain evolution of, 9
    and gaze-tracking reflex, 13–14
    and peer instincts of humans, 12–13
    and prosociality, 36
prison and crime prevention initiatives,
    123–25
Private Truths, Public Lies (Kuran), 94
privatization, 172
product placements, 100, 124–25
progressive change, societal lag in, 94–95
Prohibition, 83–87, 88, 95
propaganda, 211
prosocial actions and attitudes, 35–39,
    44–45, 52–55
Proust, Marcel, 19
psychology and grassroots movements, 157
public health interventions, 91
punctuality standards, 151–54
Puritans and Thanksgiving day tradition,
    129, 130
Putnam, Robert, 184

Quinn, David, 118–19
Quito, Ecuador, 152–54

race
  bias training, 193, 200
  and discrimination, 192, 200
  and inequity, 191–93
  and integration, 95
  racial characteristics, 25–26
Raffles, Thomas Stamford, 15, 16
the Raj, 157
Rakuten, 27
rallies, 209–10
"rape culture," xvii
rationality, xxix
"reach across the aisle" sentiment, 181
"Real Beauty" campaign of Dove, 109
red-blue dialogue programs, 190
Reddit, 167–68
referral programs, 197–98, 201
religions
  and ceremonies, 70
  cloistering/isolation of members,
    115–16
  religious behaviors/attitudes, 62
  religious cults, 114–16
  religious diversity, 203, 207
  religious extremism, 116
  religious ideals, 163
  religious symbols, 43, 49
  and timing of holy days, 140
  as tribal traditions, 207
  violent conflict associated with, 207
Renaissance, 79–80
Renault, 27
Republican Party, 180–81, 184, 186–91
Republic of Georgia, 130–31
reputation mindedness, 36–38, 52–54, 55
resonant framing, 139–43
resource dilemma games, 216
résumés, 194–96
"re-tribalization," xxvii
"retro" brands, 142
revenge porn, 167
"reverse discrimination," 193
revisionist histories, 129
right-wing groups, 209–10, 213
risk taking, xv, 51, 110–11
Ritual (Xygalatas), 67
rituals
  and children, 70
  and comfort in continuity, 72–73
  and emergence of Homo sapiens, 62

fantastical/counterintuitive elements of, 64
framing for familiarity, 140
painful or risky, 67
replication/repetition in, 64, 66
sense of meaning associated with, 66–67
and social learning, 66
See also ancestor instinct/codes; traditions
    and traditionalism
Roach, Neil, 4, 5
"Rockin' in the Free World" (Young), 122
Rogers, Todd, 102
role models, influence of, 106–7, 116, 120
Romani people, 206
Roosevelt, Franklin, 128
Rosen, Lawrence, xxvii
Rose Revolution, 161
Rugby World Cup (1995), 141–42
Russia, 172–73
Russian soccer team, xv–xvi
Rutgers Business School, 197
Rwanda, Hutu-Tutsi conflict in, 108–9

Sabido, Miguel, 107–8
Sachs, Jeffrey, 171
safe-sex practices, 107–8
Salt Lake Temple, 132–33
Salt March, 156
same-sex marriage, 158–59
Sanahuja, Ramon, 212
Sanders, Bernie, 158
San Marcos, California, 96–98
San people of the Kalahari Desert, 5
Santoro, Erik, 190
Sarajevo, Yugoslavia, 203, 205
Sarandos, Ted, 111–12
satire, 122
satyagrahis, 156
scarcity, 215
Scared Straight! crime-prevention initiative,
    122–23, 124
science, attitudes toward, 116
Scientology, 115
Scott, Ridley, 101
Second Amendment, 159
The Secret of Our Success (Henrich), 65
sectarian conflict, 207–8, 213–14
Seder meal and Jewish Passover, 64
selective recall, 137–39
self-interest, 215
Senegal, 161–63

September 11, 2001, terrorist attacks, 30, 72–73, 211
Serbia, 147, 203–5, 208–9, 211
Serbian Orthodox Church, 204–5, 208
sexual assault/exploitation, 93–94, 117–19
Shakespeare, William, 33
shame, 53–54
Sheikh, Hammad, 75
shills, 92–93
Shinola, 136
shock therapy, 155, 172–73
signals. *See* precedent signals; prestige signals; prevalence signals; tribal signals
signs as tribal triggers, 19
Singapore, 15–17, 26, 155
Skinner, B. F., 106
slavery, 177
Slovenia, 204
smiling in photographs, 13, 88–89, *89*
smoking and tobacco campaigns, 124–25, 166–67, 171
soap operas, social influence of, 103–5, 107–9
soccer
    Harvard's soccer team, 119
    and mutually mistrustful communities, 201
    Socceroos soccer team, Australia, xv, xviii
    South Korea's Reds, ix–xiv, xviii, xix, xx, xxx, 87–88
social affiliations, 51
social animals, humans as, xxiii
social brain hypothesis, 9
social embeddedness, 51–52
social intelligence
    and brain evolution, 9–12
    central importance of, 8
    encoding and enactment of, 10–11
social learning
    biases in, xxvii
    and cultural evolution, xxvi–xxvii
    effect on early humans, 11
    from elders, ancestors, and precedents, 66, 129–43
    from heroes, role models, and prestigious figures, 39, 106–14
    from peers and prevalence, 89–99
social media, 185, 189
"sock puppet" groups, 160

soda bans, 166–67
Sodexo, 197
Sounds Like Hate podcast, 193
South Africa, 140–42, 156
Southern Poverty Law Center (SPLC), 192–94, 197–200, 202
Southern Slavic peoples, 203
South Korea
    Reds soccer team, ix–xiv, xviii, xix, xx, xxx, 87–88
    women's hockey team in 2018 Olympics, 148
Soviet Union, 94
Spain, 212
sports teams
    changing cultures of, 117–19
    and "contact" hypothesis, 200–201
    diversity in, 148
    and multiculturalism, 212
South Korea's Reds soccer team, ix–xiv, xviii, xix, xx, xxx, 87–88
South Korea's women's hockey team, 148
and Springboks and Mandela, 140–42
Springboks rugby team, 141–42
Springsteen, Bruce, 122
Starbucks branch in Beijing, 144–45, *144*
Start-Up Chile, 93
status-seeking, xxix
Stop the Steal, 181
St. Patrick's Cathedral in New York, 132
substance abuse, 101
suicide bombings, 117
Sullivan, Andrew, 181
Sunday, Billy, 84
Sungir archaeological site, 62
Super Bowl, 96
Super Glide motorcycle, 142
superstition, 216
sustainable consumption, 215–16
Swann's Way (Proust), 19
Swanson, Ron (character), 122
Sweden, 164–66, *165*, 171, 207
switching between cultural frames, xix, 22–25
symbols, 39–44, 49–50, 66, 79
synchronous activities, 70–72
Syrian immigrants, 207

Tamil Tigers, 117
Tanzania, 107–8

Tea Party movement, 160
technology, 185
teen smoking campaigns, 124
telenovelas, 104–5, 106, 107
television shows and advertising, 103–5, 106, 107–9, 120–21, 123
temperance movement, 83–87, 88, 95, 155
terrorism
    and counterterrorism, xviii
    September 11, 2001, terrorist attacks, 30, 72–73, 211
    and social networks, 51
    and tribal rage concerns, 191–92
Texas's anti-littering ad campaign, 120–21
Thanksgiving Day tradition, 126–29, 133, 140
"they" used as singular pronoun, 91
think tanks, 160
"Three Strikes and You're Out" laws, 123–24
TikTok, 96
Time, 181–82
timeliness standards, 151–54
tipping-point dynamic, 91
tolerance, 211
Topa, Giorgio, 197
top-down change, 165–67, 171–77
Tostan, 161–63
totaalvoetbal ("total football"), x–xi, xiii, xv–xvi, xviii
totem animals, 43–44
toxic tribalism, 181–82, 191, 195, 199
traditions and traditionalism, 126–48
    and ancestor instinct, xxvii
    and anxiety, 74
    bias toward continuity with, xxvii
    and children, 65–66
    and creation of collective memories, 134
    and cultural appropriation, 144–45, *144*
    and cultural hegemony, 145–46
    in dangerous/threatening contexts, 74, 78–79
    and death/mortality, 74–76
    and deference to authority, 171
    and demographic trends, 76
    and female circumcision, 161–63
    and fictional histories, 136
    followed blindly, 65
    and grassroots movements, 157
    human's inclination to perpetuation, xxx
    and inclusiveness, 148
    invented, 134

    and Joan of Arc, 67–69
    lessons preserved in, 63–64
    and mass violence, 206, 207
    and multiculturalism, 211
    negative perceptions of, xxix
    and peer-instinct conformity, 183
    and precedent signals, 129–30
    relationship to ceremony, 251n70
    and sense of obligation, 72
    of South Korean soccer team, xii–xiii
    Thanksgiving Day, 126–29, 140
    as tool of changemakers, 147–48
    See also ceremonies and rituals
traffic laws, 164–66, *165*, 171
tragedy of the commons, 215–16
trends focus, 92
tribal instincts
    about, xxvii–xxviii, 10–11
    and evolution of humans, xxx, 10
    and Fukushima plant disaster, 78–79, 80
    impacts of, 11
    and partisan conflicts in US, 182
    power of, xxx, xxxii
    three layers of, xxvii–xxviii
    and tribal signals, 87
    See also ancestor instinct/codes; hero instinct/codes; peer instinct/codes
tribal signals
    about, 87
    cultural codes shaped/changed by, xxxi, 85, 87
    and tribal instincts, 87
    unconscious effects of, xxxi
    See also precedent signals; prestige signals; prevalence signals
tribal triggers
    about, xxx, 23–24
    ceremonies as key triggers of ancestor codes, 70
    cultural codes activated by, xix, xxx, 85
    and Fukushima plant disaster, 78–79
    signs as key triggers of peer codes, 19
    symbols as key triggers of hero codes, 42
    and South Korea's Reds soccer team, xix
    and temperance movement, 85
tribe (term/concept), xxv, xxviii–xxix
triggers. *See* tribal triggers
Triumph of the Will (film), 209, *209*
Trobriand Islanders, 74
Trojans, 205

Truffaut, François, 121–22
Trump, Donald J., 158, 179–80, 186, 189
trust, 61
Truth and Reconciliation Commission, 141
tsunami, 2004 (Indian Ocean), 64
Tukanoan people, 65
Tulip Revolution, 161
Tutu, Desmond, 141
Twende na Wakati ("Let's Go with the
    Times"), 107–8
two-party political system, 181, 183

ubuntu, spirit of, 141
Ukraine, 161
UNESCO, 146–47
Unification Church of Reverend Moon,
    114–15
United Kingdom, 212
United Nations diplomats, 18
"Unite the Right" rally (Charlottesville),
    193, 210
University of California, Berkeley, 190
University of Chicago, 132
University of North Carolina at
    Chapel Hill, 98
University of Pennsylvania, 189–90
Urban Rural Action, 190
"Us" and "Them" dynamic, 44, 182–83, 191,
    195, 214
U.S. Department of State, xix
U.S. Intelligence Community, xix
U.S. Supreme Court, 158, 184

values, cultural, 108–9
Ven Conmigo ("Come with Me"), 107
Vikings' 2022 season, 31
Volksverhetzung law, 210
Volkswagen, 27, 142
voter mobilization, 96, 102

Wałęsa, Lech, 172
Warsaw Pact, 204
wars/wartime, 121–22, 205–6

Washington, George, 127, 129, 130, 140
Wasserman, Dave, 187
The Weeknd, 96
West Bank, 75
WeWork, 99
Wheeler, Wayne, 85
white coat ceremony of medical students, 72,
    135, 253n72
white nationalism, 198
white supremacy ideology, 199
Whitman, Walt, xix
"Who Doesn't?" (Lange), 18
Will & Grace (television series), 158
Willer, Robb, 188
wine and signals of antiquity,
    130–31, 132
Winslow, Edward, 127
Winter Olympics (1984), 203
Winter Olympics (2018), 148
women and family planning,
    104–5, 107
"work from home" practices, 14
Working Families for Walmart, 160
World Cup soccer, ix–xiv, xx–xxi, *xxi*
world heritage sites, 146–47
worldviews, 186–87
Wrangham, Richard, 6

Xhosa tribe, 141
Xygalatas, Dimitris, 67

Yadin, Yigael, 138
Yale University, 190–91
Yeltsin, Boris, 172–73
Yom Kippur attack, 30
Yoo Sang-chul, xiii–xiv
Yoplait, 146
Yoshizawa, Atsufumi, 77–78
Young, Alexander, 127, 128
Young, Neil, 122
Yugoslavia, 203–5, 208–9

Zelenskyy, Volodymyr, 45